ISBN 978-1-5278-1529-2
PIBN 10894372

This book is a reproduction of an important historical work. Forgotten Books uses state-of-the-art technology to digitally reconstruct the work, preserving the original format whilst repairing imperfections present in the aged copy. In rare cases, an imperfection in the original, such as a blemish or missing page, may be replicated in our edition. We do, however, repair the vast majority of imperfections successfully; any imperfections that remain are intentionally left to preserve the state of such historical works.

1976 ARCHEOLOGICAL INVESTIGATIONS

Trash Dump Excavations,
Area Surveys,
and Monitoring of Fort Construction and Landscaping

BENT'S OLD FORT NATIONAL HISTORIC SITE
Colorado

by
Douglas C. Comer

June 1985

U.S. Department of the Interior / National Park Service

CONTENTS

INTRODUCTION   1

HISTORICAL BACKGROUND   6

EXCAVATION METHODS   15

REMOTE SENSING: METHODOLOGY AND RESULTS   20

MONITORING   26

EAST BASTION EXCAVATIONS   30

STATISTICAL TECHNIQUE   36

RANDOM SAMPLING PROCEDURE   41

WEST DUMP STRATIGRAPHY   42

MAIN DUMP STRATIGRAPHY   45

DATING   47

MAIN DUMP FEATURES   49

DISCUSSION OF ARTIFACTS   52
    Comparison of Ages of Main and West Dumps   52
    Trade Network   55
    Indian Trade Items in the West and Main Dumps   56

DIET   59

FURS TRADED AT THE FORT   62

DETERMINATION OF SOCIOECONOMIC LEVEL   63
    Ceramics Considered in the Socioeconomic Analysis   63
    Ceramic Characteristics with Socioeconomic Significance   66
    Evaluating the Socioeconomic Indicators   67

RECOMMENDATIONS   70

REFERENCES CITED   72

APPENDIX A: OBSERVED AND PREDICTED DISTRIBUTION
            OF ARTIFACTS, WEST DUMP   75

APPENDIX B: OBSERVED AND PREDICTED DISTRIBUTION
              OF ARTIFACTS, MAIN DUMP   97

APPENDIX C: OBSERVED AND PREDICTED DISTRIBUTION
              OF ARTIFACTS, FEATURE 1, MAIN DUMP   129

APPENDIX D: FAUNAL ANALYSIS   133

APPENDIX E: POLLEN ANALYSIS   161

APPENDIX F: MEAN CERAMIC DATES, WEST AND MAIN DUMPS   173

APPENDIX G: ARTIFACT DESCRIPTION BY PAUL INASHIMA   177

LIST OF FIGURES

1. Location Map and Historic Views of Bent's Old Fort   2
2. Map of Bent's Old Fort in Historical Context   3
3. Site Map of Bent's Old Fort   4
4. Archeological Plan Map   16
5. Composite Photograph of the West Dump Excavations   18
6. Archeological Plan Map of Leonard's Features 92 and 94   31
7. Archeological Plan Map of the Main Dump Depicting Comer's
    Features 1, 2, and 3   50

LIST OF TABLES

1. Items Traded at Bent's Fort   14
2. Bone   53
3. Ceramics   54
4. Beads   57
5. Distribution of Various Ceramic Types and Percentages   69
6. Distribution of Various Ceramics Based on Cost by Percentage   69

INTRODUCTION

The report deals with the archeological excavation, monitoring, and other archeological investigations conducted intermittently from February 20 to June 28, 1976, in association with site development activities at Bent's Old Fort National Historic Site, La Junta, Colorado (see figures 1 and 2). The investigations were supervised by Douglas C. Comer of the Denver Service Center, National Park Service, in accordance with section 106 of the National Historic Preservation Act of 1966. Monitoring of all site development involving ground surface disturbance--i.e., parking lot and new entrance road, construction, installation of a leach field and septic tank, trenching for utility lines, reconstruction of historic trails, and landscaping around the fort, was performed in the above period.

Excavations and other subsurface investigations were carried out in the area threatened by landscaping and construction of a historic trail. The area, measuring roughly 200' x 150', was located north-east of the northeastern wall of Bent's Old Fort (see figure 3). Two historic trash deposits were known to be located within this area and had been previously tested by Jackson W. Moore during his 1963-66 excavation, which dealt primarily with the fort interior. Moore had recorded, in his report, the approximate horizontal distribution of the trash deposits. From his description, it could be seen that one of the deposits, which he had designated the West Dump, lay entirely within the area to be landscaped, while perhaps the western 30 percent of the area that Moore called the Main Dump would be affected by the proposed landscape alteration. Moore had also presented the tentative finding that the deposits, at least within the area to be impacted, were relatively shallow (Moore 1973:59 & 60).

In light of this, five basic objectives were identified. Excavation was deemed necessary in the West Dump and affected Main Dump areas in order to further evaluate the extent and importance of the deposits, and, should the latter be found to be sufficient, to salvage as much archeological information from the deposits as time and available money allowed. Given the proximity of the area to be landscaped to the fort, it was also decided to explore the area systematically for hitherto unknown trash deposits or other features before the landscaping was to be done.

Another objective concerned two features discovered by Robert W. Leonard, Jr., from the Laboratory of Public Archeology at Colorado State University, during his monitoring of the trenching for the reconstructed walls of the fort. These features were also to be explored by means of excavation. Leonard had designated these as features 92 and 94. Feature 94 was a deposit of midden-like soil located at the juncture of the north-east (front) wall of the fort and the North East Bastion. Leonard had suspected this to be a part of a possible midden deposit he had found beneath the floor of the North East Basion. Feature 92 was an intrusive pit found in the north wall of the trench dug for the foundation of the northeast wall of the fort and was located 8.75 feet east or the northwest corner of the entrance to the fort.

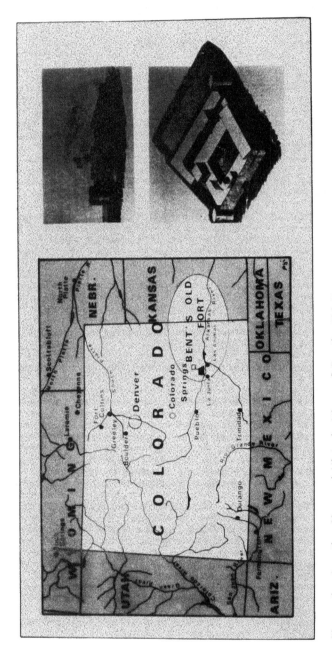

Figure 1. Location Map and Historic Views of Bent's Old Fort

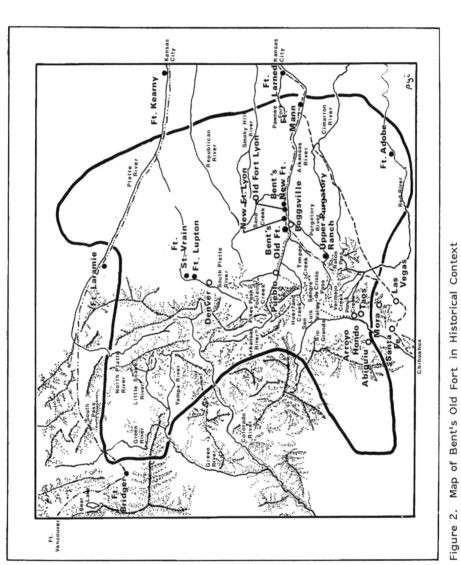

Figure 2. Map of Bent's Old Fort in Historical Context

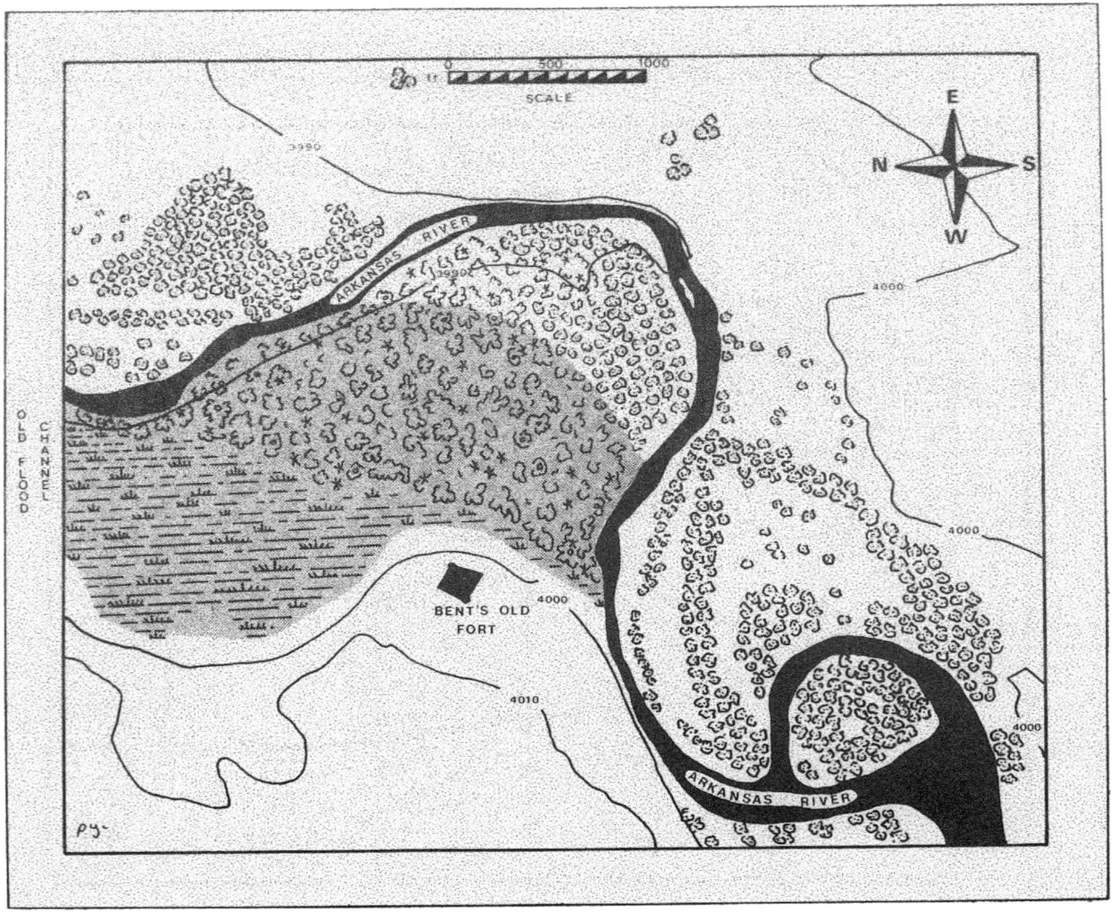

Figure 3.   Site Map of Bent's Old Fort

The final objective was to utilize remote sensing techniques in an effort to locate several historically recorded but unidentified features. These included an ice house separate from the main body of the fort (Stinson 1965:22) the path of the Mountain Branch of the Santa Fe Trail as it ran into and out of the fort, a racetrack, Indian campsites, and other previously undiscerned features.

Included in this report are a description and interpretation of cultural materials found during the course of the investigations, by provenience. Since it was originally expected that landscaping would obliterate all of the West Dump and about 30 percent of the Main Dump, a statistically based sampling method was used during the excavation of these areas in order to be able to generalize about quantities and percentages of artifacts and other sorts of cultural material contained in the total area, including those unexcavated portions. This procedure, its statistical basis, and its results is also presented.

HISTORICAL BACKGROUND

Bent's Old Fort was probably built between 1828 and 1832 by the trading firm of Bent, St. Vrain and Company. This firm had been created by the brothers Bent (Charles and William) and Ceran St. Vrain. The fort was the second they had built in the area. The first, really a stockade, had been put up near present day Pueblo, Colorado, on Fountain Creek in about 1826, but the location was not a successful one. Sometime shortly after the construction of Bent's Old Fort, and before 1840, the partnership constructed Fort St. Vrain on the South Platte River, just below St. Vrain's Fork; and Adobe Fort on the South Canadian River. In 1849, William Bent abandoned Bent's Old Fort and built a new trading post at Big Timber, near the present location of Lamar, Colorado. The new post is sometimes referred to as Bent's New Fort.

Of all of these, and the other trading posts built by other firms in that area, Bent's Old Fort was the most historically significant. It was the first permanent outpost in the Southwestern frontier. The other posts were ancillary to Bent's Old Fort, in that goods were brought from them to Bent's Fort, which was located on the Mountain Branch of the Santa Fe Trail. Also, Bent's Old Fort was located on the Arkansas River, the border between the United States and Mexico at the time it was built, and would serve as a staging area prior to the brief and successful Mexican War.

The United States at that time was in the throes of becoming an industrial nation and a world power. This transformation had begun in earnest just a few years earlier, with the conclusion of the War of 1812. In 1815, the British were soundly defeated at the Battle of New Orleans, to the great enthusiasm of the United States population. More importantly, that same year the United States Navy established itself as a serious contestant on international seas with the raid freeing the American ships and prisoners held by the pirates of the Barbary Coast. In 1816, tariffs were introduced as a protection against the dumping of British goods in the U.S., a measure taken to bolster the incipient industrialization of this country. 1817 was the year construction began of the Erie Canal, the first of the large-scale internal improvements made to provide for the inexpensive transport of the resources of the western frontier to the urban centers of the East.

By 1828, Congress had passed what was known in the Southern states as the "Tariff of Abominations" which controlled the import of foreign goods. The South, of course, was more interested in the availability of cheap European merchandise than in stimulating Northern industry. Also in 1828, the construction of the first U.S. railroad, the Baltimore and Ohio, was begun. The completed railroad two years later was the most efficient device thus far for linking the frontier with the East. The frontier in this case was the Ohio Valley.

Bent's Old Fort was not only west of the Ohio Valley, it was beyond the Mississippi Valley. It was linked to the East only by a few wagons which made their infrequent, hazardous way across the prairies and deserts between Indpendence, Missouri and Santa Fe, at that time a town in

6

Mexico. It was roughly as far south-west as one could travel and remain in the United States. Moreover, at the time the Bent's arrived, it was already occupied by people whose culture differed greatly from that of the East.

In considering the location of Bent's Old Fort, it is well to keep in mind that, more than being a way-station for those involved with the Santa Fe trade, it was conceived as a place at which to trade with the Indians. Included in this Indian trade would be trade with the trappers and hunters from the East, and the "mountain men" who traded the same goods as did the Indians and oftentime lived with them. Jackson Moore (1973:1) mentions that the first trading stockage built by Bent, St. Vrain and Company was badly located because it was far from the Santa Fe Trail and west of the main buffalo-hunting grounds. While these were probably factors contributing to the stockade's demise, it seems likely also that the eventual site of Bent's Old Fort was selected because the Indians had been trading near there for some time.

In his dissertation on the trade system of the Plains Indians, Donald Blakeslee suggests a moving locus in the trade network--a trading rendezvous--which he believes may have been on the Cheyenne River of present-day South Dakota at one time. He presents the idea that the location of the rendezvous moved southward in order to be closer to the herds of Spanish horses. From the Cheyenne it may have been moved to the South Platte, near the location of Denver today. After this, it may have been relocated to the Arkansas River. It is known that a rendezvous was held for several years prior to the building of Bent's Old Fort at a place on the Arkansas River. Of this place, Blakeslee says ". . . the construction of Bent's fort within 30 miles of the site indicates that this section of the Arkansas River retained its importance as a trading center for years" (1975:217).

These rendezvous, as Blakeslee described them, were large enough to have generated a good deal of trade in themselves. At the Arkasnas River rendezvous, Blakeslee reports the attendance of Cheyenne, Arapaho, Kiowa, Commanche, and Shoshone in a camp with more than 700 tepees. The rendezvous lasted from mid-November until mid-December.

In fact, the factor which limited the duration of the rendezvous provides a hint as to why Bent's Old Fort was built at a location 30 miles from the historically recorded rendezvous spot. After about one month, all of the local wood was consumed, necessitating the disbanding of the rendezvous. Therefore, the rendezvous must have been held at locations some distance apart from year to year, and a place as much as 30 miles distant from that of the year before may not have been unusual. Also, the location of the fort may have been selected to be 30 miles from the last rendezvous site in order to ensure a supply of the wood that was used in the construction of the fort.

It seems probable that a large part of the considerable success the Bents enjoyed in trading with the Indians may have been due to the fact that they appreciated the existence of the Indian culture, and fit their Operation to it. One measure of the extent of this is that William Bent, who managed the fort, married a Cheyenne woman, and then her sister when the first died. Kit Carson, an intermittent employee, frequent visitor to the fort, and close friend of the Bents* also had a Cheyenne wife during one of his terms of employment. It would seem in character, then, that the Bents would settle upon a location for the trading post that was already in use by the Indians for trade.

It was for similar considerations, apparently, that the "ancillary" posts of Fort St. Vrain and Adobe Fort were established. George Bird Grinnell (1923:42) maintains that Fort St. Vrain was built for trade with the Sioux and the northern bands of the Cheyenne and Arapaho, who infrequently traveled as far south as the Arkansas River. He also says that the Kiowas, Comanches, and Apaches requested that Adobe Fort be built on the South Canadian, because these groups, who lived south of the Arkansas, had been fighting with the Cheyenne and Arapaho for some time, and were hesitant to encounter their enemies at Bent's Old Fort.

THE NATURE OF THE TRADE

Trade in the Southwest had proven to be a highly lucrative enterprise by the time of the completion of Bent's Old Fort. The Bent trading caravan of 1832 returned to Missiouri with $100,000 in Mexican dollars and other currency, along with $90,000 in Mexican goods and mules. In 1833, their train of 93 wagons brought back another $100,000 in paper money and a large amount of property (Grinnell 1923:48). It is not clear whether or not these figures, taken from Grinnell, include the proceeds from the fur trade with the Indians and trappers. Among all historians who write of the fur trade in the Southwest during this time, though, there is a consensus that Bent, St. Vrain and Company was the dominant mercantile presence there. It is likely, then, that the fur trade either contributed substantially to the above totals, or provided an appreciable addition to them.

In general, although with some exceptions, the trade in which the Bents engaged consisted of exchanging the products of the industrial eastern United States and western Europe for currency, gold and silver from the Mexicans, and furs from the Indians. Both the Mexicans and the Indians were willing to pay dearly for these industrial goods; the Mexicans because their alternate source was, principally, via far off Vera Cruz, the Indians because the goods the Bents offered could be had less expensively and with less hazard. Moreover, it is likely that the Indians had a great deal more trust for the Bents than in other potential trading partners.

---

* Grinnell (1923:36) relates the story that Kit Carson, running away from his apprenticeship as a saddler, first went to Santa Fe with one of Charles Bent's wagon trains. Later, he helped in the construction of Bent's Old Fort.

The wagons were loaded in Independence, Missouri, with an assortment of items including arms, ammunition, blankets, cloth, beads, brass wire, axes, kettles, lead, sugar, tobacco, coffee, and molasses. At Bent's Old Fort, some of these would be exchanged for "buffalo robes" (buffalo hides), mules and horses from the Indians, and beaver pelts and other furs from the trappers. Both of these groups were interested in most of the goods just listed, and more besides. The Indians were the primary market for beads, hoop iron (from which was made arrow points), bells, brass wire and tacks (used for the embellishment of saddles, clothing, etc.), abalone shells, and vermillion.* In Santa Fe, the remainder of the Independence goods would be exchanged. Again, the arms, tools, dry goods, and foods which were difficult to obtain in the region brought high prices. Josiah Gregg, in his remembrances of the Santa Fe trade originally published in 1844, mentions that cloth was scarce enough in Santa Fe, ". . . common calicoes and even bleached and brown domestic goods . . ." to bring two or three dollars per Spanish yard (of thirty-three inches) (Gregg 1967:7). Gold and silver was a form of payment readily accepted by the Bents in Santa Fe, along with currency, mules, and blankets from Mexico, made by the Pueblos, or, in some cases, by the Navajo.

Some of the trade items collected on the outbound phase of the trading expedition were kept there or left there to be traded in turn. The Mexican, Pueblo, and Navajo blankets were prized by the Cheyenne, for example, the Cheyenne sometimes purchased horses and mules, although more frequently they would offer them for sale. As time went on, another market developed which was within the Bent's Old Fort sphere of mercantile influence. Emigrants to California and those returning often traveled to the north of the fort, and were eager to purchase supplies and fresh horses and mules. Payment in these instances was usually in currency, silver, or gold.

This very profitable trading situation existed until after the Mexican War. By that time, the influx of traders, emigrants, and soldiers had devastated the native cultures of the area. Armed conflict between the various Indian groups and the whites, and especially diseases such as cholera and smallpox had decimated the Indian population. As a part of the resulting social dislocation, as Moore notes (1973:4), ". . . more war parties than bands intent on trading were in the fort's vicinity." Many Indians were hesitant to visit the fort for fear of encountering these war parties and of contracting the diseases introduced by the newcomers. Thus by the late 1840s, the Indian trade had drastically declined. The beaver trade had already largely fallen off, due to a change in preference in the material used for fashionable clothing in the late thirties. A lrge trading post such as Bent's Old Fort, with its numerous employees, would be difficult to maintain given this much reduced trading activity.

---

* Grinnell (1923:58) reports that a single abalone shell, to be used for jewelry and other decorative purposes, would bring four dressed bufallo robes.

For these and personal reasons, William Bent grew dissatisfied with the operation of Bent's Old Fort. His brother, Charles Bent, had been killed in 1847 during an uprising in Taos, shortly after being appointed as governor of the new U.S. territory of New Mexico. His first wife had died not long before. He told friends that the fort contained too many memories which were painful to recall. About this time he tried to sell the fort to the U.S. Army.

Since William Bent felt that the Army was somewhat indebted to him after his cooperation in the use of Bent's Old Fort during the Mexican War, he was gravely disappointed when the Army would not meet the price he asked for the fort. Rather than accept the lower price the Army offered, William abandoned and burned the fort in 1849. He resumed his trade on a smaller scale at Big Timbers, 40 miles downstream from the site of Bent's Old Fort.

THE DESIGN OF THE FORT

Bent, St. Vrain and Company designed the fort within the constraints and in order to take advantage of the characteristics of the environment of the Southwest. Log construction was probably never seriously considered, the number of suitable trees in the region being very few. Instead, the adobe construction of New Mexico, and particularly Taos, was used. The adobe offered several advantages over log construction. Adobe was much more comfortable, the rooms being cooler in the summer and warmer in the winter. If properly maintained it was more durable. Finally, adobe could not be burned during attacks on the fort by Indians or other groups.

The plan of the fort was essentially a rectangle described by four contiguous room blocks meeting at right angles, enclosing a large plaza. Two observation towers, or bastions, were situated at the east and west junctures.* The long sides of the rectangle, between the front (north-east) and back (south-west) row of rooms, was 142 feet. The short sides (north-west to south-east) measured 122 feet. The basic rectangular shape was modified by additions on the south-east and south-west sides. On the south-east was a triangularly shaped open-roofed enclosure which ran along that entire side of the fort. This is referred to by Moore (1973:15), as the "inner canal." On the south-west were two other additions, each a long rectangle similar to the room blocks but without the interior partitioning into rooms. Situated closest to the south-west row of rooms, separated only by an alleyway, was the wagon house. Immediately along side the wagon room, is the wider area used as the main corral. The plan of the fort is presented in figure 1.

---

* The walls of the fort were not aligned precisely with the cardinal directions of the compass, but the front of the fort (the side with the entrance to the plaza had a generally north-east alignment.

Outside the fort were, reputedly, several structures associated with it. Several sources mention an ice house, about 200 yards southwest of the fort, toward the river. Others mention a racetrack west of the fort, a graveyard to the northwest, and a wood pile also to the northwest. An additional feature was an "acequia," or irrigation ditch, dug to provide water during the illfated attempts to grow vegetables at the fort. This, from one source, came towards the fort from the northwest and then curved off toward the east (Stinson 1965:23& 24).

For a more complete description of the fort and the historical references to the uses of its various rooms and features, the reader is directed to the Historic Structures Report, Bent's Old Fort National Historic Site (Stinson 1965).

ACTIVITIES AT THE FORT

Trading was the purpose of the fort, but hardly the only activities which took place there. Some were necessitated by the isolation of the fort from its parent culture; the rest were certainly shaped by that factor.

Several activities were concerned with the maintenance of equipment, tools, and the fort itself. Several sources mention a blacksmith shop and a carpenter shop, each with its own room at the fort. These activities almost certainly took place at the fort, as vital as they would have been to its operation. With parts of wagons, tack, weapons, or the structural elements of the fort not readily available, it was probably often necessary to repair broken ones or fashion new ones from metal or wood. Visitors to the fort later in its history report seeking a gunsmith and a tailor, whose presence would also seem reasonable.

There were apparently separate rooms for food preparation and consumption. One visitor to the fort spoke of a "common dining hall" used by ". . . traders, trappers, and hunters, and all employees" (Stinson 1965:70). A number of other sources mention a cook for the fort, some by name. It would seem, then, that cooking and eating were normally done within the room blocks.

The number of people, and probably their occupation and sex, inhabiting the fort varied over the years. It also differed according to the season. In the summer, for instance, most of the employees were accompanying the annual wagon train to Westport, Missouri. The Indians, incidentally, were usually off on their summer buffalo hunt at this time. This is at least a partial explanation for the various accounts of the popuation at Bent's Old Fort. Estimates of numbers of people seem to range from about 60 to 200. The numbers of women and children are also uncertain, although George Bent, son of William by his Cheyenne wife, remembers, ". . . 100 employees, most of whom had families" (Stinson 1965:71).

George Bird Grinnell recorded an interesting description of the occupants of the fort, although he does not specifically say so in this instance, it is generally thought that Grinnell was greatly influenced in his portrayals of Bent's Old Fort from George Bent. It should be kept equally in mind that George Bent was six years old when he left Bent's Old Fort, and that he had not seen the fort for 59 years at the time he talked to Grinnell. The information related in the following quote from Grinnell (1923:51), might be the sort, however, that if not remembered from the age of six might have been obtained from those around him as George Bent was growing up:

> The traders, clerks, mechanics, trappers, hunters, teamsters and common laborers at Bent's Fort were of many races. Most of the traders, clerks and mechanics were Americans, with a few Frenchmen. The hunters and trappers were American, Frenchmen, and eastern Indians, particularly Delawares and Shawnees. Black Beaver, the Delaware, was one of the most famous of the Bent hunters. The teamsters were mostly American, with some Frencmen from Missouri, while the herders and common laborers were usually Mexicans. There were also two or three negroes at Bent's Fort--Dick Green and his brother Andrew, the servants of Charles and William Bent, and, according to some authorities, Charlotta, a negress, was also employed at the fort. Most of the men at the fort had taken Indian wives from one tribe to another, and the fort was plentifully peopled with women and children as well as men.

Where all of the above people would have been quarteres is uncertain. Many sources mention private rooms for the owners and visitors, but barrack-like accommodations for the rest of the employees.

Reference is made in a few historic accounts of life at Bent's Old Fort to attempts at growing vegetables and raising food animals there. The horticultural effort occasioned the digging of the acequia, or irrigation canal, in front of the fort. None of these efforts were successful because of trampling of the plants by animals roaming near the fort and because of pilferage. Animals menticned in historic records include piegeons, turkeys, and chickens. One, a Dr. F.A. Wislizenus, described the livestock at the fort in 1839 as follows: "In the ample courtyard were many barnyard fowl. In addition they have cattle, sheep and goats and three buffalo calves that peacefully graze with the rest of the herd" (Grinnell, 1923:41). A number of historic informants report a goat kept as a pet at the fort, which clambered over the rooftops to the amazement of the Indians, who were unfamiliar with this type of animal. This being so, one wonders if the single goat might have been transformed by Dr. Wislizenus' imagination into sheep and goats. Bent also had peacocks that were kept as pets.

Trade was carried out at the fort, in part, in a room referred to in some places as a "store." Here were kept various sorts of luxuries, such as crackers, candy, and preserved ginger. It is probable that some trading took place also in the plaza, in the center of which was the fur press.

SUBSEQUENT HISTORY

After the abandonment of Bent's Old Fort by William Bent in 1849, the site remained uninhabited for some time, but was eventually reoccupied. The authors of the historic structures report (1965) for the fort have identified several periods in the fort's history that are presented here:

Bent Period 1833 (date of fort's completion to 1849--The period just discussed, during which the fort served as headquarters for Bent, St. Vrain and Company.

Firt Interim Period 1849 to 1861--The ruins of the fort were unoccupied.

Stagecoach Period 1861 to 1881--The Barlow-Sanderson Overland Mail and Express Company repaired a portion of the structure, probably just the rectangle of room blocks. It is used as a "home station" and general repair shop on the line from Kansas City to Santa Fe. The persistance of the stage line to 1881 might be explained by the fact that the first railroad did not enter Santa Fe until 1880. Mr. Sanderson resided at the stage station.

Cattle Period 1881 to 1884--Again abandoned, the ruins are scavanged for adobe by settlers.

Second Interim Period 1884 to 1920--Deterioration continues. A monument was put up by the Daughters of the American Revolution in 1912, and in 1920 the DAR was granted title to the site.

Terminal Period 1920 to 1963--In 1921 the Arkansas River flooded and largely obliterated what remained of the structure. Due to lack of funds needed to create an interest in the fort among the public, the DAR deeded the site to the state of Colorado in 1954. That year the state funded a limited archeological excavation there and marked the location of the fort foundation with adobe walls.

On June 3, 1960, Bent's Old Fort National Historic Site was established, and on October 31, 1961, the United States acquired title to the site. The National Park Service began its administration of the site on March 15, 1963.

Table 1
Items Traded at Bent's Fort

To Indians	From Indians	From Mexicans
molasses	buffalo robes	silver
arms	horses	blankets
ammunition	mules	Pueblo blankets
tobacco		mules
blankets (blue, white, and black)		
coffee		
red cloth		
beads (white, red, and blue)		
brass wire		
hoop iron		
butcher knives		
small axes		
vermillion		
powder and ball		
abalone shells		
Mexican blankets		
Pueblo blankets		
kettles		
lead		
sugar		
Navajo blankets		
brass tacks		
shells		

To Emigrants and Gold Prospectors	From Emigrants and Gold Prospectors	From Mountainmen
horses	silver	beaver pelts
mules	gold	

From Independence	To Independence	To Mexicans
manufactured iron	buffalo robes	arms
	furs	cloth
	silver	powder
	gold	lead
		molasses ?
		annumition
		tobacco ?
		coffee
		brass wire
		hoop iron
		butcher knives
		axes
		kettles

Animals at Fort
pigeons
chickens
turkeys
several peacocks
one goat

EXCAVATION METHODS

The West Dump and the western portion of the Main Dump, both previously located by Moore, and two features (designated F 92 and F 94) discovered during Robert W. Leonard's monitoring of the trenching for the reconstructed fort walls were known to be located in the area north-east of (or in front of) the fort (see figure 4). This entire area was to undergo landscaping and trail construction and, accordingly, these known resources were to be mitigated in face of the anticipated impacts. Therefore, a control grid was imposed to include all of the above features and deposits. In order to facilitate the recognition of spatial relationships among the fort, the known dump and features, and any other undiscovered features, the front wall (or north-east side) of the fort was employed to demarcate the base line of the grid, with the alpha datum point being located 20 feet east of the northern corner of the fort along the 109° (from magnetic north) line formed by the front of the fort. Site meridian was therefore not aligned with either true or magnetic north, but extended from the alpha datum at 19° (again, from magnetic north).

Alpha datum was designated N0, E0, and the two dimensional locations of all features or cultural material located within the grid were thereafter expressed in terms of north ad east coordinates. Grid units are referred to according to the coordinates of the corner nearest alpha datum (the southwestern corner of the grid unit). For example, the grid unit nearest alpha datum (immediately to the northeast) would be N0/E0. The unit adjacent to the north would be N3/E0, the one just east of N0/E0 would be N0/E3. The location of the alpha datum was 109° 30 feet and 93 feet from the site datum, situated just across the parking lot on a small rise, 1.73 feet above alpha datum. The elevation of the site datum was 4,004.95 feet, being 4.91 feet below the elevation of the C-1 brass cap that served as the reference point for the datum. Elevation of the C-1 brass cap was 4,009.86 feet and site datum was 94° and 256 feet from the cap.

Previous to and during excavation of the Main and West Dumps, an effort was made to locate additional dumps or other features within the gridded area by means of core samples taken at 20-foot intervals along the N20 to N180 grid lines. Initial attempts at obtaining core samples with a simple, manually operated coring device and a gasoline-powered posthole digger proved to be too time consuming, primarily because of a gravel and rock layer that covered much of the ground surface of the area. Fortunately, Las Animas District of the Soil Conservation Service kindly agreed to lend the services of their truck mounted coring mechanism, and two of their personnel to operate it.

About 50 corings were taken to a depth of between 2 feet and 6 feet with this device in approximately seven hours. Cores were 2 inches in diameter. Soil from the cores was spread out with a trowel and visually examined. No previously undiscovered cultural deposits were located within the grid area, although the procedure aided greaty in delimiting the extent of the West and Main Dumps, and of Leonard's F 94.

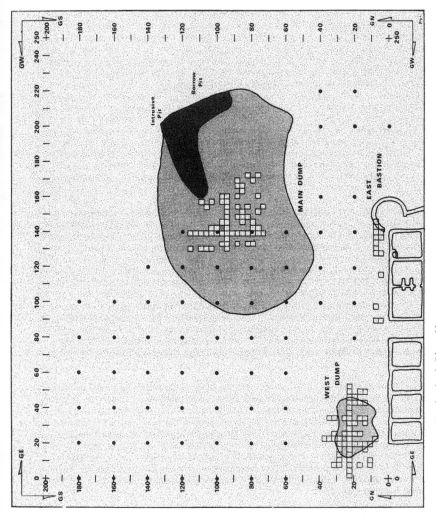

Figure 4.   Archeological Plan Map

16

The basic grid unit employed was a 3-feet-by-3-feet square; the smallest unit that could feasibly be excavated to any depth. Besides providing greater control over the horizontal distribution of cultural material, the small excavation unit was decided upon because it facilitated the probabilistic sampling technique, described in detail in a later section of this report. Such a small excavation unit decreases the volume of earth that must be excavated to obtain a sample from which dependable satistical inferences may be drawn about the population being sampled (in this case, the population of cultural material, by grid unit, in the dumps). This is so because the adequacy of a sample is determined not so much by the percentage of the population sampled as by the absolute number of samples obtained.

A non-random configuration of excavation units complemented the probabilistic sampling design. Units were selected randomly for excavation so that generalizations could be made about the total cultural content of both trash dumps. This would not, however, supply all of the pertinent information about the dumps. Besides content, it was necessary to determine the extent of the dumps and the manner in which material contained in the dumps was deposited. In order to investigate these matters, cross-trenches were excavated through both of the trash dumps. The placement of these trenches, arbitrary only from a probabilistic viewpoint, was selected after considering Moore's findings in the area and the results of the coring described just above. An attempt was made to locate the intersection of the cross-trenches in the center, and, it was hoped in the deepest part, of the trash dumps.

As may be seen in figures 4 and 5, the (grid) north-south (actually northeast-southwest) trench in the West Dump had to be modified because of an unexpected encounter with one of Moore's backfilled exploratory trenches. The northsouth trench here was comprised of units along the E18 line from N9 to N30. At N30, the alignment of the trench was shifted by the width of one excavation unit to E21. The trench then continued in a northerly direction and terminated at grid unit N36/E21.

All earth removed from the West and Main Dumps was screened, except soil known positively to be overburden. Four-fifths of the soil was screened through 1/4inch mesh screen, and one-fifth through 1/8-inch mesh screen in an effort to retrieve a sample of items of cultural material typically diminutive in size, such as trade beads and percussion caps. This was accomplished by placing one shovelful of dirt in five of the finer-meshed screen. All cultural material found in situ or in the screens was bagged according to the 3-feet-by-3-feet grid unit stratum and level (as appropriate) in which it was found.

The excavation of the West Dump was begun on February 20, 1976, and concluded on April 1, 1976, with a crew which, besides the principal investigator, consisted of three other members: Roxie Hoss, Jack Herron, and Cathy Johnson. Excavation of the Main Dump was delayed until May 19, 1976, because two construction sheds were located over a portion of this dump and could not be moved until then. The crew for the Main Dump excavation, completed on June 7, 1976, was the same, except for the replacement of Jack Herron by Brian Avazion. Leonard's Feature 94 and 92 were also investigated during this later period.

Figure 5. Composite Photograph of the West Dump Excavations

The English system of measure (feet and inches) was used instead of the metric system for two reasons. First, the fort was built in feet and inches, and it was thought to be more convenient if discovered features were described in the same terms as might be found in historic records. Also, data recorded from the archeological excavation would be relayed to architects and engineers, who worked in feet and inches.

REMOTE SENSING: METHODOLOGY AND RESULTS

In an attempt to discover the locations of historically recorded features associated with the fort (such as the ice house, race track, the intersection with the fort of the Mountain Branch of the Santa Fe Trail and, possibly, the acequia--the Spanish term for an agricultural irrigation ditch--whose locations had been lost with the passing of years) black and white, as well as color infrared, photographs of the general vicinity of the fort were obtained and inspected. It was thought, too, that the use of these remote sensing techniques might also reveal other features associated with the fort for which there were no historical evidence. Some possibilities were additional trash dumps, burial sites, and historically cultivated areas.

STEREO PAIRS

The black and white photographs were taken by a private company, which had been contracted for the purpose by the Department of Surveys, Denver Service Center. These were taken with the camera mounted beneath the plane, so that the line of sight through the lens would be perpendicular to the ground surface. The plane was flown over the Bent's Old Fort area in parallel transects so that the series of photographs taken at each transect could be fitted together. Moreover, photographs were taken during the course of the transect frequently enough so that any given location appeared in more than one of the photographs, and were therefore viewed from a slightly different perspective in each photograph.

By focusing on the same spot in two different photographs simultaneously with a device called a stereoptiscope the surface of the ground might be seen in relief. Topographic patterns were thus seen where they were not apparent while walking over the ground surface. Pairs of photographs showing the same location were referred to as "stereo pairs." The black and white photographs examined were taken on June 18, 1974. The scale of the photographs was about 1:2,000--large enough to permit the recognition of shapes only a few feet across.

Inspection of the black and white stereo pairs with the aid of a stereoptiscope by Robert Henson of the Bureau of Land Management Remote Sensing Laboratory at the Denver Federal Center revealed two anomolies within the area where historic written records and the crude maps indicate the ice house may have been located. About 25 feet west of the fork of a southern extension of the entrance road (or eastern arc of the loop road around the fort) was a raised area that appeared to be roughly rectangular. In fact, when one of the black and white stereo pairs was viewed without the steroscope, a rectangular pattern could be seen, comprised of circular light (perhaps bare) spots. Nearer to the present river channel was another small area of higher ground, located on the east side of the road. The vegetation here was different from that surrounding the area, being various types of short grasses and low shrubs in contrast to the taller grasses around the area.

A number of core samples to a depth of 6 or 7 feet were taken at each of the suspected areas. At both, nothing aside from the expected stratigraphy was recovered from the samples.

An additional anomaly was observed to be about 40 feet west of the entrance road and roughly 450 feet north of the north corner of the fort. This was a shallow, circular depression approximately 30 feet in diameter at the crest of a small hill. This location did not conform to any historically recorded feature associated with the fort and time limitations prevented an investigation of this anomaly, which was not disturbed by reconstruction activities. The location and regularity of the anomaly are intriguing, however, and it has been recorded as BWA 3 in hopes that it will be thoroughly examined sometime in the future.

Also visible, particularly in the stereo-pairs, were crop marks over the entire area west of the entrance road and of the fort. The crop marks are not apparent when the area is viewed from the ground.

Ground surface examination of the many small light or white circles, which were seen in the black and white photographs, proved them to be anthills.

The location of the portion of the Main Dump to the east of the entrance road corresponded to an area of more verdant vegetation, which appeared darker than the surrounding vegetation in the black and white photographs. However, no inequality in the topography could be seen with the stereoptiscope. As described previously in this paper, the mound that had once existed there had been leveled with a bulldozer. As exemplified by this, recent intensive farming activities in the area west of the entrance road may have had a similar effect upon the topographic manifestations of other historic cultural features that may have exited there.

COLOR INFRARED PHOTOGRAPHS

On Sunday, July 18, 1976, aerial color infrared photos of Bent's Old Fort and the immediate vicinity were taken from a small private airplane by Mr. Emil Gimino, one of the partners in the construction company contracted to rebuilt the fort. Mr. Gimino, who had previously arranged the flight in order to obtain conventional color and black and white aerial photographs for his personal use, kindly agreed to take the additional infrared photographs. A 35mm camera using Kodak Ektachrome Infrared film with a Kodak Wratten Filer No. 12 was employed for these latter.

METHODOLOGY

Very briefly, color infrared photographs record the normally invisible infrared waves reflected or transmitted by an object by means of a color film sensitized to infrared. The width of the infrared band produces several different colors that may be exhibited on the color infrared photograph. The color infrared film is also sensitive to green and red visible light (and to blue that is screened out by the use of a yellow filter). The film is manufactured and processed so that infrared shows up as red on the photographic print. Similarly, green appears as blue and red as green in the print. The infrared image may be mixed with reflected green and red, producing the range of possible colors that can be displayed on an infrared photograph. Because of the color changes, infrared photography is sometimes called "false-color" infrared photography.

It should be noted here that infrared color photography records only near-red radiation, and not heat radiation. The object reflecting or emitting this radiation need not be hot itself. If film more sensitive to heat waves were produced it would be very difficult to prevent it from being overexposed by the heat present in normal situations.

The addition of the infrared component to the red and green transmitted or reflected from the subject results in colors on the finished photograph that are characteristic of specific subjects. For example, healthy deciduous green foliage is seen as red; diseased or deficient foliage as greenish or bluish, and conifers as dark purple. Non-botanical color modifications include venous blood as red-brown, arterial blood as green-brown, and fluorite crystal as buff. Just as important as the color exhibited by particular subjects in an archeological application of color infrared photography is the fact that contiguous subjects or subject areas may appear in contrasting colors whereas there may be little or no difference in the visible light colors of these.

Examination of the color infrared photographs was done, again, with the aid of Robert Hanson from the Remote Sensing Laboratory of the Bureau of Land Management at the Denver Federal Center.

The plane from which the photographs were taken was not equipped with a camera mount that would have allowed the photographs to be taken at an angle directly perpendicular to the ground surface. In addition, the wings on the plane were located below the windows, so that the photographs could only be taken over the wings as the plane rolled over on its side in a steep bank. These circumstances not only prevented the photograph from being taken from the most revealing angle, but also made it very difficult to adjust for the changes in lighting that occurred rapidly with the movement of the plane. For this latter reason, many of the photographs were either darker or lighter than one would wish for. Kodak's infrared photography manual states that ". . . with infrared color film, exposure should be held to within $\pm\frac{1}{2}$ stop of the best exposure." This would imply that an error on the negative side would be even more critical and may explain why many of the photographs are too dark to display detail with much clarity. In addition, there may have been some defect in the film itself, as the reds are more purple and the greens bluer than they should be in most of the photographs. This defect may very well have resulted from improper storage of the film, which is sensitive to heat. The film must be stored at -18° to -23° C before use, and, after exposure, stored again at below 4° C until it can be developed. Failure to do this results in a reduced sensitivity to infrared and a shift in the color balance towards cyan, a greenish-blue color. In fact, this shift towards cyan fits in very wel with the color modification observed just above.

HISTORIC RIVER CHANNEL

Examination of the color infrared photographs, incidentally but interestingly, yielded some indication of the relative chronology of the changes in the course of the Arkansas River to the east of the fort. Evidence of these changes may also be seen in the black and white aerial photographs but are more strikingly illustrated in the color infrared photos.

The grade of the area east of the entrance road is generally steeper next to the entrance road and becomes progressively lower to the east, up to the edge of the forest within the arc formed by the present river channel. One would expect that the most recent course of the river was through the area lowest at present, as this would have been the space occupied by the river when it flowed between the entrance road and the forest. It is likely that the river moved gradually to the east, probably as a result of more erosion occurring along the eastern bank of the river.

The color of the vegetation between the entrance road and the forest as it appeared in the infrared color photographs supported this idea. At the lower elevation near the forest edge, the vegetation appeared greenish-blue, a color that represents deficient foliage. Vegetation near the entrance road was reddish, indicating that it was healthy. This difference in vegetation was probably not attributable to a difference in the availability of water to the vegetation since one would normally find more water at the lower elevation. It is more probably, then, due to a difference in soil. Topsoil in the most recent channel would have been scoured away by the shallow, often rapidly flowing river. In the older river course, a new topsoil might have developed with time, as evidently has happened. The development of the topsoil just east of the entrance road was probably facilitated by the deposition of colluvial soil from the higher elevations to the west of the road, as well as by soil precipitating out of receding flood waters.

The sandbar that was built up in the 1921 flood and which redirected the river flow to its present channel is evident in the aerial photograhs. In the color infrared photos, it may be seen that the eastern end of the sandbar lines up very well with the western edge of the scoured area of poor vegetation, which extends in a north-easterly direction from here, and almost touches the approximate eastern boundary of the Main Trash Dump. The scoured area may then be seen to proceed in a more easterly direction than does the entrance road, which is aligned more to the north. Since it would seem that the scoured area was the course of the river in 1921 and that the river channel had been moving to the east up until that time, the western edge of the river during the fort's occupation must have been at the western edge of the scoured area as revealed in the color infrared photographs. All of this would indicate that the river flowed very near the fort during the time it was occupied.

FEATURES

Of the anomalies found in the examination of the black and white stereo pairs, only BWA 3 was evident in the color infrared photographs.

Perhaps this was because the color infrared shots of the area in which features BWA 1 and BWA 2 were located were generally underexposed. The vegetation in the slight depression of A 3 appeared reddish, probably due to water that had collected there.

However, several roughly linear anomalies not detected in the black and white photographs were seen in the color infrared photos. All three were bluish-green and lighter than their surroundings. All other linear configurations visible in the photographs may be explained by crop marks. The narrow CA 1 runs on either side of the mid-portion of the entrance road, and its presence here might well be attributed to the existence and construction of the road. However, as the entrance road approaches Highway 50, C 1 moves away from the entrance road to the east and runs for a distance parallel to and south of Highway 50. CA 1 also seems to go around to the west of the historic graveyard in the direction of the fort entrance, while the entrance road passes the graveyard to the east. CA 2, also quite narrow, joins with CA 1 just north of the graveyard and from this point extends to the west. In some of the color infrared photographs showing CA 2, the western end of the anomaly seems to pass through the current boundary of the historic area into a cultivated field for about 100 feet before it disappears. CA 3 is parallel to and north of CA 2, although much wider, and also appears to extend into the cultivated field in some of the color infrared photographs.

C 1 and C 2 may be residual manifestations of the Sante Fe Trail. The path described by the anomalies is at least a reasonable one. Historically, the trail from the east approached the fort on the north side of the Arkansas River, and was thought to have followed the north bank of the river west of the fort for some time before crossing the river at one of two fords further upstream. As to the alignment of CA 1 it is a logical location for the historic entrance road. We have seen that the channel of the river during the fort's occupation must have been quite near to the present-day entrance road in the near vicinity of the fort. It is quite possible that the historic road ran along much the same path as does the present-day road, especially if it were following the north bank of the historic river channel. It seems less likely from the evidence at hand to have been to the west of the entrance road. If the river channel had been further east of the entrance road, and had the trail run through the area between the entrance road and the hypothetical channel further east, one might expect at least some trace of the trail through this area to appear in the color infrared photographs. This area has not undergone disturbance to a degree comparable to that which the area west of the entrance road has been subjected. No such evidence of a former trail appears in this area. Although representing a more recent occurrence, the twin wheel tracks of automobiles or trucks that had driven through the area can be seen clearly in several places.

That the CA 2 also represents the Santa Fe Trail is likewise reasonable, if not at all certain. CA 2 is on the north bank of the historic river channel, and approaches the fort at its main entrance.

What, if anything, CA 3 represents is a matter of more speculation. The wide anomalie might be the result of earlier or later alignments of the trail, camping activity, or it could even be the remnant of the race track

24

mentioned historically. A surface inspection of the area yielded no material to support any of the ideas.

SUMMARY

The application of black and white stereoscopic and color infrared remote sensing techniques resulted in the discovery of several interesting anomalies. Core samples taken at BWA 1 and BWA 2 yielded no evidence of anything but the expected stratigraphy at these locations. However, the reliability of this method in detecting the presence of certain types of features is not absolute. This is particularly true of the detached ice house, which were constructed of adobe, and seems to have been used only a short time. We have seen, also, that the position of the anomalies are somewhat consistent with the historical descriptions and maps of the ice house location.

The inspection of the color infrared photographs tentatively revealed the possible path of the Santa Fe Trail in the immediate vicinity of Bent's Old Fort. It is recommended that professional quality color infrared photographs be obtained of the vicinity of the fort from an altitude of about 20,000 feet. This altitude would allow recognition of a feature of the trail's size, but might also enable portions of the trail that have already been discovered on either side of the vicinity of the fort to be connected up with those tentatively identified in the present analysis, and also, perhaps, to identify sections of the trail not heretofore located.

Aside from the aerial photographs examined for this study, only satellite photographs, taken from an extremely high altitude are currently available for the area around the fort. However, there are commercial aerial photography companies operating in the region of southeastern Colorado with the capability of making the photographs described above. If the photographs are taken during a flight in which similar photographs of a nearby area are also taken as may be prearranged, the 1976 cost of obtaining the photographs would be only a few hundred dollars.

It is further recommended that further exploration of anomalies BWA 1, 2, and 3 be carried out sometime in the future prior to any grond disturbance in these areas. at BWA 1 and 2, this could be very limited test pitting. At BWA 3, more extensive test pitting is recommended.

MONITORING

The proposed site development called for, in general, the removal or concealment of all post-1846 innovations in the vicinity of the fort, and alteration of the landscape near the fort to 1846 appearance. It was necessary also to connect utility lines to facilities located, and concealed, within the reconstructed fort. As mentioned previously, all activities involving ground disturbance were monitored. The results of this surveillance are presented here.

ENTRANCE ROAD CONSTRUCTION

A new entrance road was constructed about 100 feet east of the existing one, running from Highway 50 to the area of the new parking lot. About 1 foot of earth was removed by a scraper before the roadbed was compacted and the asphalt poured.

A road scraper makes a shallow, smooth, and clean cut in which it is quite easy to discover features or cultural material should they be present. Two irregularly shaped areas, about 3 feet in diameter containing charred wood and a thin layer of fire-scorched earth were noticed in the scraped entrance road easement. Further inspection revealed numerous pine needles and a few strands of tinsel. Mr. John Patterson, park superintendent, later volunteers that these were probably spots where he ahd burnt Christmas trees. Also found in the easement were modern red brick fragments, slightly rusted pieces of what appeared to be modern farm implements, and several window pane and white ceramic fragments.

PARKING LOT CONSTRUCTION

The scraper, described above, was used here also. The parking lot area was scraped down, and the dirt piled up on the south side of the lot, in order to block the view of the parking from the fort.

While inspecting the area where the parking lot was to be located, a small, crudely made, corner notched projectile point was found on the ground surface. This proved to be the only artifact recovered during the monitoring of the parking lot construction.

As the dark A horizon was scraped away and the pale-brown loam beneath was exposed, plow scars, running roughly east-west and spaced about 1 foot apart, became evident. The ground here is commonly known to have been cultivated, whic may partially explain the lack of artifacts found. The fort, as I have been told many times by local informants, was a very popular spot`for pothunting, and several of the collectors from the area I have spoken to have assured me that a recently plowed field was a good place to find artifacts.

In addition to the plow scars, a maze of rodent-runs were visible on the top of the C1 horizon. No other features could be seen in the parking lot area. No historic farm artifacts, or, for that matter, any other artifacts were found in this area.

LEACH FIELD AND SEPTIC TANK INSTALLATION

A 30-foot by 10-foot by 12-foot pit was dug for the septic tank and a 125-foot by 75-foot by 7-foot area was excavated for the leach field just south of the main corral. At the investigator's request, the A horizon in the leach field area was removed by the scraper. A bulldozer was then employed, because of the extreme hardness of the C horizon, to bring the area down to the required depth. The pit for the septic tank was dug by a hydraulic hoe with a bucket capacity of three-quarters of a yard. This is not an implement that greatly facilitates archeological monitoring, as it removes great chunks of earth very rapidly.

While the A horizon was being scraped from the leach field area, several circular features of mixed light tan and dark brown soil with diameters of 6 to 8 feet were discovered. The soil within these features was loose and contained a great number of twigs and wood chips, the former being still fresh enough to snap when broken. Upon inquiry, several persons working on the fort's reconstruction recalled that pits had been dug for percolation tests in what they recalled as being the same spots. The twigs in the fill of the features could very reasonably be attributed to tumbleweeds blown into the open pits. In fact, any open pit in the area is soon similarly filled. As for the wood chips, logs used in the reconstruction of the fort were usually hand-hewn at that particular location and were probably deposited in the test pits. Subsequent scraping of the area yielded no other material in the features.

Several pieces of charcoal were found in the back-dirt from the septic tank pit. While inspecting the east wall of the pit, a stratum of what appeared to be typical A horizon soil thoroughly mixed with a tan soil and a small amount of charred wood was found to extend from ground surface to a few inches in depth. The length of the stratum was about 15 feet and tapered off gradually to the north and south. This appeared to be the remains of a recent wood fire.

Riverine gravels and cobbles were only about 4 feet below ground surface at the southern end of the leach field although 9 feet of overlying earth was removed before they were found in the septic tank pit.

HISTORIC TRAIL

As the historic trail to the fort is believed to have followed the same path as did the former entrance road, trail construction north of the existing Daughters of the American Revolution monument consisted mianly of removing the asphalt paving from the road and otherwise obliterating evidence of modern construction. Pieces of concrete brick and some black plastic sheeting was found during the scraping of the trail a few feet north of the historic graveyard.

As the historic trail follows the previous entrance road around to the east of the fort it passes over the western portion of the Main Dump. In fact, the eastern edge of the former entrance road here was the eastern limit of the portion of the Main Dump excavated by the author, since no site development was proposed to the west of this line.

After several discussions with Mr. Ike Erickson, owner of the construction company contracted to do the site development work, it was decided that it was not necessary to go more than a few inches in depth in cutting the bed for the historic trail. This section of the entrance road, which had looped around the fort, had not been paved. The cutting of the bed was done with a road grader, and no cultural material was observed to be disturbed by this portion of the trail reconstruction. The cutting operation was done after the Main Dump excavation had been concluded, and the open grid units filled in. During the excavation of the dump it was noted that there was generally several inches of overburden on top of the trash deposit. The scraping most probably removed only this overburden.

Water was sprinkled oer the trail cut by means of a water truck, which was then driven over the trail several times to cmpact the trail bed. A small sheepsfoot roller was also employed for this purpose. The effect of this was to disturb the upper few inches of the dump beneath the trail.

LANDSCAPING

The most extensive landscaping in the vicinity of the fort was proposed for the area in front, or north-east of the north-eastern wall, of the fort. It had originally been thought that landscaping in front of the fort would largely or completely destroy the Main Dump and portion of the West Dump located there. It was known that the general area had been bulldozed, probably in the early 1950s by the then adjacent land owner (Moore 1973:59), and it was believed that the remaining trash deposits would be quite shallow in most places. This turned out not to be the case.

All phases of the reconstruction of the fort, including archeological investigations, had to be completed by the late July 1976 deadline. Site development was scheduled for a time near the conclusion of the reconstruction of the fort so as not to interfere with construction and the contract for site development not let until the excavation of the dumps had been begun. It was therefore impossible to determine prior to beginning the excavations in front of the fort the exact location and extent of ground disturbances there, since the site developer was unavailable for counsel.

Nonetheless, it is to the credit of Mr. Ike Erickson, the site development contractor, that the West Dump and Main Dump were ultimately not disturbed during the landscaping. By the time Mr. Erickson could be conferred with concerning the matter, the limits of the West and Main Dumps were known. A subsurface investigation of the area in front of the fort had also been conducted, and no other features had been found. When this information had been conveyed to Mr. Erickson, along with the

National Park Service's concern for the conservation of the remaining trash deposits, he devised a strategy by which the landscaping specifications could be met but which would avoid the West and Main Dumps.

The specifications called for the leveling and graveling of an area immediately in front of the fort and the construction of a broad, shallow swale running to the northeast of the fort for drainage. The majority of the swale was positioned between the two dumps. The southwestern end of the swale and a part of the area to be gravelled were over the West Dump. Fortunately, only about 0.5 foot had to be removed here from the ground surface. As had been determined during the excavation of the West Dump, the A horizon over the dump was about 1.2 feet in depth in most places, and contained material unrelated to the dump itself. The best cultural material was not disturbed by the landscaping.

To the north-west of the fort, the asphalt paving of an existing parking lot was taken up, and a line of trees running through the middle of the parking lot was removed. The area was then found to be at the correct elevation and graded smooth. The soil beneath the paving was found to be primarily gravel fill, brought in as bedding for the parking lot.

On the south-east side of the fort there was no disturbance of the ground below the existing ground surface. Mounds of sand, which had been placed there during the reconstruction of the fort, were removed, and afterward what remained of this material was smoothed. No cultural material or features were found on the north-west or south-east sides of the fort.

SUMMARY

The monitoring of the landscaping at the fort was both disappointing and rewarding. No cultural material or features of any significance were discovered. On the other hand, through the cooperation of the site contractor, none of the known cultural resources in the area landscaped were damaged by that activity.

EAST BASTION EXCAVATIONS

The test excavations done in the area of the east bastion (hereafter referred to as "the bastion") were prompted by Robert W. Leonard's findings in the summer of 1975. The bastion area had been examined by means of excavation twice before Leonard's work. Both Jackson Moore and Herbert Dick had tested the area in order to determine the location of the bastion. Leonard reported that he dug more deeply than did Moore or Dick and discovered a midden deposit. He then dug two test trenches outside the bastion to determine whether the bastion had been built over the deposit, or if the deposit had been made within the bastion after its construction. If the bastion had been built over the midden, dating the midden would provide a date before which the bastion could not have been built.

In a trench dug from the juncture of the north wall of the fort with the bastion due magentic north, in excess of 9 feet long Leonard found midden-like soil in both the east and west walls. The midden-like deposit extended 9 feet from the north wall of the fort. Leonard noted that the dark soil in the deposit appeared very similar to that found inside the bastion. Both contained bits of charcoal.

Leonard had also noted a dark soil stratum while monitoring the trenching for the modern foundation for the north wall of the reconstructed fort. Thus it seemed to him, as he suggested to me, that this might also be a part of the midden. If it were, it would run from the bastion to a point just east of the main entrance to the fort.

Accordingly, I opened up grid units N3, E126, and E6, E126 (see figures 4 and 5) to find the extent of the midden-like deposit Leonard had discovered near the bastion. The coordinates for the junction of the north wall and the bastion were almost exactly N0, E144 and the north wall of the fort runs very closely along the N0 line. When the 3-feet-by-6-feet trench formed by these two units was taken down to the depth of about 0.75 feet, a very distinct straight line could be seen in the floor of the trench a few inches east of the west wall of the trench. This was designated feature 30. The soil to the east of the line was dark, while that to the west was much lighter. Having had some experience in the identification of previously dug archeological trenches in the area by this time, the characteristics of the feature at hand suggested to me that it might be yet another of these trenches. In an attempt to determine if the feature indeed represented a previous archeological excavation unit, the two grid units just to the east of N6, E126--units N6, E129 and N6, E132--were opened. Also, grid unit N3, E114 was excavated in order to further test for the extent of the feature.

A few inches east of the west wall in N3, E114, feature 31 was found, which looked, in plan, almost identical to the feature found in N6, E126--that is, a straight, north-south line of division with dark soil to the east and light soil to the west. Units N3, E135 and N6, E135, located near Leonard's trench but adjacent to grid unit N6, E132, which had just been opened, were then rapidly excavated. At a depth of 2 feet in N6, E135, an east-west line of division could be seen on the floor of the

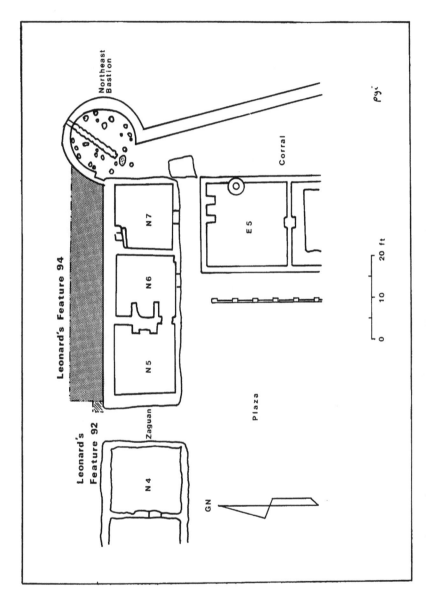

Figure 6. Archeological Plan Map of Leonard's Features 92 and 94

31

units, just 0.2 foot from the northern wall. The soil here was darker to the south of the line, and lighter to the north. The darker soil was designated feature 32. Finally, further cleaning of the floor in unit N6, E129 revealed two additional north-south lines of division. The line furthest west was located from 1 foot to 1.6 feet east of E129 and provided the eastern edge of the trench first noticed in unit N6, E126. About 0.5 foot east of this line, or from 0.9 foot to 1.4 feet west of E132, was another distinct linear soil transition, dark soil to east and light tan soil to the west. It seemeed likely that this dark soil, called feature 33, might join with the east-west line observed in unit N6, E135 to form the north-east corner of a backfilled square or rectangular archeological excavation unit (see figure 5).

Excavation near the bastion was halted at this point, and the available records of the locations of previously excavated archeological units were examined. Unfortunately, as noted earlier in this report, the plan map of Moore's excavation could not be found after having been sent to the fort a number of years earlier. There remained only an aerial photograph that Moore had taken of his excavation units, and the sketches in his excavation notes. Unfortunately, the aerial photograph had been taken before all units had been completely excavated. It was a bit difficult to determine the exact placement of the units because the photos had been taken from an oblique angle (from the east). Also, the sketches by definition were not drawn to scale.

Even so, when the photographs were inspected each showed that a square excavation pit had been dug at the juncture of the north wall and the bastion. The aerial photograph also revealed that three test trenches had been excavated between the square by the bastion and the main gate. These looked to be about 3 feet in width and 9 or 10 feet long, stretching north of the north wall of the fort.

Two things then seemed quite obvious: 1) that we had found Moore's excavation units in our units N3, E114, and N3, E126, and N3, E126; and 2) that Leonard must have dug his test rench from the juncture of the north wall and the bastion through an excavation square previously dug there. It also seemed possible that the corner found in N3, E135 and N6, E135 was the northwest corner of the Moore's excavation square. Finally, all of the above conclusions seemed even more likely since we had found very few artifacts in the backfill taken from bastion excavation units, and none of these could positively be dated as historic.

Investigations near the bastion were therefore abandoned, at least for the moment, and we returned our attention to the very pressing matter of completing the West Dump excavation. The erection of scaffolding near the bastion for the purpose of plastering the walls dictated that units opened there be backfilled. It was felt, though, that these units could quickly be reexcavated should that need arise in the future, particularly since the earth near the bastion was inordinately loose and friable in comparison with the hardpacked clay encountered over most of the area in front of the fort.

A subsequent visit with Mr. Leonard at the Laboratory of Public Archeology at Colorado State University engendered some doubts in regard to my conclusions (explained in the two preceding paragraphs).

In the first place, Leonard had taken historic artifacts from his trench at the bastion wall juncture. One of these was a wagon hub, and from directly beneath the hub had come the articulated skeleton of a small mammal. Secondly, Leonard displayed color prints and soil samples taken of the midden-like deposit inside the bastion and in the trench. Both were remarkably similar.

To finally resolve the controversy, additional excavation was carried out in the area to the west of the bastion on June 5, 6, and 7, 1976. It was conducted specifically to test the following explanations that had been offered for the findings made in Leonard's test trench:

1. That the northern end of Leonard's trench had revealed a midden deposit that was just north of Moore's excavation square.

2. That the western wall of Leonard's trench was dug in Moore's square, but that the eastern wall was located in the midden.

3. That the eastern edge of Moore's excavation square was not aligned with magnetic north, but to the west of north. Leonard's trench, aligned with magnetic north, could then have been excavated in a midden next to the bastion.

4. That the southeast corner of Moore's excavation square was not at the bastion northern wall juncture, but a few feet to the west. Again, this would have allowed Leonard's trench to have been dug through a midden next to the bastion.

5. That the surface of the ground when Moore dug his excavation square was higher than it was when Leonard dug his trench; thus, Moore may not have dug deeply enough to discover the midden-like deposit found in Leonard's trench.

Statements 1 through 4 above could not be absolutely disproven prior to further excavation since it was impossible to determine with precision from either the aerial photograph or the sketch map in Moore's notes the dimensions, position, or shape of Moore's square. As to the dimension of the square, it looked small in the sketch and somewhat larger in the photograph. There was also the chance that the square had been altered after the photograph had been taken. Explanation 5 could not be discounted beforehand with total confidence because elevations of Moore's square could not be located.

THE SEARCH FOR MOORE'S EXCAVATIONS

On June 5, 1976, units N6, E132; N6, E135; N6, E138; N3, E128; N6, E141; and N6, E144 were opened or reopened, depending upon the particular unit. At a depth of 1.0 foot in unit N6, E141, the outline of the test trench Leonard had dug was plainly visible in the floor of the unit (see figure 5). As the units to the east and west were excavated to a depth of 1.75 feet, it became clearly apparent that the northern edge, feature 33, previously noted in N6, E135, extended from that grid unit to the east through N6, E138 and matched up with a soil change line in N6,

E143. The soil to the south of this line in N6, E143, moreover, appeared identical to that within feature 33 in units N6, E135 and N6, E138. The north end of Leonard's test trench extended about 0.6 foot beyond the northern edge of feature 33 as seen in N6, E138 (see figure 5). It seemed very probable, then, that Leonard had excavated his trench within feature 33. This was confirmed when N6, E141 was taken down to a depth of 3.0 feet. On the floor of the unit at this depth, below that excavated by Leonard, the northern boundary of feature 33 joined with the boundary of the feature visible in units N6, E138 and N6, E141. Furthermore, as the excavation of unit N6, E144 proceeded, the northeast corner and eastern boundary of feature 33 were discovered on the floor of the unit at 23 feet and in the southern wall.

Feature 33 is judged to be Moore's square excavation unit that he dug at the juncture of the north wall of the fort and the bastion by virtue of the following:

1. The position of the feature coincides with that presented for Moore's excavation unit in his notes and the aerial photograph taken of his excavation, although it does extend further to the east than either of these would indicate.

2. No other feature that might be interpreted as Moore's excavation unit was found within feature 33.

3. Most exclusively artifactual material removed from feature 33, although partially comprised of historical items, included material of very recent manufacture, i.e., wire nails and fragments of plaster. Some of this recent material was found at the lowest depth of the feature excavated.

In summary, Leonard has presented persuasive evidence for a true midden deposit located beneath the floor of the bastion. However, the feature tentatively identified by Leonard (my feature 33, found by Leonard in his unit II-1 and designated by him feature 94) as a western extension of this refuse pit outside the walls of the bastion was found in subsequent investigations to be an exploratory pit excavated by Moore during his work at the fort. Thus, it would seem that the refuse pit discovered by Leonard was confined specifically to the area within the bastion since Moore did not report a midden-like deposit in his exploratory unit (feature 33) dug just west of the bastion.

LEONARD'S FEATURE 94

My feature 33 (Moore's square pit in the corner formed by the bastion and the northeast wall) is a portion of Leonard's feature 94, which he originally thought to be connected to his feature 85 (the refuse pit beneath the floor of the bastion). Leonard first observed feature 94 in the north wall of the trench dug for the foundation of rooms N5, N6, and N7 noting that it ran from near the bastion westward for 52.6 feet while decreasing in thickness, as seen in the northern trench all, from 1.9 feet to 0.45 foot at about 0.5 foot below 100 grade. I recorded a similar stratum in the north wall of his excavated east-west trench comprised of grid units N6, E132; N6, E135; N6, E138; N6, E141; and N6, E143. The north wall of this trench, then, was 9 feet north of the northeast wall of the fort, or 0.85 foot beyond the edge of Leonard's feature 85 (my feature 33) at 8.15 feet from the northeast wall of the fort. The stratum in the north wall stretched the entire length of the trench and was also about 0.5 foot below ground surface and varied in thickness from 0.1 foot to 0.5 foot. The composition of the stratum was largely homogenous and appeared identical to the contents (fill) of feature 33 proper. There is little reason to doubt that the stratum was deposited at the same time that feature 33 was backfilled. Given the extent of the stratum, this was very likely an intentional effort to raise the grade of the area in conformance with construction specifications. The approximately 0.5 foot of overburden above the stratum probably represents a continuation of this effort at a later date. This interpretation would apply equally to the stratigraphy recorded by Leonard in the western reaches of his feature 94: the portion of the feature to the west of the western edge of Moore's excavation square.

LEONARD'S FEATURE 92

Leonard also noted an intrusive pit in the north face of the trench dug for the foundation of the northeast wall of the fort, located 8.75 feet east of the northwest corner of the bastion (1978:45-47). To investigate the nature of this feature (Leonard's feature 92), the 3-foot-by-3-foot grid unit N6, E88, 6 feet north of the position at which Leonard had discovered the feature, was opened. Because of time limitations, soil from the unit was not screened although care was taken to examine it for cultural material as it was removed by trowel and shovel. For the same reason, the unit was excavated only to a depth of 2.0 feet below ground surface, at which the feature was still visible in the floor of the units. In both the north and south walls at this depth a very straight, vertical line of soil transition could be seen at E90. To the east of this was a homogenous tan, sandy soil while to the west the earth looked to be a mix of tan, brown, and blackish soils. This arrangement was apparent also in the floor of the unit.

It cannot be stated positively that the feature represents a trench dug during an archeological investigation of the area just to the front of the fort. No cultural material was recovered from N6, E88 and therefore no date was obtained for the feature. If it were an excavation unit one would hope for some modern material in the backfill. Even so, the pronounced regularity of the soil transition and the alignment of the western edge of the feature perpendicularly with the front wall of the fort certainly suggests that the feature was an excavation unit. The total absence of artifactual material supports this to some degree.

There are no surviving records that indicate that Moore had excavated a trench at this location, and as Leonard has stated (1978:45) Moore does not recollect doing so. Therefore, if the feature is in fact an archeological trench, it may have been dug by Herbert Dick during his 1956 excavation. Final resolution of the matter must await either the discovery of an archeological plan map exhibiting a trench at this location, or further excavation of the feature and subsequent analysis that might provide a reliable modern date for the feature or point to a nonarcheological function.

STATISTICAL TECHNIQUE

A further discussion of the sampling method and statistical technique used in the excavations of the dumps is necessary here. Individual pieces of cultural material cannot be sampled directly in an excavation since they may not be selected one at a time. In practice they are selected en masse as the excavation units that contain them are excavated. Therefore, the procedure of excavating randomly selected grid units is properly an application of cluster sampling, and the calculations employed in the interpretation of the sample must be those appropriate for cluster sampling rather than element sampling.

A random sampling procedure was employed in the excavations of the West and Main Dumps in order to predict the proportions and absolute numbers of various types of items of cultural material contained within the areas to be disturbed. This was done, as previously stated, because time and funds were not available to excavate these areas in their entirety. A sample probabilistically selected is preferable to one selected non-probabilistically for three reasons: it is a more unbiased sample, inferences concerning the population from which the sample was taken may be drawn, and a measure of the accuracy of the inferences drawn is provided for with the application of the proper statistical analysis to the sample.

Briefly, the randomly collected data was treated in the following manner: The proportion of elements of a given type of cultural material (blue transfer-printed pearlware, for example) to elements of cultural material of all types (or the total number of items of cultural material) in a stratum was calculated from the grid units randomly selected and excavated. Then, the variance for the proportion was calculated, and the standard deviation for the proportion determined from this. At various confidence levels (95 percent and 80 percent), confidence limits for the proportion were determined. Confidence limits for the total number of elements of the given type were, in turn, calculated from the confidence limits of the proportion.

These statistics appear in appendixes A and B. The first column shows the number of items of the given type of cultural material that were found within the randomly selected units excavated, for each stratum. The next column presents the proportion that the number in the first column represents of the total number of artifacts excavated from randomly selected units in the given stratum. Unless the type of cultural material described is a sub-type of a more general type. In this case, the second column shows a proportion for the number of elements of the sub-type to the number of elements of the type that were found in the random units excavated in the stratum. This was done in order to produce a more meaningful statistical results. It is generally more instructive to talk about proportions when both the fraction and the whole are related in some significant way than when this relationship is tenuous or ill-defined. In this situation, the most important relationship is (the judgment, at least) that the artifacts are essentially of the same type, but that there is enough variation in ancillary characteristics to justify the positing of sub-types. Therefore, a proportion based upon the number of elements of the sub-type to the number of elements of the type was thought to be most important.

None of the foregoing has any effect on the accuracy of subsequent statistical calculations. The proportion, which is the basis for those calculations, is derived from numbers of artifacts found in randomly selected clusters, in any case. The proportion is valid, whether it is produced from comparing the number of a type of cultural material to the total number of items to cultural material, or from comparing the number of a sub-type to the total number of items of a type.

The last two columns in appendixes A and B present the results of the statistical technique per se. The third column gives the first statistical prediction, which along with the fourth column are at the 80 percent confidence level. The number here is that of the elements of this type or sub-type that one might expect to find in the entire stratum, including the unexcavated portion. The measure of the degree of certainty with which one might expect this range of numbers to be accurate is the confidence level for the statistic, and is expressed as a percentage at the top of the table. A 95 percent confidence level, for instance, would mean that one could expect the estimate to be accurate 95 out of 100 times. A 50 percent confidence level would mean that the estimate might be expected to be accurate in only half the cases in which it were made. The final column, labeled "percents" gives the estimated percentage for the representation of the type or sub-type of artifact, in the same way that artifact proportion was figured in the second column; e.g., a comparison of the numbers of items of types to total number of items, except when numbers of items of sub-types are being considered, which are then compared to the total number of items of the type. The confidence level at the top of the table applies to these estimates also.

G.S. Vecelius has applied this basic statistical method in predicting proportions of given types of ceramic sherds for an area randomly sampled. Very interestingly, though, a National Park Service statistician based at the Denver Service Center with whom the author conferred, Albert Calipeau, discovered that the formula for variance, which Vecilius had used, to be in error as it was presented in his widely read and cited paper. Calipeau discovered the correct formula for variance for unequal clusters to be that given by Leslie Kish (1965:187-189). A comparison of Kish's formula and Vecilius' formula using Kish's notational system revealed that Vecelius had misplaced a bracket.

Kish's formula, and an explanation of his notation, is as follows:

a = number of sample clusters

A = number of population clusters

$f = \dfrac{A}{a}$ = sampling fraction

y = total elements of variable of interest in all sample clusters (estimate of Y)

x = total elements in all sample clusters = EX_x (estimate of X)

$r = {}^{Y}/_{x}$ = proportion of variable of interest in all sample clusters

y_α = number of elements of variable of interest in a single sample cluster

x_α = total elements in a single sample cluster

$\overline{y_\alpha} = {}^{y_\alpha}/_{x_\alpha}$ = proportion of sample of interest in a single sample cluster

The standard deviation for the propotion is arrived at by taking the sqaure root of var (r) (the variance of the proportion $^Y/_x$)

$$SD(r) = \sqrt{var(r)}$$

The confidence limits for the proportion are calculated by choosing the appropriate t value from a Students' t table, multiplying the value by the standard deviation, and adding and subtracting the result from the proportion (r). The selection of the appropriate t value is determined by the number of degrees of freedom and the confidence level desired, where the number of degrees of freedom equals the number of sample clusters (randomly selected grid units) minus X (df = a-1).

$$\text{confidence limits} \qquad r = r \pm t \, \sigma \, r$$

The confidence limits for the total number of elements of a given type of cultural material in a stratum (confidence limits n) are calculated from the above by multiplying the proportions at both ends of the confidence limits (one at a time) by the estimate of the total number of elements of all types of cultural material in the stratum.

$$\text{confidence limits } n = r \pm t \, \sigma r \, A \left(\tfrac{x}{a}\right)$$
$$\text{or}$$
$$\text{confidence limits } n = \text{confidence limits } r \, A \left(\tfrac{x}{a}\right)$$

Confidence limits n is at the same confidence level as was confidence limits r.

Of course, the clusters being sampled are not described fully by the grid units; they are also defined by the strata or levels within the grid units. If the site is dug stratigraphically, therefore, it is possible that sampling fractions may be different for particular strata because each strata may not be present everywhere within the site. Where this was so, then a population predicted upon the number of grid units contained within the occurrence of the strata was determined, and the sampling fraction calculated as the percentage of randomly selected grid units excavated from that population of grid units.

To summarize the discussion of the statistical implicants of variation in strata depth, the measure of the population expressed either volumetrically or areally is to some extent an estimation since the only means of measuirng the population size precisely would be to excavate it completely. Randomly selecting 2-dimentional grid units of equal size should, by the nature of the process, result in an aggregate sample which approximates a sample of mean volume multiplied by the number of grid units selected, since the depth of the randomly selected units should tend to vary normally around the mean depth for all grid units in the population. As the number of grid units selected (and subsequently excavated) becomes greater, the probability that the total sample approximates one composed of an equal number of samples of mean depth increases. In fact, since the proper variance formula for cluster sampling is weighted for clusters of unequal sizes, it makes no difference whether the source of variation is from the unequal volume of the clusters or from the unequal distribution of items between clusters. Therefore, validity of inferences statistically drawn from the sample depends entirely on the accuracy of the calculated sampling fraction. While there should be little difficulty in arriving at the total sample size, care must be taken in the estimation of population size.

The statistical technique described here should provide for a valid estimate of the degree of representation of artifacts by proportion and by actual count. This estimate will be expressed as a range (between stated confidence limits) which may be regarded as being reliable to a known degree of confidence (confidence level), expressed as a percentage for all the samples which might be drawn which would in fact yield accurate confidence limits. Any error introduced by variation in strata thickness should be minor. In general, such error would tend to be reduced as more cluster samples were taken of the stratum in question.

A possible criticism of the use of this sampling procedure, and one that actually may introduce some error, is that strata are normally not of uniform depth. There are two implications to this: 1) The randomly selected samples (grid units) will in all likelihood be of unequal size. 2) For the same reason, the population (in this case the stratum) size may not be precisely determined. To state the problem in another way, both the population and the sample are expressed in 2-dimensional terms (as x number of 2-dimensional grid units) although they exist in 3-dimensions. In effect, the third dimension is taken to be constant.

An obvious solution would be to calculate the volume of both the strata in question and the individual samples taken from the strata and compute the sampling fraction from these. In practice, however, this would be not only very time-consuming, but would still allow an indeterminant degree of error. It would be impossible to discover the exact dimension of the stratum unless it were entirely excavated. Also, it would be very difficult to precisely calculate the volume of the solid geometrical form represented by the stratum within the grid unit, since the upper and lower limits of this might, in many instances, be quite irregular.

That the samples are of unequal size does not, per se, affect the validity of the results of the analysis. The number of items per sample would expectedly vary even if the samples were of equal volume. It is only in the computation of the ratio of the aggregate sample to the population (the sampling fraction) that a problem arises. Since a volumetric determination of this would have been, as we have seen, both imprecise and prohibitive in terms of time, it was felt that a total sample-population comparison by numbers of grid units would serve almost as well.

RANDOM SAMPLING PROCEDURE

The approximate locations of the boundaries of the dumps were determined from maps drawn by Moore (1973:14) and by the results of the core camples mentioned previously. In the case of the West Dump, a few test squares were dug to supplement this information. The cross-trenches were, again, dug through the middle of these areas. The gridded areas also provided the population from which the randomly selected grid units to be excavated were chosen.

Grid units within the approximate limits of the dumps were numbered from left to right working from the bottom row of units to the top row. A table of random numbers was consulted, and a list of the enumerated grid units in the order they appeared in the table was prepared for each dump. As many of these units as time allowed were then sequentially excavated. When a unit was found to be outside or on the perimeter of a dump, the boundary was redefined accordingly. In each of these instances, the population was decreased. Occasionally, a unit was discovered to be in the fill of a trench or other excavation unit dug by Moore or Dr. Herbert Dick. These units were discarded from the sample, although these previously excavated areas could not be subtracted from the population as they represented a portion of the material originally deposited even though they had been disturbed.

In the West Dump, 21 randomly selected grid units were excavated out of a population of approximately 97 grid units within the finally determined boundaries of the dump, yielding a sampling fraction of 22 percent. An additional 18 grid units were excavated to form the cross-trenches, and three grid units were dug for the purpose of better defining the boundary of the dump.

WEST DUMP STRATIGRAPHY

The stratigraphy of the West Dump proved to be extremely complex, being comprised for the most part of lenses as opposed to strata. These lenses were of ash, charcoal, sand, gravel, loam, clay, and combinations of any or all of these materials. They apparently represent numerous episodes of trash dumping, trash burning, and the covering of organic material with soil, sand, or gravel.

The stratigraphy here was not, however, quite as dumbfounding as it seemed at the outset of the excavations. Because maps showing the precise location of Moore's test trenches outside of the fort were unavailable, and perhaps also because of a psychic unity among archeologists concerning the most promising areas in which to dig, which in this case at least spans the decades, my first test pit and, subsequently, first cross-trenches were placed almost directly over Moore's trenches. The units, of course, contained amazingly homogenous fill with no stratigraphy whatsoever. These first units were accordingly excavated in arbitrary levels. When other units were excavated that displayed stratigraphy, it was suspected that the first units had been excavated through fill. It was decided, nonetheless, to continue the excavation of the later units both stratigraphically and by arbitrary levels. This was done by beginning a new collection bag whenever the lower limit of either an arbitrary level or a lens was encountered, labeling the collection bag accordingly. This practice was continued throughout the excavation of the West Dump, but was not practical during the excavation of the Main Dump.

The only strata that were present across the entire trash deposit were the two uppermost, designated in the field as strata A and B. These two strata were, respectively, a light brownish-gray clay loam and a slightly lighter brownish-gray loam. Stratum A was usually about 9 inches in depth, while the average thickness of stratum B was 5 inches. These were later identified as the A1 and A2 horizons of the Numa Clay Loam profile typically found in the vicinity of the fort and were lumped together as stratum A in the statistical treatment of the cultural material by stratum.

Stratum A is not a part of the midden, but represents a natural deposition by wind, or by the water, which has frequently inundated the floodplain of the Arkansas River. When compared to its occurrence at the locations, the depth of stratum A was greater over the West Dump. It is probable that soil collected in a slight depression that formed as the trash deposits settled in.

Thirty-one other discontinuous, discrete deposits were found below stratum A in the cross-trenches or the randomly placed 3-feet-by-3-feet squares. While, as just stated, none of these could be seen to run the complete length of either the cross-trenches, they were arranged in a discernable pattern.

The entire West Dump measures approximately 25 feet (grid north-south) by 50 feet (grid east-west). There is, though, a central, deeper deposit that contained almost all of the charcoal and ash found within the dump and a greater density of cultural material than the surrounding area. While the (grid) north-south width of this area was 24 feet, or about the same as the dump in its entirety, it measured only 28 feet from edge to edge along (grid) east-west. An inspection of the profile of the east-west cross-trench will show that the strata within this central area ended abruptly at locations that correspond to sudden slopes in the floor of the dump. Just east of the eastern edge of this area is another depression in the dump floor, which may be seen to be about 10 feet in length in the east-west profile. For reasons subsequently explained this was not considered to be a part of the central area.

During the excavation, a careful examination of the dump floor at these points showed the marks of tools that had been used to dig out the depression. The soil below the A horizon here is a sandy clay that is very suitable for use in the making of adobe bricks (Superintendent Patterson, personal communication). It is probable that the depression was dug as a borrow pit for this purpose (that is, clay was removed here for the purpose of making the adobe bricks for the fort), and later utilized as a trash receptacle. Moore has postulated this same scenario in regards to the comma-shaped pit he located on the eastern edge of the Main Dump (1973:60).

Adobe brick fragments and almost complete adobes were found in lenses of soils, which varied greatly in their composition from just below stratum A to the bottom of the pit in this central area. Adobe material was not found in the otuer portions of the dump. Charcoal and ash were present in lenses up to a foot thick in the middle of the dump, and most of the other lenses below the A horizon here contained at least a small amount of charcoal or ash. The only charcoal and ash discovered on the dump periphery were three rather thin, superimposed lenses near the extreme western end of the east-west cross-trench. Central lenses tended to be sands or gravels, while stratigraphy on the edges consisted mainly of loams and sandy clays. Finally, as noted above, artifact density was higher in the central area than in the outer area.

From the foregoing, it seems that most of the trash had been deposited and burned in the deeper area in the middle of the dump, while more sterile soils had been used to fill in the edges. For this reason, the deposits on edges of the dump were lumped together as stratum B during the statistical stratigraphic analysis of the dump material.

Since true strata were also absent in the interior portion of the dump, a similar lumping of the lenses present here was done for the purposes of the stratigraphic analysis. All lenses directly above sterile soil in the central area of the pit were included in stratum D, while those above D, within the circular periphery provided by stratum B and below A were collectively designated as stratum C.

While it was recognized these latter designations are to a certain extent arbitrary, they do reflect the actual stratigraphic makeup of the deposit. The error, if one has been made, is probably in splitting the central deposit at all, since the same types of materials and soils were found from top to bottom. However, an inspection of the cross-trench profiles will show that the lenses comprising stratum C, while they may be discontinuous, overlap in a way that would not permit an intrusion from or through C into stratum D; therefore, the lenses in stratum D must have been deposited before those in C. This, of course, does not imply that the time difference was necessarily great.

The great majority of material coming from the portion of the West Dump excavated in 0.25-foot arbitrary levels could be fitted into this gross stratigraphy with certainty. Where this could not be done, the material was excluded from the stratigraphic sample.

An analysis based upon the arbitrary levels was also done, although any analysis based upon actual stratigraphy would have to be preferable to one of this sort. Therefore, the stratigraphic analysis will be the one discussed in this report. A breakdown of the artifactual material by arbitrary level has been done, and is available upon request.

As an additional note here, it was feared initially that stratigraphic excavation might not lend itself to the type of random sampling method employed in the investigations of the West and Main Dumps for two reasons. First, because recognition and excavation of strata in the small grid unit might require an inordinate amount of time, and secondly because strata from an isolated unit might not reliably be matched up with strata found in other units. As it developed, stratigraphic excavation took no longer than excavation by levels, especially after a few units had been dug in an area with stratigraphy and some knowledge of the general stratigraphy of the dump gained. As to the second concern, because of the number of grid units excavated, which includes both units selected randomly and those excavated to form the cross-trenches, one was never more than several feet away from its nearest neighbor. If this sampling method were used in a larger area with a smaller number of units being excavated, one might envision the necessity of opening intermediate non-random units to facilitate strata identification.

MAIN DUMP STRATIGRAPHY

Even though the Main Dump, like the West Dump, contained numerous discrete lenses of varying compsoition, the stratigraphy of the portion of the Main Dump excavated by the author was much more clear-cut than that of the West Dump.

The vicinity of the Main Dump had been bulldozed prior to Moore's 1963-66 excavation by the owner of land adjacent to the fort (Moore 1973:59). Moore proposed that this disturbance had probably scraped off all but early Bent materials from the Main Dump. Moore's speculation may have resulted from the fact that the bulk of his excavation took place in the eastern part of the Main Dump. Deposits in the western one-third of the dump excavated, on the other hand, were assigned to a late Bent period for reasons that will be discussed later in this paper.

Be that as it may, the scraping had displaced the A horizon, which is present everywhere else over the entire area surrounding the fort including over West Dump. Midden deposits were encountered immediately below several inches of sand, gravel, and rock overburden. These materials had been packed to a hardness similar to that of concrete by the passage of vehicles and equipment associated with the reconstruction of the fort over the area.

Beneath this cap were four additional strata, which were found to be present in almost all the grid units opened. Fortunately, contiguous strata possessed dissimilar characteristics of color and soil composition. All contained lenses of sand, gravel, ash, and charcoal. Cultural materials taken from these lenses were bagged and cataloged separately. For the purposes of this analysis, though, the artifacts will be discussed in terms of their provenience within the following four macrostrata:

> Stratum B: tan sandy clay and small gravel. Its depth was usually between 0.75 foot and 1.0 foot, sometimes exceeding this. There were many inclusions here of thin ash and charcoal bands, some of which were several feet in width. Also present were lnses of yellowish-brown sand, tan sandy clay, brown sand and large gravel, and light brown sand.

> Stratum C: ash and charcoal. This stratum was present everywhere between strata B and D, although its thickness ranged from a fraction of an inch to more than 0.5 foot.

> Stratum D: light brown fine sandy clay and small gravel. As with B, there were many lenses of charcoal and ash within this stratum, along with lenses of brown clay, brown sands, and brown gravels of various sizes. Stratum D was generally not as thick as stratum B, D being usually between 0.25 foot and 0.75 foot.

> Stratum E: ash and charcoal, usually only a few tenths of a foot in thickness. This stratum was not present throughout the dump, but was indicated as a separate stratum because it was found over much of the bottom of the dump. It does not appear on the profile

drawings of the Main Dump cross-trenches because it did not appear in these units.

No evidence was detected to suggest that this section of the dump had been dug out as a borrow pit, as were the West Dump and the eastern end of the Main Dump. No tool marks were found on the floor of the dump. Also, the dump did not display any abrupt edges. The depth of the deposits increased gradually to the northeast, which merely suggests a slope in that direction (towards the probable former course of the river) slightly greater than that of the ground surface at present.

Since the stratigraphy was uniform throughout the portion of the West Dump excavated, the strata probably represent the same chronological period regardless of horizontal loci within the strata. Accumulation of trash over the entire area of the Main Dump dealt with here, judging from the stratigraphy, seems to have been quite regular. Trash must have accumulated at about the same rate in all locations. Moore found mostly early Bent artifacts in the borrow pit on the eastern edge of the dump. Once the pit had been filled, the dump evidently expanded in the direction of the fort since that was the only direction in whcih the dump could expand. The western end of the dump would expectedly contain material deposited at a later time during the Bent occupation of the fort.

DATING

A dependable date after which the trash in the portion of the Main Dump excavated must have been deposited was obtained from two sherds of ceramic. The dark blue "transfer-printed ware" displayed a portion of a "Gentleman's Cabin" pattern. One of these showed the GENT portion of the "Gentleman's Cabin" inscription, which is characteristic of this pattern. They were taken from stratum D in unit N102, E138, one of the non-random squares in the north-south trench. (There is no stratum E in this unit.) The two sherds would have been among the first deposited in the unit, and were almost certainly among the first deposited within the approximately 30 percent of the dump excavated. Stratum E, after all, is not present everywhere over the floor of the dump. As an indication of this, out of 35 random grid units excavated (excluding those that turned out to be in previously dug trenches), stratum E was found in only 17. Stratum E may have been deposited at a slightly earlier time, but it represents only a small percentage of the total content of the dump. It is only a few tenths of an inch in thickness in most places where it is present. All cultural material found above stratum E would, in any case, have to have been deposited later than the date indicated by the two ceramic fragments.

The "Gentleman's Cabin" pattern was registered on September 2, 1841, by J. & T. Edwards, potters in Staffordshire, England (Godden 1965:159). On a plate, this pattern depicts a scene in a ship's cabin with four men gathered around a table. Below this is the inscription "Gentleman's Cabin." Around the edge of the plate are four sailing ships, their names inscribed beneath: the Britannia, Acadia, Columbis, and Caledonia. The pattern is applied by transfer printing, a process in which engraved copper plates are inked and the pattern transferred first to tissue-thin paper and, finally, from the paper to the earthenware or soft paste porcelain vessel. All "Gentleman's Cabin" sherds from the Main Dump exhibited dark blue ink under a pearlware glaze.

Sherds of the "Gentleman's Cabin" type were also found in strata C and B, but none of these fit together with each other or with the fragments from stratum D. Only 11 fragments of this sort were found in the excavated portion of the Main Dump (including both random and non-random grid units), and of these, three displayed a portion of the "Gentleman's Cabin" inscription. Since this was printed only once on a vessel, the 11 fragments were of at least three different vessels.

No artifactual material that could be dated later than 1841 was removed from any part of the Main Dump excavated. Of particular interest is the fact that no cartridge casings or percussion caps were found during the Main Dump excavation. The first successful metal cartridge was patented by Smith and Wesson in 1854, and was first produced for revolvers in 1857 (Logan 1959:6). Although some Confederate troops still were not equipped with cartridge firing weapons at the beginning of the Civil War, by the end of the 1860s they had largely supplanted percussion firearms.

There was a similar gradual, and to some extent regional, adoption of the use of guns utilizing percussion caps in the years before this. A

47

percussion cap was patented in England as early as 1816 (Logan 1959:3). The caps offered a method of carrying priming powder, whcih was safe and convenient, and which also protected the powder from moisture. Moreover, a flint-lock could be converted to a cap-lock quite easily. In view of this, the length of the delay in the acceptance of percussion cap weapons, particularly in the West, might seem quite surprising (Russell 1957:242). It might be speculated that the supply of powder and flints were more dependable than the supply of percussion caps in frontier regions.

The Model 1842 musket was the first regulation percussion weapon issued by the U.S. military (Logan 1959:4), although percussion guns were in use by civilians before then. They would certainly have been present at Bent's Old Fort in 1846 when General Kearney's Army of the West arrived there (Don Rickey: personal communication). How much longer they had been in use at the fort before that time is less clear. An incident described in notes compiled in the early 1900s by the historian F.W. Craigen in preparation for a book that was never published is pertinent to this question, if accurately reported. It was apparently relayed to Craigen in a letter from a Milo H. Slater in September, 1903, although this is unclear because Craigen's notes are in an unorganized state. Slater recalled that during . . . "the regular fall buffalo hunt at Bent's Fort" (he mentions five of these) in 1838, a young man called Blue borrowed a rifle from the leader of the hunt, Ike Chamberlain of Taos, so that he could go along. Two weeks after the hunt began, the lock on the rifle broke and the young man had to return to Taos because only flint-lock muskets could be had at the fort at the time which were ". . . useless for hunting buffalo". This would indicate that percussion caps were being used by occasional visitors to the fort as early as 1838, although not at all frequently.

Whatever the case, the absence of percussion caps in the Main Dump suggests, at least, that the part of the dump excavated was deposited before 1846, when General Kearney's troops arrived and many percussion caps would have been in use at the fort. Of course, the fort was abandoned in 1849. The dates between which the western 30 percent of the dump examined was deposited apparently were 1841 and 1846, or more certainly, 1841 and 1849.

MAIN DUMP FEATURE 1

Main Dump feature 1 is very irregular, but is basically a v-shaped trench. It runs a little west of north through the section of the Main Dump excavated. The width of the feature varies considerably in the excavation units where it was examined, but it seems to average about 6 feet (see figure 7). The feature was first noted in three of the grid units in the east-west cross-trench: N93, E147; N93, E150; and N93, E153. It was later seen in units opened in the north-south cross-trench, which was aligned along E138. The north coordinates of these units were N105, N108, N111, and N114.

The trench appears wider in the north-south trench because, first of all, the north-south trench crosses it at a more oblique angle than does the east-west trench. Secondly, the southern edge of the trench appears to have been dug in steps, in the profile of the east wall, with the upper two steps adding about 4.5 additional feet to the width than it would be if the trench had been dug in a more regular V-shape at this point. In the profile of the west wall the trench conforms more to a V-shape.

This is also true in the north and south wall profile in the east-west cross-trench where the feature passes through it. In the north wall, the feature exhibits a width of only about 3.5 feet. The situation in the south wall is more complex. Here may be seen two trenches with a broad V-shape, a larger one to the west and another substantially smaller just to the east.

It was thought from the first that feature 1 might be another of Moore's test trenches. Although the walls of the feature were not straight and were, in fact, asymmetrical, the profiles exhibited by others of Moore's trenches in the area in front of the fort (which were exploratory units dug primarily in an effort to locate features) had been seen to be also somewhat irregular. Examination of field photographs taken by Moore had shown that some of his exploratory trenches had been excavated with one or both sides slanting or stepped in order to facilitate soil removal. For reasons that will be dealt with shortly, it was also felt that the feature was not the acequia, for which there is some historical reference. Because time was limited and feature 1 seemed to be a test trench, not much of it was excavated. In fact, when the feature was encountered in an excavation unit, that unit was abandoned.

The fill in the feature taken from the few grid units excavated within it did not contain artifactual material that was overly instructive. However, two of these were used to date the fill to a time later than that for the portion of the West Dump through which the feature ran. The first of these was a 0.3-foot length of barbed wire, which was not used until the 1870s. It was formed of two double strands of wire twisted around each other. Knots of wire were at either end of the piece with the ends of the short lengths of wire used for the knots protruding as the barbs. The other was a tin can, which was in an advanced state of corrosion and was removed in fragments. Two of the fragments could be pieced together to form one of the circular ends of the can measuring 2¼ inches

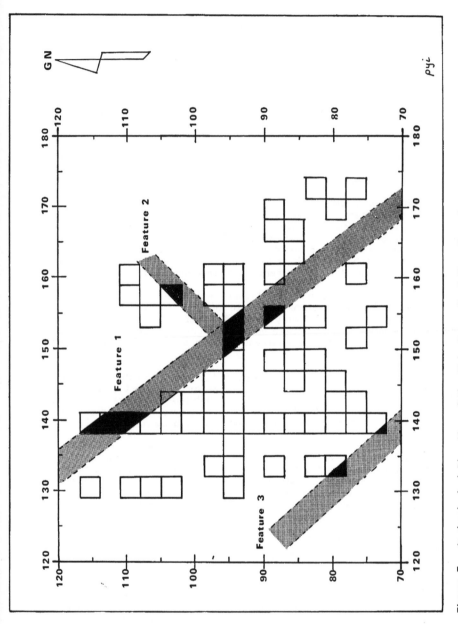

Figure 7. Archeological Plan Map of the Main Dump Depicting Comer's
Features 1, 2, and 3

in diameter. Another displayed the juncture of the other end and the can side that could be seen to be a crimped double seam. Equipment capable of producing this type of seam was not developed until 1897. In turn, the seam allowed the production of the open-top can, which began replacing hole-in-top cans by 1902 (Fontana and Greenleaf 1962:72-73).

Since the feature was dug through a portion of the West Dump probably deposited in the late Bent period, it could not have been dug until after that time--the middle to late 1840s. This makes it quite unlikely that feature 1 is the acequia that is mentioned historically. In 1846, a Lt. Abert who visited the fort that year with General Kearny's troops during the Mexican War and the year before with Fremont's 1845 expedition wrote that, ". . . Traces of the 'acequia' . . . are yet visible," which would imply that it had not been used for some time. Also, a rough sketch drawn from memory by a former employee at the fort during the years 1844-45, William M. Boggs, shows what Boggs labled "an old ditch" running in front of the fort. If this refers to the acequia, this would also seem to indicate that it had been dug sometime before Boggs' stay at the fort (Stinson 1965:24).

MAIN DUMP FEATURE 2

Another trench was found in the West Dump area, this one oriented towards the east, joining feature 1 almost at right angles. It was first discovered in grid unit N102, E156, just below the overburden, at a depth of 0.7 foot, and the excavation of the unit was suspended at that level. The southern edge of the trench was found in the north-east corner of unit N96, E156. In both squares, the edge of the trench could be seen to be very straight. It was not encountered to the east of feature 1.

Feature 2 is believed to be one of Moore's test trenches, as he was known to have been working in this area, sometimes aligning his trenches with the magnetic points of the compass.

MAIN DUMP FEATURE 3

The edge of another feature aligned with magnetic north was found in the south-west half of random square N78, E132, and in the very tip of the southwest corner of N72, E138. It was located on the extreme southwestern perimeter of the trash deposit, and therefore the eastern edge of the feature was not located, and the shape of the feature was not ascertained. The edge discovered was more or less parallel with feature 1 and perpendicular to a line drawn through the length of feature 2.

The fill in the part of the feature excavated was very similar to that in feature 1: a friable dark brownish-black loam. Like feature 2, feature 3 is thought to be one of Moore's trenches.

A listing of the cultural material found in the Main Dump features is presented below. All of these were fragments, most of them very small, with the exception of two found in MDF 1, all items could date to either Bent or Stagecoach times.

DISCUSSION OF ARTIFACTS

This discussion will deal primarily with those artifacts presented in appendixes A and B. These are the artifacts recovered from the randomly selected portion of the West and Main Dumps. Artifacts found in non-random grid units are generally of the same sorts, and are described in other sections of this report.

COMPARISON OF THE AGES OF THE MAIN AND WEST DUMPS

It should be remembered that all cultural material taken from the portion of the Main Dump excavated can be assigned to a period later than 1841 with some certainty, with the exception of material found in stratum E. This date probably applies to stratum E also, because it shares the floor of the excavated section of the Main Dump with stratum D. An upper date for all strata may be set at 1849, the year of the abandonment of the fort by the Bents, since nothing dating to the Stagecoach Period (1861-1881) was found in any of the excavated strata. In fact there is reason to believe as discussed elsewhere that the upper limit for the section of the West Dump dealth with here might be better regarded as 1846, the date of the arrival of General Kearney's Army of the West at the fort.

The dating of the material in the West Dump involves different considerations. Here, there is no artifact or characteristic of an artifact that supplies a useful <u>terminus post quem</u>, or date after which the material must have been deposited. The date thus supplied would have to be after 1828 to be of value. While percussion caps occur in the lowest strata, there are only a few of these. They are not numerous enough not to be explained by the infrequent use of firearms using percussion caps at Bent's Old Fort prior to the arrival of the Army of the West. In fact, the Mean Ceramic Dating method produces an extremely early date for the West Dump, although the method may not be refined enough for use with early 19th century ceramics to yield exact dates.

By all appearances the West Dump is a remnant of the Bent period. The Mean Ceramic Dating method does indicate an early date, certainly one before the Stagecoach period. This is reinforced by the absence of any artifact in the trash deposits proper of the West Dump, which was made after the mid-1800s. Also, there is the presence of the "wasters" at the lower depths of the trash deposit. These are broken adobes, present in quantity. A reasonable explanation for their presence is that they are the flawed or broken bricks discarded during construction. The most convenient place to dispose of them might have been the borrow pit, which provided the clay from which they were made.

There is also the location of the dump, just a few feet from the fort. The largest number of artifacts found in the West Dump were bone, often comprising about 40 percent of such items in a trash strata (see figure 7). It is probably safe to assume that these bones were not clean when placed in the dump. If they were not, they would have constituted a pronounced annoyance, if not a health hazard. The many episodes of burning represented in the stratigraphy probably occurred to allay this. The burning would have been done frequently, to judge from the amount of faunal material and ash. While the odor of burning trsh may be somewhat less disagreeable than that of decaying flesh, I would venture that most people would seek not to be exposed to either if at all possible. Garbage would also attract vermin of various sorts, including rats and snakes. Therefore, the proximity of the West Dump to the fort is puzzling.

Table 2
Bone

| | West Dump | | Main Dump | |
Stratum	Proportion	Projected Percentage	Proportion	Projected Percentage
A	.34	28 - 40	.76	60 - 90
B	.41	18 - 62	.48	43 - 52
C	.46	40 - 49	.64	58 - 69
D	.40	30 - 50	.63	58 - 67
E			.68	63 - 72

It may be that the dump was in use only during the construction of the fort, while the builders were living away from it in a temporary stockade. That the dump was probably used during the building is evidenced by the presence of adobe wasters there.

Additional, and persuasive, evidence for a very early period date for the lower strata (B, C, and D) of the West Dump is supplied by the faunal analysis conducted by John S. Applegarth (appendix C). In comparing the composition of the bone collections he examined from three different areas: the Main Dump, strata B, C, and D of the West Dump, and stratum A of the West Dump (which, again, contains Stagecoach Period and later artifacts), Applegarth discovered some striking differences. In the Main Dump were found five domestic species (chicken, mule, pig, goat, and sheep). Domestic species are totally absent from the West Dump. While domesticated animals are not present in the three lower strata, wild game remains such as fish, box turtle, and wild birds are there in quantity. These wild game species are much less well represented in the Main Dump and in stratum A of the West Dump, where some of these species are absent. On the other hand, the Main Dump is much richer in deer and pronghorn antelope remains than are either the lower strata of the West Dump or stratum A there. And, finally, the only remains of domestic cat are found in stratum A of the West Dump.

The findings reinforce the interpretation suggested by the other material contained in the dumps. Although bison bones are found in strata B, C, and D in the West Dump, this food source is well supplemented by the kind of game one might obtain within the immediate vicinity of the fort, espeically along the banks of the Arkansas River. These might be the game species that the builders would exploit as they were occupied with

53

the construction of the fort and before the later hunting parties were organized. Also, as the completed fort became better known and the site of more frequent visitation by Indians and trappers from other locales, the species indigenous to the fort might decrease in availability as the influx of people put greater stress on the local environment. The larger numbers of people at the fort may have also required a larger new supply that was more economically had in the larger game species.

This might be what is indicated by the Main Dump faunal deposits. The game species that might have been easily killed had near the fort decreased in representation, while those that might be better hunted some distance from the fort, in groups, and by horseback--deer and antelope--increase drastically in representation. Again, all of this lends credence to the idea that B, C, and D in the West Dump predate the Main Dump, and actually date to the time of the construction of the fort. The distribution of faunal material is presented in Table 2.

The presence of one class of artifacts among those found in the West Dump might cast some doubt upon this interpretation: ceramics. Ceramics are found in all strata of the West Dump. These include not just utilitarian wares, but also dinnerware. It seems somewhat incongruous to imagine the builders of Bent's Old Fort eating from decorated, English ceramics while living in a stockade. Of course, it might seem unusual to think of such ceramics at Bent's Old Fort at all, until one becomes aware of all the historically recorded aspects of life there. Perhaps some of these same activities (dinners for visitors from the East and Santa Fe, for example) were occurring while the stockade served as a residence. One would expect these activities to occur more frequently during the occupation of the fort, however. This could be reflected in the ceramic percentages displayed in Table 3. West Dump stratum A should be disregarded in this comparison, as it was deposited after the Bent Period, being overburden that contains artifacts from the Stagecoach Period and later. Similarly, Main Dump stratum A should also probably not be considered, as it has been disturbed to some extent by recent activities. When examining ceramic percentages, both those observed and predicted, for strata B, C, and D of the West Dump compared to strata B, C, D, and E of the Main Dump, it can be seen that ceramic percentages for Main Dump strata are uniformly higher than those for West Dump strata.

Table 3
Ceramics

| | West Dump | | Main Dump | |
Stratum	Proportion	Projected Percentage	Proportion	Projected Percentage
A	.036	2 - 4	.029	0 - 5
B	.016	0 - 2	.065	5 - 7
C	.03	2 - 3	.029	2 - 3
D	.018	1 - 2	.04	1 - 6
E			.03	1 - 4

The West Dump midden strata (B, C, and D), in summary, are considered to have been deposited during the Bent Period. There is, in fact, some evidence to suggest that all or, more certainly, the lower portion of the West Dump strata B, C, and D was deposited during the construction of the fort.

TRADE NETWORK

Bent's Old Fort existed because of a trade network that provided for the exchange of goods between three quite different economies, those of the eastern United States, the Plains Indians, and New Mexico. Very generally, the valuables supplied by each were: manufactured goods from the East, furs from the Plains Indians, and currency--silver and gold--from New Mexico.

This system was linked to a larger system of trade. The linkage, from historical accounts, was not to the same systems for the three economies involved. The Plains Indians had been involved in an extensive trading system for hudnreds of years (Blakeslee 1975). It is probable that some of the furs traded at Bent's Old Fort arrived there via this network. New Mexico had economic ties with Mexico, and the United States traded extensively with Europe.

All this, of course, is not reflected equally in the archeological record. What appears most clearly is trading relationships between the United States and Europe. This should not be unexpected, since the items traded by the Indians (furs) do not long survive in an archeological context, while those from New Mexico (currency, gold and silver) would not likely find their way to the dump.

The trade between the United States and Europe is seen most clearly in five classes of artifacts. The first of these is ceramics. Almost all the non-utilitarian ceramics recovered from the trash deposit were, or could have been, produced in England. Most of those not produced in England were copies of English ceramics. Generally, efforts in ceramic technology had been to produce non-utilitarian ceramics that most closely resembled porcelain, and the English were the undisputed leaders in this. Another English import in evidence at the Bent's Old Fort trash dumps was the Kaolin (clay) smoking pipe. These were made in numerous small shops in both England and Scotland. They were produced and sold for so little that they were often given with the purchase of small amounts of smoking tobacco. The third class of artifact produced in Europe came from Italy--the glass trade beads, which for hundreds of years had been manufactured primarily in Venice.

Gunflints, made in both England and France, comprise the fourth type of European artifact. English flints are gray to black, while those from France are honey-colored. During the time of flink-lock firearms, gunflints, like kaolin pipes, were cheap and plentiful. Flint is a variety of crypto-crystalline quartz that is found in Europe but not in the United States. There are a variety of cryptocrystalline quartzes in the United States that are extremely similar to flint (jasper and chert, in particular) and which are sometimes referred to generally as "flint." In fact, these materials were sometimes fashioned into gunflints. Nonetheless, they did not possess precisely the same qualities as did quartz, most notably the quality of reliably producing a spark when struck against iron. Since producing a spark might be vital, in every sense of the word, to the individual wielding a firearm, gunflints made in England and France were much preferred to those of United States manufacture.

There is a fifth type of artifact of European origin which is represented in some quantity in the randomly collected samples. This is the dark green bottle glass found in both the Main and West Dumps. A seal of this same dark green glass was found among the randomly selected excavation units, and several more were discovered in the backfill of Moore's trenches, which probably had come originally from the West and Main trash deposits. These glass seals identified the contents of the bottles to which they were once affixed such as Medoe, from a French vintner. Although it is impossible to be absolutely sure, many of the dark green glass fragments recovered were likely from such bottles, also.

While not many, there were a few artifacts that evidenced trade links with non-European economies. A portion of a bowl of a caltinite pipe was recovered, for instance. This was a valued item among the Plains Indian groups. The distinctive red caltinite from which the pipe was made is found only in the area of what is now Minnesota. The caltinite was shaped into pipes shortly after being quarried, while it was soft and easy to work. The finished pipes were traded over much of the central portion of the United States. Trade with a different Native American group was represented in the dumps by the presence of a few sherds of pottery. The clay body contained flecks of mica, which produces a glistening surface to the pottery. Such micaceous pottery is particular to Taos Pueblo, in New Mexico (near the present-day location of the city of Taos).

INDIAN TRADE ITEMS IN THE WEST AND MAIN DUMPS

Trade items recovered from the trash excavations include those mentioned in historical documents and others that are not. Beads ("common," mandrel-round, and plychrome), described elsewhere in this paper, were found in strata excavated. Blue and white were the colors of the great majority of these beads. Historic accounts report that these were the colors preferred by the Arapahoe, incidentally. Beads were by no means the best represented of the artifacts, but as Table 4 illustrates, the probability is that they comprise at least a few percent of the material collection of most strata.

Gunflints, percussion caps, lead balls, lead shot, lead, and various parts of firearms were found in trash deposits. These were all traded to the Indians. Of course, the particular artifacts discovered may not have been intended for that purpose, but may have been used by the inhabitants of the fort.

Various items made of brass were valued by the Indians. Notable among these were brass tacks. Only the caps of brass tacks were found, although a few were found with short segments of the shank still adhering to the cap. These shanks were all square. All tack heads measured to 0.4 inch (1 cm) in diameter. Brass tacks were widely employed for decorative purposes by white frontiersmen and Indians alike. They have been found, to cite just a few examples, on clothing, gun stocks, and knife sheaths. Brass tack caps comprised very small projected percentages, at either the 80 percent or 95 percent confidence levels, in strata B and C in the West Dump, and stratum C in the Main Dump. Confidence limits at the 80 percent confidence level for the numbers of brass tacks predicted for these strata ranged from 0 to 9 in West Dump stratum C to 1 to 14 in West Dump stratum B. As this indicates, the tacks were not abundant. The small number of tacks found might be due in part to corrosion, although recovered brass objects were usually in fairly good condition. The brass tacks might have been well looked after, being trade items they were valuable to a certain degree. Another possibility was that they were never traded in large numbers.

Table 4
Beads

Stratum	West Dump		Main Dump	
	Proportion	Projected Percentage	Proportion	Projected Percentage
A	0.0034	0 - 4		
B			0.0035	0 - 4
C	0.054	0 - 10	0.06	0 - 11
D	0.022	0 - 3	0.03	0 - 5
E			0.008	0 - 1

Other brass artifacts that might have been trade items were brass wire, scraps of sheet brass, and small brass buckles. A small brass bell, commonly called a "hawk" bell, was found in stratum A of the West Dump. These bells are likely trade items but this particular bell was found in a provenience that includes many artifacts dating after the Bent Period.

Several mollusk shells, or fragments thereof, were found. Most were oyster shell, and the largest number of these recovered from a trash stratum were taken from stratum D in the Main Dump. At an 80 percent confidence level, one then might expect to recover from 14 to 29 of these shells were all of stratum D in the western 30 percent of Main Dump excavated. Like many of the other trade items, these were not well represented in the trash deposits. It may be significant that no abalone shell was recovered, since this was very valuable, bringing up to four buffalo skins per shell in trade. The oyster shells may not have been worth quite as much, since the interior of the oyster shell is not as lustrous as that of an abalone shell. It was, of course, the mother-of-pearl interior, cut into segments, which was used to embellish various objects. Also, the oyster shell is smaller. A single dentalium shell was recovered, also from stratum D of the Main Dump. These were also prized by the Plains Indians, and were used for decorative purposes.

The majority of the identified metal artifacts, aside from those of brass already discussed, do not seem to have been trade items. The exception may be a 2½-inch length of solid copper wire, ¼ inch in diameter. This was from stratum C in the Main Dump. The unidentified pieces of iron, and the much fewer unidentified pieces of copper, may have been parts of trade items such as hoop iron or knives.

DIET

We can gather a good idea of the variety of meat in the diet from Applegarth's faunal analysis (appendix C). The composition of the meat diet seems to have changed through time. More exactly, it may be that the diet was different during the construction of the fort then it was during the fort's occupation.

The widest range of wild animal species were represented in strata B, C, and D of the West Dump. This is the deposit that might represent the very early Bent Period: the construction of the fort itself. These species include those that may have been obtained along the Arkansas River as it ran near the fort. Such species include fishes such as channel catfish and the goldeye, a salmonoid fish.*

Freshwater mussels were also found. Bird species were present, including Canadian geese, surface eeding ducks, green-wing teal, quail, blue grouse, sage grouse, sharp-tailed grouse, and wild turkey. Other birds were represented that may or may not hav been eaten: the sandhill crane, the great blue heron, crows, jays, magpies, and ravens. The western box turtle and softshell turtles were probably eaten. Other animals found in the "early" deposit could have come from a greater distance from the fort. Small mammals were the black-tailed jackrabbit and the cottontail rabbit. Large mammals identified among them were a few bones from elk and mule deer, many more from the pronghorn antelope and the white-tailed deer, and, most by far, the buffalo (bison). There were no domesticated animal bones.

The Main Dump included all of the above species, although the fishes, turtles, and wild birds are much less well represented. Perhaps, in a way, taking their place are domesticated species: chicken, pig, goat, and sheep. The considerable variety in the meats consumed at Bent's Old Fort was thus maintained, and even enhanced.

If one judges by the relative weight of the faunal material from the excavation units examined by Applegarth (an admittedly rough measure), one would say that in the very early Bent Period (as reflected in strata B, C, and D in the West Dump, buffalo was by far the most plentiful meat, followed by pronghorn antelope, deer, catfish, box turtle, miscellaneous wild birds, wild turkey, and Canadian goose. In the later Bent Period (as evidenced by the faunal remains in the Main Dump), the meat most often eaten would again be buffalo, followed again by pronghorn antelope and deer (but these being more frequently represented here than in the West Dump), followed by domestic mammals.

---

* The individual who identified the fish remains, Dr. William J. Kaster of the University of New Mexico, noted that the western limit of the goldeye's range had been thought to be 300 miles east of Bent's Old Fort. Since the goldeye had not before been reported in Colorado, it may not be there today.

Weight for faunal remains of all other species drop off sharply as a percentage of total faunal weight.

Compared to the abundance of data concerning meat diet, not much is known about the vegetable diet at the fort. A few corncobs and pinyon nut shells were found during the excavations. Corn seems the likeliest cereal grain to have been eaten at the fort, as it was a staple of the Southwest in that time. Indeed, several grinding stones were found in the fort trash deposits. These may well have been used by the Mexican population of the fort in grinding meal from corn. Pinyon nuts, harvested from the low, scrubby pinyon trees in the fall, were another widely exploited food source in the Southwest and Great Basin areas. To some Great Basin Shoshonean groups who did not practice agriculture, pinyon nuts represented a major part of their caloric intake. These, too, could be ground into meal. While they might have been used in this way at the fort, they might also have been regarded as a condiment or as a snack, as they are today. Pinyon trees do not grow near the fort, but there are many of them in the foothills some 40 or so miles to the southwest, in the direction of Taos and Santa Fe.

References are made in historical accounts of life at the fort to attempts at growing vegetables in a "kitchen garden." For this reason, an irrigation ditch, or **acequia**, was dug. These attempts were reported to have been intermittant, being frustrated by the trampling of the garden by stock and by pilfering of the vegetables.

On the chance that evidence of cultigens might be obtained, pollen samples were take at various locations within both dumps. A stratigraphic column sample was not taken, since it was felt that the deposits hd been layed down rapidly, and environmental information was not being sought in any case. Rather, samples were taken from proveniences for which it was felt firm dates could be obtained, and where conditions seemed most favorable for the preservation of pollen.

Of the plants very probably growing quite near the fort are a number that could have been consumed. These plants were insect-pollinated, as opposed to being wind-pollinated. Dr. Gerald K. Kelso, who conducted the pollen analysis, states that "Even a few grains of insect-dispersed pollen are . . . a good indicator that such plants were not growing too far from the sampling site." In his analysis, Dr. Kelso mentions that these plant species prefer disturbed soil and therefore may have been growing right on the dumps. Interestingly, the observed species list prepared as part of the master plan for the development of Bent's Old Fort lists none of these edible species in a list of species observed near the fort today.

Probably none of these edible plants were regarded as a staple, but they might have contributed to the variety of the diet at Bent's Old Fort. The plant that conceivably might have provided the most calorically of these is the sunflower. Like the pinyon, sunflower seeds have comprised a significant percentage of the dietary makeup of some U.S. native populations. They are prepared and consumed in much the same way as are pinyon nuts. Finally, a member of the chicory tribe (dandelions) was growing near the fort.

That pollen of other sorts of edible plants was not discovered in the samples taken from the dumps does not mean that such plants were not being grown at the fort. A dump environment usually promotes the deterioration of pollen as Kelso says. "Dump deposits are loose and by their nature subject pollen to repeated wetting and drying which rapidly oxydizes it. Decaying organic material in trash deposits accelerate oxydation, and pollen-destroying fungi are often present." Moreover, many cultigens are insect-pollinated. These plants not only produce less pollen than do wind-pollinated plants, but the adhesive substance, which attaches the pollen to the legs of the transporting insects also prevents the pollen from detaching from the flower. To quote from Kelso's pollen analysis report again, ". . . the pollen of such plants is rare in natural deposits . . ., and its absence from a soil sample does not necessarily mean that the plants were not present."

Piecing together the diet at Bent's Old Fort would benefit from the data supplied by a number of sources. One of these is archeological. Archeology tells us that the fort inhabitants enjoyed a variety of meats, and identifies a number of them. It also suggests several plant species that might have been grown at the fort as food. Ethnohistoric information tends to agree with these findings. The vegetal diet of the inhabitants of the Southwest, both the Mexican and Indian populations, was centered around corn, and included pinyon nuts and sunflower seeds. Another major component of the Southwestern diet, beans, was not represented in the archeological deposits. As discussed, though, this does not prove that it was not consumed at the fort. Dried beans, along with rice, and the corn for which there is archeological evidence, could be transported and kept for long periods of time without spoiling. We know of other foods consumed at the fort, such as crackers, candy, and molasses, from historical sources. In the absence of specific historical accounts, of course, we can never know positively which of the inhabitants of the fort were consuming what of the foods. All available evidence would indicate, though, that the occupants of the fort enjoyed a plentiful, varied, and perhaps surprisingly well-rounded diet.

OTHER CULTIVATED PLANTS

Some results of the pollen analysis revealed, rather unexpectedly, that some plants may have been grown at the fort for decorative purposes. They include the evening primrose, members of the rose family, the mistletoe, and members of the nightshade family. All are insect-pollinated, and therefore in all probability were growing near to the dumps. All are not indigenous to the area of the fort, and do not grow in the fort's vicinity at present.

FURS TRADED AT THE FORT

Evidence for the variety of furs being traded at the fort comes from historic accounts but is supplemented by the analysis of faunal material recovered from the trash deposits. Buffalo furs and beaver pelts are the furs generally thought of as being traded. Buffalo bones (<u>Bison bison</u>), of course, comprise, by far, the greatest percentage of the total faunal remains in both dumps. Beaver bones are also present in both dumps, although not in the quantity approaching the buffalo bones. Beaver would, as a matter of course, be skinned where it had been trapped. Deer and pronghorn antelope are represented in appreciable amounts of bone, especially in the Main Dump. It is likely that these animals were skinned, even if their hids are not mentioned as contributing to the fur trade.

It seems, though, that two other species were skinned and their furs probably traded. Foot bones were recovered for these species, which might indicate that the feet, as was done, were left on the hide at the initial skinning, and then removed during processing of the hide at the fort. One of these species is fox, the other may be the gray wolf.

DETERMINATION OF SOCIOECONOMIC LEVEL

It seems safe to assume that the socioeconomic status of the various fort inhabitants varied, and perhaps greatly. The financial circumstances of William Bent, or the other Bent brothers and Ceran St. Vrain when they were present, would have been much different from that of the Mexican laborers residing at the fort or the trappers and mountainmen who stayed there occasionally. Yet the debris produced by the activities of all these groups found their way into the same trash deposits.

In considering socioeconomic level, as with other questions in historic site archeology, one must be guided by what the field of history and ethnoanthropology have to offer. With this in mind, those items of material culture most indicative of a higher socioeconomic status are assumed, for the purposes of this interpretation, to have belonged to the owners of the fort or their associates who occupied the same or a higher socioeconomic status. For this reason, the question of socioeconomic status will be addressed only in regards to the owners of the fort.

In general, material recovered from the trash deposits does recommend a fairly high socioeconomic status for the owners of the fort. This is true (as the term "socioeconomic" itself might imply), both because of the expense of some of the artifacts found, and because some of these items were generally used by individuals of the upper social strata.

The indication of high socioeconomic status for the owners of Bent's Old Fort is derived primarily from an interpretation of the ceramic collection obtained from the trash dumps. At present in historic sites archeology, ceramic analysis and examination of faunal remains; to determine the cut of meat represented; are regarded as the most reliable indicator of socioeconomic status. (Given the amount of faunal material and the funds available for analysis, the latter study was not done.) Many other artifacts indicative of high social and economic status are carefully curated and seldom found in a dump context.

Given the central position of the ceramic collection in the interpretation of socioeconomic status here, it is necessary to preface the analysis with some clarification of the sense in which various terms are used, and some comments regarding these.

CERAMICS CONSIDERED IN THE SOCIOECONOMIC ANALYSIS

Definitions

Earthenware.   Pottery that is not vitrified and therefore is porous unless glazed.

Stoneware.   Pottery composed of clay in which has been mixed a certain amount of crushed stone, which vitrifies during firing, making the finished pot impervious to liquids even if it is not glazed. Salt or lead glazes were sometimes applied as embellishment. It first appeared in England in the late 1600s, probably coming from Germany.

Creamware. An earthenware developed by Josiah Wedgewood in 1760. The body is composed of whitish clay and calcined flint mixed with the typical earthenware clay. A clear lead glaze, which may be seen to be actually of a faint yellow or green color where it has gathered in crevices, was applied over this; this was also commonly called "Queen's-ware."

Pearlware. Josiah Wedgewood's refinement of creamware, which he began producing in 1779. It contained a greater proportion of white devon clay and calcined flint in the body, and was covered by glaze that was tinted slightly blue by the inclusion of a small amount of cobalt. Over time, the body became whiter and the use of the bluish glaze was discontinued.

Porcelain. A porcelain body is of kaolin clay and feldspathic rock. The latter vitrifies upon firing, producing a kind of glass. The commonly held criteria of translucency holds only for European porcelain. Chinese porcelain may be thick enough to preclude translucency, but will emit a ringing note if tapped sharply. Chinese porcelain has been imported to Europe since the 14th century.

Two of the ceramic types, pearlware and creamware, might have been classified as sub-type of earthenware, since the former two terms principally refer to a type of glaze over a basically earthenware body. This was not done for three reasons. First of all, it was felt that had this been done these might have been instances in which a sherd could not be fully described in terms of the five categories. Secondly, there are ratios of constituents in the clay bodies themselves of both of the wares peculiar to each. And finally, these are the three terms usually employed in referring to the respective wares. To call a ceramic an earthenware implies that it is neither pearlware nor creamware, but an earthenware that lacks the features of either of these.

It may be noticed that annular pottery is listed in appendixes A, B, and C under both creamware and pearlware. "Annular" refers to a style, popular in the late 18th and early 19th centuries found on jugs, mugs, and bowls, which featured horizontal bands of color. Sometimes these were rills or grooves. This style was popular on pearlwares from 1795-1815, but it may have been originated as early as 1785, at which time it was found on creamwares (Hume 1969:131).

Peculiar sorts of annular ceramics are "marbled" annularware and what Moore termed "blue mocha" (1973:74). The second of these at least superficially resembles true "mocha" pottery, which displayed brown fern-like ornamentation on a broad, horizontal band, this band was usually white on annular creamware. The fern-like ornament (sometimes characterized as dendritic) on the sherds found at Bent's Old Fort was blue. Moore believed this ceramic to have a creamware body, and to be of American origin. Marbled pottery results from the swirling of slips of various colors, usually green and light brown, between colored bands on annular pearlware ceramics. The technique was popular in the late 18th and early 19th centuries (Hume 1974:132).

A common variety of pearlware, but one not particularly well represented among the ceramic fragments from the Bent's Old Fort dumps, is (to use

Ivor Noel-Humes terminology) shell-edged pearlware. Shell-edged here refers mostly to the slightly scalloped edge of this ceramic, and not to any particular pattern that may be molded on the edge. It is therefore the same as Moore's description of this as crinkle-edged (1973:70). The edge of this ceramic is painted either blue or green, although no pieces with a green edge were found during the dump excavations.

Shell-edged pearlware may be divided into groups: those that have been painted by drawing the paintbrush inward, thus enhancing the feather edge effect, which is sometimes imprinted in the clay of the edge; and those that have been painted by merely drawing the paintbrush laterally around the edge. Very few examples of the former, which date to about 1780-1795, were found in the dumps. Laterally painted specimens date to later than 1800. This date applies also to shell-edged pearlware having edges embossed with various designs (Hume 1974:31). All embossed-edged pearlware from the Main and West Dumps had been painted laterally.

"Transfer-printing" is a technique by which decorative designs are applied to ceramic vessels. The term "transfer-printed ware," then, refers to any ceramic so decorated.* In transfer printing, a copper plate is etched with a design. The plate is then "inked" with the pigment to be applied to the ceramic vessel. After the plate has been wiped off so that pigment remains only in the crevices of the etching, a thin sheet of paper is pressed against the upper plate. The impression of the design is transferred to the plate and then to the ceramic when the paper is pressed against the vessel.

Transfer-printing on pearlware was begun in 1787, although the process had been used on other sorts of clay bodies from 1756. The great majority of transfer-printed sherds from the Bent's Old Fort dumps were much too small to be recognized with certainty as pearlware. However since pearlware generally comprises the largest percentage of ceramics found at sites of the early 1800s (Hume 1974:129-230), all transfer-printed sherds were tentatively classified as pearlware in the absence of evidence to the contrary, for the purposes of the statistical analysis. The dark-blue transfer-printed "Gentleman's Cabin" pattern, previously discussed, definitely appeared on pearlware.

A floral spray pattern, exhibiting red and/or blue flowers and buds growing from a black line stem with green leaves, was observed on white sherds found in the two dumps. These sherds proved to be pearlware, as attested to by the characteristic blue glaze seen where it had gathered above footings. Moore had assigned an approximate 1810-1839 date to this design (1973:73). Both black and red rim stripes were observed on various of the sherds (although most sherds were not of rims).

---

* This is an example of the inconsistent use of the term "ware." Thus one could have transfer-printed ware on pearlware.

Some very small fragments of "copper lustre" decorated pearlware, which appeared to be identical to those described by Moore (1973:69), were taken from strata in both dumps. The copper lustre is so termed because of its color--it is actually produced with gold. On sherds recovered from the trash deposits with a white background, the color of the lustre is as much purple as copper. This is due to deterioration of the decorative lustre work.

All examples of "spatter ware" found at Bent's Old Fort trash dumps were of the red and green spattered areas alternating on a white earthenware background. Other colors used in this pattern, which was made in England between 1825 and 1850, were blue and puce. Spatterware is so called because the decoration consists of what seem to be spatters of color that appear to have been flung on the ceramic as if from a small paintbrush. Actually, they were applied with sponges.

Undecorated fragments comprised sizable proportions of both the earthenware and pearlware sherds found in almost all strata in both dumps. White sherds of earthenware were more numerous than decorated ones.

Only a few sherds of porcelain were found, and these were not of a high quality. Like the great majority of all sherds recovered, they were too small to reveal an identifiable pattern. The design was painted on in shades of blue over a slightly bluish-white background. One sherd appeared to depict leaves on a tree branch.

Tableware, as opposed to utilitarian ceramics, would seem to have been represented in both dumps mainly by pearlwares and earthenwares, along with some creamwares. Utilitarian ceramics (crocks, jugs, in general, storage vessels) appeared to be, as they are almost invariably at historic sites, of stoneware.

CERAMIC CHARACTERISTICS WITH SOCIOECONOMIC SIGNIFICANCE

Three considerations in regard to a ceramic or collection of ceramics have been shown to have particular input in the determination of socioeconomic status of those who owned them (Otto 1977; Miller 1980). These are decorative technique (how the decoration was applied), form, and (for a collection of ceramics) whether or not ceramics were purchased as a part of a matched set.

John Solomon Otto conducted a statistical test of the idea that ceramic form and status were associated (1977). Otto used the term "form" in the same manner as South (1972:71) who defined it as ". . . a generalized term which includes shape, as well as those other attributes from which type are defined." The results of his test Otto stated as being that, ". . . the distribution of these ceramic forms should be a sensitive indicator of social status" (1977:107). The specific forms he found to be significant in his study were banded (annular) bowls and transfer-printed serving flatware. Working with sites at an Antebellum plantation, he found that the former were most frequent at slave sites, slightly less frequent at overseer sites, and not at all frequent at planter family sites.

Just the reverse was true of transfer-printed serving flatware. Fragments of this type of ceramic comprised a large percentage of the ceramic collection from planter sites, a smaller percentage from overseer sites, and the smallest percentage at slave sites. He advances two plausible reasons for this, which, together, do much to explain the phenomena. the first of these has to do with the bowl versus the platter shape. Since members of lower socioeconomic groups consume a high percentage of less-expensive cuts of meat, these, the argument goes, were most frequently stewed in order to tenderize the meat. Stews were served in bowls. Economically well-off families, however, consumed more expensive cuts of meat, which were not stewed, but broiled or fried. These were served on flatware. Secondly, transfer-printed ware cost more than did banded bowls.

After much documentary research into the historic price of ceramics, George Miller (1980) has determined that, excluding porcelain, the major determinant of price was decorative technique. He has devised a method of indexing by which the cost of a collection of ceramics is compared with the cost of the same collection in undecorated, or "cream-colored" ware manufactured in the same year. This produces the index value, indicating the relative values of ceramics decorated with various techniques. Unfortunately, Miller's index cannot be used with the Bent's Old Fort ceramic collection. Ceramic sherds in the collection are unusually small, perhaps as a result of crushing by the numerous heavy bones discarded in the dumps. Whatever the reason, most sherds are so small as to preclude the possibility of recognizing the shape of the vessel from which they were produced. Unfortunately, the method devised by Miller depends upon being able to reconstruct the collection of vessels represented by the sherds. Even if this could be done, it would not provide an infallible measure of the collection owner's socioeconomic status. As Miller perceptibly notes, the subtle correlation between ceramic price and socioeconomic status has got to be precisely determined.

Jeff Miller (personal communication) has pointed out that ceramics and porcelain of all sorts could be purchased secondhand, one piece at a time, for a price reduced from the original. In areas away from population centers, miscellaneous ceramics were frequently offered by traveling salesmen. The indication of an upper socioeconomic status, then, is the possession of matched sets of decorated ceramics. Not only does this signify the ability to pay for the entire set, but the set would be recognized as a symbol of membership in the upper socioeconomic groups by other members of the group.

EVALUATING THE SOCIOECONOMIC INDICATORS

In evaluating the ceramic fragments recovered from the Bent's Old Fort trash deposits, all the above have been considered. Given the special problems with the collection (mostly having to do with size of the fragments and inability to determine which of the fort's inhabitants were using the intact ceramics), it can be seen that the evaluation is somewhat problematic.

Table 5 presents percentages of various non-utilitarian ceramic types found in the Bent's Old Fort trash strata in the West and Main Dumps. Table 6 shows percentages of non-utilitarian ceramics lumped into relative price ranges as determined by decorative technique for both the West and Main Dumps. It also includes the few sherds of porcelain found in the Main Dup. In Otto's study, he notes that porcelain fragments are rarely found in trash deposits, probably because porcelain was so well cared for. He did, though, find a much greater percentage of transfer-printed ware at high socioeconomic status sites-about 62 percent at planter sites. Thus these figures alone would not indicate high socioeconomic status. One must again remember, though, that the percentage of transfer-printed sherds may be depressed by the number of sherds contributed by members of other socioeconomic groups at the fort.

The more general concept of what South and Otto refer to as "form," though, does not seem to indicate a higher status. As noted before, sherds were too small to allow for reconstruction of ceramic shape or estimate of vessel count. Nonetheless, many of the sherds of transfer-printed ware, spatterware, and the copper lustre seem to have come from tea servings. In fact, copper lustre was produced almost entirely, if not entirely, as tea servings (Jeff Miller, personal communication). These servings were used only on special, somewhat formal occasions. The presence of the tea servings may manifest a variation of what South calls the "British Tea Ceremony." South generalizes that, "the tea ceremony was an important ritual in eighteenth century British colonial life, relating to status even in the remote corners of the British Empire" (1977:42). A similar sort of ritual may have been engaged in at Bent's Old Fort, conducted with visitors from the East and from Santa Fe.

Finally, at least three vessels represented the blue transfer-printed "Gentleman's Cabin" pattern. This could indicate the purchase of a matched set of this most expensive decorated ceramic. Not only was the set expensive, but it is likely tha it would be purchased for use only at more formal social occasions.

A non-ceramic indicator of a higher socioeconomic status is the evidence of consumption of French wine at the fort. The numerous fragments of blackish-green bottle glass may indicate that the wine was present at the fort in some quantity. Again, one would expect the more expensive alcoholic beverage to be consumed most often at more formal social occasions.

While the evaluation is not certain, one is lead to suspect that the owners of the fort shared some of the trappings and rituals common to the upper socioeconomic group of the day. Their business was certainly profitable enough for them to do so. The presence of the French wine, the copper lustre, and the matched transfer-printed ceramics suggest that they were consciously selecting these objects in order to reinforce their status in the upper socioeconomic milieu.

Table 5
Distribution of Various Ceramic Types
by Percentage

	West Dump Strata B-D	Main Dump Strata B-E	Total
Undecorated	43	43	44
Yellow ware	8	5	5
Edged	8	3	4
Annular	10	4	9
Spatterware	10	7	7
Painted	14	24	24
Transfer-printed	6	10	10
Porcelain		1	1

Table 6
Distribution of Ceramics Based Upon Cost
by Percentage

	West Dump Strata B-D	Main Dump Strata B-E	Total
Undecorated - least expensive	43	43	44
Decorated - more expensive (annular, copper lustre, edged, spatterware, painted)	51	46	45
Decorated - most expensive (transfer-printed)	6	10	10
Porcelain			

Note: Using George Miller's scheme of assigning a value of 1.00 to undecorated white ceramics, the value of the "more expensive" group here would be approximately 1.30, the "most expensive" decorated about 3.00, and the porcelain just as roughly 4.00.

RECOMMENDATIONS

As mentioned previously here, it appeared prior to the excavation of the trash dumps that those parts of the dumps that were located in the area to be graded for landscaping and trail construction would very probably be destroyed. This would have been the entire West Dump and about the western 30 percent of the Main Dump. After determining that there were indeed undisturbed trash deposits in these areas and gaining some idea of the extent of the deposits it became apparent that there was not enough time before the scheduled beginning of construction, nor were there available funds, for a complete excavation of the affected dump areas. Because of this the probabilistic field methodology described in this report was carried out.

As eventually happened these deposits were not destroyed during construction. While grading the area, it was decided that the lowering of the ground surface, to facilitate drainage away from the fort, did not have to be to such an extent that the trash deposits would be disturbed. By this time, of course, the archeological sampling excavations of the trash dumps had been completed.

This was an extremely fortunate turn of events. In retrospect, with the benefit of the subsequent analysis of the material from the site it seems clear that the trash dumps at Bent's Old Fort represent a cultural resource of the first order of significance. rich, undisturbed trash deposits from the extreme fringe of the frontier, which date to the beginning of United States industrialization, westward expansion, and development into a nation taking its place in the world arena are few in number. Adding to its significance is the fact that the fort comprised a juncture with, or perhaps an intrusion into, not one but two cultures: the Plains Indians and the Colonial Spanish. This is reflected in artifact collections retrieved from the dumps.

While the inferences drawn from the portion of the dumps excavated and examined are useful and, arguably, valid in at least a statistical sense, the unexcavated deposits nonetheless retain a great deal of significance. Because the deposits are unique in respect to their unquestionable association with pivotal cultural events that took place within a short time (a few years in fact), information to be gained from specific items of cultural material contained therein are unlikely to be redundant to the generalizations obtained for the cultural material through the sampling procedure. It would be informative, for example, to simply increase the number of identifiable artifacts of certain kinds, such as ceramics, beads, bottles, and metal hardware. Regarding the questions to be addressed at this site, a qualitative analysis would be very complementary to an essentially quantitative one, such as that presented here. It would also provide a test for the quantitative methods.

One area might especially benefit from future research. While the faunal analysis carried out by John Applegarth yielded many significant findings, there was simply not enough time allowed him to examine enough bones to comprise a significantly unimpeachable sample. Such an extensive study would yield even more precise information about diet, hunting and trapping practices, butchering methods, preferred cuts of meat, environment, and historic utilization of faunal remains. in regard to this last, Applegarth observes, "many fragments of mature long bone shafts of roughly bison-size mammal . . . appear deliberately broken beyond what would be necessary for marrow extraction, bear a striking resemblance to remnants of glue boiling . . ."

Until the time that a research-oriented excavation is done of the remains of the Main and West trash dumps at Bent's Old Fort, they should be stringently protected.

REFERENCES CITED

Blakeslee, Donald
    1975   The Plains Interband Trade System: An Ethnohistoric and Archeological Investigation. Unpublished Ph.D. dissertation, University of Wisconsin, Milwaukee.

Fontana, Bernard L. and J. Cameron Greenleaf
    1962   Johnny Ward's Ranch, A Study in Historic Archaeology. Kiva 28 (1 and 2).

Godden, Geoffrey O.
    1965   British Pottery and Porcelain 1780-1850. A. Barker, London.

Gregg, Josiah
    1967   The Commerce of the Prairies. University of Nebraska Press, Lincoln.

Grinnell, George Bird
    1923   Bent's Old Fort and Its Builders. Collections of the Kansas State Historical Society, 1919-22, 15:28-91.

Hume, Ivor Noel
    1969   Historical Archaeology. Alfred O. Knopf, New York.

Hume, Audrey Noel
    1974   Archeology and the Colonial Gardner. Colonial Williamsburg Foundation, Williamsburg.

Kist, Leslie
    1965   Survey Sampling. John Wiley and Sons, New York.

Leonard, Robert
    1978   Archaeological Surveillance and Excavations, Bent's Old Fort National Historic Site, LaJunta, Colorado. MS. Midwest Archeological Center, Lincoln.

Logan, Hershel C.
    1959   Cartridges. Stackpole Company, Harrisburg.

Miller, George
    1980   Classification and Economic Scaling of Nineteenth Century Ceramics. Historical Archeology 114:1-40.

Moore, Jackson W., Jr.
    1973   Bent's Old Fort, An Archeological Study. Pruett Press, Boulder.

Otto, John Solomon
    1977   Artifacts and Status Differences. In Research Strategies in Historical Archeology, edited by Stanley South, Academic Press, New York.

Russell, Carl P.
    1957   Guns of the Early Frontier. University of California Press,
            Los Angeles.

Savage, Newman
    1974   Illustrated Dictionary of Ceramics.

Stinson, Dwight E., Jr.
    1965   Bent's Old Fort. Historic Structure Report, part 2.
            Unpublished MS, National Park Service, Midwest Region,
            Omaha.

South, Stanley
    1972   Evolution and Horizon as Revealed in Ceramic Analysis in
            Historic Archeology. The Conference on Historic Site
            Archeology Papers 6:71-106.

    1977   Method and Theory in Historical Archeology. Academic Press,
            New York.

A[...] with 80% Confidence Level

Number of Grids Dug in Stratum A = 13 as follows:

009-006	009-009	012-015	012-018	012-030	015-055	015-018
000-033	015-0[..]	[...]-020	018-042	018-045	021-00[.]	024-025	022-030
021-069	[...]				

[...] under [...] [...] in Stratum A = [...]

[...] of samples clusters = 18

[...] of [...] clusters = 62

Sampling fraction .290323

1.3330

75

WEST DUMP   80% CONFIDENCE LEVEL

CLASS	NUMBER OF ELEMENTS	PROPORTION	PREDICTED TOTAL FOR STRATUM	PREDICTED PERCENTS
BEAD	8	0034 1	17 - 37	0 - 0•
COMMON	4	.50000	7 - 20	27 - 72
OPAQUE WHITE	4	1.00000	13 - 13	100 - 100[x]
MANDREL WOUND	4	.50000	7 - 20	27 - 72
OPAQUE WHITE	4	1. 00	13 - 13	100 - 100[x]
ROUND	4	1. 0	13 - 13	100 - 100[x]
BONE	808	.34442	2331 - 3234	28 - 40
BURNT	147	.18193	287 - 724	10 - 26
BOTTLE	547	.23316	1655 - 2112	20 - 26
BROWN	9	.01645	0 - 66	0 - 3
GREEN	7	.01280	0 - 51	0 - 2
BASE	1	.14286	3 - 3	14 - 14
WHITE	8	.01463	0 - 59	0 - 3
LIP	1	.12500	3 - 3	12 - 12
BRASS TACK	2	.00085	1 - 12	0 - 0•
CAP	2	1.00000	6 - 6	100 - 100[x]

•Less than 1%

[x]Sample too small

WEST DUMP   80% CONFIDENCE LEVEL

CLASS	NUMBER OF ELEMENTS	PROPORTION	PREDICTED TOTAL FOR STRATUM	PERCENTS
BUTTON	5	.00213	8 - 25	0 - 0°
BONE	1	.20000	0 - 7	0 - 41
UNIDENTIFIED	1	1.00000	3 - 3	100 - 100[x]
MILITARY	1	1.00000	3 - 3	100 - 100[x]
CLOTH ON METAL	1	.2 000	0 - 7	0 - 41
EYE	1	1.00000	3 - 3	100 - 100[x]
METAL	1	.20000	0 - 6	3 - 36
EYE	1	1.00000	3 - 3	100 - 100[x]
MOTHER OF PEARL	1	.20000	0 - 6	3 - 36
FOUR HOLE	1	1.00000	3 - 3	100 - 100[x]
PLASTIC	1	.20000	0 - 7	0 - 41
FOUR HOLE	1	1.00000	3 - 3	100 - 100[x]
CARTRIDGE	7	.00298	13 - 35	0 - 0°
38 CALIBER	1	.14286	0 - 7	0 - 30
41 CALIBER	1	.14286	0 - 6	0 - 27
44 CALIBER	1	.14286	0 - 6	0 - 27
45 CALIBER	1	.14286	0 - 6	0 - 27
50-56 CALIBER	1	.14286	0 - 7	0 - 30
56 CALIBER	2	.28571	2 - 11	10 - 46
CEMENT	2	.00085	1 - 12	0 - 0°

77

CLASS	NUMBER OF ELEMENTS	PROPORTION	PREDICTED TOTAL FOR STRATUM	PERCENTS
CERAMIC	84	.03581	211 – 366	2 – 4
CREAMWARE	2	.02381	0 – 12	0 – 4
ANNULAR	1	.50000	0 – 6	9 – 90
WHITE BAND→	1	1.00000	3 – 3	100 – 100[x]
YELLOW	1	.50000	0 – 6	9 – 90
EARTHENWARE	56	.66667	169 – 216	58 – 74
BROWN	1	.01786	0 – 6	0 – 3
SPATTER DECORATED	21	.37500	36 – 107	19 – 55
TURQUOISE	1	.01786	0 – 7	0 – 3
WHITE	33	.58929	80 – 146	41 – 76
PEARLWARE	18	.21429	40 – 83	14 – 28
ANNULAR	2	.11111	0 – 14	0 – 24
MARBLED	2	1.00000	6 – 6	100 – 100[x]
COPPER LUSTRE	1	.05556	0 – 6	0 – 10
FLORAL SPRAY	4	.22222	6 – 21	10 – 34
TRANSFER PRINTED	9	.50000	21 – 40	34 – 65
BLUE	3	.33333	8 – 12	27 – 39
BROWN	2	.22222	0 – 13	0 – 44
GREEN	1	.11111	1 – 5	3 – 18
PURPLE	2	.22222	2 – 11	7 – 36
RED	1	.11111	0 – 7	0 – 25
WHITE	2	.11111	2 – 11	3 – 18
STONE	8	.09524	12 – 42	4 – 14
GRAY-LIGHT BROWN	3	.37500	3 – 17	12 – 62

CLASS	NUMBER OF ELEMENTS	PROPORTION	PREDICTED TOTAL FOR STRATUM		PERCENTS	
CIGARETTE	1	.00043	0	- 7	0 -	0•
PACK	1	1.00000	3	- 3	100 -	100^x
LUCKY STRIKE	1	1.00000	3	- 3	100 -	100^x
FLINT	1	.00043	0	- 7	0 -	0•
ENGLISH	1	1.00000	3	- 3	100 -	100^x
BLACK	1	1.00000	3	- 3	100 -	100^x
METAL	582	.24808	1790	- 2218	22 -	27
BRASS	36	.06186	62	- 185	3 -	9
BELL	1	.02778	0	- 7	0 -	6
HAWK	1	1.00000	3	- 3	100 -	100^x
EYELET	1	.02778	0	- 6	0 -	5
HOOK	1	.02778	0	- 7	0 -	6
UNIDENTIFIED	33	.91667	106	- 120	86 -	97
IRON	543	.93299	1807	- 1932	90 -	96
AX HEAD	1	.00184	0	- 7	0 -	0•
HARNESS BUCKLE	1	.00184	0	- 7	0 -	0•
HORSESHOE	1	.00184	0	- 7	0 -	0•
NAIL	81	.14917	226	- 331	12 -	17
SQUARE CUT	23	.28395	49	- 109	17 -	39
10 PENNYWEIGHT	1	.04348	0	- 7	0 -	9
2 PENNYWEIGHT	1	.04348	0	- 6	0 -	7
30 PENNYWEIGHT	1	.04348	0	- 6	0 -	7
3 PENNYWEIGHT	2	.08696	0	- 13	0 -	17

CLASS	NUMBER OF ELEMENTS	PROPORTION	PREDICTED TOTAL FOR STRATUM	PERCENTS
44 PENNYWEIGHT	2	.08696	2 - 10	3 - 13
5 PENNYWEIGHT	3	.13043	3 - 16	4 - 21
6 PENNYWEIGHT	4	.17391	6 - 20	8 - 26
7 PENNYWEIGHT	1	.04348	0 - 6	0 - 7
8 PENNYWEIGHT	1	.04348	0 - 6	0 - 7
UNIDENTIFIED	459	.84530	1528 - 1633	81 - 87
LEAD	3	.00515	2 - 18	0 - 0*
UNIDENTIFIED	3	1.00000	10 - 10	100 - 100^x
MUSKET BALL	2	.00085	1 - 11	0 - 0*
FIRED	1	.50000	0 - 6	9 - 90
54 CALIBER	1	.50000	0 - 6	9 - 90
OCHRE	1	.00043	0 - 7	0 - 0*
RED	1	1.00000	3 - 3	100 - 100^x
PERCUSSION	5	.00213	7 - 26	0 - 0*
MUSKET	1	.20000	0 - 6	3 - 36
PIPE	15	.00639	38 - 64	0 - 0*
BOWL	4	.26667	4 - 22	9 - 43
TYPE IH	1	.25000	0 - 7	0 - 52
TYPE I	3	.75000	6 - 14	47 - 102

.WEST DUMP   80% CONFIDENCE LEVEL

CLASS	NUMBER OF ELEMENTS	PROPORTION	PREDICTED TOTAL FOR STRATUM	PERCENTS
PLAIN	11	1.00000	37 – 37	100 – 100[x]
5/64" DIAMETER	9	.81818	27 – 34	71 – 92
6/64" DIAMETER	1	.09091	0 – 6	0 – 17
WINDOW GLASS	276	.11765	705 – 1195	8 – 14

WEST DUMP

Number of grids dug in Stratum B = 9 ae follows:

006-021 009-006 009-009 009-018 010-015 012 030 012-048

015-006 021-006

Total number of artifacts in Stratum B = 551

Number of sample clusters = 9

Number of population clusters = 37

Sampling fraction = .243243

T Value = 1.3970

WEST DUMP   80% CONFIDENCE LEVEL

CLASS	NUMBER OF ELEMENTS	PROPORTION	PREDICTED TOTAL FOR STRATUM	PREDICTED PERCENTS
BONE	224	.40653	421 – 1420	18 – 62
BURNT	128	.57143	240 – 812	26 – 88
BOTTLE GLASS	43	.07804	19 – 333	0 – 14
BRASS TACK	2	.00363	1 – 14	0 – 0°
CAP	1	.50000	0 – 7	4 – 95
BUTTON	2	.00363	2 – 14	0 – 0°
BONE	1	.50000	0 – 7	4 – 95
FIVE HOLE	1	1.00000	4 – 4	100 – 100^x
MILITARY	1	1.00000	4 – 4	100 – 100^x
METAL	1	.50000	0 – 7	4 – 95
EYE	1	1.00000	4 – 4	100 – 100^x
MILITARY	1	1.00000	4 – 4	100 – 100^x
CERAMIC	9	.01633	7 – 66	0 –
PEARLWARE	2	.22222	1 – 14	5 – 39
TRANSFER PRINTED	1	.50000	0 – 7	4 – 95
PURPLE	1	1.00000	4 – 4	100 – 100^x
WHITE	1	.50000	0 – 7	4 – 95
STONEWARE		.77778	22 – 35	94

CLASS	NUMBER OF ELEMENTS	PROPORTION	PREDICTED TOTAL FOR STRATUM	PREDICTED PERCENTS
GRAY-LIGHT BROWN	4	.57143	3 - 29	12 - 100
SALT-GLAZE	3	.42857	0 - 25	0 - 67
GRAY-BROWN	3	1.00000	12 - 12	100 - 100[x]
FLINT	1	.00181	0 - 9	0 - 0•
ENGLISH	1	1.00000	4 - 4	100 - 100[x]
BLACK	1	1.00000	4 - 4	100 - 100[x]
LITHIC	1	.00181	0 - 5	0 - 0•
FLAKE	1	1.00000	4 - 4	100 - 100[x]
PETRIFIED WOOD	1	1.00000	4 - 4	100 - 100[x]
YELLOW	1	1.00000	4 - 4	100 - 100[x]
UTILIZED	1	1.00000	4 - 4	100 - 100[x]
METAL	235	.42650	469 - 1462	20 - 64
BRASS	5	.02123	9 - 31	0 - 32
UNIDENTIFIED	5	1.00000	20 - 20	100 - 100[x]
IRON	230	.97872	934 - 956	96 - 99
WALL	38	.16522	89 - 203	11 - 21
SQUARE CUT	4	.10526	0 - 36	0 - 23
10 PENNYWEIGHT	1	.25000	0 - 7	5 - ﾍ
3 PENNYWEIGHT	1	.25000	0 - 9	0 - ﾟﾟ
4 PENNYWEIGHT	2	.50000	4 - 11	27 - 72

84

WEST DUMP 80% CONFIDENCE LEVEL

CLASS	NUMBER OF ELEMENTS	PROPORTION	PREDICTED TOTAL FOR STRATUM	PREDICTED PERCENTS
PIPE	7	.01270	9 - 48	0 - 2
BOWL	1	.14286	0 - 9	0 - 31
TYPE IH	1	1.00000	4 - 4	100 - 100^x
STEM	6	.85714	19 - 29	68 - 100
PLAIN	6	1.00000	24 - 24	100 - 100^x
5/64" DIAMETER	2	.33333	3 - 12	15 - 50
6/64" DIAMETER	4	.66667	12 - 20	49 - 84
WINDOW GLASS	27	.04900	56 - 165	

WEST DUMP

Number of grids dug in Stratum C = 14 as follows:

| 009-009 | 012-015 | 012-018 | 012-030 | 015-018 | 015-033 | 015-042 | 018-030 |
| 018-042 | 018-045 | 021-015 | 021-030 | 021-042 | 030-021 | | |

Total number of artifacts in Stratum C = 2023

Number of sample clusters = 14

Number of population clusters = 62

Sampling fraction = .225806

T Value = 1.3500

CLASS	NUMBER OF ELEMENTS	PROPORTION	PREDICTED TOTAL FOR STRATUM	PREDICTED PERCENTS
BEAD	110	.05437	3 - 970	0 - 10
COMMON	97	.88182	407 - 451	83 - 92
OPAQUE BLUE	27	.27835	111 - 127	26 - 29
OPAQUE GREEN	2	.02062	2 - 15	0 - 3
OPAQUE PURPLE	1	.01031	3 - 5	0 - 1
OPAQUE WHITE	66	.6804 1	276 - 307	64 - 71
TRANSLUCENT WHITE	1	.01031	0 - 11	0 - 2
MANDREL	2	.10909	35 - 70	7 - 14
OPAQUE WHITE	10	.83333	34 - 54	64 - 100
OVAL	1	.10000	2 - 5	6 - 13
ROUND	9	.90000	38 - 41	86 - 93
TRANSLUCENT AMBER	1	.08333	0 - 10	0 - 20
ROUND	1	1.00000	4 - 4	100 - 100[x]
TRANSLUCENT BLUE	1	.08333	0 - 10	0 - 20
ROUND	1	1.0 000	4 - 4	100 - 100[x]
TUBE	1	.00909	0 - 11	0 - 2
OPAQUE WHITE	1	1.00000	4 - 4	100 - 100[x]
BONE	901	.44538	3583 - 4396	40 - 49
BURNT	174	.19312	286 - 1254	7 - 31
BOTTLE	120	.05932	399 - 663	4 - 7
GREEN	1	.00833	0 - 9	0 - 1
WHITE	11	.09167	0 - 106	0 - 20

CLASS	NUMBER OF ELEMENTS	PROPORTION	PREDICTED TOTAL FOR STRATUM	PREDICTED PERCENTS
BRASS TACK	1	.00049	0 - 9	0 - 0$^{\bullet}$
CAP	1	1.00000	4 - 4	100 - 100^{x}
BUTTON	8	.00395	18 - 52	0 - 0$^{\bullet}$
BONE	6	.75000	21 - 31	60 - 89
FIVE HOLE	5	.83333	16 - 27	63 - 100
MILITARY	5	1.00000	22 - 22	100 - 100^{x}
FOUR HOLE	1	.16667	0 - 9	0 - 36
MILITARY	1	1.00000	4 - 4	100 - 100^{x}
MOTHER OF PEARL	2	.25000	3 - 13	10 - 39
FOUR HOLE	2	1.00000	8 - 8	100 - 100^{x}
CERAMIC	62	.03065	205 - 343	2 - 3
CREAM	10	.16129	19 - 69	7 - 25
ANNULAR	6	.60000	18 - 34	41 - 78
BLUE MOCHA	2	.33333	0 - 17	0 - 66
WHITE RILLED	4	.66667	8 - 26	33 - 100
YELLOW	4	.40000	9 - 25	21 - 58
EARTHENWARE	22	.35484	71 - 123	26 - 44
RED	1	.04545	0 - 8	0 - 8
BLACK STRIPE	1	1.00000	4 - 4	100 - 100^{x}
SPATTER DECORATED	5	.22727	7 - 36	8 - 37
WHITE	16	.72727	59 - 82	60 - 84

88

WEST DUMP   80% CONFIDENCE LEVEL

CLASS	NUMBER OF ELEMENTS	PROPORTION	PREDICTED TOTAL FOR STRATUM	PREDICTED PERCENTS
FLORAL SPRAY	6	.25000	9 - 43	9 - 40
SHELL EDGED	5	.20833	11 - 32	11 - 30
EMBOSSED	2	.40000	4 - 12	21 - 58
LATERAL STRIPE	3	.60000	9 - 17	41 - 78
TRANSFER PRINTED	3	.12500	5 - 20	5 - 19
BLUE	1	.33333	0 - 8	0 - 66
BROWN	1	.33333	0 - 8	0 - 66
PURPLE	1	.33333	0 - 8	0 - 66
WHITE	7	.29167	22 - 39	21 - 36
STONEWARE	6	.09677	0 - 52	0 - 19
SALT-GLAZED	6	1.00000	26 - 26	100 - 100[x]
GRAY-BROWN	5	.83333	15 - 28	59 - 100
GRAY-ORANGE	1	.16667	0 - 10	0 - 40
CIGARETTE	1	.00049	0 - 9	0 - 0°
FILTER	1	1.00000	4 - 4	100 - 100[x]
FLINT	4	.00198	9 - 26	0 - 0°
ENGLISH	3	.75000	8 - 18	48 - 100
BLACK	2	.66667	4 - 13	33 - 100
GRAY	1	.33333	0 - 8	0 - 66
FRENCH	1	.25000	0 - 9	0 - 51

WEST DUMP 80% CONFIDENCE LEVEL

CLASS	NUMBER OF ELEMENTS	PROPORTION	PREDICTED TOTAL FOR STRATUM	PREDICTED PERCENTS
GRINDING STONE	1	.00049	0 - 9	0 - 0°
LOWER	1	1.00000	4 - 4	100 - 100[x]
LITHIC	1	.00049	0 - 9	0 - 0°
POINT BASE	1	1.00000	4 - 4	100 - 100[x]
QUARTZITE	1	1.00000	4 - 4	100 - 100[x]
BROWN	1	1.00000	4 - 4	100 - 100[x]
CORNER	1	1.00000	4 - 4	100 - 100[x]
METAL	628	.31043	2484 - 3077	27 - 34
BRASS	16	.02548	36 - 105	1 - 3
EYE	2	.12500	3 - 14	4 - 20
GUN SIDE P	1	.06250	0 - 9	0 - 13
"DN" (INSCRIPTION)	1	1.00000	4 - 4	100 - 100[x]
UNIDENTIFIED	12	.75000	44 - 61	63 - 86
WIRE	1	.06250	0 - 10	0 - 14
IRON	611	.97293	2669 - 2741	96 - 98
CARRIAGE BOLT	1	.00164	0 - 9	0 - 0°
NAIL	60	.09820	211 - 320	7 - 11
SQUARE	3	.05000	5 - 21	2 - 7
6/64" DIAMETER	1	.33333	0 - 8	0 - 66
8/64" DIAMETER	1	.33333	0 - 8	0 - 66
UNIDENTIFIED	550	.90016	2378 - 2493	87 - 92

CLASS	NUMBER OF ELEMENTS	PROPORTION	PREDICTED TOTAL FOR STRATUM	PREDICTED PERCENTS
PERCUSSION CAP	5	.00247	14 - 29	0 - 0°
PIPE	56	.02768	160 - 335	1 - 3
BOWL	22	.39286	70 - 124	28 - 50
TYPE IB	1	.04545	0 - 10	0 - 10
TYPE IH	1	.04545	0 - 9	0 - 10
TYPE I	16	.72727	61 - 80	62 - 82
PLAIN UNIDENTIFIED	2	.09091	3 - 14	3 - 14
TYPE VB	1	.04545	1 - 7	1 - 7
TYPE VC	1	.04545	0 - 10	0 - 10
STEM	34	.60714	123 - 177	49 - 71
PLAIN	34	1.00000	150 - 150	100 - 100[x]
4/64" DIAMETER	2	.05882	2 - 15	1 - 10
5/64" DIAMETER	23	.67467	79 - 124	52 - 82
6/64" DIAMETER	9	.26471	18 - 61	12 - 40
SEED	1	.00049	0 - 10	0 - 0°
PINE CONE	1	1.00000	4 - 4	100 - 100[x]
WHETSTONE	1	.00049	0 - 9	0 - 0°
WINDOW GLASS	122	.06031	382 - 698	4 - 7
WOOD	1	.00049	0 - 9	0 - 0°
HANDLE	1	1.00000	4 - 4	100 - 100[x]

TEST DUMP

Number of grids dug in Stratum D = 9 as follows:

012-030   015-033   035-042   018-030   018-045   021-015   021-030
021-042   030-021

Total number of artifacts in Stratum D = 892

Number of sample clusters = 9

Number of population clusters = 62

Sampling fraction = .145161

T Value = 1.3970

CLASS	NUMBER OF ELEMENTS	PROPORTION	PREDICTED TOTAL FOR STRATUM	PREDICTED PERCENTS
BEAD	20	.02242	40 – 234	0 – 3
COMMON	15	.75000	69 – 137	50 – 99
OPAQUE BLUE	2	.13333	2 – 24	2 – 24
OPAQUE WHITE	13	.86667	78 – 100	75 – 97
MANDREL	5	.25000	0 – 68	0 – 49
OPAQUE BLUE	1	.20000	4 – 9	12 – 27
OVAL	1	1.00000	6 – 6	100 – 100[x]
OPAQUE GREEN	2	.40000	8 – 19	24 – 55
ROUND	2	1.00000	13 – 13	100 – 100[x]
OPAQUE WHITE	2	.40000	5 – 21	15 – 63
ROUND	2	1.00000	13 – 13	100 – 100[x]
ONE	361	.40471	1893 – 3080	30 – 50
BURNT	89	.24654	482 – 744	19 – 29
BOTTLE	79	.08857	382 – 706	11
GREEN	13	.16456	0 – 190	0 – 34
BASE	1	.07692	5 – 7	6 – 8
LIP	1	.07692	5 – 7	6 – 8
SEAL	1	.07692	0 – 19	0 – 21
WHITE	3	.03797	0 – 46	0 – 9
BUTTON	1	.00112	0 – 15	0 – 0*
BRASS	1	1.00000	6 – 6	100 – 100[x]
EYE	1	1.00000	6 – 6	100 – 100[x]

CLASS	NUMBER OF ELEMENTS	PROPORTION	PREDICTED TOTAL FOR STRATUM	PREDICTED PERCENTS
CERAMIC	16	.01794	67 - 153	1 - 2
CREAMWARE	3	.18750	11 - 29	10 - 27
ANNULAR	1	.33333	0 - 14	0 - 70
WHITE RILLED	1	1.00000	6 - 6	100 - 100^x
YELLOW	2	.66667	6 - 21	29 - 100
EARTHENWARE	6	.37500	15 - 67	14 - 60
SPATTER DECORATED	2	.33333	6 - 21	14 - 51
WHITE	4	.66667	19 - 35	48 - 85
PEARLWARE	7	.43750	23 - 73	20 - 66
FLORAL SPRAY	1	.14286	0 - 16	0 - 33
SHELL-EDGED	1	.14286	0 - 16	0 - 33
EMBOSSED	1	1.00000	6 - 0	100 - 100^x
TRANSFER PRINTED	1	.14286	0 - 14	0 - 30
BROWN	1	1.00 00	6 - 6	100 - 100^x
WHITE	4	.57143	15 - 39	32 - 81
FLINT	1	.00112	0 - 15	0 - 0$^•$
FRENCH	1	1.00000	6 - 6	100 - 100^x
GOOSE SHOT	1	.00112	0 - 15	0 - 0$^•$
LITHIC	1	.00112	0 - 15	0 - 0$^•$
FLAKE	1	1.00000	6 - 6	100 - 100^x

CLASS	NUMBER OF ELEMENTS	PROPORTION	PREDICTED TOTAL FOR STRATUM	PREDICTED PERCENTS
METAL	330	.36996	1586 – 2960	25 – 48
IRON	328	.99394	2245 – 2273	98 – 100
NAIL	29	.08841	119 – 280	5 – 12
SQUARE CUT	3	.10345	0 – 47	0 – 23
3 PENNYWEIGHT	1	.33333	6 – 0	33 – 33
40 PENNYWEIGHT	1	.33333	6 – 0	33 – 33
UNIDENTIFIED	299	.91159	1979 – 2140	87 – 94
LEAD	2	.00606	0 – 27	0 – 1
UNIDENTIFIED	2	1.00000	13 – 13	100 – 100^x
OCHRE	4	.00448	0 – 59	0 – 0°
RED	4	1.00000	27 – 27	100 – 100^x
PERCUSSION CAP	2	.00224	2 – 25	0 – 0°
PIPE	25	.02803	75 – 269	1 – 4
BOWL	14	.56000	68 – 124	39 – 72
TYPE I	14	1.00000	96 – 96	100 – 100^x
STEM	11	.44000	47 – 104	27 – 60
PLAIN	11	1.00000	75 – 75	100 – 100^x
4/64" DIAMETER	1	.09091	0 – 15	0 – 20
5/64" DIAMETER	9	.81818	51 – 72	67 – 95
6/64" DIAMETER	1	.09091	0 – 14	0 – 19
TOOTH	1	.00112	0 – 14	0 – 0°

WEST DUMP   80% CONFIDENCE LEVEL

CLASS	NUMBER OF ELEMENTS	PROPORTION	PREDICTED TOTAL FOR STRATUM	PREDICTED PERCENTS
WINDOW GLASS	46	.05157	220 - 413	3 - 6
WOOD	4	.00448	0 - 59	0 - 0*
HANDLE	4	1.00000	27 - 27	100 - 100^x
INCISED	4	1.00000	27 - 27	100 - 100^x

MAIN DUMP 80% CONFIDENCE LEVEL

Number of grids dug in Stratum A = 11 as follows:

| 078-132 | 078-168 | 084-150 | 087-138 | 087-147 | 087-159 | 087-165 | 087-168 |
| 093-159 | 096-144 | 099-141 |

Total number of artifacts in Stratum A = 589

Number of sample clusters = 11

Number of population clusters = 191

Sampling fraction = .057592

T Value = 1.3720

MAIN DUMP   80% CONFIDENCE LEVEL

CLASS	NUMBER OF ELEMENTS	PROPORTION	PREDICTED TOTAL FOR STRATUM	PREDICTED PERCENTS
BONE	445	.75552	6243 – 9210	61 – 90
BURNT	50	.11236	630 – 1106	8 – 14
BOTTLE	28	.04754	61 – 910	0 – 8
BLUE	1	.03571	0 – 42	0 – 8
BROWN	3	.10714	9 – 94	2 – 19
GREEN	6	.21429	25 – 182	5 – 37
WHITE	5	.17857	30 – 143	6 – 29
LIP	1	.20000	5 – 29	6 – 33
CARTRIDGE	1	.00170	0 – 45	0 – 0*
44 CALIBER	1	1.00000	17 – 17	100 – 100[x]
CERAMIC	17	.02886	42 – 548	0 – 5
EARTHENWARE	5	.29412	36 – 137	12 – 46
SPATTER DECORATED	1	.20000	0 – 40	0 – 46
WHITE	4	.80000	46 – 92	53 – 100
PEARLWARE	6	.35294	45 – 162	15 – 55
COPPER LUSTRE	1	.16667	0 – 40	0 – 39
FLORAL SPRAY	1	.16667	0 – 36	0 – 34
SHELL EDGED	1	.16667	0 – 36	0 – 34
EMBOSSED	1	1.00000	17 – 17	100 – 100[x]

CLASS	NUMBER OF ELEMENTS	PROPORTION	PREDICTED TOTAL FOR STRATUM	PREDICTED PERCENTS
TRANSFER PRINTED	2	.33333	18 – 50	17 – 48
BROWN	1	.50000	0 – 34	0 – 99
PURPLE	1	.50000	0 – 34	0 – 99
WHITE	1	.16667	0 – 40	0 – 39
STONEWARE	6	.35294	29 – 178	10 – 60
SALT-GLAZED	5	.83333	63 – 109	61 – 100
BROWN-ORANGE	1	.20000	0 – 44	0 – 51
GRAY-ORANGE	4	.80000	42 – 96	48 – 100
WHITE	1	.16667	0 – 40	0 – 38
LITHIC	1	.00170	0 – 45	0 – 0*
FLAKE	1	1.00000	17 – 17	100 – 100^x
QUARTZITE	1	1.00000	17 – 17	100 – 100^x
GRAY	1	1.00000	17 – 17	100 – 100^x
METAL	58	.09847	728 – 1285	7 – 12
IRON	57	.98276	967 – 1012	96 – 100
NAIL	10	.17544	59 – 287	6 – 29
SQUARE CUT	6	.60000	65 – 142	37 – 82
3 PENNYWEIGHT	1	.16667	0 – 36	0 – 34
4 PENNYWEIGHT	1	.16667	0 – 36	0 – 34
7 PENNYWEIGHT	1	.16667	0 – 40	0 – 39
8 PENNYWEIGHT	1	.16667	0 – 36	0 – 34
UNIDENTIFIED	47	.82456	702 – 929	70 – 93
LEAD	1	.01724	0 – 40	0 – 3
UNIDENTIFIED	1	1.00000	17 – 17	100 – 100^x

MAIN DUMP   80% CONFIDENCE LEVEL

CLASS	NUMBER OF ELEMENTS	PROPORTION	PREDICTED TOTAL FOR STRATUM	PREDICTED PERCENTS
PIPE	6	.01019	1 - 207	0 - 2
BOWL	1	.16667	2 - 32	2 - 31
TYPE IB	1	1.00000	17 - 17	100 - 100^x
STEM	5	.83333	71 - 101	68 - 97
PLAIN	5	1.00000	86 - 86	100 - 100^x
5/64" DIAMETER	5	1.00000	86 - 86	100 - 100^x
REFLECTOR	1	.00170	0 - 45	0 - 0$^\bullet$
RED	1	1.00000	17 - 17	100 - 100^x
PLASTIC	1	1.00000	17 - 17	100 - 100^x
SHELL	2	.00340	0 - 75	0 - 0$^\bullet$
OYSTER	1	.50000	0 - 34	0 - 99
PINON	1.	.50000	0 - 34	0 - 99
TOOTH	1	.00170	0 - 42	0 - 0$^\bullet$
WINDOW GLASS	29	.04924	70 - 936	0 - 9

MAIN DUMP

Number of grids dug in Stratum B = 35 as follows:

072-153	075-141	075-150	075-159	075-171	078-141	078-144	078-168
081-147	081-153	081-171	084-144	084-147	084-150	084-162	084-165
087-132	087-138	087-147	093-147	093-159	096-132	096-138	096-144
096-156	096-159	099-141	102-129	102-141	105-129	105-153	108-129
108-156	108-159	114-129					

Total number of artifacts in Stratum B = 3438

Number of sample clusters = 35

Number of population clusters = 191

Sampling fraction = .183246

T Value = 1.3060

MAIN DUMP 80% CONFIDENCE LEVEL

CLASS	NUMBER OF ELEMENTS	PROPORTION	PREDICTED FOR STRATUM %L	PREDICTED PERCENTS
BEAD	12	.00349	43 - 87	0 - 0•
COMMON	6	.50000	18 - 46	28 - 71
OPAQUE BLUE	2	.33333	3 - 18	10 - 56
OPAQUE GREEN	2	.33333	3 - 18	10 - 56
OPAQUE WHITE	2	.33333	3 - 18	10 - 56
FACET	1	.08333	0 - 10	0 - 16
TRANSLUCENT BLUE	1	1.00000	5 - 5	10 - 100[x]
MANDREL	5	.41667	16 - 37	25 - 57
OPAQUE WHITE	3	.60000	10 - 21	39 - 80
ROUND	3	1.00000	16 - 16	100 - 100[x]
TRANSLUCENT AMBER	1	.20000	0 - 9	3 - 36
ROUND	1	1.00000	5 - 5	100 - 100[x]
TRANSLUCENT BLUE	1	.20000	0 - 11	0 - 42
ROUND	1	1.00000	5 - 5	10 - 100[x]
BONE	1650	.47993	8230 - 9778	43 - 52
BURNT	181	.10970	652 - 1323	7 - 14
BOTTLE	370	.10762	1665 - 2372	8 - 12
BLUE	12	.03243	11 - 119	0 - 5
BROWN	43	.11622	123 - 345	6 - 17
LIP	2	.04651	0 - 21	0 - 9
GREEN	141	.38108	040 - 898	31 - 44
BASE	9	.06383	19 - 78	2 - 10
LIP	2	.01418	1 - 20	0 - 2

MAIN DUMP   80% CONFIDENCE LEVEL

CLASS	NUMBER OF ELEMENTS	PROPORTION	PREDICTED TOTAL FOR STRATUM	PREDICTED PERCENTS
WHITE	129	.34865	593 – 814	29 – 40
BASE	1	.00775	0 – 12	0 – 1
BUTTON	2	.00058	2 – 19	0 – 0•
BONE	2	1.00000	10 – 10	100 – 100[x]
FIVE HOLE	1	.50000	0 – 10	7 – 92
MILITARY	1	1.00000	5 – 5	100 – 100[x]
UNIDENTIFIED	1	.50000	0 – 10	7 – 92
CERAMIC	225	.06545	1079 – 1376	5 – 7
ABORIGINAL	1	.00444	0 – 12	0 – 0•
MICA	1	1.00000	5 – 5	10 – 100[x]
BLACK INSIDE/BLACK OUTSIDE	1	1.00000	5 – 5	10 – 100[x]
CREAMWARE	22	.09778	37 – 203	3 – 16
ANNULAR	20	.90909	98 – 119	82 – 99
BLUE MOCHA	1	.05000	0 – 13	0 – 11
BLUE RILLED	1	.05000	0 – 13	0 – 11
WHITE BAND	1	.05000	0 – 13	0 – 11
WHITE RILLED	17	.85000	76 – 109	70 – 99
YELLOW	2	.09091	0 – 21	0 – 17
EARTHENWARE	92	.40889	436 – 567	35 – 46
GREEN RIM STRIPE	1	.01087	0 – 11	0 – 2
SPATTER DECORATED	11	.11957	39 – 80	7 – 16
WHITE	80	.86957	414 – 458	82 – 91

CLASS	NUMBER OF ELEMENTS	PROPORTION	PREDICTED TOTAL FOR STRATUM	PREDICTED PERCENTS
PEARLWARE	86	.38222	412 - 525	33 - 42
ANNULAR	9	.10465	13 - 84	2 - 17
MARBLED	9	1.00000	49 - 49	100 - 100[x]
COPPER LUSTRE	12	.13958	43 - 87	9 - 18
FLORAL SPRAY	15	.17442	55 - 108	11 - 23
SHELL EDGED	5	.05814	14 - 40	2 - 8
EMBOSSED	4	.80000	15 - 27	58 - 100
BRUSH DRAWN INWARD	1	.20000	0 - 11	0 - 41
TRANSFER PRINTED	33	.38372	141 - 218	30 - 46
BLUE	8	.24242	27 - 59	15 - 32
BROWN	2	.00061	2 - 18	1 - 10
DARK BLUE	8	.24242	21 - 65	11 - 36
GENTLEMAN'S CABIN PATTERN	7	.87500	31 - 44	72 - 100
GREEN	6	.18182	16 - 48	9 - 26
PURPLE	6	.18182	19 - 45	10 - 25
RED	3	.09091	6 - 26	3 - 14
WHITE	12	.13953	41 - 89	8 - 19
PORCELAIN	3	.01333	2 - 30	0 - 2
BLUE	3	1.00000	16 - 16	100 - 100[x]
STONEWARE	21	.09333	90 - 139	7 - 11
BEIGE	1	.04762	0 - 12	0 - 10
GRAY-LIGHT BROWN	2	.09524	0 - 22	0 - 19
SALT-GLAZED	16	.76190	70 - 103	61 - 90
GRAY-BROWN	5	.31250	13 - 40	15 - 46
GRAY-GRAY	4	.25000	8 - 35	9 - 40
	7	.43750	22 - 54	25 - 62

MAIN DUMP   80% CONFIDENCE LEVEL

CLASS	NUMBER OF ELEMENTS	PROPORTION	PREDICTED TOTAL FOR STRATUM	PREDICTED PERCENTS
FLINT	8	.00233	26 – 61	0 – 0•
ENGLISH	4	.50000	15 – 28	35 – 64
BLACK	3	.75000	10 – 22	49 – 100
GRAY	1	.25000	0 – 11	0 – 50
FRENCH	4	.50000	15 – 28	35 – 64
INSULATOR	1	.00029	0 – 12	0 – 0•
WHITE	1	1.00000	5 – 5	100 – 100^x
CERAMIC	1	1.00000	5 – 5	100 – 100^x
USA	1	1.00000	5 – 5	100 – 100^x
LITHIC	11	.00320	36 – 83	0 – 0•
FLAKE	11	1.00000	60 – 60	10 – 100^x
CHALCEDONY	1	.09091	0 – 11	0 – 18
PINK	1	1.00000	5 – 5	100 – 100^x
CHERT	2	.18182	2 – 19	4 – 31
GRAY	1	.50000	0 – 10	7 – 92
YELLOW	1	.50000	0 – 10	7 – 92
JASPER	6	.54545	24 – 41	40 – 68
RED	3	.50000	9 – 22	30 – 69
YELLOW	3	.50000	9 – 22	30 – 69
QUARTZITE	2	.18182	2 – 19	4 – 31
GRAY	2	1.00000	10 – 10	100 – 100^x

MAIN DUMP   80% CONFIDENCE LEVEL

CLASS	NUMBER OF ELEMENTS	PROPORTION	PREDICTED TOTAL FOR STRATUM	PREDICTED PERCENTS
METAL	664	.19314	3027 - 4219	16 - 22
BRASS	1	.00151	0 - 11	0 - 0•
UNIDENTIFIED	1	1.00000	5 - 5	100 - 100ˣ
COPPER	4	00602	1 - 41	0 - 1
TUBE	3	.75000	9 - 23	43 - 100
UNIDENTIFIED	1	.25000	0 - 12	0 - 56
IRON	654	.98494	3536 - 3601	97 - 99
CHAIN	1	.00153	0 - 12	0 - 0•
NAIL	178	.27217	837 - 1105	23 - 30
SQUARE CUT	61	.34270	234 - 431	24 - 44
LARGE	1	.01639	0 - 11	0 - 3
10 PENNYWEIGHT	1	.01639	0 - 11	0 - 3
2 PENNYWEIGHT	4	.06557	10 - 32	3 - 9
3 PENNYWEIGHT	7	.11475	20 - 55	6 - 16
4 PENNYWEIGHT	7	.11475	23 - 53	6 - 15
5 PENNYWEIGHT	10	.16393	36 - 72	10 - 21
6 PENNYWEIGHT	8	.13115	27 - 60	8 - 18
7 PENNYWEI GT	5	.08197	14 - 39	4 - 12
8 PENNYWEI GT	3	.04918	5 - 26	1 - 8
THIMBLE	1	.00153	0 - 12	0 - 0•
UNIDENTIFIED	474	.72477	2452 - 2721	68 - 76
LEAD	5	00753	14 - 39	0 - 1
UNIDENTIFIED	5	1.00000	27 - 27	100 - 100ˣ

CLASS	NUMBER OF ELEMENTS	PROPORTION	PREDICTED TOTAL FOR STRATUM	PREDICTED PERCENTS
MUSKET BALL	2	.00058	0 - 24	0 - 0*
50 CALIBER	2	1.00000	10 - 10	100 - 100[x]
PIPE	74	.02152	314 - 492	1 - 2
BOWL	26	.35135	92 - 191	22 - 47
TYPE IA	9	.34615	9 - 88	6 - 62
TYPE IB	7	.26923	3 - 72	2 - 51
5/16" DIAMETER	6	.85714	24 - 40	64 - 100
TYPE IE	1	.03846	0 - 11	0 - 8
TYPE I	6	.23077	10 - 54	7 - 38
5/16" DIAMETER	1	.16667	0 - 11	0 - 35
PLAIN UNIDENTIFIED	2	.07692	3 - 18	2 - 12
STEM	48	.64865	212 - 311	52 - 77
LINE-DOT PATTERN	2	.04167	0 - 23	0 - 9
PLAIN	46	.95833	238 - 263	90 - 100
4/64" DIAMETER	5	.10870	12 - 41	5 - 16
5/64" DIAMETER	28	.60870	124 - 181	49 - 72
6/64" DIAMETER	5	.10870	11 - 42	4 - 17
SHELL	23	.00669	10 - 240	0 - 1
OYSTER	23	1.00000	125 - 125	100 - 100[x]
TAIL LIGHT	1	.00029	0 - 12	0 - 0*
RED	1	1.00000	5 - 5	100 - 100[x]
TOOTH	12	.00349	18 - 112	0 - 0*

MAIN DUMP

Number of grids dug in Stratum C = 35 as follows:

072-153	075-141	075-150	075-159	075-171	078-141	078-144	078-168
081-132	081-147	081-153	081-171	084-144	084-147	084-150	084-162
084-165	087-132	087-147	087-165	087-168	093-147	093-159	096-132
096-138	096-144	096-156	096-159	099-141	102-129	102-141	105-129
105-153	108-129	108-159					

Total number of artifacts in Stratum C = 4500

Number of sample clusters = 35

Number of population clusters = 191

Sampling fraction = .183246

T Value = 1.3060

MAIN DUMP   80% CONFIDENCE LEVEL

CLASS	NUMBER OF ELEMENTS	PROPORTION	PREDICTED TOTAL FOR STRATUM	PREDICTED PERCENTS
BEAD	271	.06022	34 - 2923	0 - 11
COMMON	252	.92989	1298 - 1451	87 - 98
OPAQUE BLUE	174	.69048	936 - 962	68 - 69
OPAQUE GREEN	10	.03968	52 - 56	3 - 4
OPAQUE WHITE	68	.26984	356 - 285	25 - 28
MANDREL	18	.06642	29 - 167	1 - 11
OPAQUE GREEN	3	.16667	9 - 23	9 - 24
OVAL	1	.33333	0 - 11	0 - 70
ROUND	2	.66667	4 - 17	29 - 100
OPAQUE WHITE	12	.66667	50 - 80	50 - 82
OVAL	4	.33333	14 - 28	22 - 43
ROUND	8	.66667	36 - 50	56 - 77
TRANSLUCENT BLUE	1	.05556	0 - 12	0 - 12
ROUND	1	1.00000	5 - 5	100 - 100[x]
TRANSLUCENT RED	2	.1	0 - 23	0 - 23
OVAL	2	1.00000	10 - 10	10 - 100[x]
POLYCHROME	1	.00369	0 - 14	0 - 0[.]
BLUE ON WHITE	1	1.00000	5 - 5	100 - 100[x]
BONE	2871	.63800	14338 - 16996	58 - 69
BURNT	775	.26994	3341 - 5116	21 - 32
BOTTLE	205	.04556	949 - 1287	3 - 5
BROWN	3	.01463	5 - 27	0 - 2

MAIN DUMP   80% CONFIDENCE LEVEL

CLASS	NUMBER OF ELEMENTS	PROPORTION	PREDICTED TOTAL FOR STRATUM	PREDICTED PERCENTS
GREEN	85	.41463	343 - 583	30 - 52
BASE	1	.01176	0 - 11	0 - 2
LIP	13 .	.15294	12 - 129	2 - 27
NECK	1	.01176	0 - 12	0 - 2
SEAL	1	.01176	0 - 12	0 - 2
PAUILLAC	1	1.00000	5 - 5	100 - 100[x]
WHITE	33	.16098	123 - 236	11 - 21
LIP	2	.06061	0 - 23	0 - 12
BRASS TACK	1	.00022	0 - 12	0 - 0°
CAP	1	1.00000	5 - 5	100 - 100[x]
BUTTON	4	.00089	6 - 37	0 - 0°
BONE	2	.50000	2 - 18	13 - 86
FIVE HOLE	2	1.00000	10 - 10	10 - 100[x]
MILITARY	1	.50000	0 - 10	7 - 92
MOTHER OF PEARL	2	.50000	2 - 18	13 - 86
FOUR HOLE	2	1.00000	10 - 10	100 - 100[x]
CERAMIC	130	.02889	564 - 854	2 - 3
CREAM	3	.02308	2 - 30	0 - 4
ANNULAR	1	.33333	0 - 11	0 - 70
WHITE RILLED	1	1.00000	5 - 5	100 - 100[x]
YELLOW	2	.66667	4 - 17	29 - 100

CLASS	NUMBER OF ELEMENTS	PROPORTION	PREDICTED TOTAL FOR STRATUM	PREDICTED PERCENTS
EARTHENWARE	56	.43 07	266 - 344	37 - 48
SPATTER DECORATED	17	.30357	69 - 116	22 - 38
WHITE	39	.69643	189 - 236	61 - 77
PEARLWARE	59	.45385	282 - 361	39 - 50
ANNULAR	3	.05085	3 - 29	1 - 9
MARBLED	3	1.00000	16 - 16	100 - 100[x]
COPPER LUSTRE	1	.01695	0 - 12	0 - 3
FLORAL SPRAY	26	.44068	114 - 169	35 - 52
SHELL EDGED	11	.18644	23 - 96	7 - 30
EMBOSSED	5	.45455	6 - 48	10 - 80
LATERAL STRIPE	6	.54545	11 - 53	19 - 89
TRANSFER PRINTED	11	.18644	35 - 84	10 - 26
BLUE	3	.27273	6 - 26	10 - 44
BROWN	2	.18182	0 - 21	0 - 35
DARK BLUE	1	.09091	0 - 11	0 - 19
GENTLEMAN"S CABIN PATTERN	1	1.00000	5 - 5	10 - 100[x]
PURPLE	5	.45455	17 - 37	29 - 61
WHITE	7	.11864	22 - 54	6 - 16
STONEWARE	12	.09231	31 - 99	4 - 14
SALT-GLAZED	12	1.00000	65 - 65	100 - 100[x]
GRAY-BROWN	1	.08333	0 - 11	0 - 17
GRAY-GRAY	2	.16667	4 - 17	6 - 26
GRAY-ORANGE	9	.75000	37 - 61	56 - 93
FLINT	5	.00111	7 - 47	0 - 0*
ENGLISH	4	.80000	15 - 28	55 - 100
BLACK	2	.50000	6 - 15	28 - 71

MAIN DUMP   80% CONFIDENCE LEVEL

CLASS	NUMBER OF ELEMENTS	PROPORTION	PREDICTED TOTAL FOR STRATUM	PREDICTED PERCENTS
GRAY	2	.50000	6 - 15	28 - 71
FRENCH	1	.20000	0 - 12	0 - 44
GRINDING STONE	1	.00022	0 - 12	0 - 0•
MANO	1	1.00000	5 - 5	100 - 100[x]
HANDLE	1	.00022	0 - 11	0 - 0•
BONE	1	1.00000	5 - 5	100 - 100[x]
INCISED	1	1.00000	5 - 5	100 - 100[x]
LEATHER	1	.00022	0 - 12	0 - 0•
HEEL	1	1.00000	5 - 5	100 - 100[x]
LITHIC	9	.00200	25 - 73	0 - 0•
FLAKE	9	1.00000	49 - 49	100 - 100[x]
BASALT	1	. 1	0 - 11	0 - 22
GRAY	1	1.00000	5 - 5	100 - 100[x]
CHERT	6	.66667	26 - 38	54 - 79
GRAY	2	.33333	2 - 19	8 - 58
WHITE	3	.50000	9 - 22	30 - 69
JASPER	1	. 1	0 - 10	1 - 20
RED	1	1.00000	5 - 5	10 - 100[x]
PITCHSTONE	1	. 1	0 - 11	0 - 24
BLACK	1	1.00000	5 - 5	10 - 100[x]

CLASS	NUMBER OF ELEMENTS	PROPORTION	PREDICTED TOTAL FOR STRATUM	PREDICTED PERCENTS
METAL	589	.13089	2731 - 3696	11 - 15
BRASS	1	.00170	0 - 11	0 - 0°
UNIDENTIFIED	1	1.0 000	5 - 5	100 - 100^x
COPPER	3	.00509	4 - 27	0 - 0°
ROLLER BAR	1	.33333	0 - 10	0 - 65
BRIDLE	1	1.00000	5 - 5	100 - 100^x
BIT	1	1 00000	5 - 5	100 - 100^x
UNIDENTIFIED	2	.66667	5 - 16	34 - 99
IRON	583	.98981	3168 - 3194	98 - 99
BRACE PIECE	1	.00172	0 - 11	0 - 0°
WAGON	1	1.00000	5 - 5	100 - 100^x
LYNCH PIN	2	.00343	0 - 24	0 - 0°
AXLE	1	.50000	5 - 5	50 - 50
NAIL	216	.37050	1025 - 1331	32 - 41
SQUARE	07	.31019	271 - 460	23 - 39
2 PENNYWEIGHT	2	.02985	1 - 20	0 - 5
3 PENNYWEIGHT	5	.07463	7 - 46	2 - 12
4 PENNYWEIGHT	3	.04478	7 - 25	1 - 6
5 PENNYWEIGHT	1	.01493	0 - 11	0 - 3
6 PENNYWEIGHT	4	.05970	7 - 36	1 - 9
7 PENNYWEIGHT	4	.05970	6 - 37	1 - 10
8 PENNYWEIGHT	1	.01493	0 - 12	0 - 3
STAPLE	1	.00172	0 - 11	0 - 0°
WROUGHT	1	1.00 00	5 - 5	100 - 100^x
UNIDENTIFIED	362	.62093	1820 - 2130	57 - 66
WIRE	1	.00172	0 - 12	0 - 0°

CLASS	NUMBER OF ELEMENTS	PROPORTION	PREDICTED TOTAL FOR STRATUM	PREDICTED PERCENTS
OCHRE	1	.00022	0 - 11	0 - 0°
RED	1	1.00000	5 - 5	100 - 100[x]
PIPE	54	.01200	227 - 361	0 - 1
BOWL	14	.25926	54 - 98	18 - 33
CATLINITE	1	.07143	0 - 11	0 - 15
TYPE IA	1	.07143	0 - 11	0 - 15
TYPE IB	1	.07143	0 - 11	0 - 15
TYPE IE	1	.07143	0 - 10	0 - 14
TYPE II	2	.14286	0 - 21	0 - 28
TYPE I	3	.21429	5 - 27	6 - 36
TYPE PLAIN·UNIDENTIFIED	3	.21429	0 - 32	0 - 43
TYPE VC	1	.07143	0 - 11	0 - 15
TYPE VIA	1	.07143	0 - 11	0 - 15
STEM	40	.74074	196 - 240	66 - 81
"ELIAS"	1	.02500	0 - 10	0 - 4
5/64" DIAMETER	1	1.00000	5 - 5	100 - 100[x]
PLAIN	39	.97500	207 - 217	95 - 99
4/64" DIAMETER	1	.02564	0 - 10	0 - 5
5/64" DIAMETER	31	.79487	155 - 183	72 - 86
6/64" DIAMETER	5	.12821	13 - 41	6 - 19
SHELL	2	.00044	2 - 19	0 - 0°
OYSTER	2	1.00000	10 - 10	100 - 100[x]

114

MAIN DUMP   80% CONFIDENCE LEVEL

CLASS	NUMBER OF ELEMENTS	PROPORTION	PREDICTED TOTAL FOR STRATUM	PREDICTED PERCENTS
WHETSTONE	1	.00022	0 - 11	0 - 0˙
WINDOW GLASS	351	.07800	1660 - 2170	6 - 8

MAIN DUMP

Number of grids dug in Stratum D = 35 as follows:

072-153	075-141	075-150	075-159	075-171	078-132	078-141	078-144
081-147	081-153	081-171	084-144	084-147	084-150	084-162	084-165
087-132	087-138	087-147	087-165	087-168	093-147	093-159	096-132
096-138	096-144	096-156	096-159	099-141	102-129	102-141	105-129
105-153	108-129	108-159					

Total number of artifacts in Stratum D = 3113

Number of sample clusters = 35

Number of population clusters = 191

Sampling fraction = .183246

T Value = 1.3060

116

CLASS	NUMBER OF ELEMENTS	PROPORTION	PREDICTED FOR STRATUM	PREDICTED PERCENTS
BEAD	90	.02891	125 - 856	0 - 5
COMMON	62	.68889	294 - 382	59 - 77
OPAQUE BLUE	41	.66129	168 - 278	49 - 82
OPAQUE PURPLE	1	.01613	2 - 8	0 - 2
OPAQUE WHITE	20	.32256	56 - 161	16 - 47
FACET	1	.0 1	2 - 8	0 - 1
TRANSLUCENT BLUE	1	1.00000	5 - 5	100 - 100^x
MANDREL	25	.27778	86 - 186	17 - 37
OPAQUE BLUE	3	.12000	2 - 30	1 - 22
ROUND	3	1.00 00	16 - 16	100 - 100^x
OPAQUE WHITE	19	.76 00	82 - 124	60 - 91
OVAL	6	.31579	6 - 58	6 - 56
ROUND	13	.68421	45 - 96	43 - 93
TRANSLUCENT AMBER	2	.08000	1 - 20	1 - 14
ROUND	2	1.00000	10 - 10	100 - 100^x
TRANSLUCENT WHITE	1	.04000	0 - 11	0 - 8
OVAL	1	1.00000	5 - 5	100 - 100^x
POLY	2	.02222	4 - 16	1 - 3
BLUE ON WHITE	2	1.00000	10 - 10	100 - 100^x
BONE	1970	.63283	9956 - 11545	58 - 67
BURNT	235	.11929	966 - 1598	8 - 14
BOTTLE	103	.03309	446 - 677	2 - 3
BLUE	1	.00971	0 - 11	0 - 2
BASE	1	1.00000	5 - 5	100 - 100^x

MAIN DUMP   80% CONFIDENCE LEVEL

CLASS	NUMBER OF ELEMENTS	PROPORTION	PREDICTED TOTAL FOR STRATUM	PREDICTED PERCENTS
BROWN	4	.03883	10 - 33	1 - 5
GREEN	74	.71845	364 - 443	64 - 78
BASE	2	.02703	1 - 19	0 - 4
LIP	1	.01351	0 - 12	0 - 2
NECK	1	.01351	0 - 12	0 - 2
WHITE	23	.22330	89 - 161	15 - 28
BASE	1	.03438	0 - 12	0 - 9
BUTTON	5	.00161	10 - 44	0 - 0*
BONE	4	.80000	15 - 27	57 - 100
FIVE HOLE	3	.75000	12 - 20	56 - 93
MILITARY	2	.66667	5 - 16	34 - 99
UNIDENTIFIED	1	.25000	1 - 9	6 - 43
METAL	1	.20000	0 - 11	0 - 42

CLASS	NUMBER OF ELEMENTS	PROPORTION	PREDICTED TOTAL FOR STRATUM	PREDICTED PERCENTS
WHITE	27	.87097	132 - 161	78 - 95
PEARLWARE	86	.67188	395 - 542	56 - 77
ANNULAR	8	.09302	0 - 91	0 - 19[x]
MARBLED	8	1.00000	43 - 43	100 - 100[x]
COPPER LUSTRE	1	.01163	0 - 13	0 - 2
FLORAL SPRAY	44	.51163	193 - 286	41 - 61
TRANSFER PRINTED	4	.04651	0 - 45	0 - 9
BLUE	2	.50000	6 - 15	28 - 71
GREEN	1	.25000	0 - 11	0 - 53
PURPLE	1	.25000	1 - 9	0 - 43
WHITE	29	.33721	129 - 186	27 - 39
STONE	6	.04688	0 - 72	0 - 10
SALT-GLAZED	6	1.00000	32 - 32	100 - 100[x]
GRAY-ORANGE	6	1.00000	32 - 32	100 - 100[x]
FLINT	3	.00096	5 - 27	0 - 0[•]
ENGLISH	2	.66667	5 - 16	34 - 99
GRAY	2	1.00000	10 = 10	100 - 100[x]
FRENCH	1	.33333	0 - 10	0 - 65
LEATHER	1	.00032	0 - 11	0 - 0[•]
SHOE SOLE	1	1.00000	5 - 5	100 - 100[x]
LITHIC	5	.00161	12 - 41	0 - 0
FLAKE	5	1.00000	27 - 27	100 - 100[x]
CHERT	1	.20000	0 - 11	0 - 41

119

MAIN DUMP   80% CONFIDENCE LEVEL

	NUMBER OF		PREDICTED TOTAL	PREDICTED
PINK	2	1.00000	10 - 10	100 - 100[x]
YELLOW	1	.20000	0 - 11	0 - 41
METAL				
BRASS	507	.16287	2405 - 3128	14 - 18
HINGE	5	.00986	11 - 43	0 - 1
HANDMADE	1	.20000	0 - 11	0 - 42
"23 RC"	1	1.00000	5 - 5	10 - 100[x]
UNIDENTIFIED	1	1.00000	5 - 5	100 - 100[x]
UNIDENTIFIED	4	.80000	15 - 27	57 - 100
COPPER	1	.00197	0 - 12	0 - 0[•]
UNIDENTIFIED	1	1.00000	5 - 5	100 - 100[x]
IRON	496	.97830	2682 - 2730	96 - 98
DRIVE PINNEL	1	.00202	0 - 11	0 - 0[•]
FISH HOOK	1	.00202	0 - 12	0 - 0[•]
NAIL	165	.33266	755 - 1045	27 - 38
SQUARE	28	.16970	94 - 211	10 - 23
2 PENNYWEIGHT	1	.03571	0 - 11	0 - 7
3 PENNYWEIGHT	1	.03571	0 - 12	0 - 7
4 PENNYWEIGHT	4	.14286	5 - 38	3 - 24
5 PENNYWEIGHT	1	.03571	0 - 11	0 - 7
6 PENNYWEIGHT	2	.07143	0 - 23	0 - 15
7 PENNYWEIGHT	1	.03571	0 - 11	0 - 7
8 PENNYWEIGHT	2	.07143	2 - 19	1 - 12
WIRE	1	.00606	0 - 11	0 - 1

MAIN DUMP   80% CONFIDENCE LEVEL

CLASS	NUMBER OF ELEMENTS	PROPORTION	PREDICTED TOTAL FOR STRATUM	PREDICTED PERCENTS
STAPLE HOOK	1	.00202	0 - 12	0 - 0*
THIMBLE	1	.00202	0 - 11	0 - 0*
UNIDENTIFIED	327	.65927	1630 - 1938	60 - 71
LEAD				
UNIDENTIFIED	5	.00986	12 - 41	0 - 1
UNIDENTIFIED	5	1.00000	27 - 27	100 - 100[x]
PIPE	75	.02409	277 - 540	1 - 3
BOWL	28	.37333	97 - 207	23 - 50
TYPE IA	1	.03571	0 - 11	0 - 7
TYPE IB	2	.07143	2 - 19	1 - 12
TYPE IH	1	.03571	0 - 11	0 - 7
TYPE II	1	.03571	0 - 11	0 - 7
TYPE I	10	.35714	35 - 73	23 - 48
5/64" DIAMETER	1	.10000	0 - 11	0 - 21
PLAIN-UNIDENTIFIED	1	.3571	0 - 11	0 - 7
PLAIN UNIDENTIFIED	11	.39286	36 - 83	23 - 54
5/64" DIAMETER	1	.09091	0 - 12	0 - 20
TYPE VB	1	.03571	0 - 11	0 - 7
6/64" DIAMETER	1	1.00000	5 - 5	100 - 100[x]
STEM	47	.62667	201 - 311	49 - 76
LINE-DOT DECORATED	1	.02128	0 - 12	0 - 4
5/64" DIAMETER	1	1.00000	5 - 5	100 - 100[x]
PLAIN	46	.97872	244 - 257	95 - 100
5/64" DIAMETER	36	.78261	182 - 210	72 - 83
6/64" DIAMETER	7	.15217	22 - 53	8 - 21
7/64" DIAMETER	1	.02174	0 - 11	0 - 4

MAIN DUMP   80% CONFIDENCE LEVEL

CLASS	NUMBER OF ELEMENTS	PROPORTION	PREDICTED TOTAL FOR STRATUM	PREDICTED PERCENTS
SHELL	6	.00193	18 – 46	0 – 0˙
DENTALIUM	1	.16667	0 – 11	0 – 34
OYSTER	4	.66667	14 – 29	43 – 89
SNAIL	1	.16667	0 – 11	0 – 34
TOOTH		.00225	9 – 66	0 – 0˙
WINDOW GLASS	213	.06842	796 – 1528	8

MAIN DUMP

Number of grids dug in Stratum E = 19 as follows:

075-159	078-141	081-147	081-153	084-144	084-147	084-150	084-162
084-165	087-132	087-138	087-147	087-165	087-168	096-132	096-144
096-159	099-141	108-159

Total number of artifacts in Stratum E = 887

Number of sample clusters = 19

Number of population clusters = 191

Sampling fraction = .099476

T Value = 1.3300

MAIN DUMP   80% CONFIDENCE LEVEL

CLASS	NUMBER OF ELEMENTS	PROPORTION	PREDICTED TOTAL FOR STRATUM	PREDICTED PERCENTS
BEAD	7	.00789	29 – 111	0 – 1
COMMON	2	.28571	5 – 34	8 – 48
OPAQUE WHITE	2	0000	20 – 20	10 – 100[x]
MANDREL	5	.71429	36 – 64	51 – 91
OPAQUE BLUE	1	.20000	0 – 22	0 – 44
OVAL	1	1.00000	10 – 10	100 – 100[x]
OPAQUE WHITE	4	.80000	27 – 52	55 – 100
OVAL	2	.50000	4 – 36	10 – 89
ROUND	2	.50000	4 – 36	10 – 89
BONE	602	.67869	5646 – 6457	63 – 72
BURNT	168	.27907	1190 – 2187	19 – 36
BOTTLE	27	.03044	183 – 359	2 – 4
GREEN	9	.33333	40 – 140	15 – 51
WHITE	3	.11111	4 – 55	1 – 20
BRASS TACK	1	.00113	0 – 22	0 – 0˙
CAP	1	1.00000	10 – 10	100 – 100[x]

MAIN DUMP   80% CONFIDENCE LEVEL

CLASS	NUMBER OF ELEMENTS	PROPORTION	PREDICTED TOTAL FOR STRATUM	PREDICTED PERCENTS
CERAMIC	27	.03044	139 - 403	1 - 4
ABORIGINAL	4	.14815	0 - 86	0 - 31
MICA	4	1.00000	40 - 40	100 - 100[x]
BROWN-BROWN	4	1.00000	40 - 40	100 - 100[x]
EARTHENWARE	7	.25926	33 - 106	12 - 39
WHITE	7	1.00000	70 - 70	100 - 100[x]
PEARLWARE	15	.55556	89 - 212	32 - 78
FLORAL SPRAY	14	.93333	127 - 154	84 - 100
WHITE	1	.06667	0 - 23	0 - 15
STONEWARE	1	.03704	0 - 21	0 - 7
SALT-GLAZED	1	1.00000	10 - 10	100 - 100[x]
GRAY-GRAY	1	1.00000	10 - 10	100 - 100[x]
FLINT	3	.00338	8 - 51	0 - 0[•]
ENGLISH	1	.33333	0 - 20	0 - 68
BLACK	1	1.00000	10 - 10	100 - 100[x]
FRENCH	2	.66667	9 - 30	31 - 100
LITHIC	3	.00338	3 - 56	0 - 0[•]
FLAKE	3	1.00000	30 - 30	100 - 100[x]
QUARTZITE	3	1.00000	30 - 30	100 - 100[x]
GRAY	1	.33333	3 - 16	12 - 53
PINK	2	.66667	13 - 26	46 - 87

MAIN DUMP   80% CONFIDENCE LEVEL

CLASS	NUMBER OF ELEMENTS	PROPORTION	PREDICTED TOTAL FOR STRATUM	PREDICTED PERCENTS
METAL	144	.16234	1169 – 1725	13 – 19
BRASS	3	.02083	0 – 62	0 – 4
UNIDENTIFIED	3	1.00 00	30 – 30	100 – 100[x]
COPPER	1	.00 84	0 – 21	0 – 1
UNIDENTIFIED	1	1.00000	10 – 10	100 – 100[x]
IRON	140	.97222	1376 – 1438	95 – 99
NAIL	58	.41429	465 – 00	33 – 49
SQUARE CUT	13	.22414	96 – 165	16 – 28
2 PENNYWEIGHT	2	.15385	7 – 32	5 – 25
3 PENNYWEIGHT	1	.07692	0 – 20	0 – 15
4 PENNYWEIGHT	1	.07692	0 – 22	0 – 17
6 PENNYWEIGHT	1	.07692	0 – 22	0 – 17
7 PENNYWEIGHT	1	.07692	0 – 20	0 – 15
UNIDENTIFIED	82	.58571	06 – 941	50 – 66

MAIN DUMP   80% CONFIDENCE LEVEL

CLASS		NUMBER OF ELEMENTS	PROPORTION	PREDICTED TOTAL FOR STRATUM	PREDICTED PERCENTS
	5/64" DIAMETER	9	.69231	64 – 116	49 – 88
	6/64" DIAMETER	3	.23077	11 – 48	8 – 37
SHELL		5	.00564	25 – 74	0 – 0˙
	DENTALIUM	1	.20000	0 – 21	0 – 43
	OYSTER	4	.80000	28 – 51	56 – 100
TOOTH		5	.00564	16 – 83	0 – 0˙
WINDOW GLASS		38	.04284	238 – 525	5

APPENDIX C

MAIN DUMP

Number of grids due in Feature 1 = 3 as follows:

078-132   087-159   111-138

Total number of artifacts in Feature 1 = 177ʹ

Number of sample clusters = 3

Number of population clusters = 191

Sampling fraction = .015707

T Value = 1.8860

MAIN DUMP   80% CONFIDENCE LEVEL

CLASS	NUMBER OF ELEMENTS	PROPORTION	PREDICTED TOTAL FOR STRATUM	PREDICTED PERCENTS
BEAD	3	.01695	0 - 417	0 - 3
COMMON	1	.33333	0 - 182	0 - 95
OPAQUE WHITE	1	1.00000	63 - 63	100 - 100^x
FACET	1	.33333	0 - 182	0 - 95
TRANSLUCENT BLUE	1	1.00000	63 - 63	100 - 100^x
MANDREL	1	.33333	0 - 182	0 - 95
OPAQUE WHITE	1	1. 00	63 - 63	100 - 100^x
ROUND	1	1 00	63 - 63	100 - 100^x
BONE	35	.19774	953 - 3503	8 - 31
BOTTLE	21	.11864	332 - 2341	2 - 20
BROWN	4	.19048	67 - 441	5 - 33
GREEN	4	.19048	28 - 480	2 - 35
WHITE	13	.61905	788 - 66	58 - 64
BUTTON	1	.00565	12 - 114	0 - 1
METAL	1	1.00000	63 - 63	100 - 100^x
EYE	1	1.00000	63 - 63	100 - 100^x
COLOUR	1	1.00000	63 - 63	100 - 100^x

130

CLASS	NUMBER OF ELEMENTS	PROPORTION	PREDICTED TOTAL FOR STRATUM	PREDICTED PERCENTS
CERAMIC	10	.05650	314 – 958	2 – 8
CREAMWARE	2	.20000	0 – 292	0 – 45
ANNULAR	1	.50000	63 – 63	50 – 50
WHITE RILLED	1	1.00000	63 – 63	100 – 100ˣ
YELLOW	1	.5 00	63 – 63	50 – 50
EARTHENWARE	4	40000	172 – 337	27 – 52
WHITE	4	1.00000	254 – 254	100 – 100ˣ
PEARLWARE	4	.40000	172 – 337	27 – 52
FLORAL SPRAY	3	.75000	87 – 294	34 – 100
TRANSFER PRINTED	1	.25000	0 – 166	0 – 65
BLUE	1	1.00 00	63 – 63	100 – 100ˣ
LITHIC	1	.00565	0 – 219	0 – 1
FLAKE	1	1.00000	63 – 63	100 – 100ˣ
CHERT	1	1.00000	63 – 63	100 – 100ˣ
WHITE	1	1.00000	63 – 63	100 – 100ˣ
METAL	78	.44 68	1606 – 8325	14 – 73
COPPER LUSTRE	1	.01282	0 – 262	0 – 5
UNIDENTIFIED	1	1.00000	63 – 63	100 – 100ˣ
IRON	77	.98718	4703 – 5100	94 – 100
NAIL	7	.09091	70 – 820	1 – 16
SQUARE CUT	4	.57143	77 – 431	17 – 96
2 PENNYWEIGHT	1	.25000	0 – 166	0 – 65
5 PENNYWEIGHT	1	.25000	0 – 166	0 – 65
6 PENNYWEIGHT	1	.25000	0 – 166	0 – 65
6 PENNYWEIGHT	1	25000	0 – 166	0 – 65

MAIN DUMP   80% CONFIDENCE LEVEL

CLASS	NUMBER OF ELEMENTS	PROPORTION	PREDICTED TOTAL FOR STRATUM	PREDICTED PERCENTS
UNIDENTIFIED	70	.90509	4081 – 4831	83 – 98
PIPE				
BOWL	6	.03390	65 – 698	0 – 6
TYPE IB	3	.50000	87 – 294	22 – 77
TYPE I	1	.33333	0 – 132	0 – 69
STEM	2	.66667	58 – 196	30 – 100
PLAIN	3	.50000	87 – 294	22 – 77
	3	1.00000	191 – 191	100 – 100 [x]
4/64" DIAMETER	1	.33333	0 – 132	0 – 69
5/64" DIAMETER	1	.33333	0 – 132	0 – 69
6/64" DIAMETER	1	.33333	0 – 201	0 – 100
SHELL	1	.00565	12 – 114	0 – 1
OYSTER	1	1.00000	63 – 63	100 – 100 [x]
TOOTH	5	.02825	0 – 1096	0 – 9
WINDOW GLASS	16	.09040	0 – 2891	0 – 25

NOTES ON THE BENT'S OLD FORT ARCHAEOFAUNA RECOVERED BY DOUGLAS C. COMER (NATIONAL PARK SERVICE, HISTORICAL PRESERVATION).

Identification of three items of mollusk shell was done by .Dr. Artie L. Metcalf of the University of Texas at El Paso. Land snails of the genus Succinea are typically found on plants at the edge of streams and ponds -- "they require a humid habitat but cannot stand immersion" (Hyman, 1967:620). Rather small, thin and delicate, the one shell recovered probably was not water-floated any great distance. Its presence suggests the vegetation along the river was rarely flooded (relative abundance of minute but environmentally informative snail shells should be tested during future archaeological sampling of the Bent's Fort deposits, using floatation and fine sieves as discussed by Struever, 1968, and Colyer and Osborne, 1965). The fragment of a freshwater mussel shell suggests the river to have been relatively silt-free; it may have been transported by water or man, but most likely was of relatively local origin.

Analysis of 159 items of fish bone was done by Dr. William J. Koster of the University of New Mexico. Six items represent a salmonoid species, the Goldeye (Hiodon alosoides); as far as Dr. Koster knows, this is an extension of the known range some 300 miles to the west and the first record for the state of Colorado. Eddy (1957:44-45) notes fish of the genus Hiodon to reach a length of 15 inches and to be "utilized to a limited extent for food, mostly as smoked goldeye in the north." The importation of a smoked fish seems unlikely, especially with the head attached (material includes preopercular and hyomandibular elements). According to Cross and Collins (1975:37) goldeyes "have been found in small tributary streams only during their reproductive migrations, usually in March or April. Goldeyes move up rivers, sometimes for many miles, to spawn in flowing water over rocky or gravelly bottoms."

More than 90% of the fish remains probably represent the Channel Catfish, Ictalurus punctatus. Dr. Koster positively

identified 96 items as Channel Catfish. He speculated
(personal communication) "probably all fragments identified
as 'Ictaluridae' are from Ictalurus punctatus. None of the
ictalurid fragments resembled anything but this species.
Further, according to the literature, only two members of the
Ictaluridae were to be expected in the region, I. punctatus
and I. melas, and almost all the 'Ictaluridae' fragments were
too large to be from I. melas. Many of the 'unidentified' are
probably also I. punctatus. They have the appearance of
ictalurid fragments." Preferred habitat of the Channel
Catfish is a relatively large river with a sandy or rocky
bottom, a relatively strong flow, and deep holes behind rocks,
logs, etc. where adults like to rest. Adults from lakes may
reach 25 inches and 30 pounds, but river fish seldom exceed
5 pounds (Cross and Collins, 1975:106). Although Dr. Koster
observed (personal communication) that "almost all fragments
came from fish of respectable, but not giant, size", scarcity
of small remains could be partly due to the relatively large,
quarter-inch mesh of the screens used to recover the bones.

Two toad bones, one of Woodhouse's Toad, Bufo woodhousei,
were recovered from adjacent levels in a disturbed part of the
west dump. Toads burrow in soft dirt and use burrows made by
other animals; the remains are probably intrusive and may
represent a single individual. Woodhouse's Toad prefers sandy
soil, relatively mesic conditions, and is generally confined
to river valleys in the Southwest (Applegarth, in press).

Of the 20 items of box turtle, 14 were identified as
Western Box Turtle, Terrapene ornata; the remainder probably
represent this species. Unmodified remains could be intrusive,
incidental or human refuse. However, from the west dump (N12,
E30, strata C & D) 11 carapace fragments, probably from one
large adult, have numerous scratch marks on the inner surface
indicating the inside of the turtle's shell was scraped out
during human fabrication of an implement, ornament or vessel
(microscopic examination shows the scratches to antedate

damage due to root etching indicating they were done prior to interment; they appear as though they were done with a sharp-edged stone implement). Box turtles are easily captured during the warm months of the year, and aboriginal exploitation has been so intense in some areas as to cause their extinction (Adler, 1970). The Western Box Turtle is a terrestial species which favors grassland with sandy soil, and sand dunes stabilized with vegetation.

Remains of softshell turtle probably represent the Spiny Softshell, Trionyx spiniferus, which now occurs in the Bent's Fort area, but lack of comparative material prevented separation from the Smooth Softshell, T. muticus, which occurs a few hundred miles to the east (west to Kearny County, Kansas, per Collins, 1974). Softshell turtles are usually found only in permanent streams and rivers. They are relatively silt-tolerant but do perfectly well in clear streams with sandy bottoms. Hence, their presence does not indicate a silty quality to the Arkansas River water. Because they rarely wander more than a few feet from water, the eight items recovered probably represent human refuse (softshell turtles were among the game exploited by Apaches in the Fort Sumner area per Jelinek, 1967).

Most of the bird remains were identified by Dr. Amadeo M. Rea (Curator of Birds and Mammals, San Diego Natural History Museum). Most of the bird species are those that would be expected along the Arkansas River. Exceptions include the grouses, most likely imported from further west or north, and the domestic chicken. Bird remains are probably human refuse, however many may have been carried about and consequently imported for cultural reasons (parts of ceremonial costumes, tools or religious paraphernalia). Regarding one item of Blue Grouse from the main dump and two items of grouse (blue or sharp-tailed) from the A stratum of the west dump, Dr. Rea noted the bones appeared partly digested, and speculated they had been swallowed by a dog (he thought the two items from the

135

west dump, when articulated, would have been too large for
a human to swallow). He also noted wild turkey leg bones
from the C stratum of the west dump had been butchered just
above and below the knee joint, cutting through the respective
heads rather than separating them or snapping the shafts.

Of the mammal bones recovered, two items of jackrabbit
and two of cottontail rabbit could be intrusive, incidental
or human refuse. The jackrabbit remains most likely represent
the Black-tailed Jackrabbit, Lepus californicus, which
generally favors open grassland with plenty of room for running.
On the other hand cottontails generally favor areas with brush
or other concealing vegetation. The single item of Yellow-
faced Pocket Gopher, Pappogeomys castanops, is probably
intrusive; this species favors sandy soils along stream margins.
Three items of Beaver, Castor canadensis, are most likely human
refuse and of relatively local origin. Beavers prefer streams
with relatively low gradients, relatively wide canyons or
valleys, and require an abundance of willows, cottonwoods or
similar trees for food and building materials.

Canid remains (from domestic dog, wolf or coyote) include
three wolf-size foot bones and a coyote-size tooth. The wolf-
size items may be Gray Wolf, Canis lupus, but probably cannot
be determined to species by morphological means (this seems
like an opportunity for an electrophoretic or serological study).
Seven foot bones recovered from the main dump represent the
Swift Fox, Vulpes velox. There is a possibility that these foot
bones are a product of partial skinning where the fox was
trapped then removal of the feet from the hide during processing
at the fort.

Purely a pet, the domestic cat, Felis catus, is represented
by two items from the A stratum of the west dump. This is in
contrast to the five potentially useful domestic species
represented in the main dump. Speculating on this, cats could
have been commonly carried by people riding stage coaches,
occasionally escaping or being left at isolated stations, but

seem unlikely as passengers on freight wagons going to a
frontier trading post. Although tenuous reasoning, the
absence of domestic cat from the main dump and lower levels
of the west dump, and presence in the upper level of the west
dump, tends to support the position that the A stratum of the
west dump is from the stage station period.

An equine bone from the main dump, intermediate in size
between horse and burro, is probably from a mule (Equus asinus
x caballus) but could represent a mule-sized horse. The other
domestic mammals represented in the main dump are pig, goat,
and a small breed of sheep.

Most of the deer remains seem closer to the White-tailed
Deer, Odocoileus virginianus, than to the Mule Deer, O. hemionus.
Although no one item was close enough to allow a "probable"
identification, viewed together most if not all probably do
represent O. virginianus. White-tailed Deer favor riparian
situations with enough brush or trees for concealment. The
Pronghorn, Antilocapra americana, and the Bison, Bison bison
(really should be Bos bison considering that fertile hybrid
lines have been produced) are species of the open plains.
Because most bones were extensively broken before being dumped
into the barrow pits, and because the bones of Bison are
difficult to distinguish from those of domestic cattle, only
a rough estimate can be made of the relative abundance of
Bison in the deposits: 67% by weight and 10% by items. There
is a virtual lack of head elements and a surprising abundance
of rib fragments ("almost invariably, the skull is left at the
scene of the kill" per Wheat, 1972:102).

An excavator's nick on an embryonic humerus of a large
bovid (Bos or Bison) from the main dump (bag 531) was enlarged
in order to count "strata" in the compact bone (Frison, 1974:
147-148); roughly 14 are present but very poorly defined,
suggesting a roughly full term embryo, and -- if this is Bison
-- a spring kill of the parent. A number of other embryonic
bones (bags 27, 390, 391, and 513) -- if Bison -- suggest the

137

parents were killed during the winter and spring. Many fragments of mature long bone shafts of roughly Bison-size mammal (e.g. in bag 514) appear deliberately broken beyond what would be necessary for marrow extraction, and bear a striking resemblance to remnants of glue boiling as illustrated and discussed by Schmid (1972:48-49). All artiodactyl remains are almost certainly human refuse.

Differneces between all three deposits (main dump, west dump lower levels, and west dump upper level) are indicated by Tables 7 and 8. Five domestic species (chicken, mule, pig, goat and sheep), represented by 12 items, are unique to the main dump. The main dump is also distinguished by the presence of fox and a relative abundance of deer and pronghorn. The lower levels (strata B-D) of the west dump are devoid of domestic species, and rich with fish, box turtle and wild birds. The upper level (stratum A) of the west dump is distinguished by the presence of domestic cat and absence of box turtle and wild turkey. The main dump with 5 domestics among 22 genera, compared to the lower part of the west dump with no domestics in 21 genera, could be mathematically significant. However mathematical tests on data so rich with biases seems questionable. Apparent differences could involve chance, who did the dumping, and separation of the deposits by a few months or a few years. Nothing contradicts the idea that the upper level of the west dump was deposited later, after the "fort" period.

Presence of some brush, willows and cottonwood trees along the Arkansas River in the general area of Bent's Old Fort is suggested by the archaeological representation of the following genera: Haliaeetus, Meleagris, Pica, Sylvilagus, Castor, and Odocoileus. Future archaeological sampling at Bent's Old Fort may be able to provide a more detailed environmental reconstruction by emphasizing the recovery of "microfauna" (mice, lizards, toads, snails, etc.).

LITERATURE CITED

Adler, Kraig. 1970. The influence of prehistoric man on the distribution of the box turtle. Annals of the Carnegie Museum (Pittsburgh) 41(9):263-280.

Applegarth, John S. (in press) Environmental implications of herpetofaunal remains from archeological sites west of Carlsbad, New Mexico. National Park Service symposium.

Collins, Joseph T. 1974. Amphibians and reptiles in Kansas. University of Kansas, Museum of Natural History, Public Education Series No. 1, x+283 pages.

Colyer, Marilyn, and Douglas Osborne. 1965. Screening soil and fecal samples for recovery of small specimens. American Antiquity 31(2, part 2):186-192 (Memoirs of the Society for American Archaeology number 19).

Cross, Frank B., and Joseph T. Collins. 1975. Fishes in Kansas. University of Kansas, Museum of Natural History, Public Education Series No. 3, viii+189 pages.

Eddy, Samuel. 1957. How to know the freshwater fishes. Wm. C. Brown Company, Dubuque, Iowa. vi+253 pages.

Frison, George C., ed. 1974. The Casper Site, a Hell Gap bison kill on the High Plains. Academic Press, Inc., New York. xviii+266 pages.

Hyman, Libbie Henrietta. 1967. The invertebrates: Mollusca I (volume VI). McGraw-Hill Book Company, New York. viii+792 pages.

Jelinek, Arthur J. 1967. A prehistoric sequence in the middle Pecos valley, New Mexico. University of Michigan, Anthropological Papers No. 31, iv+176 pages and 16 plates.

Schmid, Elisabeth. 1972. Atlas of animal bones for prehistorians, archaeologists and Quaternary geologists / Knochenatlas für Prähistoriker, Archaologen und Quartärgeologen. Elsevier Publishing Company, Amsterdam. viii+159 pages.

Struever, Stuart. 1968. Flotation techniques for the recovery of small-scale archaeological remains. American Antiquity 33(3):353-362.

Wheat, Joe Ben. 1972. The Olsen-Chubbuck site. A paleo-Indian bison kill. Society for American Archaeology Memoir No. 26, x+180 pages.

STATISTICS ON BENT'S OLD FORT ARCHAEOFAUNA RECOVERED BY DOUGLAS C. COMER (weight is in grams; items include fragments, whole bones, and co-adherent groups of bones; MNI are the minimum number of individuals represented by the recovered items; and an asterisk indicates inclusion of items of probable identity).

Table 1. Statistics for the main dump, part of the random samples, all strata.

common name (scientific taxon)	weight	items	MNI
mollusks (Mollusca)			
succineid land snails (Succinea)			
freshwater mussels (Unionidae)			
unidentified mollusk			
bony fishes (Osteichthyes)	3.8	12	1
Goldeye (Hiodon alosoides)			
freshwater catfishes (Ictaluridae)	3.4	10	1
Channel Catfish (Ictalurus punctatus)	2.8*	7*	1
unidentified fish	0.4	2	0
toads (Bufo)			
Woodhouse's Toad (Bufo woodhousei)			
turtles (Testudinata)	4.7	6	3
box turtles (Terrapene)	1.8	2	1
Western Box Turtle (Terrapene ornata)			
softshell turtles (Trionyx)	2.9	4	2

140

Table 1, continued.

common name (scientific taxon)	weight	items	MNI
birds (Aves)	17.1	14	7
waterfowl (Anseriformes)	2.0	2	1
Canada Goose (Branta canadensis) . .	2.0*	2*	1
Green-winged Teal (Anas crecca)			
Turkey Vulture (Cathartes aura) . . .	1.0.	1	1
buteo hawks (Buteo)	1.3	1	1
Bald Eagle (Haliaeetus leucocephalus)			
Domestic Chicken (Gallus gallus) . .	4.9	4	1
grouses (Tetraonidae)	1.1	2	2
Blue Grouse (Dendragapus obscurus) .	0.5	1	1
sage grouse (Centrocercus)			
sharp-tailed grouse (Pedioecetes) . .	0.6*	1*	1
Wild Turkey (Meleagris gallopavo) . .	4.6	3	1
Great Blue Heron (Ardea herodias)			
Sandhill Crane (Grus canadensis)			
Black-billed Magpie (Pica pica)			
Common Raven (Corvus corax)			
unidentified bird	2.2	4	0
mammals (Mammalia)	8799.2	1594	20
jackrabbits (Lepus)	2.2	2	1
cottontail rabbits (Sylvilagus) .	0.6	1	1

Table 1, continued.

common name (scientific taxon)	weight	items	MNI
mammals, continued			
Yellow-faced Pocket Gopher (Pappogeomys castanops)			
Beaver (Castor canadensis)	6.2	2	1
dogs, wolves & coyote (Canis)	11.1	3	2
Swift Fox (Vulpes velox)	3.2	7	1
Domestic Cat (Felis catus)			
Domestic Mule (Equus asinus x caballus)	80.1*	1*	1
artiodactyls (Artiodactyla)	3057.4	129	13
Domestic Pig (Sus scrofa)	45.3	3	1
deer and elk (Cervidae)	319.8	18	2
deer (Odocoileus)	307.8	15	2
Pronghorn (Antilocapra americana)	401.4	22	2
cattle or bison (Bos or Bison)	1038.2	16	5
Bison (Bison bison)	738.7	5	2
Domestic Goat (Capra hirca)	13.8	1	1
Domestic Sheep (Ovis aries)	44.9	3	1
unidentified mammal	5638.4	1450	0
unidentified vertebrate	98.4	317	0
TOTALS	8923.2	1947	31

142

STATISTICS ON BENT'S OLD FORT ARCHAEOFAUNA RECOVERED BY DOUGLAS C. COMER (weight is in grams; items include fragments, whole bones, and co-adherent groups of bones; MNI are the minimum number of individuals represented by the recovered items; and an asterisk indicates inclusion of items of probable identity).

Table 2. Statistics for the west dump, random samples, strata B through D.

common name (scientific taxon)	weight	items	MNI
mollusks (Mollusca)			
succineid land snails (Succinea)			
freshwater mussels (Unionidae)			
unidentified mollusk			
bony fishes (Osteichthyes)	42.3	120	3
Goldeye (Hiodon alosoides)	<0.1	1	1
freshwater catfishes (Ictaluridae)	38.7	98	2
Channel Catfish (Ictalurus punctatus) . . .	37.7*	89*	2
unidentified fish	3.5	21	0
toads (Bufo)			
Woodhouse's Toad (Bufo woodhousei)			
turtles (Testudinata)	22.8	18	4
box turtles (Terrapene)	20.0	16	1
Western Box Turtle (Terrapene ornata) .	16.7	12	1
softshell turtles (Trionyx)	2.8	?	1

143

Table 2, continued.

common name (scientific taxon)	weight	items	MNI
birds (Aves)	28.0	29	10
waterfowl (Anseriformes)	7.5	4	2
Canada Goose (Branta canadensis) . .	6.7	2	1
Green-winged Teal (Anas crecca) . . .	0.4*	1*	1
Turkey Vulture (Cathartes aura) . . .	2.6	2	1
buteo hawks (Buteo)			
Bald Eagle (Haliaeetus leucocephalus)			
Domestic Chicken (Gallus gallus)			
grouses (Tetraonidae)	1.6	4	3
Blue Grouse (Dendragapus obscurus) .	0.9	2	1
sage grouse (Centrocercus)	0.3*	1*	1
sharp-tailed grouse (Pedioecetes) . .	0.4*	1*	1
Wild Turkey (Meleagris gallopavo) . .	8.2*	6*	1
Great Blue Heron (Ardea herodias) . .	2.0	2	1
Sandhill Crane (Grus canadensis) . . .	4.0	2	1
Black-billed Magpie (Pica pica) . . .	1.6	8	1
Common Raven (Corvus corax)			
unidentified bird	0.5	1	0
mammals (Mammalia)	3872.5	963	7
jackrabbits (Lepus)			
cottontail rabbits (Sylvilagus) . . .	0.3	1	1

144

Table 2, continued.

common name (scientific taxon)	weight	items	MNI
mammals, continued			
Yellow-faced Pocket Gopher (Pappogeomys castanops)			
Beaver (Castor canadensis) . .	1.0	1	1
dogs, wolves & coyote (Canis)			
Swift Fox (Vulpes velox)			
Domestic Cat (Felis catus)			
Domestic Mule (Equus asinus x caballus)			
artiodactyls (Artiodactyla)	1842.2	62	3
Domestic Pig (Sus scrofa)			
deer and elk (Cervidae)	64.7	3	1
deer (Odocoileus)	64.7	3	1
Pronghorn (Antilocapra americana)	60.9	8	1
cattle or bison (Bos or Bison)	956.3	10	1
Bison (Bison bison)	495.4	4	1
Domestic Goat (Capra hirca)			
Domestic Sheep (Ovis aries)			
unidentified mammal	2029.0	899	∠
unidentified vertebrate	68.2	234	0
TOTALS	4033.8	1364	22

145

STATISTICS ON BENT'S OLD FORT ARCHAEOFAUNA RECOVERED BY DOUGLAS C. COMER (weight is in grams; items include fragments, whole bones, and co-adherent groups of bones; MNI are the minimum number of individuals represented by the recovered items; and an asterisk indicates inclusion of items of probable identity).

Table 3. Statistics for the west dump, random samples, stratum A.

common name (scientific taxon)	weight	items	MNI
mollusks (Mollusca)			
succineid land snails (Succinea)			
freshwater mussels (Unionidae)			
unidentified mollusk			
bony fishes (Osteichthyes)	1.0	6	1
Goldeye (Hiodon alosoides)			
freshwater catfishes (Ictaluridae)	0.7	4	1
Channel Catfish (Ictalurus punctatus)	0.7*	4*	1
unidentified fish	0.3	2	0
toads (Bufo)			
Woodhouse's Toad (Bufo woodhousei)			
turtles (Testudinata)	1.0		1
box turtles (Terrapene)			
Western Box Turtle (Terrapene ornata)			
softshell turtles (Trionyx) . . .	1.0		1

Table 3, continued.

Common name (scientific taxon)	weight	items	MNI
birds (Aves)	2.0	2	2
waterfowl (Anseriformes)	1.5	1	1
Canada Goose (Branta canadensis)	1.5	1	1
Green-winged Teal (Anas crecca)			
Turkey Vulture (Cathartes aura)			
buteo hawks (Buteo)			
Bald Eagle (Haliaeetus leucocephalus)			
Domestic Chicken (Gallus gallus)			
grouses (Tetraonidae)	0.5*	1*	1
Blue Grouse (Dendragapus obscurus)			
sage grouse (Centrocercus)			
sharp-tailed grouse (Pedioecetes)			
Wild Turkey (Meleagris gallopavo)			
Great Blue Heron (Ardea herodias)			
Sandhill Crane (Grus canadensis)			
Black-billed Magpie (Pica pica)			
Common Raven (Corvus corax)			
unidentified bird			
mammals (Mammalia)	1381.5	510	6
jackrabbits (Lepus)			
cottontail rabbits (Sylvilagus)			

Table 3, continued.

common name (scientific taxon)	weight	items	MNI
mammals, continued			
Yellow-faced Pocket Gopher (Pappogeomys castanops)			
Beaver (Castor canadensis)			
dogs, wolves & coyote (Canis)	3.7	1	1
Swift Fox (Vulpes velox)			
Domestic Cat (Felis catus)	7.0	2	1
Domestic Mule (Equus asinus x caballus)			
artiodactyls (Artiodactyla)	455.4	30	4
Domestic Pig (Sus scrofa)			
deer and elk (Cervidae)	15.8	2	1
deer (Odocoileus)	4.4	1	1
Pronghorn (Antilocapra americana)	27.5	5	2
cattle or bison (Bos or Bison)	326.7	9	1
Bison (Bison bison)	202.3	3	1
Domestic Goat (Capra hirca)			
Domestic Sheep (Ovis aries)			
unidentified mammal	915.4	477	0
unidentified vertebrate	63.5	228	0
TOTALS	1449.0	748	10

STATISTICS ON BENT'S OLD FORT ARCHAEOFAUNA RECOVERED BY DOUGLAS C. COMER (weight is in grams; items include fragments, whole bones, and co-adherent groups of bones; MNI are the minimum number of individuals represented by the recovered items; and an asterisk indicates inclusion of items of probable identity).

Table 4. Statistics for the west dump, random plus nonrandom samples, strata B-D.

common name (scientific taxon)	weight	items	MNI
mollusks (Mollusca)	0.1	2	2
succineid land snails (Succinea) . . .	<0.1	1	1
freshwater mussels (Unionidae)			
unidentified mollusk	<0.1	1	1
bony fishes (Osteichthyes)	44.4	137	3
Goldeye (Hiodon alosoides)	0.4	5	1
freshwater catfishes (Ictaluridae) . .	40.1	107	2
Channel Catfish (Ictalurus punctatus) . . .	39.0*	96*	2
unidentified fish	3.9	25	0
toads (Bufo)			
Woodhouse's Toad (Bufo woodhousei)			
turtles (Testudinata)	24.5	20	?
box turtles (Terrapene)	21.7	18	1
Western Box Turtle (Terrapene ornata) .	18.4	14	1
softshell turtles (Trionyx)	2.8	?	1

Table 4, continued.

common name (scientific taxon)	weight	items	MNI
birds (Aves)	28.5	31	11
waterfowl (Anseriformes)	7.5	4	2
Canada Goose (Branta canadensis)	6.7	2	1
Green-winged Teal (Anas crecca)	0.4*	1*	1
Turkey Vulture (Cathartes aura)	2.6	2	1
buteo hawks (Buteo)			
Bald Eagle (Haliaeetus leucocephalus)			
Domestic Chicken (Gallus gallus)			
grouses (Tetraonidae)	1.6	4	3
Blue Grouse (Dendragapus obscurus) . . .	0.9	2	1
sage grouse (Centrocercus)	0.3*	1*	1
sharp-tailed grouse (Pedioecetes)	0.4*	1*	1
Wild Turkey (Meleagris gallopavo)	8.2*	6*	1
Great Blue Heron (Ardea herodias)	2.0	2	1
Sandhill Crane (Grus canadensis)	4.0	2	1
Black-billed Magpie (Pica pica)	1.6	8	1
Common Raven (Corvus corax)	0.2	1	1
unidentified bird	0.8	2	0
mammals (Mammalia)	4733.6	1231	9
jackrabbits (Lepus)			
cottontail rabbits (Sylvilagus)	0.3	1	1

Table 4, continued.

common name (scientific taxon)	weight	items	MNI
mammals, continued			
Yellow-faced Pocket Gopher (Pappogeomys castanops)	0.5	1	1
Beaver (Castor canadensis) . .	1.0	1	1
dogs, wolves & coyote (Canis)			
Swift Fox (Vulpes velox)			
Domestic Cat (Felis catus)			
Domestic Mule (Equus asinus x caballus)			
artiodactyls (Artiodactyla)	2157.3	93	4
Domestic Pig (Sus scrofa)			
deer and elk (Cervidae)	86.5	15	1
deer (Odocoileus)	64.7	3	1
Pronghorn (Antilocapra americana)	90.7	13	2
cattle or bison (Bos or Bison)	1151.3	15	1
Bison (Bison bison)	592.1	6	1
Domestic Goat (Capra hirca)			
Domestic Sheep (Ovis aries)			
unidentified mammal	2574.5	1135	2
unidentified vertebrate	95.6	314	0
TOTALS	4926.7	1735	27

STATISTICS ON BENT'S OLD FORT ARCHAEOFAUNA RECOVERED BY DOUGLAS C. COMER (weight is in grams; items include fragments, whole bones, and co-adherent groups of bones; MNI are the minimum number of individuals represented by the recovered items; and an asterisk indicates inclusion of items of probable identity).

Table 5. Statistics for the west dump, random plus nonrandom samples, stratum A.

common name (scientific taxon)	weight	items	MNI
mollusks (Mollusca)	0.6	1	1
succineid land snails (Succinea)			
freshwater mussels (Unionidae)	0.6	1	1
unidentified mollusk			
bony fishes (Osteichthyes)	1.4	9	2
Goldeye (Hiodon alosoides)	0.2	1	1
freshwater catfishes (Ictaluridae)	0.8	5	1
Channel Catfish (Ictalurus punctatus) . . .	0.7*	4*	1
unidentified fish	0.4	3	0
toads (Bufo)			
Woodhouse's Toad (Bufo woodhousei)			
turtles (Testudinata)	1.0	2	1
box turtles (Terrapene)			
Western Box Turtle (Terrapene ornata)			
softshell turtles (Trionyx) . . . . ‥	1.0		1

Table 5, continued.

common name (scientific taxon)	weight	items	MNI
birds (Aves)	7.7	7	3
waterfowl (Anseriformes)	1.5	1	1
Canada Goose (Branta canadensis) .	1.5	1	1
Green-winged Teal (Anas crecca)			
Turkey Vulture (Cathartes aura)			
buteo hawks (Buteo)			
Bald Eagle (Haliaeetus leucocephalus) .	4.9	3	1
Domestic Chicken (Gallus gallus)			
grouses (Tetraonidae)	1.2*	2*	1
Blue Grouse (Dendragapus obscurus)			
sage grouse (Centrocercus)			
sharp-tailed grouse (Pedioecetes)			
Wild Turkey (Meleagris gallopavo)			
Great Blue Heron (Ardea herodias)			
Sandhill Crane (Grus canadensis)			
Black-billed Magpie (Pica pica)			
Common Raven (Corvus corax)			
unidentified bird			
mammals (Mammalia)	1749.4	784	6
jackrabbits (Lepus)			
cottontail rabbits (Sylvilagus)			

Table 5, continued.

common name (scientific taxon)	weight	items	MNI
mammals, continued			
Yellow-faced Pocket Gopher (Pappogeomys castanops)			
Beaver (Castor canadensis)			
dogs, wolves & coyote (Canis)	3.7	1	1
Swift Fox (Vulpes velox)			
Domestic Cat (Felis catus)	7.0	2	1
Domestic Mule (Equus asinus x caballus)			
artiodactyls (Artiodactyla)	494.7	33	4
Domestic Pig (Sus scrofa)			
deer and elk (Cervidae)	15.8	2	1
deer (Odocoileus)	4.4	1	1
Pronghorn (Antilocapra americana)	27.5	5	2
cattle or bison (Bos or Bison)	326.7	9	1
Bison (Bison bison)	202.3	3	1
Domestic Goat (Capra hirca)			
Domestic Sheep (Ovis aries)			
unidentified mammal	1244.0	748	0
unidentified vertebrate	100.6	326	0
TOTALS	1860.7	1129	13

STATISTICS ON BENT'S OLD FORT ARCHAEOFAUNA RECOVERED BY DOUGLAS C. COMER (weight is in grams; items include fragments, whole bones, and co-adherent groups of bones MNI are the minimum number of individuals represented by the recovered items; and an asterisk,indicates inclusion of items of probable identity).

Table 6. Statistics for disturbed deposit and deposit outside of west dump.

common name (scientific taxon)	weight	items	MNI
mollusks (Mollusca)			
succineid land snails (Succinea)			
freshwater mussels (Unionidae)			
unidentified mollusk			
bony fishes (Osteichthyes)	0.7	1	1
Goldeye (Hiodon alosoides)			
freshwater catfishes (Ictaluridae)			
Channel Catfish (Ictalurus punctatus) .	0.7	1	1
unidentified fish			
toads (Bufo)	0.3	2	1
Woodhouse's Toad (Bufo woodhousei) .	0.2	1	1
turtles (Testudinata)			
box turtles (Terrapene)			
Western Box Turtle (Terrapene ornata)			
softshell turtles (Trionyx)			

Table 6, continued.

common name (scientific taxon)	weight	items	MNI
birds (Aves)	0.2	1	1
waterfowl (Anseriformes)			
Canada Goose (Branta canadensis)			
Green-winged Teal (Anas crecca)			
Turkey Vulture (Cathartes aura)			
buteo hawks (Buteo)	0.2	1	1
Bald Eagle (Haliaeetus leucocephalus)			
Domestic Chicken (Gallus gallus)			
grouses (Tetraonidae)			
Blue Grouse (Dendragapus obscurus)			
sage grouse (Centrocercus)			
sharp-tailed grouse (Pedioecetes)			
Wild Turkey (Meleagris gallopavo)			
Great Blue Heron (Ardea herodias)			
Sandhill Crane (Grus canadensis)			
Black-billed Magpie (Pica pica)			
Common Raven (Corvus corax)			
unidentified bird			
mammals (Mammalia)	40.0	22	1
jackrabbits (Lepus)			
cottontail rabbits (Sylvilagus)			

Table 6, continued.

common name (scientific taxon)	weight	items	MNI
mammals, continued			
Yellow-faced Pocket Gopher (Pappogeomys castanops)			
Beaver (Castor canadensis)			
dogs, wolves & coyote (Canis)			
Swift Fox (Vulpes velox)			
Domestic Cat (Felis catus)			
Domestic Mule (Equus asinus x caballus)			
artiodactyls (Artiodactyla)			
Domestic Pig (Sus scrofa)			
deer and elk (Cervidae)			
deer (Odocoileus)			
Pronghorn (Antilocapra americana)			
cattle or bison (Bos or Bison)			
Bison (Bison bison)			
Domestic Goat (Capra hirca)			
Domestic Sheep (Ovis aries)			
unidentified mammal	40.0	22	1
unidentified vertebrate	4.6	12	0
TOTALS	45.8	38	4

157

COMPARATIVE STATISTICS ON BENT'S OLD FORT ARCHAEOFAUNA RECOVERED BY DOUGLAS C. COMER

Table 7. Total weights and items (weight in grams / number of items) comparing the main dump (MD) with the B through D strata (WD-BD) and the A stratum (WD-A) of the west dump, random plus nonrandom samples.

animal species or group	MD	WD-BD	WD-A
Goldeye (fish)		0.4 / 5	0.2 / 1
catfish	3.4 / 10	40.1 / 107	0.8 / 5
box turtle	1.8 / 2	21.7 / 18	
softshell turtle	2.9 / 4	2.8 / 2	1.0 / 2
Canada Goose	2.0 / 2	6.7 / 2	1.5 / 1
grouses	1.1 / 2	1.6 / 4	1.2 / 2
Wild Turkey	4.6 / 3	8.2 / 6	
other wild birds	2.3 / 2	10.8 / 16	4.9 / 3
Domestic Chicken	4.9 / 4		
Beaver	6.2 / 2	1.0 / 1	
Swift Fox	3.2 / 7		
deer	307.8 / 15	64.7 / 3	4.4 / 1
Pronghorn	401.4 / 22	90.7 / 13	27.5 / 5
Bison	738.7 / 5	592.1 / 6	202.3 / 3
other wild mammals	2.8 / 3	0.8 / 2	
domestic mammals	184.1 / 8		7.0 / 2
TOTALS	1667.2 / 91	841.6 / 185	250.8 / 25

COMPARATIVE STATISTICS ON BENT'S OLD FORT ARCHAEOFAUNA RECOVERED BY DOUGLAS C. COMER

Table 8. Percent weights and items (percent of total weight per Table 7 / percent of total items per Table 7) comparing the main dump (MD) with the B through D strata (WD-BD) and the A stratum (WD-A) of the west dump, random plus nonrandom samples.

animal species or group	MD	WD-BD	WD-A
Goldeye (fish)	-------	<0.1 / 2.7	1.0 / 4.0
catfish	0.2 / 11.0	4.8 / 57.8	0.3 / 20.0
box turtle	0.1 / 2.2	2.6 / 9.7	-------
softshell turtle	0.2 / 4.4	0.3 / 1.1	0.4 / 8.0
Canada Goose	0.1 / 2.2	0.8 / 1.1	0.6 / 4.0
grouses	0.1 / 2.2	0.2 / 2.2	0.5 / 8.0
Wild Turkey	0.3 / 3.3	1.0 / 3.2	-------
other wild birds	0.1 / 2.2	1.3 / 8.6	2.0 / 12.0
Domestic Chicken	0.3 / 4.4	-------	-------
Beaver	0.4 / 2.2	0.1 / 0.5	-------
Swift Fox	0.2 / 7.7	-------	-------
deer	18.5 / 16.5	7.7 / 1.6	1.8 / 4.0
Pronghorn	24.1 / 24.2	10.8 / 7.0	11.0 / 20.0
Bison	44.3 / 5.5	70.3 / 3.2	80.7 / 12.0
other wild mammals	0.2 / 3.3	0.1 / 1.1	-------
domestic mammals	11.0 / 8.8	-------	2.8 / 8.0
TOTALS	100.1 / 100.1	100.0 / 99.8	100.2 / 100.0

POLLEN ANALYSIS OF SAMPLES FROM
TWO TRASH DUMPS AT BENT'S OLD FORT

Gerald K. Kelso, Ph.D.
Laboratory of Paleoenvironmental Studies
University of Arizona, Tucson, Arizona 85721

OBJECTIVES

A trash dump is not the most favorable environment for the preservation of pollen. Dump deposits are loose and by their nature subject pollen
to repeated wetting and drying which rapidly oxidizes it. Decaying organic
materials in trash deposits accelerate oxidation, and pollen-destroying
fungi are often present. As a consequence, soil samples from trash deposits
often contain little pollen and frequently a high proportion of the pollen
grains recovered are so eroded as to be unidentifiable.

The present analysis of ten trash dump samples from Bent's Old Fort,
a major fur-trade era post on the Arkansas River in southeastern Colorado,
is largely exploratory. Samples were taken from various locations and
depths (Table 1) in the main and west dumps at the fort for the purpose
of determining the state of pollen preservation within the dumps and to
ascertain, provided sufficient well-preserved pollen remained, whether there
was variability in the pollen content of the deposits. A stratigraphic
column was not taken.

METHODS

Analysis of the samples was undertaken at the Laboratory of Paleo-
enviornmental Studies, University of Arizona. Mehringer's (1967) mechanical/
chemical method was used to extract the pollen and pollen residues were
mounted in glycerol for analysis. Two hundred identifiable pollen grains
per sample were tabulated (Table 2) with a compound transmitted-light
microscope at a magnification of 400 X. Problematical pollen grains were
examined under oil emersion at 1000 X. Identification of pollen types is
based on the pollen reference collection of the Laboratory. Terminology
follows Mehringer (1967) except that the Compositae have been divided
into "Ambrosia-type" and "other Compositae" categories rather than his
"low-spine" and "high-spine" groupings.

Absolute pollen frequencies per gram of sample were computed to
determine if the samples contained quantities of pollen comparable to those
of undegraded soil samples, which could therefore be confidently inter-

preted. The data are, however, presented in terms of relative pollen frequencies (Diag. 1). Absolute pollen frequencies are of limited utility in the absence of information on the rate at which the deposits accumulated, as was the case at Bent's Old Fort.

RESULTS

The pollen recovered from the Bent's Old Fort dump samples was well preserved and may be considered generally representative of the pollen originally deposited. The amount of pollen too badly degraded to be identified averaged only 3.85%, and did not exceed 7.5% in any one sample. All samples contained over 2000 pollen grains per gram (Table 3).

Arboreal Pollen Types

Pinus. Sample No. 6 excepted, pine pollen is not a prominent element in the Bent's Old Fort counts. None of the pine pollen grains which were sufficiently well preserved to warrant close examination displayed the gemmae ("belly-warts") in the proximity of the germinal colpus which distinguish the Haploxlon pine sub-genus. This sub-genus includes the piñon pines. Pine pollen may be wind transported hundreds of miles (Potter and Rowley, 1969: 5). The pine pollen in the Bent's Old Fort dump deposits is apparently derived from Diploxlon Pinus species which grow at higher altitudes and include P. ponderosa and P. contorta.

The high pine pollen percentage of sample No. 6 could be the product of a short-term variation in the environmental parameters (temperature, humidity, precipitation) which control pollen emission. The wind direction or season during which a particular lot of trash was deposited are equally likely causes.

Juniperus and Quercus. Juniper and oak pollen are low, but persistent elements in the BEnt's Old Fort pollen spectra. These pollen types may be transported by wind considerable distances, although apparently not so far as pine pollen (Potter and Rowley, 1969: 5). Oak, at least, is a prolific pollen producer (Wodehouse, 1971: 87), and although the counts suggest populations of these trees (or shrubs) in the region, they cannot have been abundant in the vicinity of the fort.

Minor Arboreal Pollen Types. Occasional grains of Betula (birch), Celtis (hackberry) and Salix (willow) pollen appear in the BEnt's Old Fort pollen counts. The first two of these are wind-pollinated genera, while the

162

third disperses its pollen largely through insects, but at least partially by wind (Wodehouse, 1971: 720). The pollen of all three may be blown considerable distances (Potter and Rowley, 1960: 5).

Colorado birches are generally found at elevations higher than that of Bent's Old Fort (Harrington, 1964: 179). The single grain of this pollen type found in sample No. 6 was most likely blown in from the mountains to the west of the fort. Both hackberry and willow are found at lower elevations and could have been elements in the bottomland vegetation along the Arkansas River not far from the fort.

Wind-Pollinated Herbs

Cheno-ams. The pollen contributed by the family Chenopodiaceae and the genus Amaranthus, which cannot be reliably differentiated, comprises the single most important pollen type in the Bent's Old Fort samples. These plants favor disturbed soils and are prominent weeds around cattle tanks and in agricultural fields.

Some cheno-am-type pollen may be carried several hundred yards from the parent plants, but large quantities of it are found only at the point of origin (Raynor, Ogden and Hayes, 1973: Fig. 4). Most of the cheno-am pollen in the Bent's Old Fort samples is undoubtedly derived from plants fostered on or very near the dumps themselves by human disturbance of the soil and natural vegetation.

The low cheno-am pollen percentages of four of the five main dump samples suggest that there was a smaller population of such plants in that area and, consequently, that there was less soil disturbance than in the west dump. Although not definitive in the absence of temporal data, the absolute pollen frequencies (Table 2) indicate that the quantities of cheno-am pollen per gram in the main dump samples are comparable to or higher than those of the west dump. The depressed cheno-am percentages in the main dump pollen spectra are very likely functions of statistical constraint brought about by increases in the contributions of grass and pine pollen to the fixed numerical sum.

Ambrosia-type. This pollen type includes the wind-pollinated members of the Compositae. It is consistantly prominent in the Bent's Old Fort pollen spectra, and second only to the cheno-ams in importance. The plants producing Ambrosia-type pollen, especially the ragweeds themselves, favor disturbed soils and the presence of large proportions of such pollen in a soil sample is a good indicator of human interference with the natural vegetation.

Although Ambrosia-type pollen may be wind-carried great distances (Raynor, Ogden and Hayes, 1973: Fig. 9), the majority of the pollen is deposited within a few meters of the source plants (Raynor, Ogden and Hayes, 1973: Fig. 6). Most of this pollen was probably produced on or very near the dumps.

Artemisia. At least one species of sagebrush (Artemisia filifolia) is currently growing at scattered locations in eastern Colorado (Harrington, 1964: 582), and the presence of some sagebrush pollen in every Bent's Old Fort sample except No. 10 suggests that there was apopulation in the vicinity of the fort during its occupation. The Artemisia relative pollen percentages, and their equivalent absolute frequencies are higher in the samples from the main dump than in those from the west dump, suggesting that this population may have been closer to, or perhaps more directly upwind of, the main dump.

Gramineae. Grasses, although dominant in the pre-agricultural vegetation of the Bent's Old Fort area, contributed little pollen to the majority of the dump samples. In both the relative and absolute pollen counts of three samples (Nos. 8, 9 and 10) from the main dump, grass pollen was, however, a significant element. It seems likely that there was more grass on or near some portions of the main dump than in the vicinity of the west dump. Whether this is due to the survival of a larger portion of the native vegetation or simply to conditions at the main dump more propituous to grass than to plants producing cheno-am and Ambrosia-type pollen could not be determined. Grass, like the latter two plant groups, is encouraged by soil disturbance.

Cyperaceae. Sedges are the only plants preferring a mesic environment which regularly contributed pollen to the Bent's Old Fort samples. The low, but consistent representation of this pollen type suggests that this pollen is derived from a stable population of plants near the dumps. Colorado sedges are found in meadow situations throughout the mixed prairie zone (Harrington, 1964: v), but this pollen is most likely derived from the Arkansas River bottomlands.

Minor Wind-Pollinated Herbs. A few pollen grains from two wind-pollinated herbs, Sarcobatus (greasewood) and Ephedra (Mormon tea), appeared in the

Bent's Old Fort counts. The closest reported populations of greasewood (Sarcobatus vermiculatus) are located about 50 miles to the southwest of the fort in Las Animas County (Harrington, 1964: 204). If these plants were present in the vicinity of the fort while the dump materials were accumulating, they must have been few in number.

Both of the Mormon tea pollen grains found in the Bent's Old Fort samples belong to Martin's (1963: 51) Ephedra torreyana-type. They were undoubtedly derived from E. torreyana itself, as the other species of Ephedra reported from Colorado produce E. nevadensis-type pollen grains (Harrington, 1964: 29). Ephedra pollen has been recovered hundreds of miles from the nearest plants (Maher, 1964: 392) and the presence of two pollen grains of this type in the fort samples does not indicate that the plants were growing in the ·vicinity.

Insect-Pollinated Plants

Insect-pollinated plants produce smaller quantities of pollen in comparison to the wind-pollinated species (Faegri and Iversen, 1974: 51). Furthermore, the sticky oils and resins through which the pollen is attached to the transporting insects also prevent the pollen from being accidentally detached from the flower (Faegri and Van der Pijl, 1971: 63). Consequently, the pollen of such plants is rare in natural deposits (Martin and Sharrock, 1964: 177), and its absence from a soil sample does not necessarily indicate that the plants were not present. Even a few grains of insect-dispersed pollen are, however, a good indicator that such plants were growing not too far from the sampling site.

"Other Compositae". The presence of this insect-transported pollen type in all but one of the Bent's Old Fort samples suggests that plants producing this pollen type were growing continuously on or very near.the dumps. Many plants whose pollen falls into this group, sunflowers for instance, are common weeds on the disturbed soils of roadsides and agricultural fields. Human activity at the dumps very likely encouraged the population which produced the pollen found in the samples.

Minor Insect-Transported Pollen Types. Minor quantities of 11 additional insect-transported pollen types were found scattered among the Bent's Old Fort samples. The plants which produced these pollen types [Iidestromia, Cichorieae (chickory tribe of Compositae), Euphorbia (spurge), Plantago (plantain), Onagraceae (evening primrose family), Malvaceae (mallow family),

165

Malvaceae cf. Sphaeralcea (mallow pollen resembling that of globe mallow),
Rosaceae (rose family), Cruciferae (mustard family), Arceuthobium (mistletoe), and Solanaceae (nightshade family)] were undoubtedly growing in the
immediate vicinity during the occupation of the fort.

SUMMARY

   Trash dumps are ideal habitats for plants which flourish in disturbed
soils. As a consequence, the Bent's Old Fort dump pollen spectra are
dominated by cheno-ams and Ambrosia-type pollen, probably from weedy species
growing right on the dumps. Grass and some insect-pollinated members of
the Compositae, very likely sunflowers, were significant components of the
local vegetation. Spurges, plantains, mallows, mistletoe, Tidestromia,
evening primroses, some relative of chicory, and members of the rose,
mustard and nightshade families were growing nearby. Populations of
sedges and sagebrush apparently existed at not too great a distance from
the fort. The pollen of six genera of trees (pine, juniper, oak, birch,
hackberry and willow) was present in the dump samples. All six arboreal
pollen types are subject to long-distance wind transport and whether these
trees were actually growing in the vicinity of the fort cannot be established
from the pollen evidence.

Literature Cited

Faegri, K. and J. Iversen, 1975. Textbook of pollen analysis. Hafner Press, New York.

Faegri, K. and L. Van der Pijl, 1971. Principles of pollen ecology. Pergamon Press, New York.

Harrington, H.D., 1964. Manual of the plants of Colorado. Sage Books, Denver.

Maher, L.J., Jr., 1964. Ephedra pollen in sediments of the Great Lakes region. Ecology 45(2): 391-395.

Martin, P.S., 1963. The last 10,000 years. University of Arizona Press, Tucson.

_____ and F.W. Sharrock, 1964. Pollen analysis of prehistoric human feces: a new approach to ethnobotany. Amer. Antiquity 30(2): 168-180.

Mehringer, P.J., Jr., 1967. Pollen analysis of the Tule Springs area, Nevada. In Pleistocene sutdies in southern Nevada, H.M. Wormington and D. Ellis (eds.), Nevada State Museum. Anthro. Pap. 13 (part 3): 120-200.

Potter, L.D. and J. Rowley, 1960. Pollen rain and vegetation, San Augustin Plains, New Mexico. Bot. Gaz. 122(1): 1-25.

Raynor, G.S., E.C. Ogden and J.V. Hayes, 1973. Dispersal of pollens from low-level, crosswind line sources. Agr. Meteorol. 9: 177-195.

Wodehouse, R.P., 1971. Hay fever plants. Hafner Pub. Co., New York.

Table 1. Pollen Sample Provenience: Bent's Old Fort

Sample No.	Provenience
1	West dump, N11-E48, Strat. F, depth 1.50-1.75 m
2	West dump, N9-E9, Strat. D, depth 0.75-1.0 m
3	West dump, N16-E6, Strat. F, depth 1.75-2.0 m
4	West dump, N18-E45, Strat. F, depth 1.75-2.0 m
5	West dump, N18-E42, Strat G, depth 1.25-1.50 m
6	Main dump, N93-E147, Strat. E, depth 1.5 m
7	Main dump, N81-E153, Strat. F, depth 1.5 m
8	Main dump, N75-E159, Strat E, depth 1.9 m
9	Main dump, N84-E150, Strat. D, depth 1.5 m
10	Main dump, N75-E150, Strat. D, depth 1.5 m

Table 2. Bent's Old Fort Dump Samples: Raw Sums

Sample No.	Pinus	Juniperus	Quercus	Betula	Celtis	Salix	Cheno-ams	Sarcobatus	Tidestromia	Artemisia	Ambrosia-type	Chichorieae	"Other Compositae"	Gramineae	Ephedra torreyana-type	Euphorbia	Plantago	Onagraceae	Malvaceae	Malvaceae cf. Sphaeralcea	Rosaceae	Cruciferae	Areuthobium	Solanaceae	Cyperaceae	Undetermined	Raw Sum	Undeterminable*
1	16	4	3	-	1	-	86	-	-	7	67	1	4	4	1	-	-	-	-	-	-	-	-	-	3	3	200	11
2	8	7	3	-	-	-	110	-	-	4	43	-	6	10	-	-	-	-	-	-	-	-	2	1	1	5	200	7
3	2	1	1	-	-	-	121	-	-	2	54	-	6	10	-	-	-	-	-	-	-	-	-	-	2	1	200	3
4	10	2	2	-	-	-	117	-	-	1	42	-	3	15	-	-	-	-	-	-	-	-	-	-	3	3	200	9
5	17	5	-	-	-	1	127	-	-	2	34	-	4	5	-	-	-	-	-	-	-	-	-	-	-	4	200	6
6	49	3	7	1	-	2	71	-	-	8	37	-	1	7	-	-	-	-	-	-	-	-	-	-	1	7	200	14
7	3	2	2	-	-	-	111	-	-	18	45	-	7	5	-	-	-	-	-	-	-	-	-	-	-	7	200	3
8	9	3	1	-	-	-	64	-	-	33	42	1	-	28	-	-	-	-	-	-	-	-	-	-	8	9	200	15
9	14	-	1	-	-	-	43	-	2	19	32	-	11	69	-	-	-	-	-	-	-	-	-	-	-	4	200	5
10	9	1	-	-	-	-	10	-	-	-	5	1	5	165	-	-	-	-	-	-	-	-	-	-	3	-	200	4

*Not included in raw sum

Table 3. Bent's Old Fort Dump Samples: Absolute Pollen Frequencies

Sample No.	Pinus	Juniperus	Quercus	Betula	Celtis	Salix	Cheno-ams	Sarcobatus	Tidestromia	Artemisia	Ambrosia-type	Chichorieae	"Other Compositae"	Gramineae	Ephedra torreyana-type	Euphorbia	Plantago	Onagraceae	Malvaceae	Malvaceae cf. Sphaeralcea	Rosaceae	Cruciferae	Areuthobium	Solanaceae	Cyperaceae	Undetermined	Absolute Sum per gram
1	185	46	35	-	12	-	997	-	-	81	777	12	46	46	12	-	-	-	-	-	-	-	45	-	35	35	2319
2	180	157	67	-	-	-	2472	-	-	90	966	-	135	225	-	-	-	-	-	-	-	-	-	23	23	112	4494
3	217	108	108	-	-	-	13120	-	-	217	5855	-	650	1084	-	-	-	-	-	-	-	-	-	-	217	108	21687
4	114	23	23	-	-	19	1336	-	-	11	480	11	34	171	-	-	-	-	-	-	-	11	-	-	34	34	2286
5	329	97	-	33	-	66	2455	66	-	39	657	-	77	97	-	-	-	-	39	-	-	33	-	-	33	77	3866
6	1606	98	229	-	-	-	2327	-	-	262	1213	-	33	229	33	-	-	33	-	33	-	-	-	-	-	229	6556
7	46	30	30	-	-	-	1686	-	-	273	683	-	106	76	-	-	905	-	-	-	-	-	-	-	-	106	3037
8	8141	2714	905	-	-	-	57891	-	-	29850	37991	903	266	25327	-	48	-	-	-	-	905	-	-	-	7237	8141	180909
9	339	-	24	-	-	-	1040	24	48	460	774	-	266	1669	-	-	-	-	24	-	-	-	-	-	398	97	4837
10	1194	133	-	-	-	-	1327	-	-	-	663	133	663	13640	-	-	-	133	-	-	-	-	-	-	-	-	26533

170

Diagram 1: Bentic Old Fort.

171

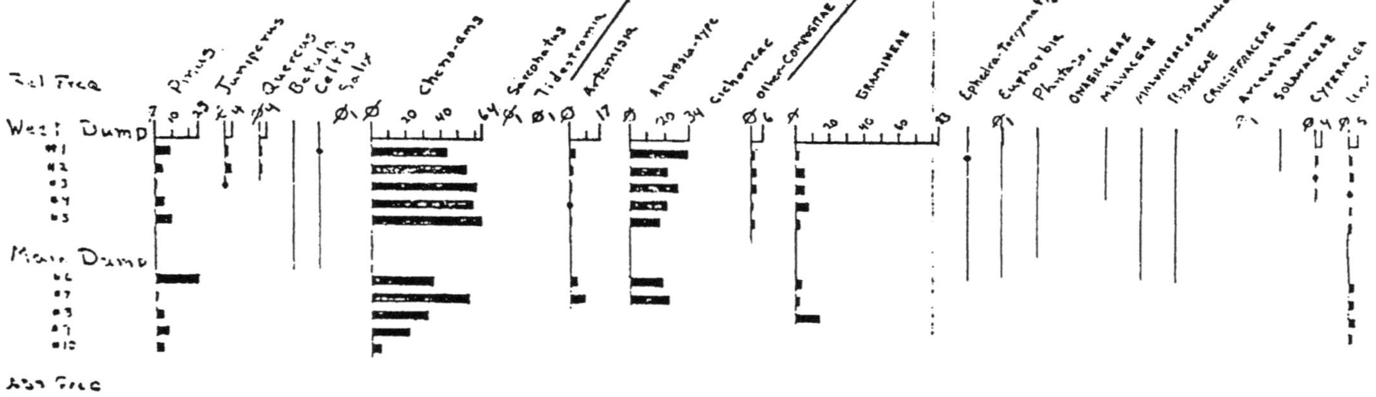

APPENDIX F

MEAN CERAMIC DATES, WEST AND MAIN DUMPS

The Mean Ceramic Dating Formula devised by Stanley South (1977:217) was applied to the ceramic collection from the Main and West Dumps. The dates realized from the calculations below (1831 for the West Dump, 1832 for the Main Dump) fit in fairly well with the dates obtained for the deposits by the archeological means, and with the dates one might expect based upon the historic record.

It was thought, from archeological evidence, that the West Dump represented a deposit from the building of the fort (sometime between 1828 and 1833). The presence of building materials and the absence of faunal remains of domesticated animal species recommended this. The Main Dump apparently dated somewhat later, as it contained some but much less construction debris but did have the faunal remains of domesticated animals. The Main Dump probably was not deposited quite as early as the Mean Ceramic date would indicate, however, because it also contained sherds of a ceramic pattern not produced until 1841. The possible reasons for this discrepancy are various: cermaics may have been incorrectly identfied, the mean dates of manufacture may not have been correctly determined, the sample may have been too small, the sampling area may have been too small (sherds are sometimes found in groups where a vessel has been tossed and broken-the finding of a single such shattered vessel can cause its type to be over-represented), or unidentified depositional or cultural factors, which have selected for the presence in quantity of a certain type of ceramic.

Main Dump
Mean Ceramic Date

Type	Median Date (x_i)	Count (f_i)	Product
Pearlware, undecorated	1805	49	88445
Earthenware, undecorated	1860	153	284580
Annular	1805	42	75810
Copper Lustre	1815	14	25410
Edged, embossed	1810	9	16290
Edged, lateral stripe	1805	1	1805
Spatterware	1837.5	32	558800
Transfer-printed	1818	48	87264
Floral spray	1822.5	99	180427.5
		447	818831.5

$$Y = \frac{\sum\limits_{i=1}^{n} x_i \cdot f_i}{\sum\limits_{i=1}^{n} f_i} = 1831.83 = 1832$$

174

Type	Median Date (xi)	Count (fi)	Product
Pearlware, undecorated	1805	11	19,855
Earthenware, undecorated	1860	20	37,200
Annular	1805	7	12,635
Copper Lustre	1815	3	5,445
Edged, embossed	1810	0	0
Edged, lateral stripe	1805	1	0
Spatterware	1837.5	7	12,862.5
Transfer-printed	1818	4	7,272
Floral spray	1822.5	7	12,757.5
		59	108,027

$$Y = \frac{\sum\limits_{i=1}^{n} xi \cdot fi}{\sum\limits_{i=1}^{n} fi} = 1830.96 = 1831$$

ANALYSIS AND DESCRIPTION OF THE ARTIFACTS FROM THE 1976
EXCAVATION OF THE MAIN AND WEST TRASH DUMPS AT
BENT'S OLD FORT NATIONAL HISTORIC SITE:
A RESTUDY

by

Paul Y. Inashima

ACKNOWLEDGEMENTS

  research and preparation of this study was facilitated by the
istance of several individuals and institutions. The library staffs of
 Harpers Ferry Center, the Department of the Interior, the Rocky
.ntain Region, the Colorado Office of the Bureau of Land Management,
 Utah Office of the Bureau of Land Management, the Library of
·gress, and the Montgomery County Library System (Maryland)
·vided their services in obtaining copies of numerous texts,
published reports, and journal articles. The staffs of Bent's Old Fort
tional Historic Site and Fort Smith National Historic Site supplied access
 various unpublished archeological and historical reports. The
-ographics Division of the Denver Service Center assisted in the
ition of National Park Service maps and drawings. In particular, Bill
/altney, Ruth Larison, Kathy Korell, Earl Locker, and Pat Van Kleeve
ε to be thanked.

·;. Dennis Stanford and David Meltzer of the Smithsonian Institution
.imined the prehistoric materials and offered valuable insights. Byron
iibury studied and commented upon the pipe collection. Jackson Moore,
 and Dick Ping Hsu of the Washington Area Service Office critiques
· section on transportation artifacts. Valerie King typed the draft
 ies of the references and the table of contents. John Ravenhörst did
ʁ bulk of the reprographic duplication of the line drawings and artifact
istrations. All of these individuals are to be thanked for their help.

CONTENTS

ACKNOWLEDGEMENTS   179

GENERAL COMMENTS   193

THE HOUSEHOLD GOODS COMPONENT   194
Introduction   194
Bottles   194
    Description--Glass Bottles   194
    Distribution--Glass Bottles   200
    Comments--Glass Bottles   200
    Description--Stoneware Bottles   208
    Distribution--Stoneware Bottles   209
    Comments--Stoneware Bottles   209
Glassware   210
    Description   210
    Distribution   210
    Comments   212
Storage and Utility Vessels   212
    Description   212
    Distribution   217
    Comments   217
Tableware   217
    Description (Introduction)   217
    Description (Series One)   221
    Distribution (Series One)   223
    Comments (Series One)   223
    Description (Series Two)   228
    Distribution (Series Two)   228
    Comments (Series Two)   228
    Description (Series Three)   230
    Distribution (Series Three)   231
    Comments (Series Three)   232
    Description (Series Four)   232
    Distribution (Series Four)   234
    Comments (Series Four)   234
    Description (Series Five)   234
    Distribution (Series Five)   237
    Comments (Series Five)   237
    Description (Series Six)   238
    Distribution (Series Six)   243
    Comments (Series Six)   243
    Description (Series Seven)   249
    Distribution (Series Seven)   250
    Comments (Series Seven)   250
    Description (Series Eight)   255
    Distribution (Series Eight)   255
    Comments (Series Eight)   255
    Description (Series Nine)   255
    Distribution (Series Nine)   257
    Comments (Series Nine)   257

Description (Series Ten)   261
Distribution (Series Ten)   261
Comments (Series Ten)   262
Description (Series Eleven)   262
Distribution (Series Eleven)   263
Comments (Series Eleven)   263
Utensils   265
   Description   265
   Distribution   266
   Comments   266

THE PERSONAL ATTIRE COMPONENT   267
Introduction   267
Beads   267
   Description   267
   Distribution   273
   Comments   273
Buckles   287
   Description   287
   Distribution   287
Buttons   287
   Distribution   299
   Comments   305
Grommets   307
   Distribution   307
Hooks and Eyes   307
   Description   307
   Distribution   307
Shoes   307
   Description   307
   Distribution   307

THE LEISURE ACTIVITIES COMPONENT   310
Introduction   310
Smoking Pipes   310
   Description   310
   Distribution   315
   Comments   315
Musical Instruments   324
   Description   324

THE FIREARMS COMPONENT   325
Introduction   325
Gun Parts   325
   Description   325
   Distribution   328
   Comments   328
Gunflints   332
   Description   332
   Distribution   338
   Comments   338

Percussion Caps   342
   Description   342
   Distribution   344
   Comments   344
Lead Round Balls   346
   Description   346
   Distribution   346
   Comments   346
Metallic Cartridges   348
   Description and Comment   348
   Distribution   351
Miscellaneous Items   351
   Description   351
   Distribution   351

THE TRANSPORTATION COMPONENT   354
Introduction   354
Harness Buckles   354
   Description   354
Horseshoes   354
   Description   354
Horseshoe Nails   360
   Description   360
Wagon Wheel Skeins   362
   Description   362
   Comments   365
   Distribution   368

THE STRUCTURAL COMPONENT   371
Introduction   371
Adobe   371
   Description   371
   Distribution   372
   Comments   374
Hinges   376
   Description   376
   Distribution   376
   Comments   377
Hooks and Eyes   377
   Description   377
   Distribution   378
   Comments   378
Latches   378
   Description   378
   Distribution   378
   Comments   378
Nails   379
   Description   379
   Distribution   379
   Comments   385
Window Glass   385
   Description   385
   Distribution   386
   Comments   386

THE MISCELLANEOUS ARTIFACT COMPONENT   390
Introduction   390
Identifiable Items   390
    Description   390
        Abrader   390
        Adz   391
        Barbed Wire   392
        Bell   393
        Brass Nails   393
        Chain   393
        Chisel   394
        Clock   394
        Cloth   394
        Container   395
        Corn   395
        Handles   396
        Hinge   396
        Insulator   396
        Nut   397
        Pencils   397
        Rivets   397
        Seal   397
        Spike   397
        Stove Plate   398
        Washers   398
        Wire   398
    Distribution   399
Unidentified Non-Amorphous Artifacts   403
    Description   403
        Brass or Copper Alloy   403
        Iron   405
        Lead   407
        Other Materials   407
    Distribution   407
Amorphous Artifacts   410
    Description   410
        Calcite   410
        Charcoal   410
        Copper   412
        Horn   412
        Iron   412
        Lead   412
        Leather   412
        Shell   412
        Slag and Clinker   413

THE NATIVE AMERICAN COMPONENT   415
Introduction   415
Lithics   415
    Description   415
        Biface   415
        Core   415
        Drill   415
        Hammerstone   418

Knife   418
Miscellaneous Crusher/Pounder   419
Ornament   419
Perforator   419
Preform   419
Projectile Point   419
Scrapers   419
Spokeshave   420
Tabular Slab   421
Utilized Flakes   421
Miscellaneous Debitage   422
Indeterminate Objects   422
Distribution   422
Comments   422
Pottery   429
Description   429
Distribution   430
Comments   430

REFERENCES   433

FIGURES

Figure 1. Bottle Terminology.
Figure 2. Seven Styles of Bottle Finishes.
Figure 3. Two Styles of Bottle Bases (a, Style One; b, Style Two).
Figure 4. Style Three Bottle Base.
Figure 5. "PAUILLAC/MEDOC" Bottle Seal.
Figure 6. Sketch of the Center Motif of the "PAUILLAC/MEDOC" Bottle Seal (Enlarged Approximately 3x).
Figure 7. Fragment of a "ST. JULIEN/MEDOC" Bottle Seal.
Figure 8. Distribution of the Bottle Glass Fragments Within the West Dump.
Figure 9. Distribution of the Bottle Glass Fragments Within the Main Dump.
Figure 10. Map of the Gironde Department, France (Reproduced from Waugh 1968:105).
Figure 11. Stoneware Bottle Fragments (a to f, Style One; g, Style Two).
Figure 12. Glassware Fragments (a, Pedestal Base; b & c, Side Panels; d, Rim; e, Base).
Figure 13. Storage and Utility Vessel Styles One Through Eight (a to c, Earthenware; d to h, Stoneware).
Figure 14. Storage and Utility Vessel Styles Nine Through Fifteen (a to g, Stoneware).
Figure 15. Selected Cross Sections of Storage and Utility Vessel Fragments (a, Style Four; b, Style Eight; c, Style Twelve).
Figure 16. Distribution of Storage and Utility Vessel Sherds and Stoneware Bottle Fragments Within the West Dump.
Figure 17. Distribution of Storage and Utility Vessel Sherds and Stoneware Bottle Fragments Within the Main Dump.
Figure 18. Annular Ware Sherds (a, Style One (b); b, Style Two; c, Style Three (b); d, Style Three (c); e and f, Style One (c); g, Style Four; h, Style One (d)).
Figure 19. Cross Sections of Tableware Sherd Styles One, Two, Three, Five, and Six.
Figure 20. Distribution of Series One to Five Tableware Styles Within the West Dump.
Figure 21. Distribution of Series One to Five Tableware Styles Within the Main Dump.
Figure 22. Purple Lustre Decorated Wares.
Figure 23. Style Six Spatter Decorated Sherds.
Figure 24. Styles Nine and Ten Sherds with Hand-Painted, Plychrome Floral Motifs (a, Style Nine; b and c, Style Ten).
Figure 25. Style Eleven Sherds with Hand-Painted, Polychrome Floral Motif.
Figure 26. Blue Edge Decorated Sherds (a, c, & d, Style Thirteen; b, Style Fifteen; e, Style Fourteen).
Figure 27. Black Transfer Printed Sherds with the "Gentlemen's Cabin" Pattern.
Figure 28. Registry Form for the "Gentlemen's Cabin" Pattern (Reproduced from Godden 1965:159).

185

Figure 29.   Red Transfer Printed Sherds (a, Style Element Four; b,
              Style Seventeen; c, Style Element Five).
Figure 30.   Purple Transfer Printed Sherds.
Figure 31.   Blue Transfer Printed Sherds (a, Style Nineteen; b, Style
              Eighteen (b); c, Style Element Six; d, Style Element Ten).
Figure 32.   Brown Transfer Printed Sherds (a, Style Element One;
              b, Style Element Two; c, Style Element Three).
Figure 33.   Green Transfer Printed Sherds (a, Style Element Seven; b,
              Style Element Eight; c, Undefined; d, Style Element Nine).
Figure 34.   Distribution of Series Six Through Eleven Tableware Sherds
              Within the West Dump.
Figure 35.   Distribution of Series Six Through Eleven Tableware Sherds
              Within the Main Dump.
Figure 36.   The Transfer Printing Process: Cutting the Transfers,
              Applying the Prints, Dipping the Dish, and Glost Placing
              (Reproduced from Copeland 1980:24-25)
Figure 37.   Hand-Painted Sherds (a, Style Element Ten; b, Undefined;
              c, Style Element Eleven).
Figure 38.   Cross Sections of Typical Undecorated Rim Sherds.
Figure 39.   Cross Sections of Typical Undecorated Basal Sherds.
Figure 40.   Miscellaneous Undecorated Basal Remnants (a, Pearlware;
              b, Unidentified).
Figure 41.   Graniteware Sherds (a, Rim; b, Footrim).
Figure 42.   Yellowware Sherds.
Figure 43.   Typical Yellowware Sherd Cross Sections.
Figure 44.   Yellowware-like Utilitarian Vessels Advertised in the 1864
              T.G. Green & Company's Church Gresley Pottery Catalog
              (Reproduced from Godden 1965:173).
Figure 45.   Fragments of Export Porcelain (a, Style Element Sixteen; b,
              Style Element Seventeen).
Figure 46.   Cross Section of Unidentified Earthenware Base.
Figure 47.   Utensil Handles (a, Wood; b to d, Bone).
Figure 48.   Styles One and Two Glass Beads (a, b, & c, Style One;
              d, Style Two).
Figure 49.   Styles Three, Four, and Five Glass Beads (a, Style Three;
              b, Style Four; c, d, e, & f, Style Five).
Figure 50.   Styles Six to Ten Glass Beads (a, Style Six; b, Style Seven;
              c, Style Eight; d, Style Nine; e & f, Style Ten).
Figure 51.   Styles Eleven to Thirteen Glass Beads (a, b, & c, Style
              Eleven; d, Style Twelve; e & f, Style Thirteen).
Figure 52.   Close-up of Style Thirteen Glass Beads Illustrating Drawn
              Glass Tubular Cores.
Figure 53.   Styles Fourteen to Sixteen Glass and Shell Beads (a & b,
              Style Fourteen; c, Style Fifteen; d & e, Style Sixteen).
Figure 54.   Distribution of Beads Within the West Dump.
Figure 55.   Distribution of Beads Within the Main Dump.
Figure 56.   Craftsmen Manufacturing Glass Beads by the Hollow Cane
              Method. (Oil Painting by Jacob van Loo, Reproduced from
              a Plate in Kidd 1979:101).
Figure 57.   Comparison of Intra-Area Percentage Distributions of "Seed"
              Beads by Color.
Figure 58.   Beadwork Remnant.

Figure 59.   Articles of Personal Attire (a, Hooks; b, Style One Eyelet; c, Style Two Eyelet; d, Buckle, e & f, Grommets).
Figure 60.   Button Terminology.
Figure 61.   Button Processing Marks (a, Drill Scar; b, Saw Scar).
Figure 62.   Bone Button Blanks.
Figure 63.   Button Styles One to Twelve.
Figure 64.   Button Styles Thirteen to Twenty-four.
Figure 65.   Buttone Styles One to Six.
Figure 66.   Button Styles Seven to Twelve.
Figure 67.   Button Styles Thirteen to Sixteen.
Figure 68.   Button Styles Seventeen to Twenty.
Figure 69.   Button Styles Seventeen to Twenty, Reverse View.
Figure 70.   Button Styles Twenty-one to Twenty-four.
Figure 71.   Button Styles Twenty-one to Twenty-three, Reverse View.
Figure 72.   Distribution of Buttons and Articles of Personal Attire Within the West Dump.
Figure 73.   Distribution of Buttons and Articles of Personal Attire Within the Main Dump.
Figure 74.   Distribution of Buttons by Material, Frquency, and Diameter.
Figure 75.   The Manufacture of Fabric-Covered Buttons (Reproduced from Luscomb 1967:69).
Figure 76.   Leather Footwear Remnants.
Figure 77.   Clay Pipe Terminology.
Figure 78.   Clay Pipe Styles One and Two.
Figure 79.   Miscellaneous Pipe Fragments (a, b, & c, Terra-cotta; d, Glazed Redware; e, Unglazed Redware; f, Catlinite).
Figure 80.   Distribution of Pipes Within the West Dump.
Figure 81.   Distribution of Pipes Within the Main Dump.
Figure 82.   Musical Instruments (a, Jew's Harp; b, Harmonica Reed).
Figure 83.   Terminology of the Flintlock Rifle.
Figure 84.   Terminology of Rifle Firing Mechanisms (a, Flintlock; b, Percussion Cap).
Figure 85.   Rifle Springs (a, Battery Spring; b, Main Spring).
Figure 86.   Gun Furniture (a & b, Side Plates; c, Butt Plate; d, e, & f, Ramrod Thimbles; g, Trigger Guard).
Figure 87.   Back Marks on Rifle Side Plates (a, "DN"; b, Linked Diamonds).
Figure 88.   Distribution of Firearms Related Artifacts Within the West Dump.
Figure 89.   Distribution of Firearms Related Artifacts Within the Main Dump.
Figure 90.   Style One Gunflints.
Figure 91.   Styles Two and Three Gunflints.
Figure 92.   Styles Four, Five, and Six Gunflints.
Figure 93.   Style Seven Gunflint.
Figure 94.   Category One and Category Two Gunflints.
Figure 95.   Size Distribution of the Gunflints in Comparison to the 1849 U.S. Ordnance Standards for Pistols, Rifles, and Muskets.
Figure 96.   Percussion Cap Terminology.
Figure 97.   Shot, Sprue, and Cherry (a, b, & c, Lead Shot; d, Copper "Jacketed" Lead Shot; e to h, Lead Sprue; i to m, Expended Lead Shot; n, Cherry).

Figure 98. Cartridge Casings and Percussion Caps (a to e, .44 Henry
            Flat; f & g, .56-56 Spencer Carbine; h, .45 Colt; i & j,
            .41 Short; k, .56-50 Spencer; l, .32 Teat Fire; m, Plain
            Percussion Cap; n, "Top-Hat" Percussion Cap; o, Fluted
            Percussion Cap; p, Nippled Percussion Cap).
Figure 99. Firing Pin Marks (a, .44 Henry Flat Lacking Typical Opposing
            Pin Marks; b, .44 Henry Flat with Typical Opposing Pin Marks;
            c, .41 Short with Single Pin Strike; d, .45 Colt with Benet
            Type Primer; e, "F.V.V. & Co" Headstamp .56-50 Spencer).
Figure 100. Firearms Associated Artifacts (a, Lead Powder Cask Plug; b,
            Lead Gunflint Pad; c, Copper Powder Flask Tube Spouts).
Figure 101. Harness Buckle, Dubbing Off Remnants, and Horseshoe Nails
            (a, Iron Harness Buckle; b & c, Dubbing Off Remnants; d to m,
            Horseshoe Nails).
Figure 102. Horseshoe Fragments.
Figure 103. Horseshoe and Horse Foot Terminology (Based on Berge 1980:
            236, 237, 242, 243; Holmstrom 1971:76-78; Watson 1977:72).
Figure 104. Horseshoes Sold in the Illustrated Catalogue of American
            Hardware of the Russell and Erwin Manufacturing Company,
            1865.
Figure 105. Horseshoe Nail Styles and Terminology.
Figure 106. Ausable Horse Nails Advertised in the Burlington Iowa
            Hawk-Eye, 1877.
Figure 107. Wagon Wheel Skeins (a, Style One; b, Remnant; c & d,
            Style Two).
Figure 108. Wagon Wheel Skein Styles and Terminology.
Figure 109. Wagon Wheel Terminology (Based on Watson 1977:86, 87).
Figure 110. Nuts, Axles, and Thimble-Skeins as Advertised in the
            Illustrated Catalogue of American Hardware of the Russell
            and Erwin Manufacturing Company, 1865.
Figure 111. Distribution of Transportation Related Hardware Within
            the West Dump.
Figure 112. Distribution of Transportation Related Hardware Within
            the Main Dump.
Figure 113. Adobe Samples (a & b, Adobe; c, Adobe Fragment with
            Whitewashed Exterior Surface).
Figure 114. Distribution of Adobe Samples, Nails, and Window Glass Within
            the West Dump.
Figure 115. Distribution of Adobe Samples, Nails, and Window Glass Within
            the Main Dump.
Figure 116. Numa Soil Series Profile (Based on U.S. Soil Conservation
            Service 1972:21).
Figure 117. Structural Hardware (a, b, & c, Strap Hinges; d & e, Hook
            and Staple Eye; f, Latch Catch or Keeper; g, Hinge Pin).
Figure 118. Spikes and Nails (a & b, Spikes; c, d, & e, Headless Cut
            Nails; f, g, & h, Clinch Nails; i to o, Common Cut Nails).
Figure 119. Frequency Distribution of the Machine-Cut Nails by
            Pennyweight and Inches ("Triangle," West Dump; "Circle,"
            Main Dump).
Figure 120. Nails and Spikes Advertised in the Illustrated Catalogue of
            American Hardware of the Russell and Erwin Manufacturing
            Company, 1865.

Figure 121. Manufacture of Cylinder or Broad Glass ("Scenes in a Glass Foundry" by Theo R. Davies, Harpers Weekly, January 1884, as Reproduced in Wilson 1976:151).
Figure 122. Manufacture of Crown Glass (Reproduced from Wilson 1976:153).
Figure 123. Broadside of Redford Crown Glass, 1837 (Reproduced in Wilson 1976:162).
Figure 124. Abraders or Whetstones.
Figure 125. Adz and Chisel Blades (a & b, Adz Blades; c, Chisel Blade).
Figure 126. Barbed Wire, Plain Wire, and Chain Links (a, Cleaveland Patent Barbed Wire; b, Baker Patent Barbed Wire; c, Twisted Chain Link; d, Flat Chain Link; e, Plain Iron Wire).
Figure 127. Copper and Copper Alloy Artifacts (a, Bell; b, Clock Gear; c, Rivets; d & e, Copper Wire).
Figure 128. Furniture Related Hardware (a, Dome-Headed Nails; b, Drawer Pull; c, Butt Hinge).
Figure 129. Fragment of Green Fabric.
Figure 130. Fragments of Charred Corn Cobs.
Figure 131. Detail of Back Marks on Drawer Pull and Butt Hinge (a, "PATENT 1855"; b, "23 RC").
Figure 132. Miscellaneous Iron Artifacts (a, Handle; b, Nut and Bolt Fragment; c, Railroad Spike; d, Rivet; e, Stove Plate; f, Washer).
Figure 133. Lead Pencils, Slate Pencil, and Lead Seal (a & b, Lead Pencils; c, Slate Pencil; d, Lead Seal).
Figure 134. Distribution of the Miscellaneous Artifacts Within the West Dump.
Figure 135. Distribution of the Miscellaneous Artifacts Within the Main Dump.
Figure 136. Copper and Copper Alloy Unidentified Artifacts.
Figure 137. Miscellaneous Iron Artifacts (a, Rectangula Bar Fragments; b, Rod Fragment; c, Unidentified; d, Band Fragments; e, Wedge-Shaped Fragment; f, g, & h, Springs).
Figure 138. Miscellaneous Artifacts (a, Lead Strainer?; b, Lead Block; c, Petrified Wood Bar; d, Wooden Ring Fragment; e to h, "Turkey Stones").
Figure 139. Calcite Fragments.
Figure 140. Wood Charcoal Fragments.
Figure 141. Freshwater Mollusk Shells.
Figure 142. Slag.
Figure 143. Stone Artifacts (a, Hammerstone; b, Tabular Stone Slab; c, Tabular Stone Spokeshave).
Figure 144. Cores (a, Black Flint; b, Chert; c, Sedimentary Stone; d, Jasper; e, Quartz).
Figure 145. Miscellaneous Lithic Artifacts (a, Biface Fragment; b, Crusher; c, Pendant Fragment; d, Projectile Point Preform; e, Scraper Preform; f, Spokeshave).
Figure 146. Lithic Implements (a, Drill; b, Thumbnail Knife; c, d, & e, Perforator/Gravers; f, Projectile Point Tip; g, Dakota Quartzite Point; h, Texas Alabase Point).
Figure 147. Scrapers and Spokeshave (a, Sidescraper; b to f, Endscrapers; g, Spokeshave).
Figure 148. Utilized Flakes.
Figure 149. Distribution of Prehistoric Artifacts Within the West Dump.
Figure 150. Distribution of Prehistoric Artifacts Within the Main Dump.
Figure 151. Pottery (a, Style One; b, Style Two; c, Style Three; d, Style Four).

TABLES

Table 1.   Distribution of Bottle Glass Finish Styles by Dump, Unit Type, and Stratum.

Table 2.   Distribution of Bottle Basal Fragments by Dump, Unit Type, and Stratum.

Table 3.   Distribution of Bottle Glass Body Fragments by Dump, Unit Type, and Stratum.

Table 4.   Distribution of Stoneware Bottle Sherds by Dump, Unit Type, and Stratum.

Table 5.   Distribution of Glassware Fragments by Dump, Unit Type, and Stratum.

Table 6.   Distribution of Storage and Utility Vessel Sherds by Dump, Unit Type, and Stratum.

Table 7.   Distribution of Style Series One, Annular Decorated Pearlware-Bodied, Sherds by Dump, Unit Type, and Stratum.

Table 8.   Distribution of Style Series Two, Purple Lustre Decorated Pearlware-Bodied, Sherds by Dump, Unit Type, and Stratum.

Table 9.   Distribution of Style Series Three, Spatter Decorated Pearlware-Bodied, Sherds by Dump, Unit Type, and Stratum.

Table 10.   Distribution of Style Series Four, Hand-Pained Floral Motif Decorated Pearlware-Bodied, Sherds by Dump, Unit Type, and Stratum.

Table 11.   Distribution of Style Series Five, Blue Edge Decorated, Sherds by Dump, Unit Type, and Stratum.

Table 12.   Distribution of Style Series Six, Transfer Printed, Sherds by Dump, Unit Type, and Stratum.

Table 13.   Distribution of Style Series Seven, Miscellaneous White Earthenware, Sherds by Dump, Unit Type, and Stratum.

Table 14.   Distribution of Style Series Eight, Graniteware, Sherds by Dump, Unit Type, and Stratum.

Table 15.   Distribution of Style Series Nine, Yellowware, Sherds by Dump, Unit Type, and Stratum.

Table 16.   Distribution of Style Series Ten, Porcelain, Sherds by Dump, Unit Type, and Stratum.

Table 17.   Distribution of Style Series Eleven, Buff-Colored Earthenware-Bodied, Sherds by Dump, Unit Type, and Sratum.

Table 18.   Distribution of Wood and Bone Handle Fragments by Dump, Unit Type, and Stratum.

Table 19.   Distribution of Style One Beads by Dump, Unit Type, and Stratum.

Table 20.   Distribution of Styles Two to Four Beads by Dump, Unit Type, and Stratum.

Table 21.   Distribution of Style Five Beads by Dump, Unit Type, and Stratum.

Table 22.   Distribution of Styles Six to Ten Beads by Dump, Unit Type, and Stratum.

Table 23.   Distribution of Style Eleven Beads by Dump, Unit Type, and Stratum.

Table 24.   Distribution of Styles Twelve to Sixteen Beads and Unspecified Fragments by Dump, Unit Type, and Stratum.

Table 25.   Presence-Absence Comparison of Comer's and Moore's
             Bead Assemblages.
Table 26.   Distribution of Miscellaneous Articles of Personal Attire.
Table 27.   Distribution of Button Styles by Dump, Unit Type, and Stratum.
Table 28.   Comparative Distribution of Buttons by Material from Comer's
             and Moore's Excavations (Ratios Based on Bone Frequency as
             the Index Value).
Table 29.   Distributional and Dimensional Aspects of Styles One and Two
             Pipes by Dump, Unit Type, and Stratum.
Table 30.   Distribution of White Clay Pipe Fragments by Style Element,
             Dump, Unit Type, and Stratum.
Table 31.   Distribution of Miscellaneous White Clay Pipebowl Fragments
             from the West Dump by Unit Type and Stratum.
Table 32.   Distribution of Miscellaneous White Clay Pipebowl Fragments
             from the Main Dump by Unit Type and Stratum.
Table 33.   Distribution of Undecorated White Clay Pipestems from the
             West Dump by Bore Diameter, Unit Type, and Stratum
Table 34.   Distribution of Undecorated White Clay Pipestems from the
             Main Dump by Bore Diameter, Unit Type, and Stratum
Table 35.   Distribution of Non-White Pipe Fragments by Dump, Unit
             Type, and Stratum.
Table 36.   Distribution of White Clay Pipestems from Moore's Excavation
             by Excavation Areas (Moore 1973:130-131).
Table 37.   Distribution of Gun Hardware by Dump, Unit Type, and Stratum.
Table 38.   Distribution of Gunflints and Gunflint Fragments by Dump,
             Unit Type, and Stratum.
Table 39.   1849 U.S. Ordnance Standards for Army Gunflints.
Table 40.   Distribution of Percussion Camp Styles by Dump, Unit
             Type, and Stratum.
Table 41.   Distribution of Shot, Lead Sprue, and Cherry by Dump,
             Unit Type, and Stratum.
Table 42.   Distribution of Metallic Cartridge Casings by Dump, Unit Type,
             and Stratum.
Table 43.   Distribution of Firearms Associated Artifacts.
Table 44.   Attributes of the Horseshoe Fragments from the West Dump.
Table 45.   Attributes of the Dubbing Off Fragments from the West
             and Main Dumps.
Table 46.   Metrical Attributes of the Horseshoe Nails from the West and
             Main Dumps.
Table 47.   Metrical Attributes of the Wagon Wheel Skein Fragments.
Table 48.   Distribution of Adobe Fragment Presence by Dump Area and
             Excavation Category.
Table 49.   Interior Fort Distribution of Excavated Adobe Finish by
             Category and Room Designation (Moore 1973:18, 22, 26, 31,
             32,35-38, 40,44).
Table 50.   Distribution of Hinge, Hook and Eye, and Latch Parts by
             Excavation Area and Unit Category.
Table 51.   Distribution of Nail Categories by Excavation Area and
             Unit Category.
Table 52.   Stratigraphic Distribution of Spikes (S), Machine-Cut (M),
             Wire (W), and Unspecified (U) Nails in the West Dump by
             Unit Category.

Table 53.   Stratigraphic Distribution of Spikes (S), Machine-Cut (M),
              Wire (W), and Unspecified (U) Nails in the Main Dump by
              Unit Category.
Table 54.   Relative Stratigraphic Density of Spikes (S), Machine-Cut (M),
              Wire (W), and Unspecified (U) Nails in the West Dump by
              Unit Category.
Table 55.   Relative Stratigraphic Density of Spikes (S), Machine-Cut (M),
              Wire (W), and Unspecified (U) Nails in the Main Dump by
              Unit Category.
Table 56.   Stratigraphic Distribution and Relative Stratigraphic Density
              of Window Glass in the West Dump by Unit Category.
Table 57.   Stratigraphic Distribution and Relative Stratigraphic Density
              of Window Glass in the Main Dump by Unit Category.
Table 58.   Distribution of Identifiable Items by Dump, Unit Type, and
              Stratum.
Table 59.   Distribution of Unidentified Non-Amorphous Artifacts by
              Dump, Unit Type, and Stratum.
Table 60.   Distribution of Copper Fragments by Dump, Unit Type, and
              Stratum.
Table 61.   Distribution of Iron Fragments by Dump, Unit Type, and
              Stratum.
Table 62.   Distribution of Lead Fragments by Dump, Unit Type, and
              Stratum.
Table 63.   Distribution of Miscellaneous Lithic Artifacts by Dump,
              Unit Type, and Stratum.
Table 64.   Distribution and Metrical Attributes of the Utilized Flakes
              by Dump, Unit Type, and Stratum.
Table 65.   Distribution and Metrical Attributes of Miscellaneous Debitage
              by Dump, Unit Type, and Stratum.
Table 66.   Distribution and Metrical Attributes of Indeterminate Lithic
              Forms by Dump, Unit Type, and Stratum.
Table 67.   Attributes and Spatial Distribution of the Pottery.

GENERAL COMMENTS

The following report was prepared under the mandate to provide a description of the artifacts recovered from the 1976 excavations of the Main and West Trash Dumps at Bent's Old Fort National Historic Site. The present analysis was conducted during the period from October 1981 to March 1982. This work was divided approximately evenly between assembling the artifact collection and original notes, examining and identifying the artifacts, preparing the illustrations, and writing up the findings.

In comparing the artifacts against the 1976 inventory, a number of discrepancies in identification were noted. As a consequence, the collection was completely reanalyzed.

In conducting this restudy, description was viewed in a broad sense. It was defined to include, as applicable, identification of item function, frequency, stylistic characteristics, metrical attributes, chronological association, materials composition, spatial distribution, and illustration. In accordance with the overall mandate, no attempts were made to provide a contextual analysis for this collection. General background information was, however, included.

In compiling the tabulations for this report, Comer's synthesized provenience designations were used rather than the original field catalogue numbers. The artifacts were tabulated in accordance with his unified strata designations and his separation of units into random and nonrandom squares.

THE HOUSEHOLD GOODS COMPONENT

INTRODUCTION

The Household Goods Component is comprised of all those articles that were utilized in the domestic activities of the home. Included within this component are bottles, glassware, storage and utility vessels, tableware, and utensils.

BOTTLES

The bottle collection can be divided into two broad categories according to material. The first category consists of bottles made of glass. The second category consists of bottles made of stoneware.

Description--Glass Bottles

The bottle glass category can be described in terms of five attributes. These characteristics are shape, bottle section or part, size, special features, and color of glass. None of the bottles included within the artifact assemblages of the two dumps is complete. Elements within this collection vary from extremely fragmentary to fragmentary.

In describing the various sections of a bottle, several conventions have been adopted (figure 1). The resting surface of the bottle when it is placed upright is called the "base." The section between the base and the point at which the bottle begins to narrow is called the "body." In describing fragments whose relationship to a particular section is not clear, the designation "body" has been applied. The portion of the bottle that narrows before achieving a uniform diameter is called the "shoulder." The section between the shoulder and the top of the bottle is designated the "neck." Special features of the various sections include the "push-up," which is a pronounced concavity of the base that occurs in some forms of bottles; the "mouth," which is the top surface of the neck; the "lip," which is the lateral surface of the neck just below the mouth; the "collar," which is a band or ring that occurs below the lip on some forms of bottles; and the "finish," which is any addition to a plain neck.

In discussing the elements within the bottle glass collection, several general categories have been utilized. These groupings are (1) styles of finish, (2) styles of base, (3) special features, and (4) miscellaneous fragments. Seven styles of finish were noted (figure 2).

The Style One finish (figure 2) consists of a series of at least three irregularly sized bands of glass that begin about 0.5 cm below the mouth. The bands have been applied manually. The mouth has been formed by the bust-off process and has been lightly fire polished to remove any jagged edges. The surface is uneven and roughly flat.

The Style Two finish (figure 2) is formed by a single irregular band applied around 0.5 cm to 0.6 cm below the mouth. The band varies in

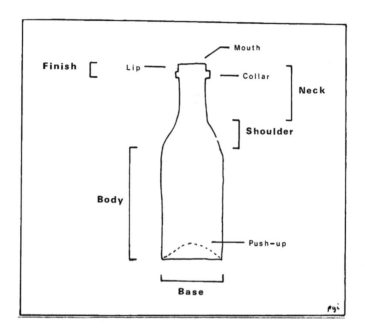

Figure 1.   Terminology of Bottle Sections.

width between 0.41 cm to 0.71 cm.   The mouth was made by the bust-off process, is roughly flat, and was fire polished.

The Style Three finish (figure 2) consists of a single band applied around the mouth to form a lip.   The band varies between 0.87 cm and 1.10 cm in width.   The band is placed irregularly around the mouth. The mouth is roughly flat, was made by the bust-off process, and was fire polished.

The Style Four finish (figure 2) consists of a single laid on band.   The band is 0.7 cm to 0.8 cm in width and occurs about 0.43 cm below the mouth.   The mouth has been crudely beveled by manually shaping the neck under heat.

The Style Five finish (figure 2) is a lip and mouth that have been formed by bending the neck back over itself under heat.   Stress lines retained along the line of the curvature document the technique used.   The lip is about 0.88 cm wide.   The mouth is rounded.

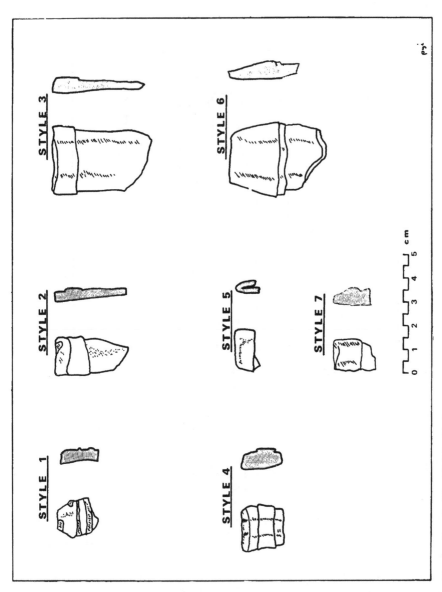

Figure 2. Bottle Finish Styles.

The Style Six finish (figure 2) is comprised of a long beveled lip applied with a lipping tool. The lip is about 2.47 cm long. The mouth is rounded.

The Style Seven finish (figure 2) is a moderately sized beveled lip that had been manually applied. The lip is about 1.18 cm wide. The mouth is rounded.

Three styles of bases were noted (figure 3). The Style One base is a narrow diameter base with a bottom-hinged mold seam. The center is marked with a jagged, glass scar from a blowpipe pontil. The estimated diameter of the base, calculated trigonometrically from the fragmentary dimensions, is 4.66 cm. The border is beveled; the center area is slightly concave. The Style Two base is a moderately wide diameter basal fragment consisting of a high push-up. A jagged, open circular glass scar from a blowpipe pontil occurs along the upper, inner surface. The borders of this artifact are absent. The Style Three base (figure 4) is a thick, circular base. The basal surface is flat. The examples are 6.74 cm and 6.29 cm (estimated) in diameter.

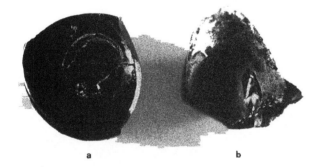

a   b

Figure 3.   Styles One and Two Bottle Bases.

Special bottle features are represented by two categories of items. These categories are bottle seals and embossed panel lettering. Two distinct seals were recovered. The first (figure 5) is a transparent, olive green disk marked, "PAUILLAC/MEDOC," around the border. The center section (figure 6) is occupied by a circular, fan-shaped design. At the center is a heart-shaped element with impressions suggesting eyebrows, eyes, and a nose (Death's Head motif). The diameter of the seal is 2.99 cm.

The seal had been applied by placing a hot glob of glass against the surface of the bottle and, then, by stamping it with a metal seal. A convex projection occurs on the interior bottle surface as a result of this process. The lettering and design are in relief. The letters are about 0.36 cm high. The center motif is 1.2 cm in diameter.

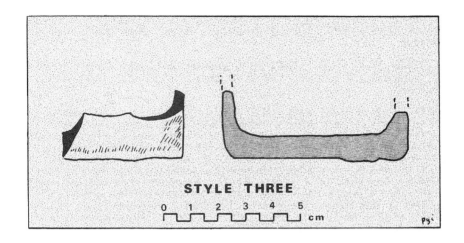

Figure 4. Style Three Bottle Base.

Figure 5. "PAUILLAC/MEDOC" Seal.

198

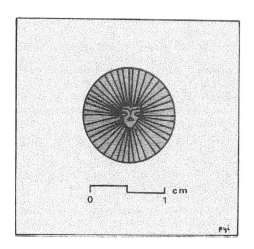

Figure 6.   Sketch of Center Motif of
"PAUILLAC/MEDOC" Seal (approximately
3 X).

The second seal (figure 7) is fragmentary.   A dotted border in relief
follows the curvature of the circular seal.   Only the letter "N" in relief is
present.   The overall design is similar to the "ST. JULIEN/MEDOC" seal
illustrated in Moore (1973:65).   The seal had been applied by affixing a
hot glob of glass to the bottle surface and stamping with a metal seal.
The diameter of the seal, estimated trigonometrically, is 2.65 cm.

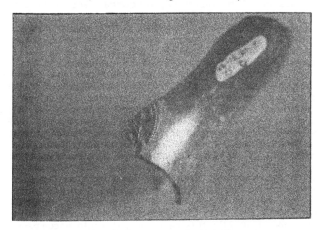

Figure 7.   Fragment of a "ST. JULIEN/MEDOC" seal.

Three fragments of clear bottle glass possess embossed lettering on panel sections. The first is the beginning letters "CO -" embossed 0.74 cm high. The second fragment has 0.59 cm high terminal letters, "US." The third has 0.85 cm high medial sequence letters, "OL." None of the sequences are sufficiently distinctive as to be related to a specific product (Baldwin 1973).

The remainder of the bottle glass collection consists of nondescript fragments. These fragments can be divided into ten categories according to general color groupings. All of the glass is translucent except for the blue and white (milk) glass. The color groupings along with their fragment frequencies are 1) dark olive green, sometimes referred to as "black," (4); 2) olive green (688); 3) light green tint (2); 4) blue tint (3); 5) blue (24); 6) dark brown (2); 7) brown (173); 8) white, usually referred to as milk glass (18); 9) amethyst, also called manganese or purple glass, (7); and 10) clear (1,538).

Distribution--Glass Bottles

The definable categories of bottle glass fragments are listed according to dump, unit type, and stratum in table 1 for finish fragments, in table 2 for basal fragments, and in table 3 for the miscellaneous nondescript fragments. The spatial distribution of the bottle glass from the combined strata are depicted in figure 8 for the West Dump and in figure 9 for the Main Dump.

Comments--Glass Bottles

The extremely fragmentary nature of the bottle glass collection precludes any detailed discussion of the historical, functional, and social aspects of this class of artifacts. Some brief comments, however, can be made. In terms of the styles of closures represented, all are cork closures. The specific forms of the finishes suggest a distinct 19th century origin. The simple laid on ring for tying off a cork was common during the period 1840-1870 (Newman 1970:73). Such tie-off related features were associated with carbonated beverages. The lipping tool applied lip began to be used prior to 1850 (Lorrain 1968:43); however, it was most commonly used during the period 1850-1870 (Newman 1970:73). The form of applied lip included within the present collection has been generally attributed to the period 1865-1875 (McKearin and McKearin 1948:424-425). Other features also indicate a 19th century origin. The rough glass scar push-up created by a blowpipe pontil was present up to the 1870s (Jones 1971:72; Newman 1970:73). Embossed lettering on paneled bottles came into practice around 1867 (Lorrain 1968:40; Newman 1970:73) and remained in use until about 1915 (Newman 1970:73). Amethyst glass, which results from the interaction of manganese included in the glass as a decolorizing agent with sunlight has been attributed to the 1880-1915 period (Munsey 1970:55). The beginnings of clear glass have been assigned to the time from 1880 on (Newman 1970:74); this early period would encompass largely manganese glass and would be evident in the artifact collection only in terms of glass that had been transformed by exposure. Non-manganese decolored glass would be undistinguishable from clear manganese glass.

Table 1. Distribution of Bottle Glass Finish Styles
by Dump, Unit Type, and Stratum

Finish	Color	Frequency	Dump	Unit Type	Stratum
Style 1	olive green	2	Main	Random	B
Style 2	olive green	1	Main	Nonrandom	C
Style 2	olive green	1	Main	Random	C
Style 2	olive green	1	Main	Random	D
Style	olive green	1	West	Nonrandom	C
Style	olive green	3	Main	Random	B
Style	olive green	1	Main	Nonrandom	C
Style	olive green	1	Main	Random	C
Style 3	olive green	1	Main	Random	E
Style 4	olive green	1	West	Nonrandom	A
Style 4	olive green	1	West	Nonrandom	C
Style 5	bluish tint		Main	Random	C
Style 6	brown		West	Nonrandom	A
Style 7	light green tint	1	Main	Nonrandom	B
NA	olive green	1	West	Nonrandom	C
NA	olive green	1	Main	Nonrandom	B
NA	light green tint	1	West	Nonrandom	A
NA	clear	1	Main	Random	A
NA	clear	1	Main	Random	C

Table 2. Distribution of Bottle Basal Fragments by Dump, Unit Type, and Stratum

Base	Color	Frequency	Dump	Unit Type	Stratum
Style 1	olive green		Main	Nonrandom	E
Style 2	olive green	1	West	Random	A
Style 2	olive green	1	Main	Random	D
Style 3	clear	1	Main	Random	B
Style 3	clear	2	Main	Nonrandom	D
NA	dark olive green	1	West	Nonrandom	A
NA	olive green	2	West	Nonrandom	A
NA	olive green	2	West	Nonrandom	C
NA	olive green	1	West	Random	D
NA	olive green	1	Main	Random	A
NA	olive green	4	Main	Random	B
NA	olive green	3	Main	Nonrandom	C
NA	olive green	1	Main	Random	D
NA	light green tint	1	West	Nonrandom	C
NA	light green tint	1	Main	Random	D
NA	bluish tint		Main	Random	D
NA	brown	2	West	Nonrandom	A

Table 3. Distribution of Bottle Glass Body Fragments
by Dump, Unit Type, and Stratum

Body	Color	Frequency	Dump	Unit Type	Stratum
Seal	olive green	1	Main	Random	C
Seal	olive green	1	West	Random	D
Panel	light green tint	1	West	Random	A
Panel	clear	1	West	Nonrandom	A
Panel	clear	2	West	Nonrandom	B
Panel	clear	1	West	Nonrandom	C
Panel	clear	1	Main	Nonrandom	B
NA	dark olive green	3	West	Nonrandom	A
NA	dark olive green	1	West	Nonrandom	B
NA	olive green	2	West	Random	OB
NA	olive green	94	West	Nonrandom	A
NA	olive green	6	West	Random	A
NA	olive green	44	West	Nonrando	B
NA	olive green	44	West	Nonrandom	C
NA	olive green	1	West	Random	C
NA	olive green	7	West	Nonrandom	D
NA	olive green	10	West	Random	D
NA	olive green	7	Main	Random	A
NA	olive green	28	Main	Nonrandom	B
NA	olive green	105	Main	Random	B
NA	olive green	123	Main	Nonrandom	C
NA	olive green	70	Main	Random	C
NA	olive green	26	Main	Nonrandom	D
NA	olive green	93	Main	Random	D
NA	olive green	7	Main	Nonrandom	E
NA	olive green	17	Main	Random	E
NA	olive green	1	Main	Random	F
NA	olive green	1	Main	Nonrandom	H
NA	olive green	3	Main	Random	H
NA	light green tint	1	West	Nonrandom	C
NA	light green tint	1	Main	Nonrandom	C
NA	blue tint	1	Main	Nonrandom	B
NA	blue tint	2	Main	Random	B
NA	blue	14	Main	Nonrandom	C
NA	blue	1	Main	Random	A
NA	blue	9	Main	Random	B

Body	Color	Frequency	Dump	Unit Type	Stratum
NA	dark brown	2	West	Nonrandom	A
NA	brown	1	West	Random	OB
NA	brown	73	West	Nonrandom	A
NA	brown	21	West	Nonrandom	B
NA	brown	9	West	Random	B
NA	brown	15	West	Nonrandom	C
NA	brown	1	Main	Nonrandom	A
NA	brown	3	Main	Random	A
NA	brown	9	Main	Nonrandom	B
NA	brown	18	Main	Random	B
NA	brown	4	Main	Nonrandom	C
NA	brown	3	Main	Random	C
NA	brown	9	Main	Random	D
NA	brown	2	Main	Nonrandom	E
NA	brown	3	Main	Random	F
NA	brown	1	Main	Nonrandom	H
NA	brown	1	Main	Random	H
NA	white	16	Main	Random	A
NA	white	1	Main	Random	B
NA	white	1	Main	Random	C
NA	amethyst	1	West	Nonrandom	B
NA	amethyst	4	Main	Nonrandom	B
NA	amethyst	2	Main	Nonrandom	C
NA	clear	45	West	Random	OB
NA	clear	215	West	Nonrandom	A
NA	clear	477	West	Radom	A
NA	clear	45	West	Nonrandom	B
NA	clear	72	West	Random	B
NA	clear	28	West	Nonrandom	C
NA	clear	88	West	Random	C
NA	clear	2	West	Nonrandom	D
NA	clear	42	West	Random	D
NA	clear	1	Main	Nonrandom	A
NA	clear	17	Main	Random	A
NA	clear	75	Main	Nonrandom	B
NA	clear	142	Main	Random	B
NA	clear	95	Main	Nonrandom	C
Na	clear	104	Main	Random	C
NA	clear	16	Main	Nonrandom	D
NA	clear	46	Main	Random	D
NA	clear	5	Main	Nonrandom	E
NA	clear	10	Main	Random	E
NA	clear	7	Main	Random	F
NA	clear	6	Main	Random	H

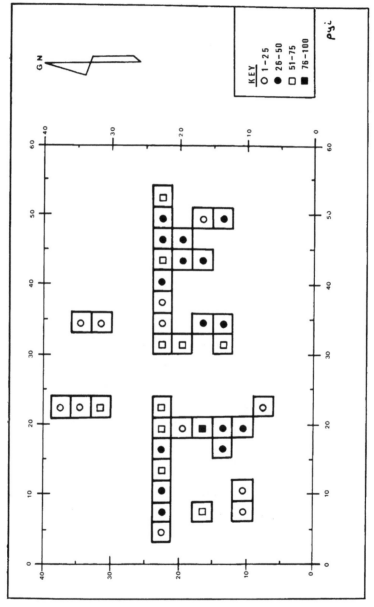

Figure 8.   Distribution of Bottle Fragments within the West Dump.

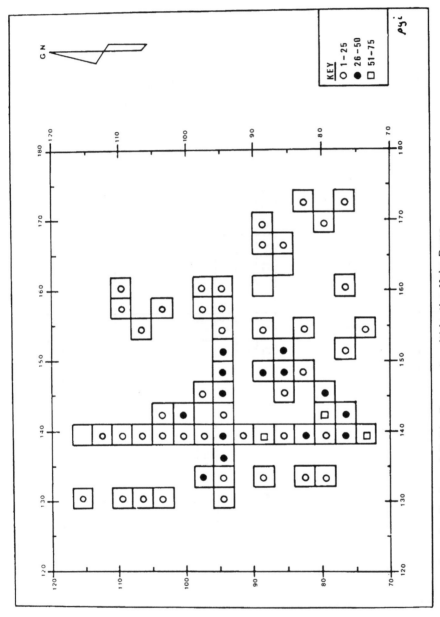

Figure 9. Distribution of Bottle Fragments within the Main Dump.

The significance of the two bottle seal fragments is somewhat problematic. Both are identical to examples of shoulder seal fragments found earlier by Moore (1973:63-65). The Medoc is one of the regions of the departement Gironde (figure 10) in France (Campbell 1972:25, 28). Brodeaux is the capital of this departement. The major product of the Medoc is a red wine usually referred to as a claret. In 1855, the courtiers or wine brokers of Bordeaux classified all the wines of the Medoc according to five divisions of prominent wines and to an unlisted category of other wines (Campbell 1972:25, 28, 31). Pauillac and St. Julien are communes within the Haut-Medoc section of the Medoc, which contain a large number of the classified vineyards.

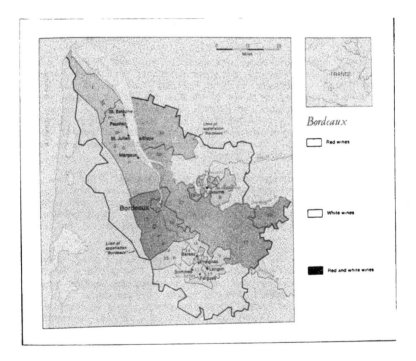

Figure 10. Map of the Gironde Departement, France.

The following comments about the qualities of the wines grown in the Medoc have been made:

[the] wines [which come from St. Julien are] of uniformly outstanding quality

[Waugh 1968:95]

. . . even a fifth-growth Medoc is far from a poor wine, on the contrary, it is something special, for out of the hundreds of Chateaus that were rated in 1855, only 62 were deemed worthy of classification.

[Waugh 1968:97]

The commune [township] of Pauillac contains the largest number of classed growths, being followed by St. Julien, then Margaux and Cantenac (often bracketed together) and St. Estephe.

[Campbell 1972:34]

Unfortunately, such references are made to the Medoc only in a general sense and may not refer to all wine products from that region. P. Guillaume (cited in Schulz et al. 1980:98) has written that, "it is customary since time out of mind to ship to the United States, under the generic name of Margaux or Saint Julien, ordinary cargo wine." Moreover, the "ST. JULIEN/MEDOC" seal was the most common one recovered from the archeological excavations of Old Sacramento, California (Schulz et al. 1980:97). The two sets of statements create some difficulty in evaluating the socioeconomic significance of the seals.

General functional categories may be inferred from the various combinations of fragment attributes, i.e., color, section form, etc. Three functional categories may be discerned. These categories are wine bottles (olive green glass, push-ups, and laid on rings), spirit bottles (brown glass with lipping tool applied lip), and patent medicine bottles (embossed paneled clear glass).

The interior fort bottle collection and the exterior fort trash dump collection are somewhat difficult to compare. The artifacts reported by Moore (1973:63-66) are complete or nearly complete bottles while those recovered from the dumps are extremely fragmentary. All of the identifiable categories of bottles from the dumps were represented in the interior fort collection; additional styles of bottles, however, were apparently located in the earlier excavations.

Description--Stoneware Bottles

The stoneware bottle collecton (figure 11) can be divided into two general groupings according to body. The first grouping consists of a number of relatively thin-walled sherds made of a stoneware clay that has been fired to vitrification. The body has been fired to three varieties of appearance. The body varies from a completely gray to a gray exterior layer and light olive green interior to a light olive green center enclosed by gray interior and exterior surface layers. Most of the sherds are completely unglazed on the interior. The exterior has been treated with

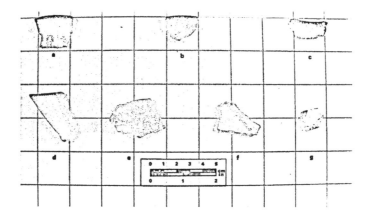

Figure 11.   Stoneware Bottle Sherds.

a brown oxide wash.   On sections of the mouth and neck, this wash has
been introduced onto the interior neck surface.   The majority of the
sherds have wall thicknesses that vary within the 0.38 cm to 0.45 cm
range.   The estimated interior diameter is 7.2 cm.

The finish fragments are all relatively similar.   The mouth has a flat
surface that is about 0.6 cm wide.   The lip extends about 1.4 cm along
the neck.   Variations in body and surface features are sufficient to
suggest that at least three distinct vessels are represented by the four
finish sherds.

The second grouping consists of a single, grayish-white stoneware sherd.
The body has been fired to vitrification.   Neither interior nor exterior
surfaces have been glazed.   The wall thickness is 0.69 cm.

Distribution--Stoneware Bottles

The distributional aspects of the stoneware bottle collection are listed in
table 4.   the spatial distribution for combined strata are depicted in
figure 16 for the West Dump and in figure 17 for the Main Dump.

Comments--Stoneware Bottles

The fragmentary nature of the stoneware bottle evidence precludes a
detailed interpretation of their functional and social significance.   The

size and form of the various sherds would suggest a medium-sized, cylindrical vessel, perhaps of the variety commonly employed for the sale of beer and ale during the 19th century.

Table 4. Distribution of Stoneware Bottle Sherds
by Dump, Unit Type, and Stratum

Grouping	Section	Wall Thickness (cm)	Frequency	Dump	Unit Type	Stratum
1	Finish	0.42	-	West	Nonrandom	B
1	Finish	NA	1	Main	Nonrandom	B
1	Finish	NA	1	Main	Random	B
1	Finish	NA	1	Main	Nonrandom	C
1	Neck	0.42-0.46	5	West	Nonrandom	B
1	Body	0.44-0.58	2	West	Nonrandom	A
1	Body	0.41-0.43	3	West	Random	A
1	Body	0.39-0.62	14	West	Nonrandom	B
1	Body	0.38-0.98	4	West	Random	B
1	Body	0.50	1	Main	Random	B
2	Body	0.69		Main	Random	B

GLASSWARE

Description

Ten fragments of glass were attributable to items other than bottles. All were made of clear glass. Portions of two pressed glass circular pedestal bases were found (figure 12 a, and unillustrated). Both sets of fragments were relatively thick and suggest kerosene lamp bases. Fragments of two pressed glass, square-sided containers were observed. The first (figure 12 b) had a section of a sunburst-type design in relief. The second (figure 12 c) had a vertically ribbed pattern. A single everted, container rim was noted (figure 12 d). The rim had been fire polished. A portion of a molded footrim (figure 12 e) was noted. In addition, three nondescript, molded fragments were recovered.

Distribution

The distribution of the general categories of glassware items is listed in table 5 according to dump, unit type, and stratum.

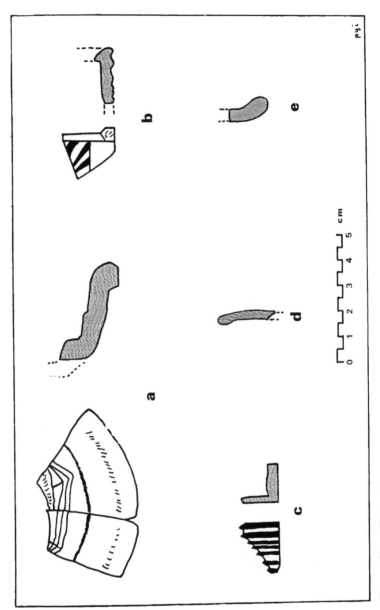

Figure 12. Glassware.

211

Table 5. Distribution of Glassware Fragments
by Dump, Unit Type, and Stratum

Descriptive Category	Frequency	Dump	Unit Type	Stratum
Pressed glass pedestal base	1	West	Nonrandom	A*
Pressed glass pedestal base	2	West	Nonrandom	B*
Pressed glass pedestal base	1	Main	Nonrandom	H
Pressed glass container	1	Main	Nonrandom	C
Pressed glass container	1	Main	Random	D
Container rim	1	West	Random	B
Molded footrim	1	Main	Nonrandom	C
Miscellaneous	1	West	Nonrandom	A
Miscellaneous	1	Main	Random	B
Miscellaneous	1	Main	Random	D

*The fragments from strata A and B mend together.

Comments

The fragmentary nature of the glassware collection prevents a detailed
interpretation of their significance Some brief comments, however, can be
made. A pressed glass machine was patented in 1827 (Lorrain 1968:43).
The period of pressed glass' greatest popularity was 1850-1900 (Kovel and
Kovel 1972:75). Comparisons with the interior fort collection cannot be
made since this class of artifacts has not been described for that
assemblage (Moore 1973).

STORAGE AND UTILITY VESSELS

Description

The sherds that belong to the Storage and Utility Vessels category can be
divided into two general groups. The first group consists of those
sherds with earthenware bodies. The second group consists of those
sherds with stoneware bodies.

The earthenware group is represented by three styles. All have bodies
that are considerably harder than most earthenwares. However, the
bodies retain a great degree of porosity. The Style One (figure 13 a)
sherd has a common clay body that has fired to an orange to red color.

212

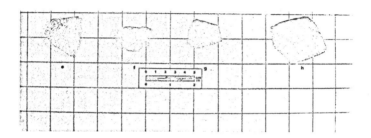

Figure 13.   Storage and Utility Vessel Fragments.

The interior has been smoothed by scraping and is unglazed.   Wall
thickness of the sherds are 0.6 cm and 0.73 cm.   The exteriors have
been lightly slipped with a gray clay that has been saltglazed.

The Style Two sherd (figure 13 b) has a common clay body that has fired
to an orange to red color.   The interior has been smoothed by scraping
and is unglazed.   One sherd exhibits interior, circumferential ribbing.
Wall thicknesses vary between 0.51 cm and 0.69 cm.   The exterior surface
has been lightly slipped with a gray clay and fired at a low heat.   The
estimated   interior   vessel   diameter,   calculated   trigonometrically,   is
20.9 cm.

The Style Three sherd (figure 13 c) has a common clay body that has
been fired to an orange to red color.   The interior has been smoothed by
scraping and is lightly coated with a clear glaze.   The wall thickness
varies between 0.73 cm and 0.94 cm.   The exterior surface has been
lightly glazed with a clear coat.   The estimated interior vessel diameter is
13.7 cm.

The stoneware group is represented by 12 styles.   Most of the bodies are
not a true stoneware but are mixtures of fine, stoneware-type gray clays
with other coarser clays.   Style Four (figure 13 d) consists of a mixed
gray   and   common   red   clay   that   has   been   fired   to   a   point   below
vitrification.   The   interior   has   been   smoothed   by   scraping   and   is
unglazed.   The interior appears a dull gray to red in color.   The wall
thickness   varies   between   0.6   cm   to   0.72   cm.   The exterior has been

213

saltglazed. The exterior glaze has worn off in spots. Three of the sherds represent mouth and lip fragments; an open crock-type vessel is suggested. The rim consists of a flat mouth that curves inward toward the body on the exterior surface (figure 15 a). The estimated interior diameter is 13.6 cm.

Style Five (figure 13 e) is a mixed clay body that has fired below vitrification. The body varies between gray and buff in color. The interior has a reddish-brown glaze. Interior circumferential ribbing is evident. The wall thickness varies between 0.50 cm and 0.65 cm. The exterior is saltglazed. The spherical curvature of some of the sherds and the interior glazing suggest a jug-type vessel. The estimated interior diameter is 15.9 cm.

The Style Six sherd (figure 13 f) is a gray clay body with pockets of a buff-colored clay. The body has been fired below vitrification. The interior has been glazed with a brown coat. Circumferential ribbing and scoring are evident. The wall thickness varies between 0.75 cm and 0.80 cm. The exterior surface has a light, clear glaze.

The Style Seven sherd (figure 13 g) is a gray body that has been fired below vitrification. The interior has been clear glazed. Interior circumferential scoring is evident. Wall thickness varies between 0.67 cm and 0.97 cm. The exterior surface has an orange-peel texture and mixed yellowish-green and gray appearance. The exact surface glaze is unknown.

The Style Eight sherd (figure 13 h) is a gray body that has been fired below vitrification. The interior surface has a red oxide wash. Interior circumferential scoring is evident. The wall thickness is about 0.8 cm. The exterior surface has an appearance similar to that of Style Nine. One of the sherds is a basal fragment (figure 15 b). The base is flat and the adjoining body section projects upward and outward.

The Style Nine sherd (figure 14 a) is a mixed body of gray and common red clays. The body has been fired to a point below vitrification. The interior is a red, unglazed surface. Circumferential ribbing and scoring are evident. The wall thickness varies between 0.6 cm and 0.96 cm. The surface is gray in color. The surface has a clear, saltglaze. The glaze has worn through in numerous areas. The spherical curvature of some of the sherds suggests a jug-type vessel. The estimated vessel interior diameter is 14.4 cm.

The Style Ten sherd (figure 14 b) consists of a mixture of buff and gray clays that have been fired to a point below vitrification. The interior surface has been coated with a reddish-brown glaze. Circumferential ribbing and scoring are evident. The body cross section suggests that the body had been constructed by applying a gray clay surface onto a buff clay backing. The wall thickness varies between 0.62 cm and 0.87 cm. The buff section remains noticeably porous. The gray clay surface lining varies in thickness between 0.28 cm and 0.36 cm. The surface has a clear, possibly alkaline glaze. One of the sherds is a rim fragment, smaller although similar in form to that sown in figure 13 a.

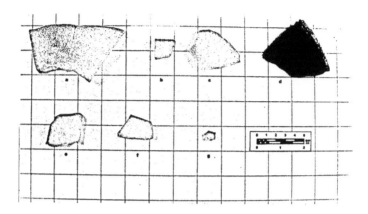

Figure 14. Storage and Utility Vessel Fragments.

The Style Eleven sherd (figure 14 c) consists of a mixed gray clay. The body is nearly vitrious. The interior surface has been covered with a brown oxide wash. Interior ribbing and scoring are present. The exterior has a clear, saltglaze coat. One of the fragments includes a portion of the base. The wall thickness varies between 0.87 cm and 0.91 cm. The form is similar to that shown in figure 15 b.

The Style Twelve sherd (figure 14 d) consists of a gray clay that has been fired to a point below vitrification. The interior surface has a brown to reddish-brown oxide coat. Interior circumferential scoring is evident. The wall thickness varies between 0.64 cm and 0.86 cm. The exterior surface has an orange-peel texture. The appearance of the glaze is a mixture of gray and yellowish-green. The type of glaze is unknown. One of the sherds is a basal fragment. The base is flat and the body extends outward at an obtuse angle (figure 15 c).

The Style Thirteen (figure 14 e) sherd consists of a mixed gray clay body which has been fired below vitrification. The interior surface varies between a gray-red to brick-red in color. The surface is unglazed and exhibits circumferential scoring. The wall thickness varies between 0.56 cm and 0.80 cm. The exterior surface has a light, clear, saltglaze coat. The estimated interior diameter is 15.1 cm.

The Style Fourteen sherd (figure 14 f) consists of a mixed gray clay which has been fired to a point below vitrification. The interior surface is unglazed and exhibits an oxidized, red surface. The wall thickness is

215

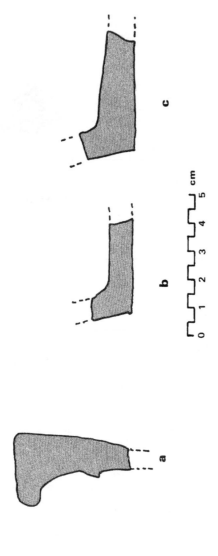

Figure 15. Miscellaneous Cross Sections of Storage and Utility Vessel Rim and Basal Fragments.

0.48 cm. The surface has a varied, glazed appearance. The surface is an irregular combination of brown, brownish-gray, and yellowish-green. The glaze variety is unknown. The sperical curvature of the sherd suggests a jug-type vessel.

The Style Fifteen sherd (figure 14 g) consists of a mixed gray clay which has been fired below vitrification. The interior surface is unglazed and exhibits an oxidized, brick-red color. The wall thickness is 0.44 cm. The exterior surface has a brown glaze.

Distribution

The distribution of storage and utility vessel fragments is listed in table 6 by dump, unit type, and stratum. The spatial distribution of the combined strata is depicted in figure 16 for the West Dump and in figure 17 for the Main Dump.

Comments

Stoneware vessels were commonly employed during the nineteenth century for the storage of a variety of liquid and solid goods. The presence of remnants of both crocks and jugs is suggested by the form of selected sherds. The estimated internal diameters of the vessels fall within the medium-to-small range of those normally encountered on nineteenth century sites.

The presence of mixed clay stoneware bodies suggests a source of manufacture away from the primary domestic and foreign sources of stoneware clays (Webster 1971). A southern states or Ohio source is likely.

Since storage and utility vessels are not reported by Moore (1973), no comparison with such items from the interior fort is possible.

TABLEWARE

Description (Introduction)

The ceramic fragments which comprise the tableware category can be described according to several criteria. These criteria are ware type, surface treatment, section, and dimensional attributes. For the purposes of this discussion, the various ware types represented in the tableware collection have been assigned to one of six groups. These groups are pearlware, common white, graniteware, yellowware, porcelain, and other. Pearlware is a ceramic entity which was created in 1779 by Wedgwood (Noel Hume 1973:232). The two components which comprise pearlware are a distinct glaze and body combination:

> The new glaze involved the use of a small quantity of cobalt to negate the inherent yellowness of the clear lead glaze, a difference most easily seen where the glaze piles up in crevices

217

Table 6. Distribution of Storage and Utility Vessel Sherds
by Dump, Unit Type, and Stratum

Style	Ware Type	Wall Thickness (cm)	Frequency	Dump	Unit Type	Stratum
Style 1	earthenware	0.60	1	West	Random	C
Style 1	earthenware	0.73	1	Main	Nonrandom	C
Style 2	earthenware	0.51-0.69	3	Main	Nonrandom	C
Style 2	earthenware	0.56-0.69	3	Main	Random	C
Style 2	earthenware	0.55	1	Main	Random	D
Style 3	earthenware	0.94	1	Main	Nonrandom	B
Style 3	earthenware	0.73	1	Main	Nonrandom	C
Style 3	earthenware	0.94	1	Main	Nonrandom	E
Style 4	stoneware	0.71	1	Main	Random	B
Style 4	stoneware	0.60-0.62	2	Main	Nonrandom	C
Style 4	stoneware	0.62-0.72	5	Main	Random	C
Style 4	stoneware	NA	1	Main	Random	E
Style 5	stoneware	0.54	1	West	Nonrandom	A
Style 5	stoneware	0.55-0.65	3	West	Random	A
Style 5	stoneware	0.56	1	West	Nonrandom	C
Style 5	stoneware	0.50-0.57	5	West	Random	C
Style 6	stoneware	0.75-0.80	2	Main	Random	B
Style 7	stoneware	0.67-0.97	4	Main	Random	B
Style 8	stoneware	0.81	1	Main	Random	A
Style 8	stoneware	0.08	1	Main	Nonrandom	B
Style 9	stoneware	0.60	1	Main	Random	B
Style 9	stoneware	0.62-0.68	3	Main	Nonrandom	C
Style 9	stoneware	0.79-0.96	3	Main	Random	C
Style 9	stoneware	0.67-0.77	5	Main	Random	D
Style 10	stoneware	0.87	1	Main	Nonrandom	B
Style 10	stoneware	0.73	1	Main	Nonrandom	C
Style 10	stoneware	0.62	1	Main	Random	C
Style 11	stoneware	0.87-0.91	2	Main	Random	3I
Style 12	stoneware	0.68	1	Main	Nonrandom	B
Style 12	stoneware	0.64	1	Main	Random	B
Style 12	stoneware	0.86	1	Main	Nonrandom	C
Style 13	stoneware	0.75-0.80	4	Main	Random	A
Style 13	stoneware	0.62-0.67	2	Main	Nonrandom	B
Style 13	stoneware	0.56-0.67	5	Main	Random	B
Style 14	stoneware	0.48	1	Main	Nonrandom	E
Style 15	stoneware	0.44	1	Main	Random	A

218

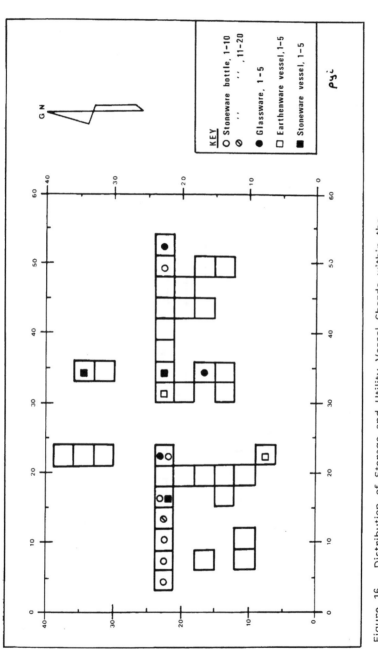

Figure 16. Distribution of Storage and Utility Vessel Sherds within the West Dump.

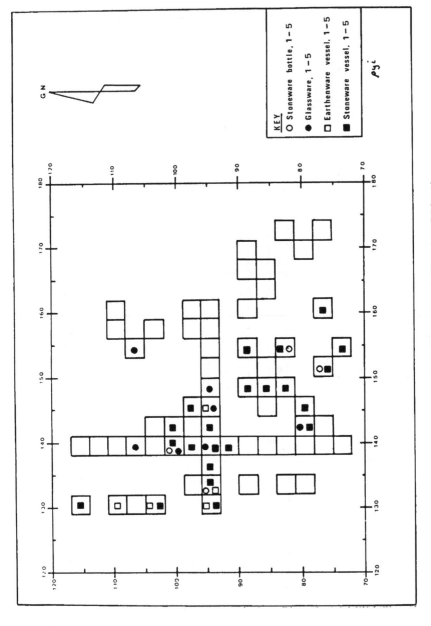

Figure 17. Distribution of Storage and Utility Vessel Sherds within the Main Dump.

under rims, handles, and within foot rings. But it was not only a whitening of the glaze that made the difference, for the body had been lightened too . . .

[Noel Hume 1973:233]

In practice, some difficulty has been encountered in distinguishing nondiagnostic sections of vessels as pearlware:

. . . pearlware can only be identified as such when a substantial area of the vessel, be it in the interior or the underside of the base, exhibits the unadorned body and glaze combination. Indeed, in the absence of the glaze, the pearlware body is visually indistinguishable from that of late creamware.

[Noel Hume 1973:242]

By convention, in this study, only those sherds which exhibit the characteristic bluing or can be related physically or stylistically to such diagnostic sherds have been classified as pearlware.

The term "common white" has been used to encompass all those white earthenware bodies which are not within the range of late creamware, pearlware, and the harder earthenwares. This group has often appeared in the literature as "whiteware." In this study, the former term has been employed. "Whiteware" has also been frequently employed by several sources in a general sense to include all earthenwares with a white appearance.

The term "graniteware" has been used in a broad sense to include a variety of ceramic wares which are physically difficult to distinguish. These wares include graniteware (in the restricted sense), stone china, hotel china, ironstone, porcelaine ^{o}paque, etc. These are essentially wares which, on the basis of marked sherds, appear to vary from a hard earthenware to a stoneware-like body.

The term "yellowware" designates a series of buff or yellowish-tan bodied ceramics. "Porcelain" refers to a series of white-bodied, translucent ceramics. The "other" group encompasses those unique body compositions which cannot be readily assigned to the more common groupings.

Surface treatment refers to the manner in which the fired body has been finished or decorated. Section refers to the portion of a vessel represented by a given sherd. Vessel parts include footrim, base, body, handle, and rim. The dimensional attributes include any measureable aspects of the sherds which may be of use in reconstructing a picture of the original vessel. Such attributes include estimated basal diameter, estimated rim diameter, wall thickness, and other measurements.

Description (Series One)

In describing the various sherds, individual styles of sherds have been grouped into general series of similar styles. Within each style designation, substyles with minor, primarily color, differences have been

221

noted. Series One encompasses decorated sherds which fall within the general category of annular. Three styles are noted.

Style One has grooved bands made by the engine turning process which occur just below the rim on the exterior surface. The interior surface is undecorated. The main portion of the exterior surface below the banded zone consists of a background color upon which have been applied swirled multicolor designs commonly known as "earthworm." Substyle "a" has a plain banded zone. The wall thickness is approximately 0.25 cm. The cross section is depicted in figure 19.

Substyle "b" (figure 18 a) has a light blue banded zone with engine turned grooves. The background of the main decorated zone is light gray. Only a fragmentary dark brown section of the earthworm is visible on the substyle sherd. The wall thickness is about 0.35 cm. The cross section is similar to that of substyle "a".

Substyle "c" (figure 18 e & f) has a light lime green banded zone with engine turned grooves. The main decorated region has a grey-blue background with an earthworm of white, dark brown, and light blue. The wall thickness is about 0.32 cm. The cross section is similar to that of substyle "a".

Substyle "d" (figure 18 h) has an undecorated banded zone with engine turned grooves. The main decorated zone is separated from this banded area by two bands. One band is a brown slip; the other, an undecorated section of the body. The main decorated zone has a background of gray with an earthworm composed of light blue, white, and dark brown. The wall thickness is about 0.32 cm. The cross section is similar to that of substyle "a".

Style Two (figure 18 b) has a dark green banded zone next to the rim. Engine turned grooves are presented. The rim is slightly everted. The background of the main body is mustard-colored. The wall thickness is about 0.26 cm. The cross section is illustrated in figure 19.

Style Three is represented by sherds with no remnant rim sections. There are three substyles. The background of the main body of sub-style "a" is a dark brown. The earthworm is implemented in white, brown, dark brown, and light blue. A brown and a partial white bands separate the main decoration from the undecorated lower portion of the vessel. The wall thickness varies between 0.36 cm and 0.53 cm. The cross section of a representative sherd is illustrated in figure 19. This piece has a footrim diameter of approximately 7.31 cm.

Substyle "b" (figure 18 c) has a mustard colored background and an earthworm painted in light blue, dark brown, and white. The wall thickness is about 0.35 cm. The cross section is similar to that of substyle "a". Substyle "c" (figure 18 d) has a grayish-tan background with an earthworm implemented in dark brown and white. The wall thickness is about 0.35 cm. The cross section is similar to that of substyle "a".

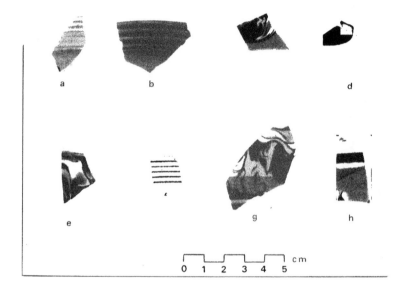

Figure 18.   Series One Annular Decorated Wares.

Style Four (figures 18 g) has a marbleized decoration in swirls of light blue, white, brown, and dark brown. A portion of the decoration is banded over with a translucent blue which is accompanied by bands of white and brown. The wall thickness is 0.40 cm.

Distribution (Series One)

The distributional characteristics of Series One are listed in table 7. The spatial distribution of the sherds is depicted in figure 20 for the West Dump and in figure 21 for the Main Dump.

Comments (Series One)

Annular wares have been considered to have been most popular during the period between 1795 and 1815 (Noel Hume 1969:131). The shape of the various sherds suggest a series of hollow vessel forms of the cup and bowl variety. Only two sherds of an annular variety are noted in Moore's report (1973:74).

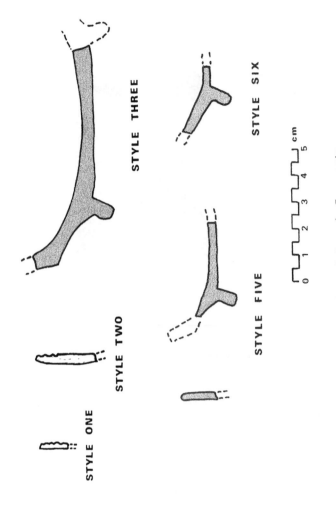

Figure 19. Miscellaneous Cross Sections of Ceramic Fragments.

224

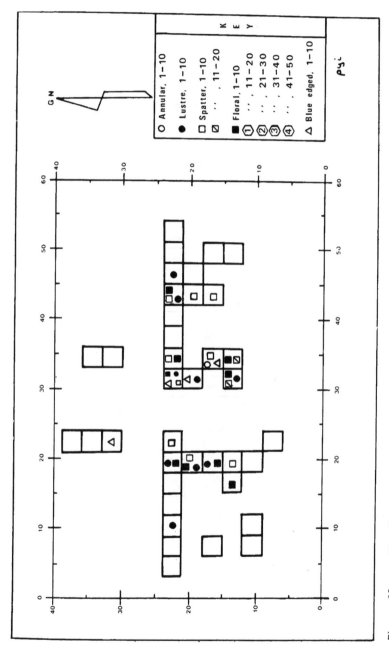

Figure 20.   Distribution of Series One to Five Tableware Styles Within the West Dump.

225

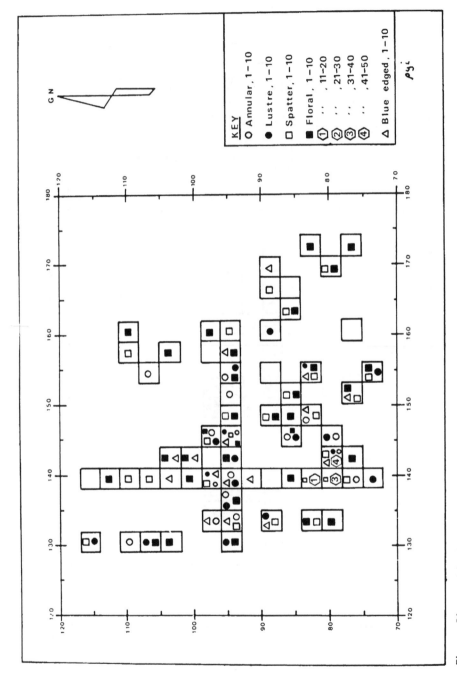

Figure 21.   Distribution of Series One to Five Tableware Styles Within the Main Dump.

Table 7. Distribution of Style Series One, Annular Decorated Pearlware-Bodied, Sherds by Dump, Unit Type, and Stratum

Style	Sub-Style	Section			Frequency	Vessel Form	Dump	Unit Type	Stratum
		Rim	Body	Base					
1	a	X			1	Hollow	Main	Nonrandom	B
1	b	X	X		1	Hollow	Main	Random	B
1	c		X		1	Hollow	Main	Random	C
1	c		X		3	Hollow	Main	Random	D
1	c	X			1	Hollow	Main	Nonrandom	E
1	d	X	X		2	Hollow	Main	Random	C
2		X	X		1	Hollow	Main	Nonrandom	C
3	a		X		2	Hollow	West	Random	A
3	a		X		3	Hollow	Main	Nonrandom	B
3	a		X		7	Hollow	Main	Random	B
3	a		X		1	Hollow	Main	Nonrandom	C
3	a		X		1	Hollow	Main	Random	C
3	a		X	X	4	Hollow	Main	Random	D
3	b		X		1	Hollow	Main	Nonrandom	C
3	c		X		1	Hollow	Main	Random	D
4			X		2	Hollow	Main	Random	D

Description (Series Two)

Series Two consists of those pearlware-bodied sherds that have been decorated with purple lustre. One style has been recognized within this series. Style Five consists of a thin, flat rim with an interior lustre band just below the top of the rim (figure 22). The band varies in width between 0.11 cm and 0.32 cm depending upon the sherd. Some of the interior surfaces also have a thin, 0.02 cm, lustre band lower into the vessel. The exterior surfaces are decorated with stylized swirls and floral designs. One of the sherds has a remnant flower reminiscent of an Adam's Rose. The wall thickness is about 0.25 cm to 0.30 cm. One of the basal sherds has an estimated footrim diameter of 4.4 cm. Cross sections of both the rim and basal sections are depicted in figure 19.

Distribution (Series Two)

The distributional characteristics of Series Two are listed in table 8. The spatial distribution of Series Two is depicted in figure 20 for the West Dump and in figure 21 for the Main Dump.

Comments (Series Two)

Purple lustre is a combination of purple of cassius (gold chloride and tin chloride) suspended in an oily fluid of sulphur and venetian turpentine suspended in ordinary turpentine. Lustre decoration was introduced into England during the early 1800s (Hughes and Hughes 1968:104) as a decorate technique (Godden 1965:24; Wills 1969:175). English lustre was popular during the early decades of the 19th century. Hollow vessel forms are suggested by the shape of the sherds. The most likely forms are cup-sized vessels. The lustre sherds reported by Moore (1973:69) apparently had motifs different from those noted on the dumps' sherds. His sherds depicted scenes with houses, trees, fences, shrubs, and a brook.

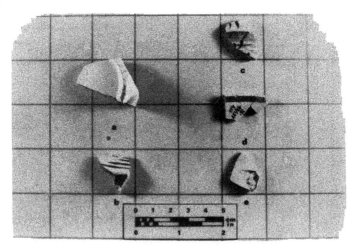

Figure 22. Series Two Purple Lustre Decorated Wares.

Table 8. Distribution of Style Series Two, Purple Lustre Decorated Pearlware-Bodied, Sherds by Dump, Unit Type, and Stratum

Style	Section Rim	Body	Base	Frequency	Vessel Form	Dump	Unit Type	Stratum
5	X			1	Hollow	West	Random	C
5	X			3	Hollow	Main	Nonrandom	B
5	X			6	Hollow	Main	Random	B
5	X			1	Hollow	Main	Random	D
5			X	1	Hollow	West	Random	A
5			X	2	Hollow	West	Random	C
5		X		1	Hollow	West	Nonrandom	A
5		X		1	Hollow	West	Nonrandom	B
5		X		3	Hollow	West	Nonrandom	C
5		X		2	Hollow	West	Random	C
5		X		1	Hollow	Main	Random	A
5		X		9	Hollow	Main	Nonrandom	B
5		X		7	Hollow	Main	Random	B
5		X		3	Hollow	Main	Nonrandom	C
5		X		2	Hollow	Main	Random	C
5		X		1	Hollow	Main	Random	D

229

Description (Series Three)

Series Three (figure 23) consists of pearlware-bodied sherds with a decorative pattern commonly referred to as spatter. Three styles are represented by the sherds within this series. The dominant style, Style Six, consists of a relatively flat rim similar to the lustre decorated rim in figure 19. On the interior surface below the rim, there is a single band, which varies between a lightly applied pinkish-red and a deep red on the various sherds. The band varies between 0.10 cm and 0.28 cm in width. The interior surfaces are undecorated except for this band and an area of green spatter within the base. The exterior surfaces have alternating vertical bands of green and red spatter that extend from the rim to a point above the base. This is a typical "rainbow" pattern. The thickness varies from 0.25 cm to 0.33 cm. A basal cross section is illustrated in figure 19. The estimated footrim diameter is 5.5 cm. The estimated interior diameter of the vessel based on one sherd is approximately 10.9 cm. A second basal section has an estimated footrim diameter of 8.0 cm.

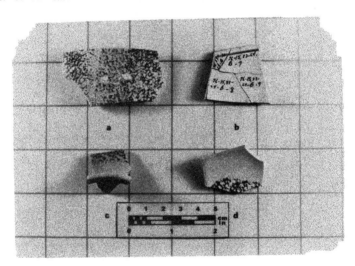

Figure 23. Series Three Spatter Decorated Pearlware Sherds.

Style Seven is represented by a single sherd. The rim is similar in configuration to the purple lustre rim in figure 19. Both the interior and exterior surfaces are covered with red spatter. The complete vessel probably consists of at least one other color. The wall thickness is about 0.26 cm.

Style Eight is represented by two sherds. These sherds have a red and green spatter decorated body with the spatter bands arranged horizontally. The wall thickness varies from 0.25 cm to 0.33 cm.

The distributional aspects of Series Three sherds are listed in table 9. The spatial distribution for combined strata is illustrated in figure 20 for the West Dump and in figure 21 for the Main Dump.

Table 9. Distribution of Style Series Three, Spatter Decorated Pearlware-Bodied, Sherds by Dump, Unit Type, and Stratum

Style	Section			Frequency	Vessel Form	Dump	Unit Type	Stratum
	Rim	Body	Base					
6	X			4	Hollow	West	Nonrandom	A
6	X			11	Hollow	West	Random	A
6	X			5	Hollow	West	Random	C
6	X			1	Hollow	West	Nonrandom	D
6	X			2	Hollow	Main	Nonrandom	B
6	X			2	Hollow	Main	Random	B
6	X			3	Hollow	Main	Nonrandom	C
6	X			4	Hollow	Main	Random	C
6	X			3	Hollow	Main	Nonrandom	D
6	X			2	Hollow	Main	Random	D
-				1	Hollow	West	Random	A
-			X	2	Hollow	Main	Random	C
6		X		1	Hollow	West	Random	OB
6		X		7	Hollow	West	Nonrandom	A
6		X		4	Hollow	West	Random	A
6		X		1	Hollow	West	Nonrandom	C
6		X		4	Hollow	West	Random	C
6		X		3	Hollow	West	Nonrandom	D
6		X		2	Hollow	West	Nonrandom	D
6		X		1	Hollow	Main	Random	A
6		X		1	Hollow	Main	Nonrandom	B
6		X		7	Hollow	Main	Random	B
6		X		6	Hollow	Main	Nonrandom	C
6		X		9	Hollow	Main	Random	C
6		X		2	Hollow	Main	Random	D
				1	Hollow	Main	Nonrandom	C
				1	Hollow	West	Nonrandom	C
				1	Hollow	Main	Nonrandom	C

231

Comments (Series Three)

Although spatterware was made in the United States, it was primarily a European and, especially, English export ware (Robacker and Robacker 1978:145-150). It was an important component of the ceramics market between 1820 and 1850; its peak period of popularity was between 1830 and 1840 (Robacker and Robacker 1978:32). The rarest colors utilized in spatterware were yellow, green, and purple. Pink and brown were common. Blue was the most popular (Robacker and Robacker 1978:37). Generally thought to have been confined to parts of the Northeast and Middle Atlantic, spatterware has been previously found as far west as Ohio in limited quanitites (Robacker and Robacker 1978:32). Spatterware similar to those from the dumps were recovered by Moore (1973:73).

Description (Series Four)

Series Four consists of those sherds that have been decorated with hand-painted motifs. This series is represented by four styles and a number of unassignable rim and body fragments. The motifs have been applied to a pearlware-type body.

Style Nine (figure 24 a) has a red band applied on the interior surface below the rim. This band is about 0.27 cm wide. The exterior surface is undecorated. The interior surface has a floral design implemented with green leaves and blue buds on a black stem. The design is vertically oriented. The wall thickness varies between 0.34 cm and 0.38 cm. The rim has a plain cross section similar to that of the purple lustre rim in figure 19. The sherds suggest a bowl-shaped vessel. An estimated interior of 16.1 cm can be calculated.

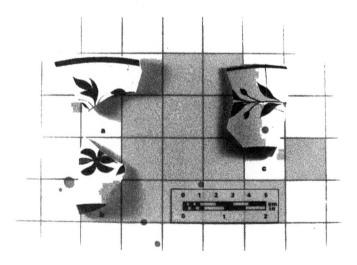

Figure 24.   Hand Painted Polychrome Floral Motifs.

Style Ten (figure 24 b & c) has a single black band below the rim on both the interior and exterior surfaces. These bands are approximately 0.13 cm wide. The interior surface is undecorated. The exterior surface has a medial, circumferential floral decoration implemented with green leaves, blue buds, red buds and flowers, and a black stem. The wall thickness varies between 0.29 cm and 0.33 cm. The rim is similar to that of the purple lustre rim in figure 19. A bowl-shaped vessel is suggested by the curvature of the sherds. An interior diameter of 9.2 cm is estimated.

Style Eleven (figure 25) has a single black band on both the interior and exterior surfaces below the rim. These bands are about 0.20 cm wide. The interior surface is undecorated. The exterior surface has a floral design implemented with green leaves, blue buds, red Adam's rose, and black stem. The design is vertically oriented. The wall thickness varies from 0.24 cm to 0.33 cm. The rim cross section is similar to that of the other rims within this series. The shape of the sherds suggests a bowl-like vessel with an estimated interior diameter of 9.3 cm. The estimated footrim diameter is 5.8 cm.

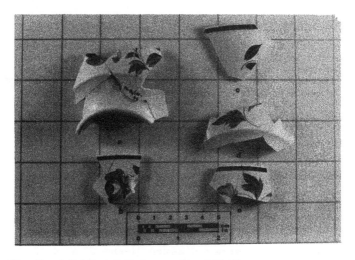

Figure 25. Hand Painted Polychrome Floral Motifs.

Style Twelve has a single black band on the interior surface below the rim. The band is about 0.19 cm wide. The exterior surface is undecorated. The interior surface has a circumferential floral design implemented with green leaves, red flowers, blue flowers, and a black stem. The treatment is similar to that of Style Ten. The wall thickness varies from 0.34 cm to 0.36 cm. The rim cross section is similar to that of others within Series Four. The sherds suggest a bowl-shaped vessel. The estimated interior diameter is 11.2 cm.

In addition, there were a number of other sherds that were too fragmentary to identify. This group of sherds could be divided into four categories. The first cateogry consisted of rim fragments with a thickness between 0.25 cm and 0.38 cm and a single black band below the rim on the interior surface. The band was about 0.20 cm wide. The second category consisted of rim fragments with a thickness between 0.25 cm and 0.33 cm. The rims had a single black band below the rim on both the interior and exterior surfaces. The width of the rim band was about 0.19 cm. The third category consisted of rims with a single red band below the rim on both the interior and exterior surfaces. The width of the band was about 0.19 cm. The wall thickness varied from 0.26 to 0.28. The last category consisted of miscellaneous decorated body sherds.

Distribution (Series Four)

The distributional characteristics of the Series Four sherds are listed in table 10. The spatial distribution is illustrated in figure 20 for the West Dump and in figure 21 for the Main Dump.

Comments (Series Four)

Very little has been written in the literature about hand-painted vessels such as those represented within Series Four. The Adam's red rose motif has been found in association with spatter and cut sponge decorated wares (Robacker and Robacker 1978:33). Its period of popularity probably encompassed the first half of the 19th century although documents to support this have not been reported. The bowl form that occurs is characteristic of vessels that have been recovered from early contexts at other sites. Similar wares were recovered by Moore (1973:68, 73).

Description (Series Five)

Series Five consists of blue edge decorated rim fragments. A border motif either molded in relief or impressed occupies the interior edge of the rim. A wide dark blue band has been applied on the rim and across the molded design. Series Five is represented by three styles.

Style Thirteen has an impressed design (figure 26 a, c, & d) on the interior border of the rim. There are three sub-styles. All of the sub-styles have impressed dots along the edge, which link with impressed, curved lines that extend inward toward the center of the vessel. All have some form of "wheat sheaf" that occurs at regular intervals along the border. Sub-style "a" (figure 26 a) has a scalloped rim. The short grooved lines occasionally terminate in circular impressions. The "wheat sheaf" is an elaborate expanded element. The blue banding does not extend to the end of all of the impressed lines. The lines curve slightly with the concave side facing right. The rim is slightly rounded and the sherd is flat. The wall thickness is 0.84 cm. The flatness of the sherd and its thickness suggest a flat, heavy vessel such as a serving platter.

Table 10. Distribution of Series Four, Hand Painted Floral Motifs on Pearlware-Bodied, Sherds by Dump, Unit Type, and Stratum

Style	Rim	Body	Base	Frequency	Vessel Form	Dump	Unit Type	Stratum
9	X	X		1	Hollow	Main	Random	B
9	X	X		1	Hollow	Main	Random	C
9	X			1	Hollow	Main	Random	D
9	X	X		1	Hollow	West	Nonrandom	C
9	X	X		4	Hollow	West	Random	E
10	X	X		1	Hollow	Main	Nonrandom	B
10	X	X		1	Hollow	Main	Nonrandom	C
10	X	X		1	Hollow	Main	Random	C
10	X	X		1	Hollow	West	Nonrandom	A
10	X	X		1	Hollow	West	Nonrandom	C
11	X	X		5	Hollow	Main	Nonrandom	C
11	X	X		2	Hollow	Main	Random	C
11	X	X		6	Hollow	Main	Nonrandom	D
11	X	X		16	Hollow	Main	Random	D
11	X	X		1	Hollow	Main	Nonrandom	E
11	X	X		2	Hollow	Main	Random	E
11		X		1	Hollow	West	Random	C
11		X		1	Hollow	Main	Random	B
11		X		7	Hollow	Main	Nonrandom	C
11		X		2	Hollow	Main	Nonrandom	D
11		X		5	Hollow	Main	Random	D
11		X		2	Hollow	Main	Random	E
11				7	Hollow	Main	Random	E
12	X	X		1	Hollow	West	Random	A
12	X	X		2	Hollow	Main	Random	C
C1				1	Hollow	West	Nonrandom	C
C1	X			3	Hollow	Main	Random	B
C1	X			1	Hollow	Main	Random	D
C2	X			1	Hollow	West	Nonrandom	A
C2	X			1	Hollow	West	Nonrandom	E
C2	X			10	Hollow	Main	Nonrandom	C
C2	X			6	Hollow	Main	Random	C
C2	X			8	Hollow	Main	Nonrandom	D
C2	X			8	Hollow	Main	Random	D
C2	X			1	Hollow	Main	Random	E
C3	X			1	Hollow	Main	Random	B
C3	X			1	Hollow	Main	Nonrandom	
C3	X			1	Hollow	Main	Random	
C3	X			1	Hollow	Main	Random	H
C4		X		2	Hollow	West	Nonrandom	A
C4		X		1	Hollow	West	Random	D
C4		X		1	Hollow	Main	Nonrandom	A
C4		X		1	Hollow	Main	Random	A
C4		X		3	Hollow	Main	Nonrandom	B
C4		X		9	Hollow	Main	Random	B
C4		X		18	Hollow	Main	Nonrandom	C
C4		X		11	Hollow	Main	Random	C
C4		X		4	Hollow	Main	Nonrandom	D
C4		X		13	Hollow	Main	Random	D
C4		X		1	Hollow	Main	Nonrandom	E
C4		X		1	Hollow	Main	Random	H

235

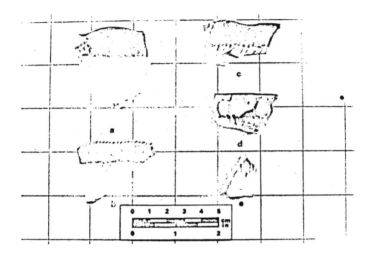

Figure 26.   Blue Edge Decorated Sherds.

Sub-style "b" (figure 26 c) has a scalloped rim. All of the grooved lines curve so that the concave side faces left. The lines extend as much as 0.7 cm below the blue banding where in Sub-style "a," they extended only as much as 0.15 cm. There are no circular impressions at the ends of the lines. The "wheat sheaf" is merely a crude elaboration of one of the regular lines. The rim is slightly rounded. The sides of the sherd are flat. The wall thickness is about 0.84 cm. The flatness of the sherd and its thickness suggest a relatively flat, heavy vessel such as a serving platter.

Sub-style "c" (figure 26 d) has a straight rim. The grooved lines curve slightly so that the concave side faces right. The lines extend up to 0.37 cm beyond the blue banding. The "wheat sheaf" appears as a swirled area between two of the lines. The rim is slightly rounded. The sides are flat. The wall thickness is about 0.90 cm. A relatively flat, heavy vessel such as a serving platter is suggested.

Style Thirteen is also represented by three thinner fragmentary sherds. These sherds vary in thickness between 0.42 cm and 0.45 cm. Their condition prevents a fuller explanation of their stylistic associations.

Style Thirteen is a shell edged rim. The impressed lines of the edging are straight (figure 26 e). The blue edging has been brushed on and follows the irregular lengths of the lines. Up to 1.0 cm of the lines are exposed. The border sections of the rim are absent on the specimens so that no elaboration of their form can be made. The wall thickness varies from 0.76 cm to 0.81 cm. A heavy serving vessel is suggested.

Style Fifteen (figure 26 b) has a flattened, scalloped rim. The edge of
the rim has a braid-like border. There is a line of distinct wheat stalks
separated at intervals by an expanded sheaf. All of the elements are
molded in relief. Up to 0.1 cm of the stalks extend beyond the blue
banding. The sheaf extends up to 0.36 cm beyond the band. The rim is
slightly rounded; the sides are flat. The wall thickness varies from 0.32
cm to 0.45 cm. A plate-type vessel is suggested.

Distribution (Series Five)

The distributional aspects of Series Five are listed in table 11. The
spatial distribution of Series Five sherds are illustrated for combined
strata in figure 20 for the West Dump and in figure 21 for the Main
Dump.

Table 11. Distribution of Series Five, Blue Edge Decorated,
Sherds by Dump, Unit Type, and Stratum

Style	Sub-Style	Frequency	Vessel Form	Dump	Unit Type	Stratum
13	a	1	Flat	West	Random	C
13			Flat	Main	Random	C
13	b		Flat	West	Random	C
13	NA	1	Flat	Main	Random	B
13	NA	2	Flat	Main	Random	C
14		1	Flat	Main	Random	B
14		1	Flat	Main	Nonrandom	D
15		2	Flat	West	Random	C
15		1	Flat	West	Random	D
15		1	Flat	Main	Random	A
15		3	Flat	Main	Nonrandom	B
15		3	Flat	Main	Random	B
15		7	Flat	Main	Nonrandom	C
15		3	Flat	Main	Random	C

Comments (Series Five)

The blue edged ware varies in quality from the relatively crudely formed
sherds of styles Thirteen and Fourteen to the more finely crafted sherds
of Style Fifteen. The existence of distinct clusters of wall thicknesses
among the sherds of Style Thirteen suggest the former existence of at
least a limited item set of dinnerware in this style. The existence of

serving platter-sized and dinner plate-sized sherds may indicate an attempt to "mix and match" to replace items within an everyday set of dinnerware; that is, the sherds may represent an effort to replace broken items within a set with similar, though not identical, items.

The chronological placement of the styles included within Series Five is elusive. Molded, blue edged wares of similar quality have been found on sites encompassing dates from the early to late 1800s. Similar sherds were recovered by Moore (1973:70) and some were felt to have come from firmly dated Bent Period contexts (1833-1849).

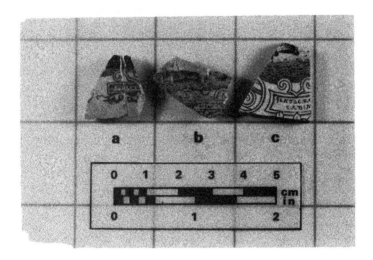

Figure 27. "Gentlemen's Cabin" Black Transfer Printed Sherds.

Description (Series Six)

Series Six consists of sherds decorated by the transfer printing technique. The series can be divided into a number of styles and motif elements. The latter comprise those sherds which are too fragmentary to assign to a style.

Style Sixteen (figure 27) is a black transfer printed design known as "Gentlemen's Cabin." The complete design (figure 28) depicts four gentlemen arranged around a dining table within a ship's cabin. A scrolled border surrounds the center scene. The border has an arrangement of sailing ships set within one of four panels. The recovered sherds represent elements of the center scene and its border. Three sets of sherds depicting parts of the "Gentlemen's Cabin" label are present in the collection. The wall thickness of the sherds varies between 0.32 cm and 0.46 cm. The shape of the sherds suggest both bowl and plate forms.

238

Figure 28. Registry Form for the "Gentlemen's Cabin" Pattern (reproduced from Godden 1965:159).

Style Seventeen (figure 29 b) is a red transfer printed design with hand painted elements. The background is a red transfer printed stipple. The edge of the stipple is bordered with hand painted diamonds with a center dot. Within the stippled area, there are hand painted tulip-like flowers. The decoration is only on the exterior surface. The interior surface is undecorated. A bowl-type vessel is suggested by the shape of the single shard of this style. The wall thickness if 0.40 cm.

239

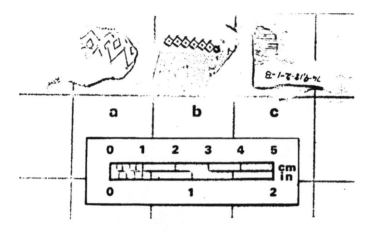

Figure 29. Red Transfer Printed Sherds.

Style Eighteen (figure 30) is a transfer printed design. There are two sub-styles. Sub-style "a" is a purple transfer print and sub-style "b" is a light blue. The exterior surface of sub-style "a" has a floral scene

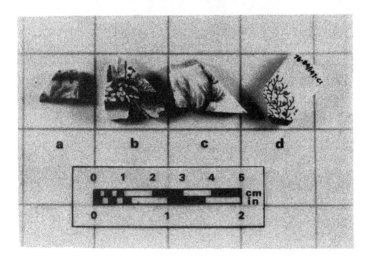

Figure 30. Purple Transfer Printed Sherds.

240

that depicts leafy plants, ferns, grass, and flowers. The rim is bordered with a stylized trim. The interior surface has a similar stylized trim below the rim. The interior surface has a main design of what appears to be an extensive bare stemmed pattern, perhaps representing thorns. Fragments of waterside scenes on portions of both the exterior surface and the interior basal surface also occur. The wall thickness varies between 0.32 cm to 0.44 cm. The rim is slightly rounded and similar to that in figure 19. The base is similar to that in figure 19. The estimated footrim diameter is 4.3 cm. A cup-sized vessel is suggested. Sub-style "b" sherds suggest a plate-type vessel.

Style Nineteen (figure 31 a) is a blue transfer printed peacock tail. The interior surface is decorated; the exterior surface is undecorated. The rim is flat. The body curves in from the rim and drops down toward the center of the vessel. The wall thickness varies between 0.34 and 0.53 cm. A plate-type vessel is suggested by the shape of the sherds.

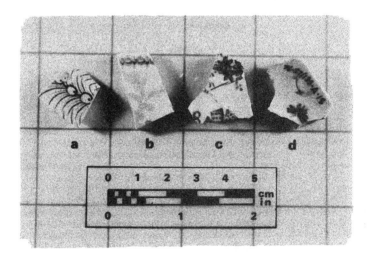

Figure 31. Miscellaneous Blue Decorated Sherds.

The remainder of the transfer printed sherds are too fragmentary and too poorly represented to define styles. A number of stylistic elements, however, can be identified. Among the brown transfer printed sherds, three stylistic elements can be recognized. The remainder of the sherds are difficult to categorize. The first stylistic element (figure 32 a) is a troubador or minstrel playing on a guitar or lute. The motif appears on the exterior surface. The second stylistic element (figure 32 b) is a floral and stipple pattern on a plate fragment. The wall thickness is about 0.28 cm. The design is on the interior surface. The third stylistic element (figure 32 c) is a wooded scene next to a body of water.

241

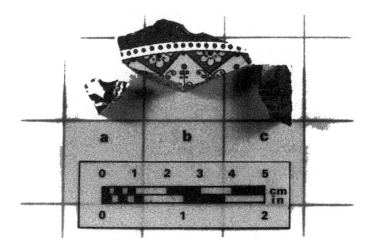

Figure 32. Miscellaneous Brown Transfer Printed Sherds.

The design is on the interior surface. The flat shape of the sherd suggests a plate-type vessel.

Stylistic elements four and five are red transfer printed motifs. Element four (figure 29 a) consists of a "V"-ed line, open diamond, and stippled zone. The wall thickness is about 0.45 cm. The design is on the exterior surface. Element five (figure 29 c) is a lined background. The wall thickness is about 0.84 cm. The exterior surface is decorated.

Some of the purple transfer printed sherds were undefined as to element. There are two recognizable stylistic elements among the miscellaneous blue transfer printed sherds and a number of uncategorizable fragments. Element six (figure 31 c) consists of a floral and domino motif. A plate form is suggested. The interior surface only is decorated. A wall thickness of 0.48 cm is noted.

Element seven (figure 33 a) is a green transfer printed design of flowers and berries. The basal sherd suggests a plate-type vessel. No wall thickness is measurable. The design is on the interior. Element eight (figure 33 b) is a partial rim border in a green transfer print. The design is a printed scalloped edge. The design is on the interior. The remainder of the green transfer printed sherds are uncategorized.

Element nine (figure 33 d) is a light lime green transfer printed design that occurs on both interior and exterior surfaces. It is a stippled floral element. The wall thickness varies from 0.28 cm to 0.33 cm.

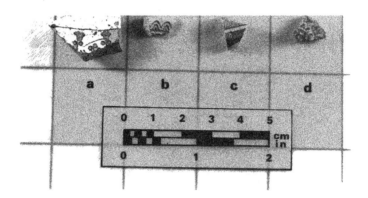

Figure 33. Miscellaneous Green Transfer Printed Sherds.

Distribution (Series Six)

The distributional aspects of Series Six are listed in table 12. The spatial distribution of the series sherds is illustrated in figure 34 for the West Dump and in figure 35 for the Main Dump.

Comments (Series Six)

The transfer printing process was in use by at least 1756. This use, however, was limited to the application of black transfers over the glaze on porcelain. Later, red and purple designs were utilized in restricted quantity (Haggar 1950:96). By 1775, a "bat-printing" process had been developed, which replaced the paper transfer with a "bat" of gelatine or glue and used oil dusted with color rather than ink. This procedure permitted finer gradations in tone and a more detailed design. By at least 1777, printing under the glaze had been developed by the Braddeleys of Shelton (Haggar 1950:98-99). In 1780, the first underglaze blue transfer print had been introduced by Thomas Turner (Coysh 1974:7). By 1784, Josiah Spode had developed the underglaze process to a commercial state (Haggar 1950:99). Most of the transfer printed designs remained to be implemented in black until after 1800 when blue began to be used in quantity (Haggar 1950:100). Pink, green, and brown were introduced about 1820 (Kovel and Kovel 1973). By the 1820s, there was an expansion of transfer printed goods and the process achieved its peak during the 1820s and 1830s (Haggar 1950:101, 104; Coysh 1974:7).

243

Style	Sub-Style	Color	Frequency	Vessel Form	Dump	Unit Type	Stratum
16		Black	4	Hollow	Main	Nonrandom	B
16		Black	1	Flat	Main	Nonrandom	B
16		Black	1	Flat	Main	Random	B
16		Black	6	Hollow	Main	Random	B
16		Black	1	Hollow	Main	Nonrandom	
16		Black	1	Flat	Main	Nonrandom	
16		Black	1	Hollow	Main	Random	C
16		Black	1	Hollow	Main	Random	D
17		Red	1	Hollow	Main	Random	B
18	a	Purple	2	Hollow	West	Nonrandom	A
18	a	Purple	2	Hollow	West	Random	A
18	a	Purple	1	Hollow	West	Nonrandom	C
18	a	Purple	1	Hollow	West	Random	C
18	a	Purple	1	Hollow	Main	Random	A
18	a	Purple	3	Hollow	Main	Nonrandom	B
18	a	Purple	1	Hollow	Main	Nonrandom	C
18	a	Purple	4	Hollow	Main	Random	C
18	a	Purple	2	Hollow	Main	Random	D
18	b	Blue	1	Flat	West	Nonrandom	
18	b	Blue	1	Flat	West	Nonrandom	A
18	b	Blue	1	Flat	West	Random	C
19		Blue	3	Flat	West	Nonrandom	A
19		Blue	2	Flat	West	Random	A
19		Blue	1	Flat	Main	Random	A
19		Blue	1	Flat	Main	Random	B
19		Blue	1	Flat	Main	Nonrandom	C
19		Blue	2	Flat	Main	Random	C

Element

Style	Sub-Style	Color	Frequency	Vessel Form	Dump	Unit Type	Stratum
1		Brown	1	Hollow	West	Random	A
2		Brown	1	Flat	West	Nonrandom	C
2		Brown	1	Flat	West	Random	D
		Brown	1	Flat	Main	Random	B
4		Red	1	Flat	Main	Nonrandom	B
4		Red	1	NA	Main	Nonrandom	C
		Red	1	Hollow	West	Random	A
		Blue	2	NA	Main	Nonrandom	B
		Blue-green	2	Flat	Main	Nonrandom	B
		Blue-green	1	NA	Main	Random	B
-		Lime green	1	NA	West	Random	A
9		Lime green	2	NA	Main	Random	B
9		Lime green	1	NA	Main	Random	D
NA		Brown	1	Flat	West	Random	A
NA		Brown	2	NA	West	Nonrandom	A
NA		Brown	1	Flat	West	Nonrandom	C
NA		Brown	1	NA	West	Random	C
NA		Brown	1	NA	Main	Random	A
NA		Brown	1	NA	Main	Random	B
NA		Brown	2	NA	Main	Random	C

Table 12 (cont.)

Style	Sub-Style	Color	Frequency	Vessel Form	Dump	Unit Type	Stratum
NA		Purple	1	NA	West	Random	B
NA		Purple	1	NA	West	Random	C
NA		Purple	1	NA	Main	Nonrandom	B
NA		Purple	2	NA	Main	Random	B
NA		Blue	1	NA	West	Nonrandom	A
NA		Blue	1	NA	West	Random	A
NA		Blue	4	NA	Main	Random	
NA		Blue	1	NA	Main	Nonrandom	
NA		Blue	1	NA	Main	Random	B
NA		Blue-green	1	NA	Main	Nonrandom	B
NA		Blue-green	3	NA	Main	Random	B
NA		Blue-green	1	NA	Main	Random	E
NA		Lime green	1	NA	Main	Nonrandom	B

245

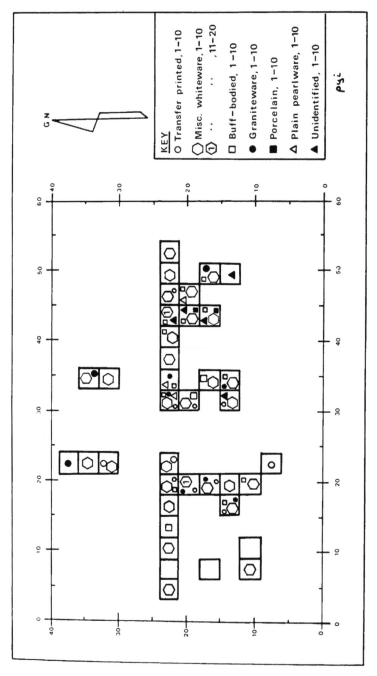

Figure 34. Distribution of Tableware Sherds within the West Dump.

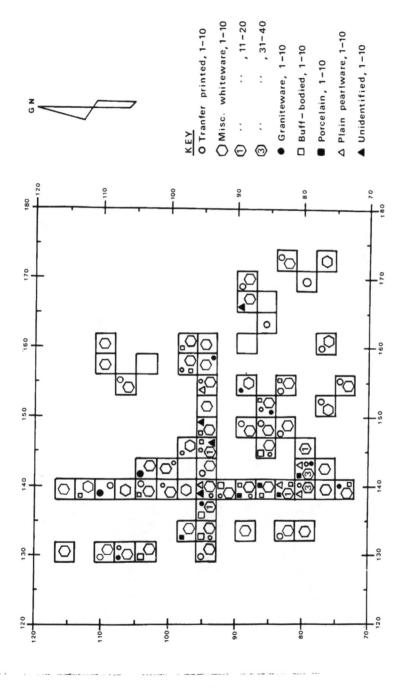

Figure 35. Distribution of Tableware Sherds within the Main Dump.

In the transfer printing process, a copper plate was engraved with the desired design. Then, the plate was inked and a transfer tissue applied to absorb the design. This tissue then was applied to the unglazed ware and removed after the design had been set. The print was allowed to dry and the ware glazed and fired. The process is illustrated in figure 36.

Figure 36. The Transfer Printing Process.

The "Gentlemen's Cabin" pattern was registered in September 1841 as part of J. & T. Edwards' "Boston Mails" Series (Godden 1965:159). This pattern in black transfer print as well as others in light blue, flow blue, red, brown, and green were recovered by Moore (1973:70-73). Moore's sherd in his figure 29, left (1973:71) has a border similar to style element nine. The interior portion of his plate is similar to style element eight.

Description (Series Seven)

Series Seven consists of miscellaneous decorated and undecorated white earthenware sherds. There are two style elements and several miscellaneous categories. Style element ten consists of hand painted blue flower and green leaf (figure 37 a). Style element eleven consists of a 0.15 cm wide blue band 0.60 cm below the rim (figure 37 c). The style element ten sherds are about 0.41 cm thick. The style element eleven sherd is 0.45 cm thick.

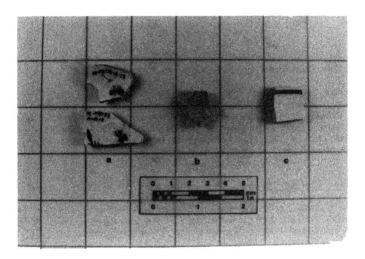

Figure 37. Miscellaneous Hand Painted Sherds.

The miscellaneous hand painted sherds vary in thickness from 0.23 cm to 0.64 cm. The miscellaneous undecorated sherds can be divided into groups according to ware type (pearlware or common white), section, and form. Three rim forms can be identified (figure 38). The rims vary in thickness from 0.24 to 0.34 cm. The body sherds can be divided into two general categories by thickness. The first group consists of those sherds with thin to moderate thicknesses, 0.2 cm to 0.5 cm. The second

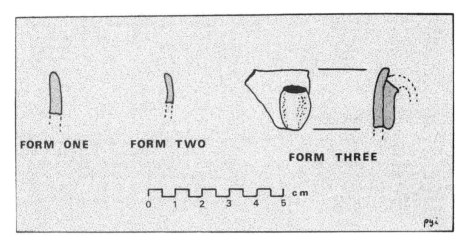

Figure 38.   Cross Sections of Typical Undecorated Rim Sherds.

group consists of relatively thick sherds, 0.7 to 0.8 cm.   Five basal
forms can be distinguished (figures 39 and 40).

Basal Forms One to Four have rudimentary footrims.   Basal From Five is
a relatively distinct rounded footrim.   The diameter of the Form Five
footrim varies from 5.6 cm (measured) to 5.8 cm (estimated).   In
addition, there are a number of unclassified basal fragments.   There is
one sherd (figure 39) that appears to be the rim of a strainer.   There
are three sherds that appear to be the rim of some sort of lid.

Distribution (Series Seven)

The distributional characteristics of Series Seven are listed in table 13.
The spatial distribution is depicted for the combined strata in figure 34
for the West Dump and in figure 35 for the Main Dump.

Comments (Series Seven)

Basal Forms One to Four suggest early plate forms (Coysh 1974:8).   Both
plate-type and cup- or bowl-type vessels are suggested by the shape of
the sherds.   Some of the sherds display blue tint in the crevices of the
footrims indicating a pearlware body and glaze.   A lid and strainer are
suggested by the rims of some sherds.

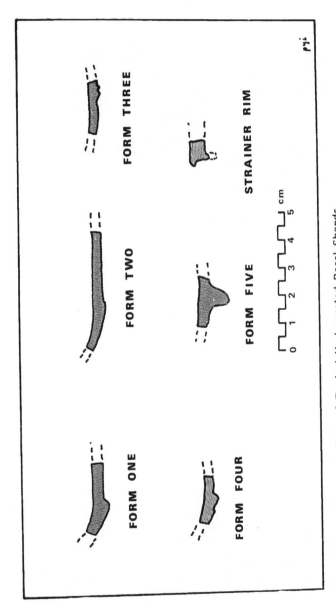

Figure 39. Cross Sections of Typical Undecorated Basal Sherds.

251

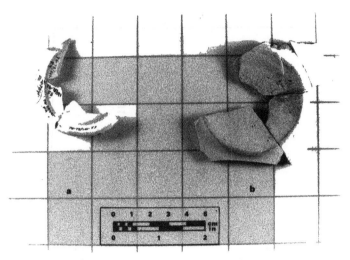

Figure 40.   Miscellaneous Undecorated Basal Remnants (a, Pearlware; b, Unidentified).

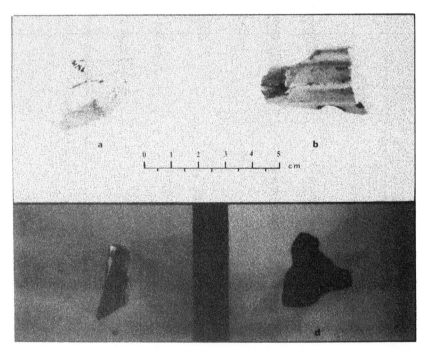

Figure 41.   Graniteware Sherds (a, Rim; b, Footrim).

Table 13. Distribution of Series Seven, Miscellaneous White Earthenware, Shards by Dump, Unit type, and Stratum

Style	Rim	Section Body	Base	Frequency	Vessel Form	Dump	Unit Type	Stratum
Element 10			X	3	Flat	Main	Nonrandom	C
Element 10				1	Flat	Main	Nonrandom	D
Element 11					NA	Main	Nonrandom	C
Misc. Handpainted		X		1	NA	West	Nonrandom	A
Misc. Handpainted		X		5	NA	West	Random	A
Misc. Handpainted		X		2	NA	West	Nonrandom	B
Misc. Handpainted		X		5	NA	West	Nonrandom	C
Misc. Handpainted		X		1	NA	West	Random	C
Misc. Handpainted		X		1	NA	West	Nonrandom	D
Misc. Handpainted		X		3	NA	Main	Random	B
Misc. Handpainted		X		3	NA	Main	Nonrandom	C
Misc. Handpainted		X		6	NA	Main	Random	C
Misc. Handpainted		X		3	NA	Main	Random	D
Misc. Handpainted		X		2	NA	Main	Nonrandom	E
Misc. Handpainted		X		1	NA	Main	Random	F
Rim Form 1	X			1	NA	Main	Nonrandom	B
Rim Form 1	X			2	NA	Main	Random	B
Rim Form 1	X			1	NA	Main	Nonrandom	C
Rim Form 1	X			2	NA	Main	Random	C
Rim Form 2				1	Hollow	Main	Random	B
Rim Form 3				1	Hollow	Main	Random	B
Undecorated		X		24	NA	West	Nonrandom	A
Undecorated		X		35	NA	West	Random	A
Undecorated		X		11	NA	West	Nonrandom	C
Undecorated		X		14	NA	West	Random	C
Undecorated		X		2	NA	West	Nonrandom	D
Undecorated		X		4	NA	West	Random	D
Undecorated		X		2	NA	Main	Nonrandom	A
Undecorated		X		2	NA	Main	Random	A
Undecorated		X		51	NA	Main	Nonrandom	B
Undecorated		X		63	NA	Main	Randon	B
Undecorated		X		59	NA	Main	Nonrandom	C
Undecorated		X		32	NA	Main	Random	C
Undecorated		X		20	NA	Main	Nonrandom	D
Undecorated		X		57	NA	Main	Random	D
Undecorated		X		3	NA	Main	Nonrandom	E
Undecorated		X		3	NA	Main	Random	E
Undecorated		X		2	NA	Main	Random	F
Undecorated		X		3	NA	Main	Nonrandom	H
Undecorated		X		2	NA	Main	Random	H

253 .

Table 13 (cont.)

Style	Rim	Section Body	Base	Frequency	Vessel Form	Dump	Unit Type	Stratum
Undecorated, Thick		X		4	Flat	West	Nonrandom	A
Undecorated, Thick		X		1	Flat	West	Random	A
Undecorated, Thick		X		3	Flat	West	Random	C
Undecorated, Thick		X		2	Flat	West	Random	D
Undecorated, Thick		X		1	Flat	Main	Nonrandom	A
Undecorated, Thick		X		4	Flat	Main	Nonrandom	C
Undecorated, Thick		X		3	Flat	Main	Random	C
Undecorated, Thick		X		2	Flat	Main	Nonrandom	D
Undecorated, Thick		X		2	Flat	Main	Nonrandom	E
Base Form 1			X	1	Flat	Main	Random	B
Base Form 2 (PW)			X	1	Flat	West	Random	D
Base Form 2			X	1	Flat	Main	Nonrandom	C
Base Form 3			X	1	Flat	Main	Nonrandom	B
Base Form 4			X	1	Flat	Main	Random	C
Base Form 5 (PW)			X	1	Hollow	Main	Nonrandom	B
Base Form 5 (PW)			X	2	Hollow	Main	Random	B
Base Form 5 (PW)			X	3	Hollow	Main	Nonrandom	C
Base Form 5 (PW)			X	1	Hollow	Main	Random	C
Base Form 5 (PW)			X	5	Hollow	Main	Random	D
Base Form 5			X	3	Hollow	Main	Random	B
Base Form 5			X	1	Hollow	Main	Random	E
Undecorated (PW)			X	2	NA	West	Random	C
Undecorated (PW)			X	1	NA	Main	Nonrandom	
Undecorated (PW)			X	1	NA	Main	Nonrandom	A
Undecorated (PW)			X	1	NA	Main	Random	C
Undecorated			X	3	NA	West	Nonrandom	A
Undecorated			X	1	NA	West	Random	A
Undecorated			X	1	NA	West	Nonrandom	C
Undecorated			X	1	NA	West	Random	C
Undecorated			X	3	NA	Main	Nonrandom	A
Undecorated			X	3	NA	Main	Random	A
Undecorated			X	6	NA	Main	Nonrandom	B
Undecorated			X	9	NA	Main	Random	B
Undecorated			X	3	NA	Main	Nonrandom	
Undecorated			X	4	NA	Main	Random	C
Undecorated			X	1	NA	Main	Nonrandom	D
Undecorated			X	6	NA	Main	Random	D
Undecorated				1	Strainer	Main	Random	C
Undecorated	X			2	Lid	West	Nonrandom	A
Undecorated	X			1	Lid	West	Random	C

Description (Series Eight)

Series Eight consists of those sherds that fall within the graniteware category. Included are hard earthenwares that commonly are known as graniteware, hotel china, ironstone, semi-vitreous, porcelaine opaque, etc. All of the sherds are undecorated except for one green banded rim, Style Element Twelve (figure 37 c). The band is 0.19 cm wide. The rim is about 0.49 cm thick and is similar to Rim Form 1 (figure 38). Two sherds have distinctive forms. One appears to be the rim of some type of open jar (figure 41 a); the other, a thick footrim (figure 41 b). The remainder of the sherds can be grouped into those which are tinted blue and those which are untinted. Wall thicknesses vary from 0.30 cm to 0.65 cm.

Distribution (Series Eight)

The distributional aspects of Series Eight are listed in table 14. The spatial distribution is depicted for the combined strata in figure 34 for the West Dump and in figure 35 for the Main Dump.

Comments (Series Eight)

Undecorated white graniteware first appeared around 1840 (Weatherbee 1981:37) although decorated forms of the ironstone and stone china wares had been known since the early part of the century. These graniteware bodies were apparently popular on the frontier for their durability.

Description (Series Nine)

The sherds included within Series Nine fall within the general category of buff-bodied earthenwares. These include both yellowware and Bennington-like fragments. The Bennington-like, Style Element Thirteen, sherds have an irregularly applied glaze that varies from a splotchy dark brown to brown with patches of the body exposed under the glaze. A second sherd, Style Element Fourteen, is a molded fragment with a dark green surface glaze. The remainder of the sherds fall within the yellowware category.

Style Twenty consists of a rounded rim with straight sides. The interior surface is clear glazed and undecorated (figure 42). On the exterior of Sub-style "a," a 0.41-cm wide blue painted band appears about 0.7 cm below the rim. Immediately after this is a white slipped zone that has been engine turned to expose alternating bands of the yellow body. Each of the slip bands is about 0.16 cm wide and the exposed bands are about 0.09 cm wide. Below the banding, white slip has been applied to form a background for a blue mocha-like decoration. Towards the base, the exterior is undecorated. Body thickness varies from 0.34 cm to 0.67 cm. Sub-style "b" has no blue band before the engine turned white slip bands.

255

Table 14. Distribution of Series Eight, Graniteware,
Sherds by Dump, Unit Type, and Stratum

Style	Section Rim	Body	Base	Frequency	Vessel Form	Dump	Unit Type	Stratum
Element 12	X			1	Flat	Main	Random	B
Blue Tint	X			1	NA	Main	Nonrandom	D
Blue Tint		X		12	NA	West	Nonrandom	A
Blue Tint		X		4	NA	West	Random	A
Blue Tint		X		6	NA	Main	Nonrandom	B
Blue Tint		X		4	NA	Main	Random	B
Blue Tint		X		2	NA	Main	Nonrandom	H
Blue Tint			X	2	NA	Main	Nonrandom	B
Blue Tint			X	1	NA	Main	Random	B
Blue Tint			X	1	NA	Main	Nonrandom	D
Undecorated		X		1	NA	West	Random	C
Undecorated	X			3	Hollow	Main	Nonrandom	B

256

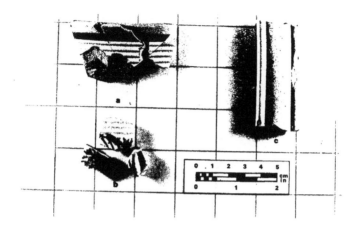

Figure 42. Yellowware Fragments.

In addition to Style Twenty sherds, there are several miscellaneous style elements. Element Thirteen is a sherd with a 0.64-cm wide slip band bordered by a single blue band on either side, 0.21 cm and 0.12 cm wide, respectively. Element Fourteen is a plain faceted surface rim. Element Fifteen is a plain rim with scalloped border. Miscellaneous cross sections are shown in figure 43.

Distribution (Series Nine)

The distributional characteristics of Series Nine are listed in table 15. The spatial distribution of Series Nine is illustrated in figure 34 for the West Dump and in figure 35 for the Main Dump.

Comments (Series Nine)

Yellowware was an inexpensive utilitarian ware that was available during the 19th century (Godden 1975:222; Kovel and Kovel 1973:28). It was made both in England (Godden 1975; Haggar 1950) and in the United States (Spargo 1974). Sherds similar to Style Twenty have been recovered at Ft. Bowie, a second half of the 19th century site (Herskovitz 1978:97-99) and are illustrated in catalogs (figure 44) from the same period (Godden 1965:173). The shape of the various fragments suggest hollow vessel forms. A pitcher and several bowl-sized vessels are indicated.

257

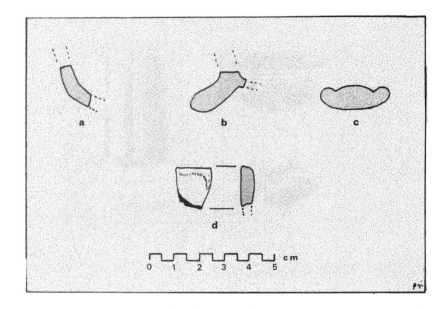

Figure 43. Miscellaneous Yellowware Sherd Cross Sections.

Figure 44. 1864 T.G. Green & Co's Church Gresley Pottery Catalog of
Yelloware-like Utilitarian Vessels (reproduced from Godden 1965:173).

Table 15. Distribution of Series Nine, Yellowware,
Sherds by Dump, Unit Type, and Stratum

Style	Sub-Style	Rim	Body	Base	Frequency	Vessel Form	Dump	Unit Type	Stratum
Bennington-like	a		X		2	NA	West	Nonrandom	A
Bennington-like	a		X		1	NA	West	Random	A
Green-glazed			X		1	NA	West	Nonrandom	B
Style 20	a		X		11	Hollow	Main	Random	B
Style 20	a				1	Hollow	Main	Random	C
Style 20	b	X			2	Hollow	Main	Nonrandom	B
Style 20	b	X			1	Hollow	Main	Nonrandom	C
Style 20	b	X			1	Hollow	Main	Random	D
Style 20	NA				1	NA	Main	Random	B
Style 20	NA		Handle		1	Hollow	West	Random	D
Style 20	NA		X		1	Hollow	West	Random	OB
Style 20	NA		X		1	Hollow	West	Nonrandom	A
Style 20	NA		X		1	Hollow	West	Random	A
Style 20	NA		X		6	Hollow	West	Nonrandom	C
Style 20	NA		X		1	Hollow	West	Nonrandom	C
Style 20	NA		X		3	Hollow	West	Nonrandom	D
Style 20	NA		X		1	Hollow	Main	Random	A
Style 20	NA		X		6	Hollow	Main	Nonrandom	B
Style 20	NA		X		3	Hollow	Main	Random	B
Style 20	NA		X		2	Hollow	Main	Nonrandom	C
Style 20	NA		X		1	Hollow	Main	Nonrandom	C
Style 20	NA		X		3	Hollow	Main	Random	D
Style 20	NA		X		5	Hollow	Main	Random	D
Style 20	NA		X		2	Hollow	Main	Random	F
Style 20	NA				2	NA	Main	Random	D
Style 20	NA			X	1	NA	Main	Random	B
Style 20	NA			X	4	NA	Main	Nonrandom	C
Style 20	NA			X	7	NA	Main	Nonrandom	D
Style 20	NA			X	1	NA	Main	Random	D
Element 13					1	NA	Main	Random	B
Element 14					1	NA	West	Random	C
Element 15					1	NA	Main	Random	C

Description (Series Ten)

Series Ten consists of porcelain sherds. Three style elements, Sixteen, Seventeen, and Eighteen, are included as well as a series of undecorated categories. The latter consist of sherds separated by general body composition, hard or soft. Element Sixteen (figure 45 a) is a blue export porcelain hand painted design. The surface is blue tinted and the wall thickness varies from 0.32 cm to 0.42 cm. The spherical curvature of the fragment suggests a teapot-type vessel. Element Seventeen (figure 45 b) is a blue export porcelain sherd with a tree design. The surface is blue tinted and the wall thickness is about 0.30 cm. The spherical curvature of the sherd suggests that it may be part of the same vessel as Element Sixteen. Element Eighteen is a molded fragment of soft paste porcelain with a tin-like blue green glaze. The remaining porcelain fragment includes a soft paste sherd with a wall thickness of 0.36 cm. There are two sherds of hard paste porcelain with wall thicknesses of 0.32 cm. Both of the sets are undecorated and suggest hollow vessels such as cups.

Distribution (Series Ten)

The distributional aspects of Series Ten are listed in table 16. The spatial distribution of the combined strata are shown in figure for 34 the West Dump and in figure 35 for the Main Dump.

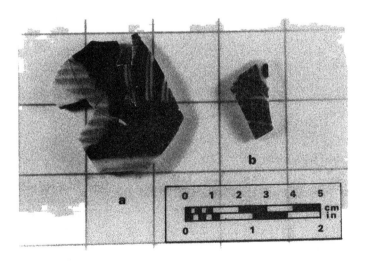

Figure 45. Export Porcelain Sherds.

Comments (Series Ten)

Cobalt blue export porcelain was mass produced by the Chinese for sale overseas well into the 19th century. At the Chinese ports, such wares were known as yang-khi or vases of the sea. Although porcelain represented very little of the worth of most ship manifests, their price was still relatively expensive. As an example, the cargo of the American ship Pearl in 1810 of teas, silks, and china had a worth consisting of 83.5 percent teas, 14.1 percent silks, and only 2.4 percent china. At that, the 50 sets of 172 pieces sold for a total of $2,290 or about $45.80 per set (Schiffer 1975:12). That can be compared to salaries of about $150 a year for a lock keeper on the C&O Canal in 1833.

Soft paste porcelain was made in England in imitation of the Chinese porcelain beginning in the 18th century (Godden 1965:xvii) and, thereafter, a hard porcelain was developed. Export porcelain has been found at a number of other frontier sites including Fort Bowie (Herskovitz 1978:96-110). No porcelain, however, was recovered by Moore during his excavations (1973:74).

Table 16. Distribution of Series Ten, Porcelain,
Sherds by Dump, Unit Type, and Stratum

Style	Frequency	Vessel Form	Dump	Unit Type	Stratum
Element 16	3	Hollow	Main	Nonrandom	B
Element 16	1	Hollow	Main	Random	B
Element 16	5	Hollow	Main	Nonrandom	C
Element 16	2	Hollow	Main	Random	D
Element 17		Hollow	Main	Nonrandom	C
Element 18		NA	West	Random	A
Soft Paste		Hollow	West	Random	A
Hard Paste	2	Hollow	West	Random	A

Description (Series Eleven)

Series Eleven consists of Style Twenty-one. Style Twenty-one is an extremely soft and porous buff-colored earthenware of unknown variety. The surface is glazed with a relatively thick grayish glaze. The bottom of the base is unglazed as are the tops of the rims. The base is illustrated in figure 40 b. The shape of the sherds suggests a saucer-shaped vessel. The base is about 5.69 cm in diameter and is concave. There is no distinct footrim. The rim is curved in vertical cross section. The wall thickness varies from 0.35 cm to 0.45 cm. A cross section of the base is shown in figure 46.

262

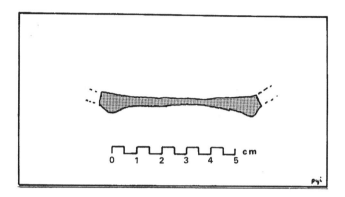

Figure 46.   Cross Sections of Base of Series Eleven.

One additional sherd has a slightly grayer glaze and a thickness of 0.63 cm.

Distribution (Series Eleven)

The distributional aspects of Series Eleven are listed in table 17.   The spatial distribution of the combined strata are depicted in figure 34 for the West Dump and in figure 35 for the Main Dump.

Comments (Series Eleven)

The body of Series Eleven does not fall within the normal range of either American or English wares.   The possibility exists that this may be a Spanish or Mexican ceramic variety.   No similar sherds were described by Moore (1973).

Table 17. Distribution of Style Series Eleven, Buff-Colored Earthenware Bodied, Sherds by Dump, Unit Type, and Stratum

| Style | Section | | | Frequency | Vessel Form | Dump | Unit Type | Stratum |
	Rim	Body	Base					
21	X			1	Flat	West	Random	A
21	X			2	Flat	East	Random	C
21	X			1	Flat	East	Random	B
21				2	Flat	West	Random	C
21			X	1	Flat	West	Random	OB
21			X	2	Flat	Main	Nonrandom	B
21			X	1	Flat	Main	Nonrandom	C
NA				1	Flat	Main	Random	A

264

UTENSILS

Description

The only remaining indications of eating utensils were fragments of wood and bone handles. The single wood handle had an intact handle length of 7.4 cm. At the end of the handle (figure 47), there were seven parallel incised lines perpendicular to the long axis. 5.1 cm in from the end were another four incised lines. There were two incised lines along the attachment end of the handle. There were two parallel incised lines along one side of the long axis. The edges of the sides were scalloped along part of the length.

Four fragments of bone handles were noted. There was a pattern of alternating sets of diagonal and straight incised lines (figure 47 b, c, & d). The end of one fragment retained saw marks. The cross section was slightly curved.

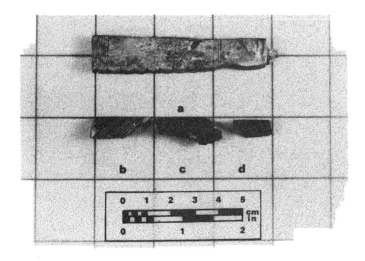

Figure 47. Wood and Bone Handle Fragments.

Distribution

The distributional aspects of the utensil artifacts are listed in table 18.

Comments

The extremely fragmentary nature of the bone precludes any further discussion. The wood handle suggests a form that could have been applied to any of the common utensil forms.

Table 18. Distribution of Wood and Bone Handle Fragments
by Dump, Unit Type, and Stratum

Material	Frequency	Dump	Unit Type	Stratum
Wood	-	West	Random	D
Bone	1	West	Nonrandom	A
Bone	1	West	Nonrandom	C
Bone	1	Main	Random	C
Bone	1	Main	Random	D

THE PERSONAL ATTIRE COMPONENT

INTRODUCTION

The personal attire component of the artifact assemblage consists of those items that were part of articles of clothing and footwear. Included within this grouping are beads, buckles, buttons, grommets, hooks and eyes, and shoes.

BEADS

Description

Sixteen styles of beads were defined in terms of six criteria. These criteria were material, methods of construction, shape, size, color, and decorative elements. The first fifteen styles were composed of glass, the last of shell.

Style One are small glass beads commonly referred to as "seed beads." These were made by the hollow cane method. The shape of these beads varies from a stubby, barrel-type to tubular to a short, donut-type. The transverse cross section is circular. The diameter varies from 0.20 cm to 0.40 cm. The length varies from 0.10 to 0.30 cm. The hole varies from 0.95 to 0.10 cm. These beads come in a number of colors; the color of the glass is uniform throughout the bead. The white beads are opaque. The light blue, silvery blue, green, and red beads are translucent. Style One beads are illustrated in figure 48 a, b, c).

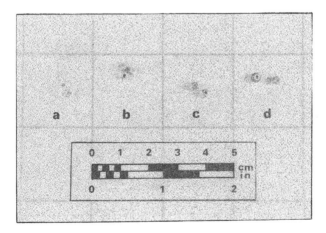

Figure 48.   Glass "Seed Beads" (a, b, c, Style One; d, Style Two).

Style Two are small glass beads of the "seed bead" category. These were made by the hollow cane method. The shape varies from a stubby, barrel-type to a short, donut-type. The transverse cross section is circular. The diameter varies from 0.12 cm to 0.41 cm. The length varies from 0.21 to 0.29 cm. The hole varies from 0.06 to 0.10 cm. Only one color of these beads was recovered. These are opaque, red beads that had been formed by rolling a white glass bead in a molten red glass. Style Two beads are shown in figure 48 d.

Style Three beads are represented by a single tubular glass bead. This bead was made by the hollow cane method. The ends of the tube have been fire polished; however, the irregular ends characteristic of beads made by breaking sections from a longer tube remain. The transverse cross section is circular. The diameter is 0.37 cm. The length is 0.86 cm. The hole is 0.10 cm. The bead is an opaque white. These are shown in figure 49 a.

Style Four beads are represented by a single tubular glass bead. This bead was made by the hollow cane method. The ends were cut and later fire polished to produce a roughly rounded contour. The transverse cross section is circular. The diameter is 0.47 cm. The length is 1.25 cm. The hole is 0.13 cm. The bead is an opaque white. Style Four beads are shown in figure 49 b.

Style Five beads are spherical glass beads made by the mandrel wound method. The transverse cross section is circular. The longitudinal cross section varies from nearly circular to slightly oval. The shoulders around the ends are rounded while the section around the hole is flat.

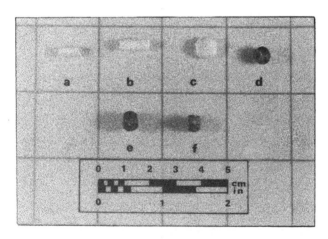

Figure 49. Glass "Necklace Beads" (a, Style Three; b, Style Four; c to f, Style Five).

268

Traces of the strands of wound glass are evident. The diameter is about 0.81 cm. The length varies around 0.75 cm. The hole is about 0.21 cm. Most of the examples of this style have been split lengthwise into nearly perfect half sections. Style Five beads come in a number of colors. The white beads are opaque. The amber, dark blue, and cobalt blue beads are translucent. These beads are illustrated in figure 49 c to f.

Style Six beads are spherical glass beads. These have been made by the mandrel wound method. Two colors of glass have been combined during the winding process. The transverse cross section is circular; the longitudinal cross section is nearly circular. The ends are rounded. The diameter is about 0.78 cm. The length is about 0.82 cm. The hole is about 0.13 cm. The only example of this style is a mixture of green and brown glass. The bead is heavily decomposed and, while at present is opaque, may originally have been translucent. This bead is illustrated in figure 50 a.

Style Seven beads are spherical glass beads. These have been made by the mandrel wound method. The bead is composed of a core of one color of glass and a surface gloss of a second color. The transverse cross section is circular. The longitudinal cross section is nearly circular. The diameter, length, and hole measurements vary around 0.81 cm, 0.75 cm, and 0.21 cm, respectively--that is, within the same general range as Style Five beads. The only examples of this style are beads with a white glass core and a light blue glass surface. These beads are opaque. Style Seven beads are illustrated in figure 50 b.

Style Eight beads are spherical glass beads. These have been made by the mandrel wound method. The transverse cross section is circular. The longitudinal cross section is nearly circular. The ends are rounded. Oval-shaped pockets or cavities have been formed on the surface of the

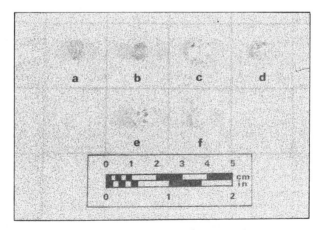

Figure 50. Glass "Necklace Beads" (a, Style Six; b, Style Seven; c, Style Eight; d, Style Nine; e,f, Style Ten).

bead. These pockets have been filled with glass of a different color than the main body of the bead. The "eyes" are flush with the surface. The single example of this style had a diameter of 0.94 cm. The length was 0.93 cm. The hole was not determinable since only a fragmentary half section was recovered. The main body was an opaque white. The glass insets that filled the eyes could not be classified accurately as to color due to heavy patination. Style Eight beads are shown in figure 50 c.

Style Nine beads are spherical glass beads. These have been made by the mandrel wound method. The transverse cross section is circular. The longitudinal cross section is nearly circular. The shoulders of the ends are rounded. The area adjacent to the hole is flat. Circular cavities or pockets have been formed on the surface. These pockets have been filled with glass of a color different from that which forms the main body. The eyes are flush with the surface. Only a single half section was found. The diameter is 0.74 cm. The length is 0.76 cm. The hole was not measurable due to the fragmentary nature of the bead. The body is an opaque white. The eye color appears to be a red or brown but is not distinct due to heavy patination of the glass. Style Nine is shown in figure 50 d.

Style Ten beads are spherical glass beads. These beads have been made by the mandrel wound method. The transverse cross section is circular. The longitudinal cross section is nearly circular. The shoulders of the ends are rounded and the section adjacent to the hole is flat. A finely incised floral design occurs along the circumference. Glass of a color different from that of the main body has been set into this design. Two of the three fragments that represent this style were measurable. The first had a diameter, length, and hole of 0.82 cm, 0.75 cm, and 0.24 cm, respectively. The second had dimensions of 0.90 cm, 0.81 cm, and 0.18 cm, respectively. The body was an opaque white. The glass inset could not be accurately defined as to color due to heavy patination of the sections of glass that had not popped out. Style Ten is illustrated in figure 50 e & f.

Style Eleven beads are glass beads that are oval in longitudinal cross section. In transverse cross section, they are circular. These beads have been made by the mandrel wound method. The shoulders taper towards the end holes. The dimensions of these beads varies somewhat by color. The white beads are °paque. Their diameter varies from about 0.54 cm to 0.65 cm. Their length varies from around 0.85 cm to 0.93 cm. Their hole varies from about 0.17 cm to 0.27 cm. Opaque light blue beads have dimensions of roughly 0.60 cm, 0.84 cm, and 0.12 cm, respectively, for diameter, length, and hole. The translucent red beads have a diameter of about 0.91 cm. Their length is about 1.19 cm. Their ho e is around 0.17 cm. Style Eleven beads are illustrated in figure 51 la, b, & c.

Style Twelve beads are glass beads that are oval in longitudinal cross section. In transverse cross section, they are circular. These beads have been made by the mandrel wound method. The shoulders taper towards the end holes. The diameter is 0.44 cm. The core of the bead is made of one type of glass. The surface has been covered with a second type of glass. The length is 0.78 cm. The hole is 0.07 cm. The

a　　b　　c　　d

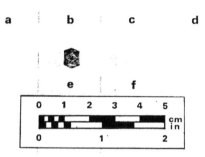

e　　f

```
0   1   2   3   4   5
■■■□■■□□■□□□□□□□□ cm
                  in
0         1         2
```

Figure 51.   Glass "Necklace Beads."

core is an opaque white.   The surface is a light brown.   Style Twelve is shown in figure 51 d.

Style Thirteen beads are faceted glass beads.   Facets have been pressed or molded on the surface.   The body of the beads has been formed around a tubular core made by the hollow cane method.   The ends are flat and hexagonal.   The circumferential facets are diamond shaped.   Two colors of beads are included within this style.   A single milky white, translucent bead was found.   Its diameter is 0.62 cm.   Its length is 0.55 cm.   Its hole is 0.23 cm.   Two examples of a dark blue, translucent color were noted.   The dimensions of the first were 0.70 cm, 0.65 cm, and 0.28 cm, respectively, for diameter, length, and hole.   The second had a diameter of 0.58 cm, a length of 0.49 cm, and a hole of 0.27 cm.   The core is an opaque white.   Style Thirteen beads are shown in figure 51 e & f.   A closeup of the end face of these beads is shown in figure 52.

Style Fourteen beads are faceted glass beads.   Facets have been pressed or molded on the surface.   The original form was probably made by the hollow cane method.   The ends are flat and hexagonal.   The circumferential facets are diamond shaped.   There is no separate core section.   Examples of two translucent colors were noted.   The lime green bead had dimensions of 0.62 cm, 0.50 cm, and 0.27 cm, respectively, for diameter, length, and hole.   The dark blue bead had a diameter of 0.67 cm.   Its length was 0.71 cm.   Its hole measured 0.22 cm.   Style Fourteen is illustrated in figure 53 a & b.

Style Fifteen beads are faceted glass beads.   Facets have been pressed or molded on the surface.   The body has been formed around at tubular core made by the hollow cane method.   The ends are hexagonal.   The facets are roughly flat single panels.   The ends are flat.   The diameter

271

Figure 52. Close-up of Style Thirteen Glass Beads Illustrating Drawn Glass Tubular Core.

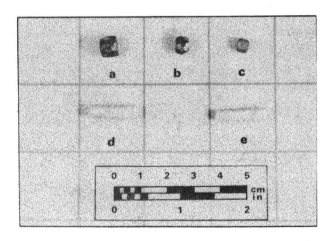

Figure 53. Glass and Shell "Necklace Beads."

is 0.43 cm. The length is 0.41 cm. The hole is 0.13 cm. The core is an opaque white. The body is a translucent, dark blue. Style Fifteen is shown in figure 53 c.

Style Sixteen beads (figure 53 d & c) are natural shell beads. These shells are roughly tubular in form. Two examples were noted. The first has a length of 1.82 cm. Its diameter tapers from 0.5 cm to 0.43 cm. Its hole varies from 0.28 cm. to 0.33 cm. The second bead has a length of 1.95 cm. Its diameter tapers from 0.5 cm to 0.37 cm. Its hole measurement ranges from 0.23 cm to 0.33 cm.

In addition to the beads that could be classified, a number of glass bead fragments were collected. These were heavily deteriorated fragments of light green and light blue glass.

Distribution

The spatial distribution of beads for combined strata is shown in figure 54 for the material from the West Dump and in figure 55 for the artifacts from the Main Dump. Provenience data by bead style, count, dump, unit type, and stratum are listed in tables 19 to 24.

Comments

Several comments may be made about the general bead terminology utilized in this discussion, the basic methods of bead production, the comparative nature of Moore's interior fort bead collection and of Comer's exterior trash dump assemblage, and other aspects. For the most part, the terminology employed to describe the various features of each bead style derive from Horace C. Beck's (1973) Classification and Nomenclature of Beads and Pendants. The "diameter" (1973:2) refers to the maximum width of the transverse cross section. The "length" (1973:3) is the distance between the two ends of a bead. The "end" (1973:2) is defined as the surface that includes the perforation. The "transverse section" and the "longitudinal section" (1973:2) have been used in a slightly different form than originally defined by Beck. The "transverse section" has been defined in this study as that cross section that is perpendicular to the axis of the perforation rather than as "that section at right angles to the axis which has the largest area." The "longitudinal section" has been defined as that cross section that is parallel to the axis of the perforation rather than as "that cross section that is parallel to the axis that includes the major radius."

The general bead categories of "seed" and "necklace" beads have been adopted after Lyle Stone's usage (1974:88) in Fort Michilimackinac, 1715-1781 to distinguish between two relatively distinct clusters of beads according to size. The "seed" bead category has a diameter below 4.0 mm and a length below 3.0 mm. The "necklace" bead category has a diameter above 6.0 mm and a length above 6.0 mm. Beads with dimensions between these have proven to be somewhat problematic (Stone

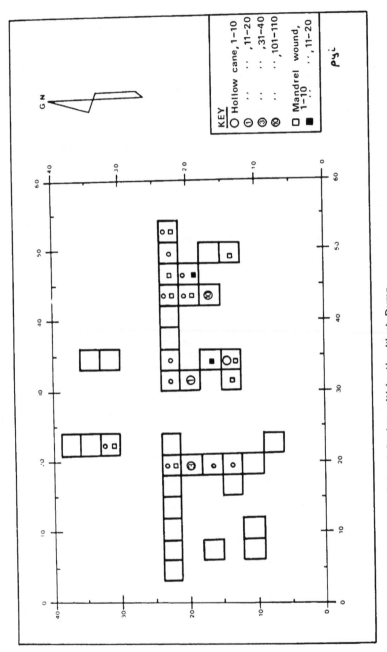

Figure 54. Distribution of Bead Styles within the West Dump.

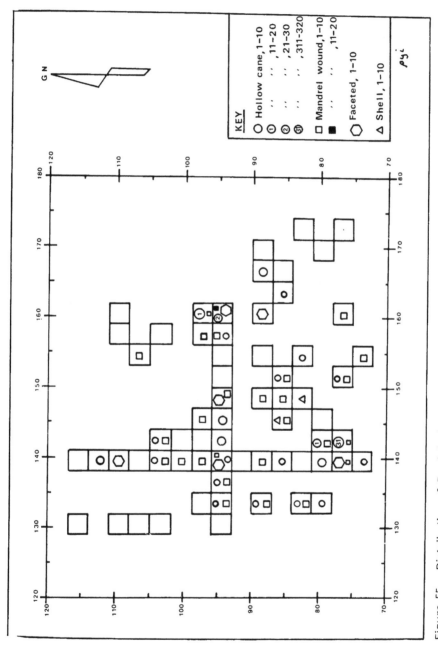

Figure 55. Distribution of Bead Styles within the Main Dump.

Table 19. Distribution of Style One Beads by Dump, Unit Type, and Strata

Style	Sub-Style	Color	Raw Frequency	Comments	Dump	Unit Type	Stratum
1	a	white	3		West	Random	A
	a	white	4		West	Nonrandom	C
	a	white	66		West	Random	C
	a	white	13		West	Random	D
	a	white	2		Main	Random	B
	a	white	4		Main	Nonrandom	C
	a	white	25		Main	Random	C
	a	white	21		Main	Random	D
	a	white	1		Main	Random	E
	a	white	1		Main	Random	F
		white	2	fragmentary	West	Random	⌐
	b	light blue	2		West	Nonrandom	A
	b	light blue	1		West	Nonrandom	B
	b	light blue	17		West	Nonrandom	C
	b	light blue	27		West	Random	C
	b	light blue	3		West	Nonrandom	D
	b	light blue	1		West	Random	D
	b	light blue	4		Main	Nonrandom	B
	b	light blue	3		Main	Random	B
	b	light blue	6		Main	Nonrandom	C
	b	light blue	200		Main	Random	C
	b	light blue	32		Main	Random	D
	b	light blue	43	fragmentary	West	Nonrandom	C
	b	light blue	3	fragmentary	West	Random	D
	b	light blue	1	fragmentary	Main	Nonrandom	C
	b	light blue	59	fragmentary	Main	Random	C
	b	light blue	3	fragmentary	Main	Random	D
	c	silver blue	1		West	Random	⌐
	c	silver blue	2		Main	Random	⌣
	d	green	1		Main	Nonrandom	D
	d	green	5		Main	Random	D
	d	green	4	fragmentary	Main	Nonrandom	B
	d	green	1	fragmentary	Main	Nonrandom	C
	d	green	2	fragmentary	Main	Random	C
	d	green	1	fragmentary	Main	Nonrandom	D
		red	1	fragmentary	West	Random	C

West Dump Subtotal   187
Main Dump Subtotal   377

Total   546

276

Table 20. Distribution of Style Two, Three, and Four Beads by Dump, Unit Type, and Strata

Style	Sub-Style	Color	Raw Frequency	Comments	Dump	Unit Type	Stratum
2		red	2		Main	Nonrandom	C
2		red	36		Main	Random	C
2		ed	1		Main		D
2		ed	1		Main	Random	D
2		ed	1		Main	Random	E
3		white	1		West	Random	C
3		white	1		Main	Random	H
					Style Two Total		41
					Style Three Total		1
					Style Four Total		1

Table 21.   Distribution of Style Five Beads by Dump, Unit Type, and Strata

Style	Sub-Style	Color	Raw Frequency	Comments	Dump	Unit Type	Stratum
5	a	white	3		Main	Random	C
5	a	white	2		Main	Random	D
5	a	white	3	f any	West	Random	A
5	a	white	1	fragmentary	West	Nonrandom	B
5	a	white	4	fragmentary	West	Nonrandom	C
5	a	white	11	fragmentary	West	Random	C
5	a	white	2	fragmentary	West	Random	D
5	a	white	1	fragmentary	Main	Nonrandom	B
5	a	white	2	fragmentary	Main	Random	B
5	a	white	3	1 any	Main	Nonrandom	C
5	a	white	5	any	Main	Random	C
5	a	white	4	any	Main	Nonrandom	D
5	a	white	13	fragmentary 2fragmentary	Main	Random	D
5	a	white			Main	Random	E
5	b	amber	1		West	Random	OB
5	b	tan	1		West	Random	C
5	b	amber	1		Main	Random	B
5	b	amber	2	fragmentary	Main	Random	D
5	c	dark blue	1		West	Random	C
5	d	balt blue	1		Main	Random	B
5	d	balt blue	3		Main	Nonrandom	C
					West Dump Subtotal		25
					Main Dump Subtotal		42
					Total		67

278

Table 22. Distribution of Styles Six, Seven, Eight, Nine, and Ten Beads
by Dump, Unit Type, and Strata

Style	Sub-Style	Color	Raw Frequency	Comments	Dump	Unit Type	Stratum
6		light blue	1		Main	Random	C
6		light blue	2		Main	Random	D
6		light lbe	1	fragmentary	Main	Random	D
7		brown & green	1		Main	Random	C
7		brown & green	2	fragmentary	Main	Random	C
8		white	1	fragmentary	Main	Random	D
9		white	1	fragmentary	Main	Random	A
10		white	1	fragmentary	Main	Nonrandom	B
10		white	1	fragmentary	Main	Random	C
10		white	1	fragmentary	Main	Random	D

Style Six Total 4
Style Seven Total 3
Style Eight Total 1
Style Nine Total 1
Style Ten Total 3

Table 23. Distribution of Style Eleven Beads by Dump, Unit Type, and Strata

Style	Sub-Style	Color	Raw Frequency	Comments	Dump	Unit Type	Stratum
11	a	white	3		Main	Random	C
11	a	white	2		Main	Random	D
11	a	white	2	fragmentary	West	Random	C
11	a	white	1	fragmentary	Main	Nonrandom	B
11	a	white	1	fragmentary	Main	Nonrandom	D
11	a	white	4	fragmentary	Main	Random	D
11	b	light blue	1		West	Random	D
11	b	light blue	1		Main	Random	E
11	c	red	2		Main	Random	C
					West Dump Subtotal		3
					Main Dump Subtotal		14
					Total		17

280

Table 24. Distribution of Styles Twelve, Thirteen, Fourteen, Fifteen, and Sixteen Beads and Unspecified Fragments by Dump, Unit Type, and Strata

Style	Sub-Style	Color	Raw Frequency	Comments	Dump	Unit Type	Stratum
12		light brown	1		Main	Random	D
13	a	milky white	1		Main	Nonrandom	D
13	b	dark blue	1		Main	Nonrandom	B
13	b	dark blue	1		Main	Random	B
14	a	lime green	1		Main	Nonrandom	C
14	b	dark blue	1		Main	Random	D
15		dark blue	1		Main	Random	F
16		white	1	natural shell	Main	Random	D
16		white	1	natural shell	Main	Random	E
NA		light green	6	fragmentary	West	Nonrandom	D
NA		light green	10	fragmentary	West	Random	D
NA		light green	4	fragmentary	Main	Random	B
NA		light blue	1	fragmentary	Main	Random	B

Style Twelve Total 1
Style Thirteen Total 3
Style Fourteen Total 2
Style Fifteen Total 1
Style Sixteen Total 2
Unspecified Fragment Total 21

1974:88). In this study, only styles One and Two fall within the "seed" bead cateogry. The rest of the styles fall for the most part within the dimensional range of the "necklace" beads.

Two basic methods of manufacture are reflected in the glass bead collection. These methods are the hollow cane or drawn glass method and the mandrel wound method. In the hollow cane method, a glob of molten glass is either folded over or blown to create a large bubble (Kidd and Kidd 1970:47-49; van der Sleen 1967:22-26). A second iron rod is attached to one end by an assistant. The bubble is pulled apart from the two ends into a long rod of glass. The rod is allowed to cool and, then, is either broken or cut into lengths suitable for further work. Figure 56 depicts glass workers making beads of these shortened lengths of tube. The final bead sections are finished by reheating in a mixture of sand and ash to smooth the rough edges of their cut ends.

Figure 56. Craftsmen Manufacturing Beads by the Hollow Cane Method. (An oil painting by Jacob van Loo, presumably of a 17th century Amsterdam scene, reproduced from a plate in Kidd 1979:101.)

In the mandrel wound method, a glob of molten glass is prepared as in the hollow cane method except that no bubble is formed. An assistant attaches a second iron rod to the glob and the two workers stretch the glass by running in opposite directions. This forms a thin solid rod of glass that is allowed to cool. This rod is then either cut or broken into shorter sections for use in making beads. These sections are reheated and wound around a wire to form beads. These beads are then tumbled in a mixture of sand and ash and heated to smooth out the rough edges of their contours.

In comparing the trash dumps' bead assemblage with that of the interior fort, only a relatively general level of comparison could be made since the interior fort collection's comprehensive inventory was not available for study. Based upon data reported in Moore (1973:102-107), a presence-absence comparison of bead categories could be made and a more specific, quantitative comparison of the "seed" bead subset could be presented.

The presence-absence comparison listed in table 25 suggests two conclusions about the relative availability of the various bead styles. The styles that occur at all three of the locations were probably the most common at the fort. For the most part, these same styles are also the most technologically simple and, hence, cheapest to produce. The styles, on the other hand, that occur at only a restricted number of locations were probably the rarest at the fort. In general, these styles are the most technologically complex and, hence, costliest to produce.

Table 25. Presence-Absence Comparison of Comer's
and Moore's Bead Assemblages

Style	Moore's Category	West Dump	Main Dump	Interior Fort
1 & 2	common bead, white	X	X	X
	common bead, blue	X	X	X
	common bead, green		X	X
	common bead, red	X	X	X
	common bead, black			X
	common bead, pearlescent	X	X	X
	common bead, yellow			X
3	NA	X		
4	NA		X	
5	round beads, white	X	X	X
	round beads, blue	X	X	X
	round beads, green			X
	round beads, black (amber)	X	X	X
6	NA		X	

283

Table 25. (cont.)

Style	Moore's Category	West Dump	Main Dump	Interior Fort
7	NA		X	
8, 9, 10	polychrome		X	
NA	cylindrical, white			X
	cylindrical, lavender			X
	cylindrical, yellow			X
	cylindrical, blue			X
NA	large egg beads, white			X
	large egg beads, blue			X
	large egg beads, green			X
11 & 12	small egg beads, white	X	X	X
	small egg beads, blue	X	X	X
	small egg beads, green			X
	small egg beads, red		X	X
	small egg beads, lavender			X
	small egg beads, yellow			X
	(light brown)		X	
13,14,15	barrel tubular faceted beads, clear			X
	barrel tubular faceted beads, blue		X	X
	barrel tubular faceted beads, red			X
	(lime green)		X	
	(milky white)		X	
16	NA		X	
NA	long tubular faceted beads, clear			X
NA	long tubular faceted beads, blue			X
	long tubular faceted beads, red			X

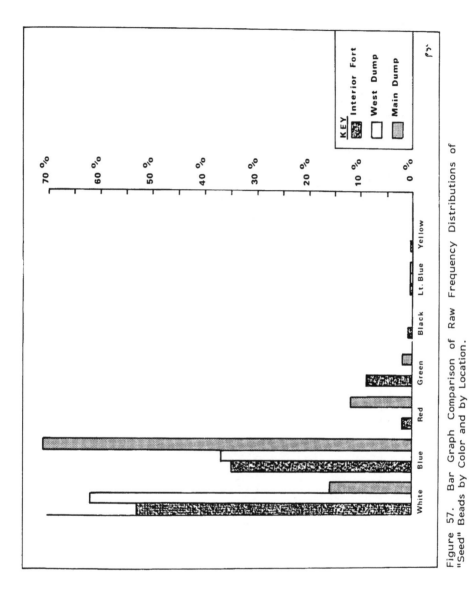

Figure 57. Bar Graph Comparison of Raw Frequency Distributions of "Seed" Beads by Color and by Location.

The quantitative comparison of "seed" beads illustrated in figure 57 suggests a relatively similar pattern of distribution of bead colors within the West Dump and the interior fort collections. The Main Dump assemblage appears to be distinct from that of the other two localities. Examination, however, of the intra-dump distribution indicates high spot densities of blue and red beads within the Main Dump. These localized clusters heavily skew the composition of the dump. Compensating for the spot densities would also bring the Main Dump into the distribution range of the interior fort assemblage.

Two final comments can be made. First, any quantitative comparison of the bead assemblage will have to accommodate the biasing factors present within the assemblage. As noted by Moore (1973:106-107), green glass beads have tended to deteriorate more rapidly than have other categories of beads. Also, in regards to the present assemblage, the differential fine mesh/quarter inch mesh technique used during the excavations skews the collection away from a full representation of beads of small size. Second, while Moore's evidence (1973:107) tended to indicate the deposition of beads primarily through random dispersal, the occurrence of bead clustering within the dumps and the presence of patterned trace depositions such as that shown in figure 58 suggest that discarding of beaded material had occurred and may, possibly, have been an important element in the discard process outside the fort.

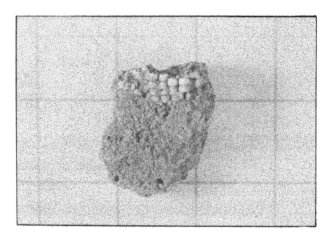

Figure 58.   Remnant of an Article of Beadwork.

BUCKLES

Description

A single, small brass buckle (figure 59 d) is included within the artifact
assemblage. The face is rectangular and measures 1.64 cm by 1.41 cm.
A design of 22 raised dots decorates the border. There is a thin center
bar. The entire piece appears to have been molded together. The plane
of the face is slightly convex.

Distribution

Provenience data are listed in table 26.

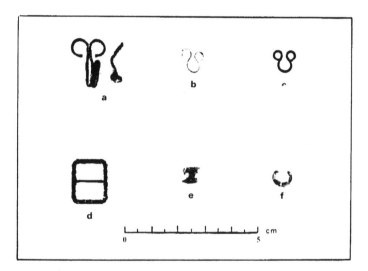

Figure 59. Miscellaneous Articles of Personal Attire.

BUTTONS

The button collection can be divided into three broad categories. These
groupings are button blanks, whole or nearly whole buttons, and
unidentifiable button fragments. Buttons can be described in terms of
shape, method of construction, material, mode of attachment, size, and
decorative elements. Based upon these criteria, 24 button styles were
noted.

In describing the buttons, a series of terms was adopted to standardize
the presentation of the discussion. Three terms were chosen to designate
the general sections of a button. The "back" was defined as that portion

Table 26. Distribution of Miscellaneous Articles of Personal Attire

Item	Material	Frequency	Dump	Unit type	Stratum
Boot Nail	Iron	1	Main	Random	D
Boot Nail	Iron	1	Main	Random	C
Buckle	Brass	1	West	Nonrandom	C
Eyelet, Style One	Copper Alloy	1	West	Random	C
Eyelet, Style Two	Copper Alloy	1	West	Random	C
Grommet	Copper Alloy	1	West	Random	A
Grommet	Copper Alloy	1	West	Nonrandom	A
Hook	Copper Alloy	2	West	Random	A
Shoe Sole	Leather	1	West	Nonrandom	A
Shoe Sole	Leather	1	Main	Random	C

of the button that rests nearest the garment when attached. The "rim" is that portion of the button that comprises the outer circumference. The "face" is that portion that is normally exposed to view when attached. On the face surface, three areas were delimited. The "border" was defined as that section of the face that comprised a distinct outer edge or band feature. The "center area" is that section of the face that lies within the border. The "center" is the physical center of the face. In describing the mode of attachment, a distinction was made between the centering hole utilized in drilling out a button blank and the actual holes used during attachment. As a convention, only the number of holes actually sewn through were listed under mode of attachment and the presence of a centering hole was noted elsewhere. These points are illustrated in figure 60.

During the process of producing bone buttons, at least four marks were left on the finished button to indicate the steps that had been used. The bone slabs from which button blanks were cut were either naturally thinned such as scapular sections or were sawed parallel to the surface to reduce the thickness. This latter operation occurred on elements such as beef ribs. As a result of this step, bone buttons frequently retain traces of the thinning as a series of either straight or slightly curved parallel ridges (figure 61 b). Bone buttons were usually cut from the prepared slab by means of a drill. This step resulted in a center hole or depression. Also evident were traces of concentric circular marks that were produced by the turning of the drill bit on the surface of the button. Finally, the drilling process left a slight circumferential ridge along the rim whose placement varied according to whether the blank had been drilled from one side or from both sides or had been snapped loose after having been partially cut. In referring to these features, the following terms were used: saw marks, drill hole, drill marks, and seam.

288

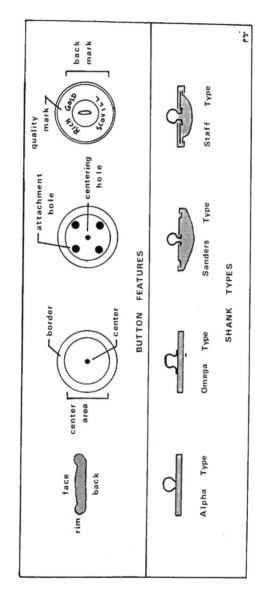

Figure 60. Button Terminology.

289

Figure 61. Button Processing Marks (a, drill cut scar; b, saw marks).

Button blanks comprise the first general category of buttons within this assemblage. Two bone button blanks (figure 62) are included in the present collection. Saw marks are evident on both surfaces. Each has a central drill hole. Only one of the blanks has distinct drill marks; the marks occur on both surfaces. Both blanks have irregular seams, which suggest that they had been drilled out from two sides.

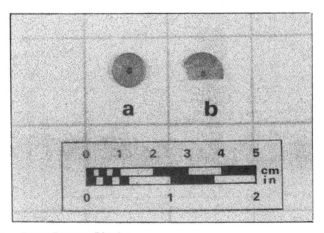

Figure 62. Bone Button Blanks.

The whole or nearly whole buttons were divided into 24 styles (figures 63 and 64) according to shape, method of construction, mode of attachment, and decorative elements. Style One is a plain shell button. The back is flat. The rim is straight. The face has a beveled border (figures 63 and 65 a). The center section is concave and has a raised, cylindrical "nose" at the center. The center section is offset from the actual physical center of the face. The four attachment holes are irregularly placed.

Style Two (figures 63 and 65 b) is a decorated shell button. The back is flat. The rim is straight. The face has a beveled border with an incised design of triangular, starburst-type points. In vertical cross section, each of the 12 points is roughly V-shaped. The center section is depressed below the border. A circular scar surrounds the four attachment holes. The holes are irregular in size and placement.

Style Three (figures 63 and 65 c) is an elaborately decorated shell button. The back is flat. The rim is straight. The border is flat. It is trimmed along the edge with finely incised, short, radial lines. Eleven starburst-type points radiate outward from the center section onto the border. The center section is concave. In vertical cross section, the points are curved; they are irregular in size. The four attachment holes are irregular in size and placement.

Style Four (figures 63 and 65 d) is a decorated shell button. The back is flat. The rim is straight. The face has a border trimmed with 24 incised V-shaped radiations. The center section is concave. Two partial scars encircle the section. There are four attachment holes.

Style Five (figures 63 and 65 e) is a plain shell button. The back is flat. The rim is straight. The face is flat. A shallow, cylindrical depression occurs at the center. There are four attachment holes.

Style Six (figures 63 and 65 f) is a shell button. The back is flat. The rim is straight. The border is flat. A circular cut separates the border from the center section. The center section is concave. A slight, cylindrical depression occurs at the center. The four attachment holes are irregularly placed.

Style Seven (figures 63 and 66 a) is a plain bone button. The back is flat. The rim is roughly convex. An irregularly placed seam is present. The border is rounded. A scar encircles a relatively flat center section. The center drill hole is slightly larger than the four attachment holes. Saw marks are evident on the back. One button within this style exhibits a misplaced drill cut scar (figure 61 d).

Style Eight (figures 63 and 66 b) is a bone button. The back is convex; concentric, circular drill marks are evident. The rim is relatively straight. The border is flat. The center section is cut below the border and is flat. A slight depression occurs at the center. The openings of the four holes are beveled.

Style Nine (figures 63 and 66 c) is a bone button. The back is flat and exhibits saw cut marks. The rim is roughly convex. The border is

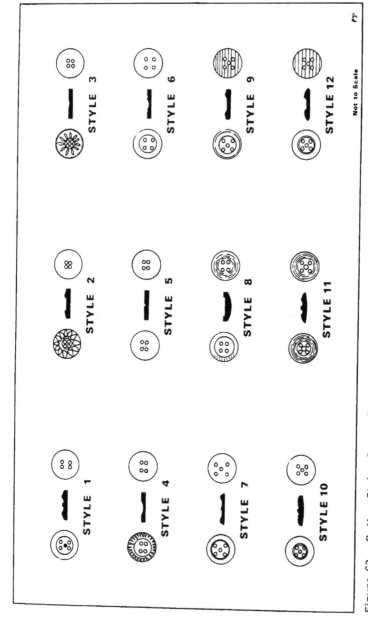

Figure 63.   Button Styles One to Twelve.

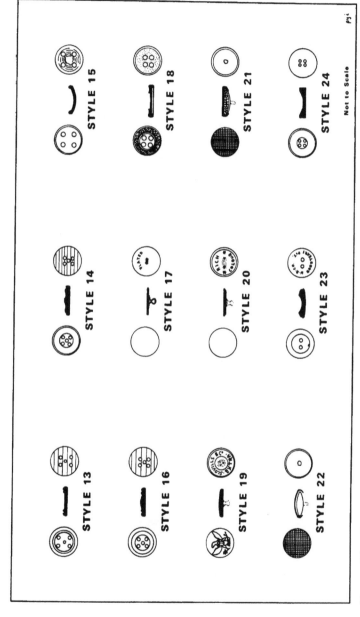

Figure 64. Button Styles Thirteen to Twenty-Four.

293

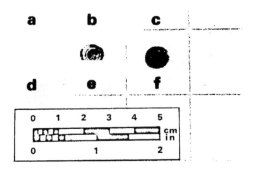

Figure 65. Button Styles One to Six (a, Style One; b, Style Two; c, Style Three; d, Style Four; e, Style Five; f, Style Six).

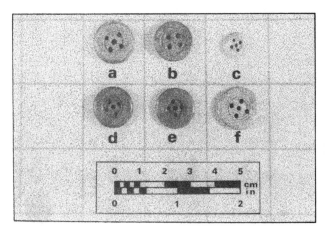

Figure 66. Button Styles Seven to Twelve (a, Style Seven; b, Style Eight; c, Style Nine; d, Style Ten; e, Style Eleven; f, Style Twelve).

rounded and is encircled along its outer edge by a scar. The central section lies below the level of the border and is flat. The placement of the four attachment holes around the center drill hole is regular.

Style Ten (figures 63 and 66 d) is a bone button. The back is slightly convex. The rim is rounded and exhibits a faint seam. The border is slightly curved. The central section is surrounded by a scar. The center section rises toward the center drill hole. (A smaller, hard, black rubber variant of this style has drill scars on its back and center face section.)

Style Eleven (figures 63 and 66 e) is a bone button. The back is slightly convex. The rim is roughly convex and exhibits an irregular, partial seam. The border merges into the rim. Drill marks are evident on both the back and the border. The center section is depressed below the level of the border. The surface of the center section is flat. The center is raised above this section. The drill hole is surrounded by four attachment holes.

Style Twelve (figures 63 and 66 f) is a bone button. The back is flat and exhibits parallel saw cut marks. The rim is convex and has a distinct seam. The border is slightly rounded. The center section is encircled by two raised, narrow rings. The center section retains faint traces of concentric, circular, drill marks. Its surface is relatively flat. There are four attachment holes and a center drill hole.

Style Thirteen (figures 64 and 67 a) is a bone button. The back is flat and possesses relatively pronounced saw marks. The rim forms an obtuse angle to the back. At the top of the rim, a seam separates the rim from the order. Two moderately wide, rounded rings encircle the flat center section. The relatively small center drill hole is surrounded by four attachment holes.

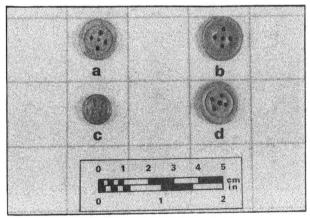

Figure 67. Button Styles Thirteen to Sixteen (a, Style Thirteen; b, Style Fourteen; c, Style Fifteen; d, Style Sixteen).

295

Style Fourteen (figures 64 and 67 b) is a bone button. The back is flat and retains traces of parallel saw marks. The rim is rounded and exhibits a seam. A narrow ring encircles the outer edge of the border. The center section drops slightly below the level of the border and then rises upward toward the center drill hole. Four attachment holes are present.

Style Fifteen (figures 64 and 67 c) is a bone button. The back is distinctly convex and has traces of fine concentric, circular drill marks. The rim is rounded and retains a medial seam. The rounded border is narrow. The center section is distinctly concave. The center is slightly indented. Faint traces of concentric, circular drill scars exist on the surface of the center section. There are four widely spaced attachment holes.

Style Sixteen (figures 64 and 67 d) is a bone button. The back is flat and retains traces of saw marks. The rim is flat and forms an obtuse angle with the plane of the back. A seam line separates the rim from the edge of the border. The border is composed of two moderately wide rounded rings. The center section drops below the level of the border and then rises toward the center drill hole. There are four attachment holes.

Style Seventeen (figures 64, 68 a, and 69 a) is an omega type (Luscomb 1967:141) brass button. Omega type buttons were machine made and had a characteristic omega-shaped wire shank brazed to the back. The back of the Style Seventeen button is flat. The word "Plated" is impressed on the back. The rim is narrow and rounded. The face is flat and plain.

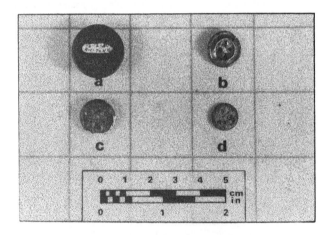

Figure 68. Button Styles Seventeen to Twenty (a, Style Seventeen; b, Style Eighteen; c, Style Nineteen; d, Style Twenty).

296

Style Eighteen (figures 64, 68 b, and 69 b) is a composite metal button. The back is a thin iron plate; its surface is flat. Part of the brass face overlaps along the edge of the iron plate to secure the surface metal to its backing. The rim is narrow and rounded. The border is a decorated band composed of narrow outer and inner rings that enclose a moderately wide band of diamond crosshatching. This design border is in relief. The center section is flat. There are four attachment holes.

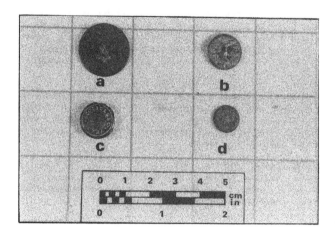

Figure 69.   Button Styles Seventeen to Twenty: Back Surfaces (a, Style Seventeen; b, Style Eighteen; c, Style Nineteen; d, Style Twenty).

Style Nineteen (figures 64, 68 c, and 69 c) is a Sanders-type (Luscomb 1967:17) brass button.   Sanders-type buttons were made by the following process:

> The upper blank was driven, by heavy pressure, into a die of hardened steel that gave it the desired shape and pattern; the under blank was similarly pressed into another die, which also "riveted" the shank into the plate.   The two dies were then pressed together, and the button was complete except for the finishing.   [Luscomb 1967:17]

The Style Nineteen button has a flat back and retains the brazed section of the loop shank attachment.   "SCOVILLS & CO./ EXTRA" is impressed around the outer edge of the back.   The face metal slightly overlaps the back plate.   The rim is rounded.   The face is convex and is decorated with an eagle and plain shield in relief.

Style Twenty (figures 64, 68 d, and 69 d) is a Sanders-type brass button.   The back is slightly concave.   The brazed section of the loop shank attachment remains.   "RICH/COLOR" is marked in relief.   The rim is stepped out toward the face.   The face is flat and plain.

Style Twenty-one (figures 64, 70 a, and 71 a) is a Sanders-type iron button. The back plate is convex. A hole remains at the attachment, which could have been either a flexible canvas or metal loop. An unidentified porous material is evident within the cavity of the button. This substance could be either cork, bone, or wood. The face plate overlaps across the back plate. The rim is rounded. The face is flat. Traces of a cross-woven fabric are imbedded within the corrosion surface of the face.

Style Twenty-two (figures 64, 70 b, and 71 b) is a Sanders-type iron button. The back plate is convex. A hole remains at the attachment, which could have been either a flexible canvas flap or a metal loop. The face plate overlaps the back plate. The rim is rounded. The face is convex. Traces of a cross-woven fabric are imbedded within the corrosion surface of the face.

Style Twenty-three (figures 64, 70 c, and 71 c) is a hard, black rubber button. The back is slightly convex. "N.R.CO./GOODYEARS/P=T" is molded in relief around the edge. The relatively straight rim is split by a medial seam. The border is beveled. The center section is concave. Two attachment holes are present.

Style Twenty-four (figures 64 and 70 d) is a translucent, yellowish-white, plastic button. The back is flat. The rim is straight. The border is a narrow, flat band. The border slopes down to a flat center section. Four attachment holes are present.

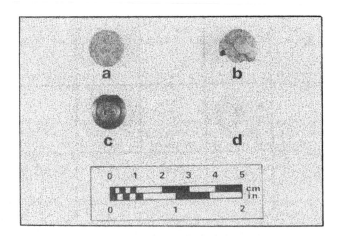

Figure 70. Button Styles Twenty-one to Twenty-four (a, Style Twenty-one; b, Style Twenty-two; c, Style Twenty-three; d, Style Twenty-four).

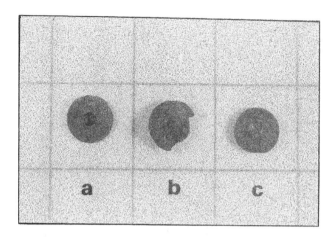

Figure 71. Button Styles Twenty-one to Twenty-four: Back Surfaces (a, Style Twenty-one; b, Style Twenty-two; c, Style Twenty-three; d, Style Twenty-four).

Several buttons due to excessive wear, fragmentation, or corrosion could not be assigned to specific styles. According to material, there were four iron, two copper alloy, and two bone buttons in this category. Two of the iron buttons, however, could be identified as being of the Sanders-type.

Distribution

The distribution of button styles by dump, provenience, and stratum is listed in table 27. Dimensional as well as other attribute data are also included. The spatial distribution of the button collection is depicted according to combined strata for the West Dump in figure 72 and for the Main Dump in figure 73.

Intra-class analysis of the button collection according to material, size (diameter), and frequency reveals a tendency toward ordered distribution or clustering. As plotted in figure 74, four cluster zones are apparent. These zones correspond roughly to homogeneous material sets. Cluster One is comprised of shell buttons with diameters of 0.79 cm to 1.01 cm. Cluster Two is comprised of bone buttons with diameters of 1.01 cm to 1.24 cm. Cluster Three is made up of brass and iron buttons with diameters of 1.27 to 1.5 cm. Cluster Four is comprised of bone buttons with diameters of 1.55 to 1.78 cm.

The four size clusters fall well below the size of the regular 19th century uniform button, 2.3 cm (Johnson 1948:19), and of present day shirt buttons, 2.0 cm. They also cluster poorly around the 19th century

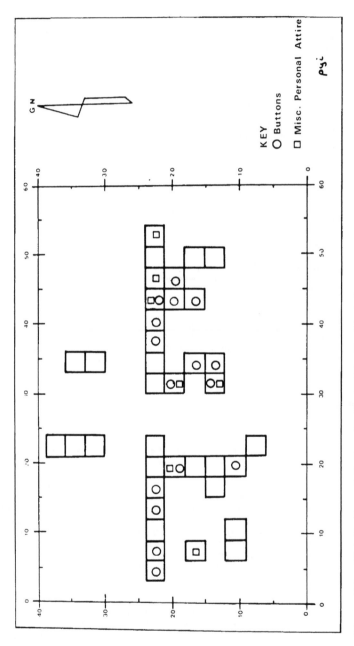

Figure 72. Distribution of Button Styles Within the West Dump.

300

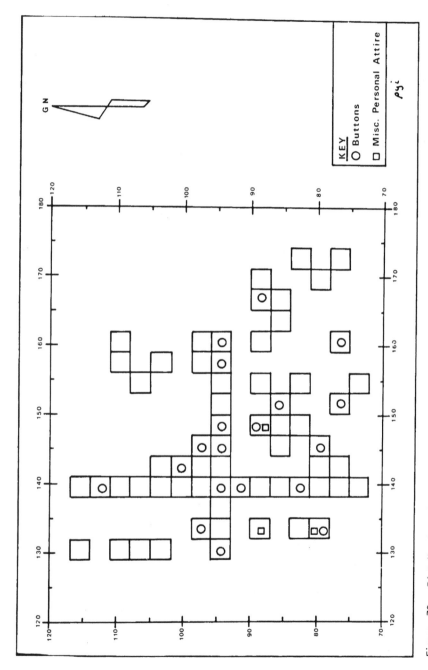

Figure 73. Distribution of Button Styles Within the Main Dump.

301

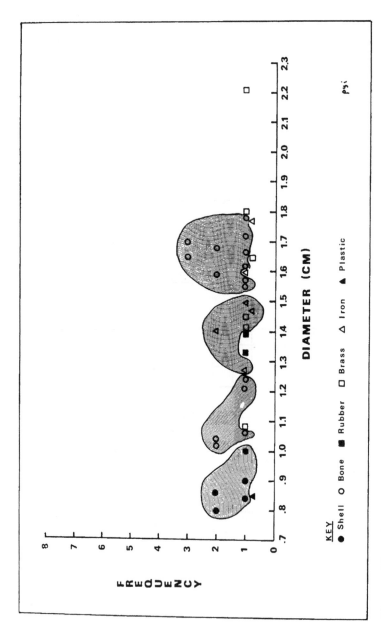

Figure 74. Intra-sample Distribution of Buttons by Material, Size (Diameter), and Frequency.

Table 27. Distribution of Button Styles by Dump, Unit Type, and Stratum

Style	Material	Diameter (cm)	Border Width (cm)	Mode of Attachment	Comments	Dump	Unit Type	Stratum
1	shell	0.79	0.18±	4-hole	worn	West	Nonrandom	D
1	shell	0.79	0.18±	4-hole	worn	West	Nonrandom	D
2	shell	0.85	0.15	4-hole	chipped	West	Random	A
3	shell	1.01	0.28	4-hole		West	Random	C
4	shell	0.90	0.19±	4-hole	heavily worn	West	Random	C
5	shell	0.86		4-hole	heavily worn	Main	Random	C
6	shell	0.83	0.09±	4-hole	heavily worn	Main	Random	C
7	bone	1.68	0.33	4-hole	drill hole	West	Random	B
7	bone	1.65	0.35	4-hole	drill hole fragmentary	West	Nonrandom	C
7	bone	1.72	0.35	4-hole	drill hole gragmentary	Main	Random	B
7	bone	1.01	0.24	4-hole	drill hole	Main	Random	D
7	bone	1.04	0.24	4-hole	drill hole	Main	Random	D
8	bone	1.59	0.26	40hole		West	Random	A
9	bone	1.04	0.23	4-hole	dirll hole	West	Nonrandom	D
9	bone	1.06	0.21	4-hole	drill hole	Main	Random	C
10	bone	1.65	0.40	4-hole	drill hole	West	Random	C
10	rubber	1.33	0.33	4-hole	drill hole	West	Nonrandom	C
11	bone	1.62	0.45	4-hole	drill hole	West	Random	C
12	bone	1.66	0.47	4-hole	drill hole fragmentary	West	Random	C
12	bone	1.70	0.44	4-hole	drill hole	West	Random	C
12	bone	1.70	0.43	4-hole	drill hble	West	Random	C
13	bone	1.65	0.41	4-hole	drill hole worn	West	Nonrandom	B
13	bone	1.68	0.44	4-hole	drill hole	Main	Random	D
14	bone	1.59	0.43	4-hole	drill hole	West	Nonrandom	C
14	bone	1.78	0.15	4-hole	drill hole	Main	Random	C
15	bone	1.21	0.15	4-hole		West	Nonrandom	D
15	bone	1.57	0.17	4-hole	fragmentary	Main	Random	D
16	bone	1.70	0.49	4-hole	drill hole	Main	Random	D
17	brass	2.11	NA	omega type	"PLATED" mark	West	Random	D
18	brass/iron	1.41	0.30	4-hole		West	Nonrandom	B
19	brass	1.45	NA	possible loop	general issue military; "SC^OVILL CO./ EXTRA" mark	West	Random	B
20	brass	1.08	NA	possible loop	"RICH C^OL^OUR" mark	Main	Random	F
21	iron, fabric, bone?	1.40	NA	possible loop		West	Random	A
21	iron, fabric, bone?	1.27	NA	possible loop shank		Main	Random	E
22	iron, fabric	1.50	NA	possible loop shank		West	Nonrandom	D

303

Table 27 (cont.)

Style	Material	Diameter (cm)	Border Width (cm)	Mode of Attachment	Comments	Dump	Unit Type	Stratum
23	rubber	1.39	0.26	2-hole	"N.R.CO./ GOODYEARS/P=T"	Main	Nonrandom	A
24	plastic	0.85	0.31	4-hole		West	Random	A
blank	bone	1.24	NA	NA	drill hole fragmentary	Main	Random	B
blank	bone	1.02	NA	NA	drill hole	Main	Nonrandom	C
NA	shell	?	?	4-hole	missing	Main	Random	D
NA	bone	1.55	unknown	unknown	heavily worn	West	Random	A
NA	bone	unknown	unknown	unknown	fragmentary	Main	Nonrandom	D
NA	copper alloy	1.65	unknown	unknown	heavily corroded	Main	Nonrandom	C
NA	copper alloy	1.80	unknown	possible loop shank	heavily corroded	Main	Nonrandom	D
NA	iron	1.60	NA	possible loop shank	heavily corroded; Sanders-type	Main	Random	B
NA	iron	1.77	NA	unknown	heavily corroded	West	Nonrandom	C
NA	iron	1.40	unknown	unknown	heavily corroded	Main	Nonrandom	D
NA	iron/bone?	1.47	unknown	possible loop shank	heavily corroded; Sanders-type	Main	Random	D

304

military vest button size, 1.2 cm (Johnson 1948:19). The clusters probably reflect a combination of socio-functional variables. The small size of this sample, however, restricts any real elaboration on this point. Nevertheless, there is some suggestion that size of button acts both to define a general category of use, e.g., shirt vs vest, as well as a finer distinction within that category, e.g., plain vs fine vests. On another plane, there is a suggestion that decorative elaboration may play a differentiating role in mediating between the level of use of any given size button, e.g., decorated fine vest buttons vs plain vest buttons. On a third plane, there is a suggestion that material also plays a refining role in the definition of button application within size groupings, e.g., brass buttons applied to fine vests vs plain bone buttons applied to regular vests.

Comments

Some notations can be made concerning the chronological and comparative aspects of the button collection. In general, all of the buttons (except the one plastic button) represent styles that were commonly available during the 19th century. The bone and shell buttons are of varieties that might also have been available earlier. In terms of chronology, a small number of buttons can be associated with general periods of manufacture. Omega-type buttons became available with machine techniques around the turn of the century and were common from about 1800 to 1850 (Luscomb 1967:141). Undecorated brass buttons with back marks such as "Rich Colour" were popular from about 1800 to 1830 (Luscomb 1967:79) before improvements in machine techniques permitted the manufacture of more elaborately decorated brass buttons. Sanders-type buttons became available after about 1825 (Luscomb 1967:17). Sanders-type buttons with fabric covers were available from about the same period (Luscomb 1967:70). These early fabric-covered buttons were generally made by machines in factories (figure 75). Later, during the 19th century, the fabric was applied by store clerks with small hand machines. Improved hard rubber was patented by Nelson Goodyear in 1851; the Novelty Rubber Company of New Brunswick, New Jersey, which used this material for producing buttons, operated between 1855 and 1870 (Luscomb 1967:140). General issue or general service military buttons were first authorized by General Order Number 1 of the Adjutant General's Office on January 20, 1854 (Ludington 1889:40). The first style of general issue buttons was supplied to enlisted personnel between 1855 and 1884 (Brinckerhoff 1972:5; Campbell 1965:5).

In order to compare the button samples collected by Comer and Moore, it was necessary to utilize a baseline ratio approach rather than the more common comparison of intra-sample percentages since not all the button frequencies were listed in Moore's report (1973:112-113). The bone button frequency was taken as the baseline or index figure and all other frequencies were compared to it to arrive at a comparative measure. The calculated ratios are listed in table 28. As can be seen, both the West Dump and Main Dump distributions are relatively similar. Both samples, however, differ markedly from that of the interior fort. The significant differences are 1) the relatively smaller presence of shell buttons in the two dumps, 2) the relatively lower presence of brass buttons in the dump

305

Figure 75. Factory Workers Applying Fabric Covers to Metal Buttons
(reproduced from Luscomb 1967:69).

Table 28. Comparative Distribution of Buttons by Material from
Comer's and Moore's Excavations (Ratios Based Utilizing
Bone Frequency as the Index Value)

Material	West Dump		Main Dump		Interior Fort	
	Raw Frequency	Index Ratio	Raw Frequency	Index Ratio	Raw Frequency	Index Ratio
shell	5	0.38	3	0.27	37	1.00
bone	13	1.00	11	1.00	37	1.00
brass	3	0.23	3	0.27	22	0.59
iron	3	0.23	4	0.36	not reported	
pewter	0	0.00	0	0.00	2	0.05
rubber	1	0.08	1	0.09	4	0.11
glass	0	0.00	0	0.00	37	1.00
plastic	1	0.08	0	0.00	0	0.00
Total	26		22			

areas, and 3) the total absence of glass buttons from the dump samples. The latter two differences might be attributed to the elimination of the upper stratum of the dump areas from the archeological retrieval operations. This process would have eliminated many of the later deposited materials. The variation in the shell samples cannot be readily explained. The other differences noted in the table can be attributed to differences in sample size.

GROMMETS

The two copper alloy grommets (figure 59 e & f) that were recovered were fragmentary. Several measurements were selected as critical dimensions. These measurements were rim diameter, bore diameter, and height. The rim diameter was defined as the maximum diameter of the grommet at one of its ends. The bore diameter was defined as the interior diameter of the aperature. The height was defined as the maximum length of the grommet from end to end. The rim diameter, bore diameter, and height of one grommet were 6.1 mm, 3.9 mm, and 6.2 mm, respectively. The second grommet had a rim diameter of 7.2 mm, a bore diameter of 3.9 mm, and a height of 3.1 mm.

Distribution

The provenience characteristics of the grommet sample are listed in table 26.

HOOKS AND EYES

Description

Two eyelets, one fragmentary hook, and one complete hook were found. All of the items had been made of a copper alloy. Each of the eyelets represented a distinct style. The Style One (figure 59 b) eyelet consists of a thin strand of wire bent into the appropriate form. The Style Two eyelet (figure 59 c) consists of a thin, flat strip of metal bent into shape.

Six dimensions were selected as critical measurements of the eyelet. These measurements included the length that was defined as the maximum distance between the end of the eye and the end of the base of the eyelet. The width of the base was defined as the maximum length of the eyelet between the outer edges of the two loops forming the attachment section. The width of the eye was defined as the maximum distance between the two sides of the eye. The eye diameter was defined as the interior diameter of the eye measured parallel to the base. The attachment eye diameter was defined as the interior diameter of one of the two attachment loops measured parallel to the base. The strand width/diameter was defined as either the diameter of the wire comprising the eyelet or the width of the metal strip measured parallel to the normal plane of the eyelet.

307

For the Style One eyelet, the critical measurements were length, 8.3 mm; width at base, 8.9 mm; width at eye, 5.1 mm; eye diameter, 3.7 mm; attachment eye diameter, 2.4 mm; and strand diameter, 0.7 mm. For the Style Two eyelet, the critical measurements were length, 8.5 mm; width at base, 8.8 mm; width at eye, 5.7 mm; eye diameter, 3.8 mm; attachment eye diameter, 1.8 mm; and strand width, 1.0 mm.

The single complete hook (figure 59 a) had been made by bending a single strand of wire into shape. Six dimensions were selected as critical measurements. These measurements included the length that was defined as the maximum distance between the end of the base and the tip of the fold in the hook. The width at the base was defined as the maximum distance between the outer edges of the attachment section. The width at the shaft was defined as the distance between the outer edges of the hook as measured parallel to the base and halfway along the shaft. The length of the hook-over was defined as the distance between the end of the fold in the hook to the tip of the section of the hook that was bent back towards the base. The diameter of the attachment eye was defined as the interior diameter of one of the attachment loops as measured parallel to the base. The strand diameter was defined as the diameter of the wire used to construct the hook. For the single complete hook, the critical measurements were length, 1.82 cm; width at base, 1.34 cm; width at shaft, 0.32 cm; length of hook-over, 1.0 cm; diameter of the attachment eye, 0.4 cm; and the strand diameter, 0.13 cm.

Distribution

The distributional characteristics of the hooks and eyes are listed in table 26.

SHOES

Description

Two sets of leather fragments (figure 76) could be identified as parts of shoes or boots. Both sets were fragments of soles and exhibited traces of threaded seam holes. Both sets had been subjected to fire and were partially scorched.

In addition, two iron boot (heel) nails were noted. Both were approximately 3/4 inch in length.

Distribution

The distributional characteristics of the shoe elements are listed in table 26.

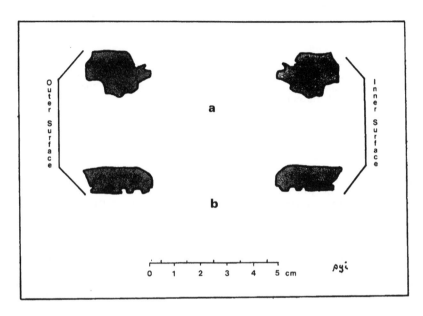

Figure 76.   Leather Footwear Remnants.

THE LEISURE ACTIVITIES COMPONENT

INTRODUCTION

The Leisure Activities Component encompasses those items within the artifact assemblage that relate to social or personal activities of a recreational nature. Included within this component are tobacco smoking pipes and musical instruments.

SMOKING PIPES

Description

The pipe collection can be divided into four general categories according to the material of which the pipes are made. These categories are 1) white clay pipes, 2) redware pipes, 3) brown terra cotta pipes, and 4) catlinite pipes. The pipes can be further described in terms of shape, size, and decoration.

In order to facilitate discussion of the pipe fragments, certain terminological conventions (figure 77) have been adopted. The top of the pipe has been defined as that part of the pipebowl that is oriented towards the aperature of the bowl. The base of the pipe has been defined as that part of the pipe that is opposite the top. The back of

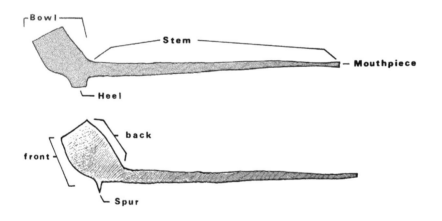

Figure 77. Pipe Terminology.

the pipebowl has been defined as that part of the bowl that faces the smoker. The front is the portion of the bowl that lies farthest away from the smoker. The sides are the sections that lie between the front and the back. The mouth is the general region of the bowl aperature. The rim is that section of the bowl that forms the mouth. The lip is the top of the rim. The body encompasses all the bowl between the rim and the base and includes any fragments that cannot be assigned to a specific region of the bowl. The junction is that portion of the pipe that includes the point at which the bowl and the stem meet. The spur is a narrow heel that projects from the bottom of the junction.

Several points of measurement have been selected. At the mouth, the length is the maximum distance between the outer surfaces of the back and front. The width is the maximum distance between the outer surfaces of the sides. The height of the bowl is the distance between the plane of the bottom of the stem to the top of the highest portion of the bowl. The interior bowl angle is the angle formed by the top of the stem and the back of the bowl along the medial or seam line. The exterior angle is the angle formed by the bottom of the stem and the front of the bowl along the medial or seam line. The exterior diameter of the stem is measured between the seam lines. The bore diameter of the stem is the diameter of the stem hole. The length of the spur is the distance from the back to the front of the spur from seam line to seam line. The width of the spur is the distance from side to side. The height of the heel is the distance from its end to its junction with the stem.

Only two sets of pipe fragments are sufficiently intact to define styles. Style One (figure 78) is a basally fluted bowl. The rim is decorated with a band of stylized oval leaves and flowers of stem motif. The flower varies from circular to oval. Below this is a band of oval bead and dot colon motif, which is bounded by circumferential line bands. The decorations are in relief. Both the front and back seams have a decoration of paired leaves that run from the base to the top. The leaves vary from distinct leaf segments to stylized ovals on the various fragments. The dimensional aspects of Style One are listed in table 29.

Style Two (figure 78) is a basally fluted bowl. The rim is decorated with an oval bead and colon bordered motif similar to Style One. Below this is a motif of thin stemmed leaf and flower. The back and front seams have a paired leaf decoration; the leaf segments are distinct. The dimensional attributes of Style Two are listed in table 29.

The remainder of the pipe artifacts are less intact. Ten sets of style elements (figure 78) can be defined. Style Element One consists of an undecorated rim and body fragment. Style Element Two consists of a single raised line below the rim and an undecorated body section. Style Element Three has a fluted body with flutes that end about 8 mm from the lip. It has paired leaf seams and a series of crosses above each flute. Style Element Four has flutes that end about 8 mm from the rim and paired leaves seams. Style Element Five has flutes that end at or within 3.0 mm of the lip and paired leaves seams. Style Element Six has flutes that end 2.5 cm below the lip. Style Element Seven has short ray lines surrounding an initial fragment that is probably "TD." Style Element

311

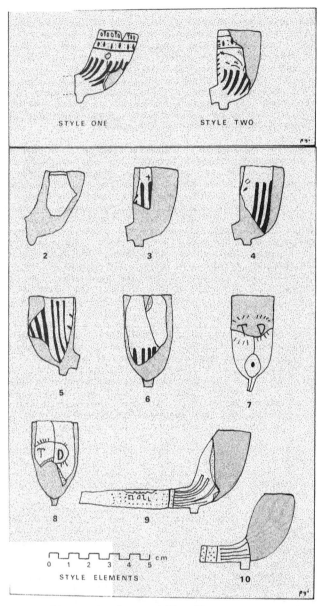

STYLE ONE   STYLE TWO

2   3   4

5   6   7

8   9

STYLE ELEMENTS   10

0 1 2 3 4 5 cm

Figure 78.   Styles One and Two Pipes.

312

Table 29. Distributional and Dimensional Aspects of Styles One and Two Pipes by Dump, Unit Type, and Stratum

Style		Section	Mouth			Spur			Bowl Angle		Hole	Stem Ext. Dia.
			Length	Width	Height	Length	Width	Height	Int.	Ext.		
One	MRA 6	bowl	2.0	1.83	3.13	0.42	0.41	0.27	32°	38°	5/64	0.93
One	MNRC 1	bowl									5/64	
One	MRA 1	bowl										
One	MNRC 1	bowl										
One	MNRC 2	bowl	2.1	1.95								
One	MNRD 1	bowl										
One	MRB 1	rim										
One	MNRC 1	rim										
One	MNRD 1	rim										
One	MRD 3	body										
One	MRE 1	rim										
One	WRC 1	rim										
One	WRC 1	body										
One	WRD 1	rim										
Two	WNRA 1	bwl				0.49	0.32	0.34	4°		4/64	
Two	WRA 1	body										
Two	WRB 1	body										
Two	WRC 1	body									5/64	
Two	MNRB 1	body										
Two	MNRC 1	body										
Two	MRD 1	body										

313

Eight is similar except the short ray lines are linked to an oval border around the letters "TD." Style Element Nine consists of a basally fluted bowl. The flutes extent partially onto the stem. Two bands and a series of dots comprise a background design for the marking, "ELIAS" and "HOLL", which appear on opposite sides of the stem. The "S" of "ELIAS" is reversed. The upper portion of the stem is covered with a leaf-like motif. The dots are aligned in single-dot columns. Style Element Ten consists of a basally lined bowl. The lined motif extends onto the stem. The stem has line banded segments with a dot design. The dots alternated from single to double.

The other white clay pipe fragments are too indistinct to assign to a specific style or style element. The bowl fragments fall into five general categories. These groups are plain, fluted, fluted with plain seam, fluted with paired leaves seam, and paired leaves seam. The plain pipestem fragments can be defined in terms of their bore diameters. The mean bore diameter is about 5/64 inch.

The second general group of pipes (figure 79 d & e) is redware pipes. Within this category, there are two varieties. The first consists of

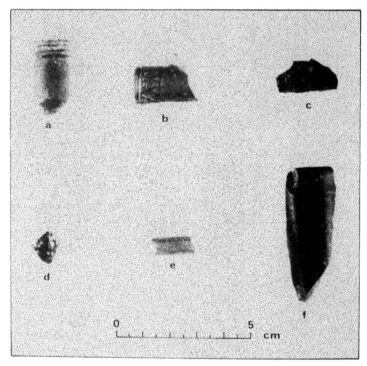

Figure 79. Miscellaneous Pipe Fragments.

314

unglazed pipestem and pipebowl fragments. The bore diameters are 5/64 inch. All of the fragments are undecorated. The second variety consists of a glazed pipebowl fragment. A partial "v"-ed line band is followed by a band of short obliquely slashed lines.

The third group of pipes are terra cotta pipes (figure 79 a, b, & c). These are of the stub-stemmed variety that took reed stems. The bowl fragments are short. Below the lip, the exterior surface has a series of three line bands in relief. Both are brown. The two stub-stems have a line band bordered zone with a series of linked "X"s. One is a yellow-brown in color. The other is a dark brown. The latter has an additional ine band between the "X" band and the tip of the stem. The interior diameter of the stems are about 0.74 cm.

The fourth group of pipes (figure 79 f) is comprised of a single catlinite pipebowl fragment. The bowl is undecorated. The fragmentary height of the bowl is 4.97 cm.

Distribution

The distributional aspects of pipe fragments are listed in a series of tables. Styles One and Two are listed in table 29. The style element fragments are listed in table 30. The miscellaneous bowl fragments are noted in tables 31 and 32. The plain white clay pipestems are listed in tables 33 and 34. The non-white clay pipe fragments are listed in table 35. The spatial distribution of the pipe fragments for combined strata is shown in figure 80 for the West Dump and in figure 81 for the Main Dump.

Comments

The pipe fragments represent varieties that were previously noted by Moore as well as additional ones. Style One is similar to Moore's Type 1b. Style Two is similar to his Type 1h. Style One pipes have also been noted at excavations in Sacramento, California (Humphrey 1968:20, 21) and Rome, New York (Hanson 1971:94, 97). The former dates to 1852 and the latter, to the period 1828-1890. Style Two pipes were also found at the Rome, New York site.

Style Elements Four and Five are similar to Moore's definition of Type 1a. Elements Seven and Eight comprise his Type 1e. Style Element Nine, the ELIAS/HOLL, stem and bowl are noted in Moore's excavations only from pipestem fragments (Moore 1973:85-86).

The terra cotta pipe fragments are similar to Moore's types Vb and Vc. These fragments are similar in execution to pipes made at Point Pleasant, Ohio (Sudbury 1979:260; 1982:personal communication). The Point Pleasant pottery appears to have made pipes from about 1850 to 1890.

Clay pipes, despite their fragile nature, were apparently retained for long periods of time. Garrard writing in 1850 (1968:154) talks of "time-worn clay pipes" and Parkman (1963:271) writing in the late 1840s

315

Table 30. Distribution of White Clay Pipe Fragments
by Style Element, Dump, Unit Type, and Stratum

Style Element	Section	Bore	Frequency	Dump	Unit Type	Stratum
One	rim		-	West	Nonrandom	A
One	rim		1	Main	Nonrandom	B
One	rim		1	Main	Nonrandom	C
One	rim		2	Main	Random	D
One	rim		1	Main	Random	E
Two	rim		1	Main	Nonrandom	B
Two	rim		3	Main	Random	C
Three	rim			West	Random	A
Three	rim			Main	Random	D
Four	rim		1	West	Nonrandom	D
Four	rim		2	West	Random	D
Four	rim		2	Main	Random	D
Four	rim		1	Main	Random	E
Five	rim		1	West	Nonrandom	C
Five	rim		2	West	Random	C
Five	rim		4	West	Random	D
Five	rim		3	Main	Nonrandom	C
Six	rim/body		2	Main	Random	C
Six	body		2	Main	Random	E
Seven	bowl	5/64	2	Main	Nonrandom	B
Eight	bowl		1	Main	Random	B
Eight	bowl		1	Main	Random	C
Nine	bowl/stem	5/64	2	Main	Nonrandom	C
Nine	stem	5/64	1	Main	Random	C
Nine	stem	5/64	1	Main	Nonrandom	D
Nine	stem	5/64	1	Main	Random	E
Ten	stem	NA	2	Main	Random	B
Ten	stem	5/64	2	Main	Nonrandom	C
Ten	stem	5/64	1	Main	Random	D
Ten	stem	5/64	2	Main	Random	E
Ten	stem	5/64		West	Nonrandom	A

316

Table 31. Distribution of Miscellaneous White Clay Pipebowl Fragments
from the West Dump by Unit Type and Stratum

Surface Treatment	Bore Diameter	Frequency	Unit Type	Stratum
Plain		1	Ramdom	
Plain		3	Random	A
Plain		1	Nonrandom	D
Fluted		2	Nonrandom	A
Fluted	5/64	1	Random	A
Fluted	6/64	1	Random	B
Fluted	7/64	1	Nonrandom	C
Fluted		4	Nonrandom	C
Fluted		12	Random	C
Fluted		4	Random	D
Fluted with Plain Seam			Random	C
Fluted with Paired Leaf Seam		1	Nonrandom	A
Fluted with Paired Leaf Seam		1	Random	C
Fluted with Paired Leaf Seam		1	Nonrandom	D
Fluted with Paired Leaf Seam		4	Random	D

Table 32. Distribution of Miscellaneous White Clay Pipebowl Fragments
from the Main Dump by Unit Type and Stratum

Surface Treatment	Bore Diameter	Frequency	Unit Type	Stratum
Plain		2	Nonrandom	B
Plain	4/64	2	Random	B
Plain	5/64	1	Random	B
Plain		3	Random	B
Plain		3	Nonrandom	C
Plain	5/64	1	Random	C
Plain	5/64	1	Random	D
Plain		4	Random	D
Plain		1	Random	E
Fluted		1	Random	A
Fluted	5/64	1	Nonrandom	B
Fluted	5/64	1	Random	B
Fluted		4	Random	B
Fluted		3	Nonrandom	C
Fluted		4	Random	C
Fluted		1	Nonrandom	D
Fluted	5/64	1	Random	D
Fluted		10	Random	D
Fluted	5/64	2	Nonrandom	E
Fluted		2	Random	E
Fluted		1	Random	F
Fluted		1	Random	H
Fluted with Plain Seam			Random	B
Fluted with Paired Leaf Seam		2	Nonrandom	C
Fluted with Paired Leaf Seam		1	Nonrandom	D
Fluted with Paired Leaf Seam		1	Nonrandom	E
Paired Leaf Seam		9	Random	B

Table 33. Distribution of Undecorated White Clay Pipestems
from the West Dump by Bore Diameter, Unit Type, and Stratum

| Stratum | Unit Type | Bore Diameter (in.) | | | |
		NA	4/64	5/64	6/64
A	Nonrandom	4	0	2	1
A	Random	2	0	8	0
B	Nonrandom	3	1	4	1
B	Random	0	0	4	3
C	Nonrandom	2	1	8	4
C	Random	2	1	24	5
D	Random	0	2	8	1
Subtotal		13	5	58	15

Total -- 91

Mean Bore Diameter 5.13/64 inch

Table 34. Distribution of Undecorated White Clay Pipestems
from the Main Dump by Bore Diameter, Unit Type, and Stratum

| Stratum | Unit Type | Bore Diameter (in.) | | | | |
		NA	4/64	5/64	6/64	7/64
A	Nonrandom	1	0	0	0	0
A	Random	0	1	3	2	0
B	Nonrandom	3	1	13	1	0
B	Random	7	2	23	7	0
C	Nonrandom	5	4	32	10	0
C	Random	2	2	28	7	0
D	Nonrandom	0	1	13	0	0
D	Random	5	3	37	4	1
E	Nonrandom	0	0	1	0	0
E	Random	0	1	9	3	0
F	Random	0			0	0
H	Nonrandom	1	0	0	0	0
H	Random	0	0	0	1	0
Subtotal		24	16	160	35	.

Total -- 236

Mean Bore Diameter 5.1/64 inch

319

Table 35. Distribution of Non-White Clay Pipe Fragments by Dump, Unit Type, and Stratum

Group	Variety	Material	Section	Bore	Frequency	Dump	Unit Type	Stratum
2	a	redware	stem	5/64	2	Main	Nonrandom	B
2	a	redware	stem	5/64	1	Main	Random	B
2	a	redware	body		1	Main	Random	C
2	b	redware	body		1	West	Nonrandom	A
3		terra ?a	bowl		1	West	Random	C
3		terra ?a	stem		1	West	Random	C
3		terra ?a	bowl		1	Main	Random	C
3		terra ?a	stem		1	Main	Random	D
4		atlinite	bowl		1	Main	Random	C

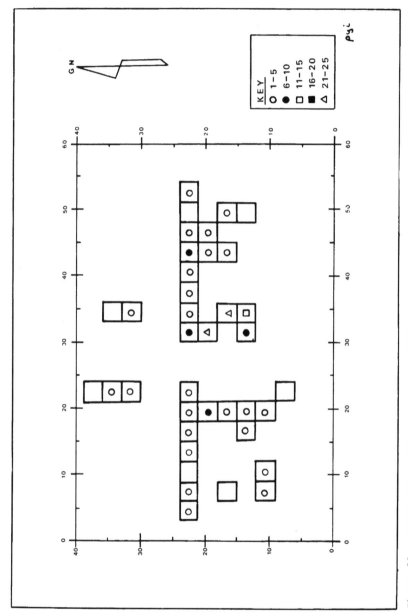

Figure 80. Distribution of Pipe Fragments within the West Dump.

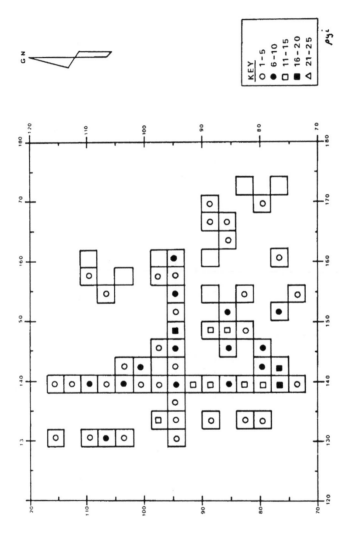

Figure 81.   Distribution of Pipe Fragments within the Main Dump.

322

speaks of the "little black pipe, as short and weather-beaten as himself [Jim Gurney]."

Moore's pipestems, like those excavated by Comer, averaged about 5/64 inch in bore diameter (table 36).

Catlinite pipes were an important part of the calumet ceremony on the Plains (Blakeslee 1975). They also were employed in a number of less formal occasions both between whites and Indians and among whites alone:

> Shaking hands [with the Cheyennes] we (St. Vrain, Folger, Chadwick, Drinker, and myself) dismounted and sat in a row with several of the principal warriors. The pipe of red marble, four inches in length, the bowl three inches in height, with a stem two feet in length, was passed around, containing a mixture of tobacco and the bark of the red willow or swamp dogwood.
>
> [Garrard 1968:27]

> On the prairie the custom of smoking with friends is seldom omitted, whether among Indians or whites. The pipe, therefore, was taken from the wall [of the trader's fort], and the red bowl crammed with the tobacco and shongsasha mixed in suitable proportions. Then it passed round the circle, each man inhaling a few whiffs and handing it to his neighbor. Having spent half an hour here, we took our leave . . .
>
> [Parkman 1963:82]

Table 36. Distribution of White Clay Pipestems from Moore's Excavation by Excavation Areas (Moore 1973:130-131)

	Bore Diameter (in.)	
Excavation Area	5/64	6/64
Trash Dumps	420	122
Plaza Trenches	74	17
North Wall	22	9
East Wall	20	10
South Wall	17	4
West Wall	108	36
Wagon Room	5	2
Billiard Room	2	1
Alley Way	28	9
Rooms A & B	1	1
Inner Corral	3	1
Subtotal	700	211

Total -- 911

Mean Bore Diameter 5.23/64 inch

MUSICAL INSTRUMENTS

Description

The only musical instruments represented in the dumps' collections are fragments of a jews harp and of a harmonica. The jews harp consists of the iron framework (figure 82 a) less the tongue. The harmonica is indicated by a single copper reed (figure 82 b) from a harmonica reed plate. Both are relatively common 19th century musical instruments.

Garrard (1968:68) speaks of the presence of a violin at the fort. However, no indication of this was found in the dumps' material.

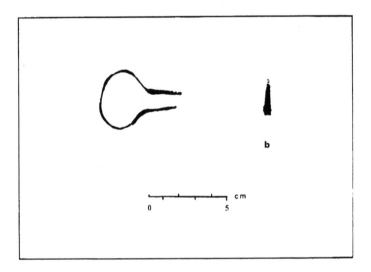

Figure 82.   Remnants of Musical Instruments.

THE FIREARMS COMPONENT

INTRODUCTION

The firearms component consists of artifacts related to guns and to their ammunition. Included within this component are gun furniture, gun springs, gunflints, percussion caps, lead shot and sprue, cherries, metallic cartridges, powder flask tubes, and powder keg plugs.

GUN PARTS

Description

The gun parts that were recovered can be divided into two general categories: gun furniture and firing mechanism parts. Gun furniture refers to the exterior accessory pieces that are applied to the basic weapon. These items include the side plate, the butt plate, ramrod thimbles, patch box covers, and trigger guards. The firing mechanism consists of various springs, the cock, the frizzen, and other parts associated with the operation of the weapon. The basic terminology of the exterior gun parts is noted in figures 83 and 84.

The only parts of the firing mechanism (figure 85) that were recovered were a fragmentary battery spring and a partial main spring. Both parts were made of iron. The battery spring is bent outward in profile. In transverse view, the spring tapers in width from one end to the other. The main spring is wider than the battery spring although it also tapers in width from one end to the other. The main spring is flat except for a curved section toward one end.

The gun furniture that is represented in the present collection (figure 86) includes side plates, a fragmentary butt plate, ram thimbles or pipes, and part of a trigger guard. One side plate is made of brass. It is curved and relatively plain. The single remaining screw hole is 0.54 cm in diameter. There is no decoration on the plate. The back is impressed with the mark, "DN" (figure 87 a). The second side plate is made of a copper alloy. It is rectangular in shape and relatively plain. The border is slighty raised and a series of fine incised parallel lines occur just inside it. Two screw holes remain. The exterior aperature of one hole is beveled; the interior opening of the other is beveled. The one complete hole measures 0.59 cm in diameter. The back is marked in relief with a series of three linked diamond (figure 87 b).

The butt plate (figure 86 c) is made of brass. The fragment is roughly triangular in shape. The two remaining holes are square in shape. The one complete hole measures about 0.33 cm square.

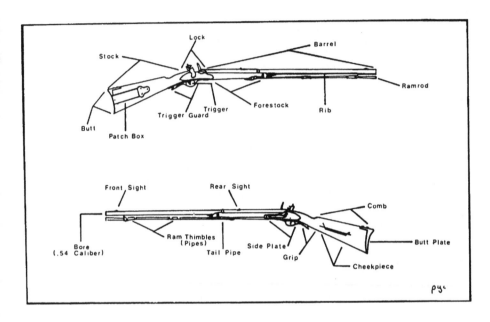

Figure 83.   Terminology of Gun Parts.

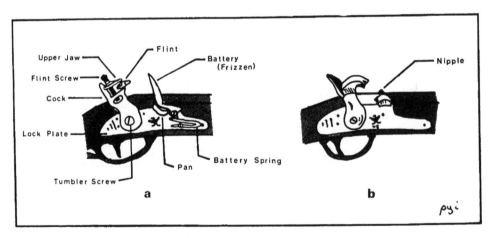

Figure 84. Terminology of Lock Parts.

326

a   b

```
L_I_I_I_I_I_I_I_I_I cm
0                 5
```

Figure

a   b   c

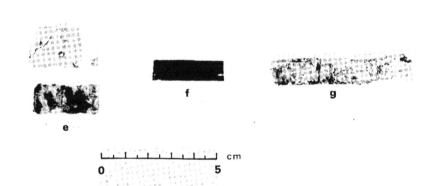

e   f   g

```
L_I_I_I_I_I_I_I_I_I cm
0                 5
```

Figure 86.   Gun Furniture.

327

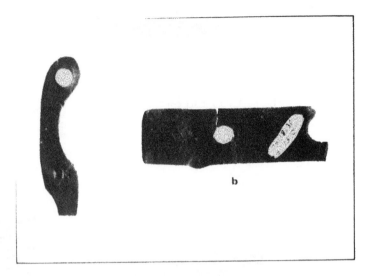

b

Figure 87.   Back Marks on Side Plate Fragments.

There are three sets of ram thimble fragments (figure 86 d, c, & f). Two of the sets of fragments are made of copper alloy, the third of brass. The two copper alloy thimbles retain segments with intact lengths. These lengths are 2.92 cm and 2.03 cm, respectively. The brass thimble retains no intact dimensions.

A fragmentary section of a trigger guard was noted (figure 86 g). The fragment is about 1.2 cm wide. It consists of two pieces that have been brazed together. Its cross section is roughly semi-circular.

Distribution

The distributional aspects of the gun parts are listed in table 37. The spatial distribution for the combined strata is illustrated in figure 88 for the West Dump and in figure 89 for the Main Dump.

Comments

The occurrence of ram thimbles suggest muzzle loading firearms. The recovery of a battery spring indicates, more specifically, flintlock weapons. The relatively plain side plates suggest common rather than more expensive weapons. None of the back marks have been identified.

Moore's (1973:87-89) excavations revealed a considerably more complete record. He found evidence of the U.S. Rifle 1841, Hudson's Bay trade

Table 37. Distribution of Gun Parts by Dump, Unit Type, and Stratum

Item	Material	Frequency	Dump	Unit Type	Stratum
Battery Spring	iron	1			
Main Spring	iron	1	Main	Random	D
Side Plate	brass	1			
Side Plate*	copper alloy	1	West	Random	A
Side Plate*	copper alloy	1	West	Random	C
Butt Plate	brass	1	Main	Random	B
Thimble	copper alloy	1	West	Random	A
Thimble	copper alloy	1	Main	Nonrandom	D
Thimble	brass	1	West	Random	A
Trigger Guard	copper alloy	1	West	Nonrandom	A

*Fragments of side plate mend together.

329

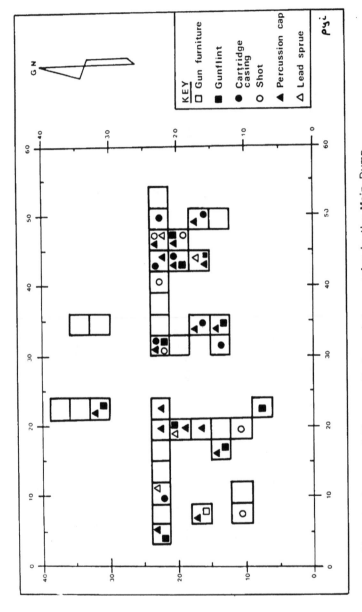

Figure 89. Distribution of Firearms Parts and Accessories in the Main Dump.

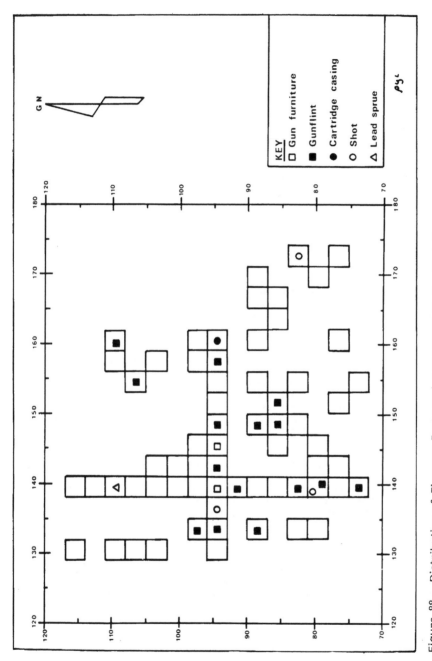

Figure 88. Distribution of Firearms Parts and Accessories in the West Dump.

331

rifles, and Derringer Indian trade rifles. His gunlocks were of both English and French design. His collection also included the remains of various dragon motif side plates that have been attributed to Indian trade rifles (Russell 1957:127-130).

GUNFLINTS

Description

Gunflints have been classified according to the techniques employed in their manufacture, their general finished form, their dimensions, and the type of flint used. Based upon appearance, seven styles of gunflints and three categories of gunflint fragments can be defined. The gunflint itself has several basic sections. These are the edge or bevel, the back, the sides, the face, and the bed (Dolomieu 1960:60; Lewis 1956:160).

Seven styles can be defined in terms of the general form of the gunflint. These styles coincide with different types of flint. Style One (figure 90) gunflints are made of a blond or light brown flint. The backs have been retouched and vary from straight to slightly rounded. The sides, also, have been retouched. The bevel is a single, long plane except where the flint has been hit by the frizzen or reworked. The bed is moderately long. The surface of the bed varies from flat to slightly concave. The face varies from slightly concave to slightly convex. The relatively intact lengths of the gunflints vary from 1.71 cm to 2.48 cm. The widths range from 1.65 cm to 2.13 cm. The heights vary from 0.44 to 0.67 cm.

Style Two gunflints (figure 91) are blond or light brown in color. The backs have been retouched and vary from slightly rounded to straight. The sides have been retouched. The bevel is a single, short plane except where it has been altered through use. The bed is relatively long and is slightly concave. The face varies from slightly concave to flat. The Style Two gunflints are noticeably thinner than the rest of the gunflints within the dumps' collections. The relatively intact lengths vary from 1.62 cm to 2.21 cm. The widths vary from 1.57 to 1.76 cm. The heights range from 0.27 to 0.44 cm.

The Style Three gunflints (figure 91) are blond in color. The back is moderately inclined. The flaking pattern suggests that the back was originally a single plane that was later chipped through use or reworking. The back is slightly rounded. The sides are retouched. The bevel is a relatively short, single plane. The bed is moderately long and is concave. The face is concave. The length varies from 1.93 cm to 2.28 cm. The width varies from 1.60 cm to 1.97 cm. The height varies from 0.47 to 0.64 cm.

The Style Four gunflints (figure 92) are black in color. The overall form of these gunflints is square. The back, the sides, and the bevel have been formed by a single strike. The back and the sides exhibit minor retouching along the edges only. The bed is moderately long and slightly concave. The opposing sides of the bed retain positive and negative bulbs of percussion. This is characteristic of the English blade technique of manufacture. The face is flat. The length varies from 1.69 cm to

332

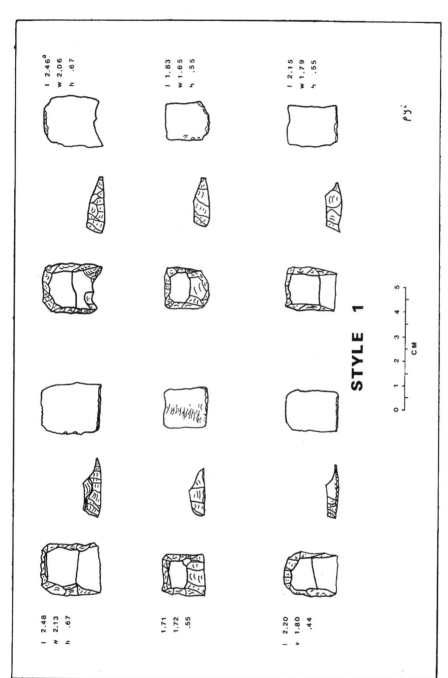

Figure 90. Style One Gunflints.

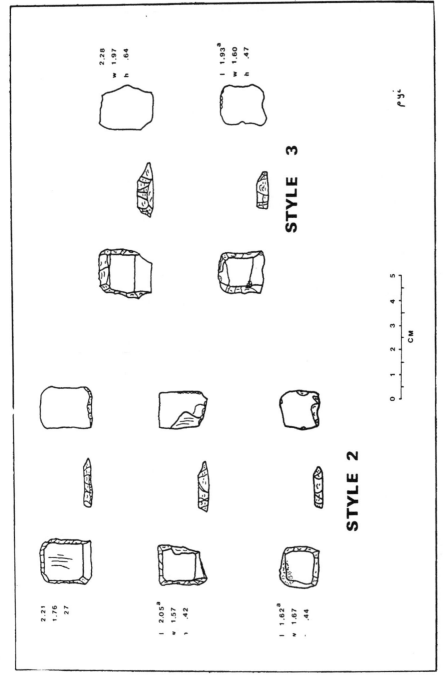

Figure 91. Styles Two and Three Gunflints.

334

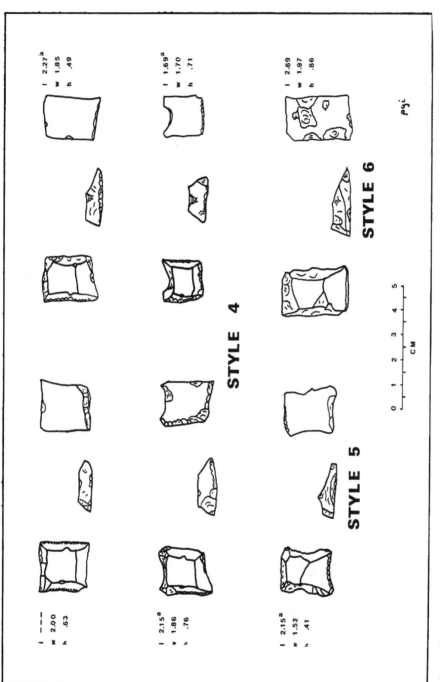

Figure 92. Styles Four, Five, and Six Gunflints.

335

2.27 cm. The width varies from 1.70 cm to 2.00 cm. The height varies from 0.49 cm to 0.76 cm.

The Style Five gunflint (figure 92) is black in color. The back is straight. The back is irregularly retouched. The sides are roughly flaked. The bed is sloped and trapezoidal in shape. The bevel is long and trapezoidal in shape. The face is convex. The length is 2.15 cm. The width is 1.52 cm. The height is 0.41 cm.

The Style Six gunflint (figure 92) is made of a gray chert. The back is straight and moderately inclined. The back and the sides have been crudely flaked. The bevel is a single, moderately long plane. The bed is moderately long and concave. The face is flat. The length is 2.69 cm. The width is 1.97 cm. The height is 0.86 cm.

The Style Seven gunflint (figure 93) is made of a gray chert. The overall form of the gunflint is square. The back is bifurcated. The sides have been roughly flaked. The bevel is a single, relatively long plane. The bed is relatively short. The face is slightly concave. Negative and positive bulbs of percussion are evident along the sides of the bed. The width is 2.5 cm. The other dimensions are not intact.

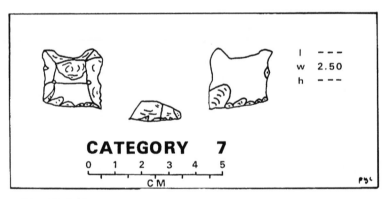

Figure 93. Style Seven.

In addition to the distinctive gunflints, there were two artifacts that might be classified as pseudo-gunflints. The first is a square-shaped item made of a yellowish-brown jasper. The item was crudely made. The second is a cortex flake of hornblende, which through accident or design has attained a gunflint-shaped form. The face, however, is irregular and no attempt apparently was made to "finish" the item.

There are at least three categories of gunflint fragments. Category One (figure 94) consists of discarded utilized gunflints whose condition preclude assignment to a style of gunflint. Category Two (figure 94)

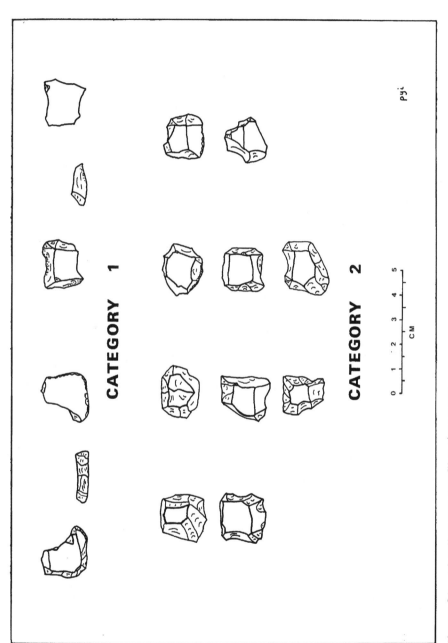

Figure 94. Miscellaneous Gunflint Fragments.

consists of utilized gunflints that were reemployed, perhaps for fireflints. Category Three consists of small fragments of gunflints.

Distribution

The distributional aspects of the gunflints are listed in table 38. The spatial distribution of the gunflints is illustrated for the combined strata in figure 88 for the West Dump and in figure 89 for the Main Dump.

Comments

Gunflints were supplied primarily by English or French sources with very few if any having been made in the United States. English gunflints have been characterized by the use of black flints (Witthoff 1966:46); French gunflints, by the use of blong flints (Witthoff 1966:39).

Although some attempts have been made to correlate the different ratios of English to French gunflints with chronological periods, the historical situation appears to have been affected by numerous factors. Hamilton has argued:

> This distinct shift from a predominance of French flints in eastern United States, representing the period from about 1750 to 1800, to a condition of slight predominance in Missouri, from about 1770 to 1820, to a position of English flint predomination on the upper Missouri, where the trade flourished from about 1810 to about 1870, seem to me to be significant. . . . It follows that when we find more French flints than English that the probabilities are that the historical period lay in the last half of the 18th century, and that English predominance indicates a historical period after 1800.
>
> [Hamilton 1960:75, 77]

On the other hand, Witthoff has found:

> At least three-fourths of them [gunflints in Pennsylvania from the period from the Revolution to the 1840s] are French blade-flints with blunted backs and edges, the remainder being equally small sized British flints. . . . As late as 1840, French flint held sway over other kinds. It was preferred then, as it is today, because it is superior material.
>
> [Witthoff 1966:41]

The gross comparison of all gunflints and fragments would indicate a predominance of English gunflints within the dumps' collections. However, a more appropriate comparison of only the intact and nearly intact gunflints indicates only a slight predominance of English gunflints; that is, 16 English to 12 French. A further complicating factor, however, is that the useful life of gunflints varied:

338

Table 38. Distribution of Gunflints and Gunflint Fragments
by Dump, Unit Type, and Stratum

Classification	Material	Frequency	Dump	Unit Type	Stratum
Style 1	blond flint	´	West	Random	C
Style 1	blond flint	2	Main	Random	
Style 1	blond flint	1	Main	Nonrandom	
Style 1	blond flint	1	Main	Nonrandom	
Style 1	blond flint	1	Main	Random	B
Style 2	blond flint		West	Random	D
Style 2	blond flint	1	Main	Nonrandom	C
Style 2	blond flint	1	Main	Nonrandom	E
Style 3	blond flint	1	Main	Nonrandom	B
Style 3	blond flint	1	Main	Random	E
Style 4	black flint	1	West	Nonrandom	A
Style 4	black flint	2	West	Random	A
Style 4	black flint		Main	Random	C
Style 5	black flint		Main	Random	C
Style 6	gray chert		Main	Nonrandom	C
Style 7	gray chert		Main	Nonrandom	A
Category 1	blond flint		West	Nonrandom	B
Category 1	black flint		Main	Nonrandom	B
Category 2	black flint	2	West	Nonrandom	
Category 2	black flint	1	West	Random	C
Category 2	black flint	1	West	Nonrandom	D
Category 2	black flint	1	Main	Nonrandom	B
Category 2	black flint	3	Main	Random	B
Category 2	black flint	2	Main	Random	C
Category 3	blond flint	1	Main	Nonrandom	C
Category 3	blond flint	1	Main	Random	C
Category 3	black flint	2	West	Random	C
Category 3	black flint	2	Main	Random	B
Category 3	black flint	1	Main	Nonrandom	D
Category 3	black flint	1	Main	Random	E

339

It was considered that a good flint would stand 50 rounds without being unfit for service, though interior grades might not last for more than fifteen.

[Lewis 1956:202]

This additional factor makes the issue of dominance difficult to address without an understanding of the relative quality of the gunflints being studied. Numerical dominance may merely represent a faster rate of discard rather than a statement either of preference or of the number of weapons utilizing a particular source of gunflints.

Gunflints were apparently relatively easy to manufacture:

A good worker can prepare 1000 good flakes in one day if he has good nodules. In one day he can make 500 gunflints. Thus, in 3 days, he alone will flake and finish 1000 gunflints.

[Dolomieu 1960:60]

The finished gunflints were then sorted into a number of catgories:

When the gunflints are finished they are sorted into different grades which have different prices based upon the degree of perfection . . . There are fine flints and common flints. They are divided into pistol flints, musket flints, and fowling-piece flints.

[Dolomieu 1960:60-61]

The cost of gunflints apparently varied according to the degree of perfection of the finished gunflint and, perhaps, according to their material durability. The price of gunflints, however, seems to have been relatively low. By 1823, a gunflint at St. Louis sold for less than one-third cent (Russell 1957:240). Farther west, on the other hand, the price of gunflints seems to have risen greatly in value. At the Great Salt Lake, gunflints sold for fifty cents a dozen or a little over four cents apiece. Like other goods, distance from the settled portions of the United States inflated the value of gunflints.

The dimensions of the gunflints, as suggested by Dolomieu, is an indication of their applications. The 1849 Ordnance Manual listed a table of acceptable ranges of gunflint sizes for military muskets, rifles, and pistols (Lewis 1956:160). This table is presented below with conversions of the original inch measurements into millimeters (Smith 1960:48).

Most of the gunflints within the dumps' collections fall outside of the Ordnance dimensions. This situation exists even when account is taken of any loss in the original dimensions due to use. This situation is partly explained by the fact that civilian rifles and pistols required smaller gunflints:

340

Table 39. Acceptable Dimensions for Army Gunflints

Dimensions	Musket		Rifle		Pistol	
	Maximum	Minimum	Maximum	Minimum	Maximum	Minimum
Whole Length	1.20 (30.5)	1.50 (38.1)	0.97 (24.9)	1.20 (30.5)	0.93 (23.6)	1.10 (27.7)
Width	1.08 (27.5)	1.13 (28.7)	0.79 (20.3)	0.88 (22.4)	0.83 (21.3)	0.92 (22.3)
Thickness at Back	0.026 (6.6)	0.33 (8.4)	0.20 (5.1)	0.29 (7.4)	0.21 (5.3)	0.27 (6.9)
Length of the Bevel	0.39 (9.9)	0.55 (13.9)	0.41 (10.8)	0.71 (18.0)	0.30 (7.6)	0.42 (10.9)

Rifles and pistol flints might serve in civilian rifles and fowling pieces. Some rifles and pistols would require flints smaller than those designated as "pistol" by the military.

[Smith 1960:48]

From the Revolution until the 1840's, the small calibre rifle and the fowling piece were standard hunting implements in Pennsylvania. Most of them had small locks and delicate vises; they took a somewhat diminutive flint, much like that made for a pocket pistol.

[Witthoff 1966:41]

The distribution of gunflints illustrated in figure 95 would suggest the presence of lighter civilian weapons at the fort.

The use of flintlock weapons did not cease with the introduction of the cap lock system of ignition. Flintlocks were made for the Northwest trade well into the 1870s (Witthoff 1966:48). Both their low initial cost and their low cost of use were important factors in their preference over other weapons. In 1861, a flintlock rifles could be purchased for $7.00 (Witthoff 1966:48) as opposed to a Henry, in 1862, for $42.00 (Williamson 1952:35). In the military, flintlocks were retained for the reserves up to the adoption of the breech-loading cartridge arms in 1866.

PERCUSSION CAPS

Description

Percussion caps were sold in three general styles. These were plain, ribbed, and hat (Russell and Erwin 1865). In addition to these common forms, the dumps' collections contain a nippled form. These styles are depicted in figure 96. Several dimensions have been selected to characterize the quantitative attributes of the caps. These measurements are the length, which is defined as the distance between the aperature of the cap and the opposing end; the exterior diameter at the head or closed end of the cap; the exterior diameter of the base or open end of the cap; and the rim diameter, on hat or musket caps, which is defined as the exterior diameter of the "brim" that surrounds the mouth.

All the percussion caps studied are made of copper. The plain percussion caps have smooth sides. Their lengths vary from 0.37 cm to 0.48 cm. None of the basal diameters are intact. The head diameters vary from 0.40 to 0.42 cm. The ribbed percussion caps have fluted sides. Their lengths vary from 0.38 cm to 0.50 cm. None of the basal diameters are intact. The head diameters are 0.44 cm. The hat caps have smooth sides and a brim comprised of at least three split sections. All of the lengths are 0.56 cm. None of the basal diameters are intact.

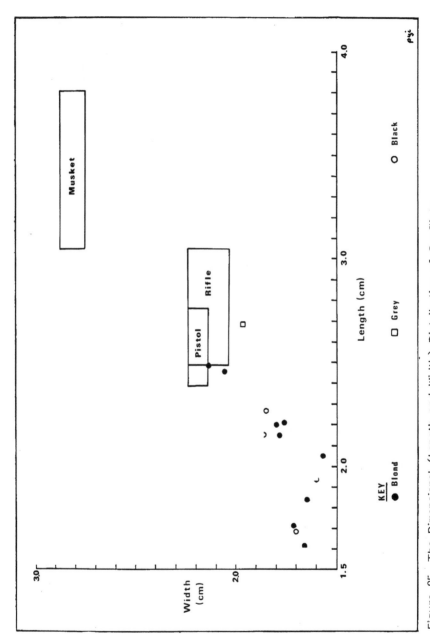

Figure 95. The Dimensional (Length and Width) Distribution of Gunflints Relative to the 1849 U.S. Army Ordnance Standards.

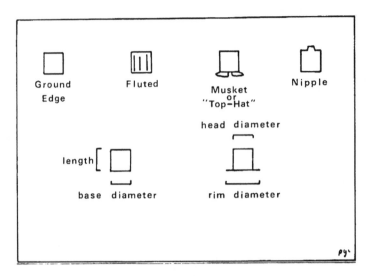

Figure 96.   General Percussion Cap Styles and Points of Measurement.

The head diameter is 0.55 cm.   The rim diameter is not measureable.
The single nippled cap has smooth sides.   Its length is 0.73 cm and its
head diameter is 0.67 cm.   The basal diameter is not intact.

Distribution

The distribution of percussion caps is depicted in figure 88 for the West
Dump and in figure 89 for the Main Dump.   The distributional aspects of
the sample are listed in table 40.

Comments

An American named Joshua Shaw first experimented with placing a mixture
of fulminate of mercury, chlorate of potash, and powdered glass into a
small metal (iron or steel cup) container as an ignition device in 1814.
By 1816, he had switched to the use of copper (Barnes 1972:301).   Cap
lock weapons were first adopted into the United States Service by the
Dragoons in 1833 (Lewis 1957:242).   They were utilized by the Santa Fe
traders in general use.

The percussion cap system had several advantages over the flintlock
system:

In 1834 experiments were conducted in England to test the
percussion principle.   First 6,000 rounds were fired from a

344

Table 40. Distribution of Percussion Cap Styles
by Dump, Unit Type, and Stratum

Style	Frequency	Dump	Unit Type	Stratum
Plain	2	West	Random	A
Plain	2	West	Nonrandom	B
Plain	3	West	Nonrandom	C
Plain	3	West	Random	C
Plain	1	West	Nonrandom	D
Plain	2	West	Random	D
Ribbed	4	West	Nonrandom	A
Ribbed	1	West	Random	A
Ribbed	1	West	Random	C
Ribbed	3	West	Nonrandom	D
Hat	3	West	Random	A
Nippled	1	West	Nonrandom	A
Total	26			

flintlock musket at the rate of 32 minutes 3 seconds per 100
rounds.   There were, in all, 922 misfires, or one in every 6½
rounds.   Then 6,000 rounds were fired under similar conditions
in a percussion musket, at a rate of 30 minutes 24 seconds per
100 rounds.   In that case there were but 36 misfires, or one in
166 rounds.   On the basis of those tests the British changed to
the percussion system.

Mordecai tested the relative efficiency of flint and percussion
ignition.   He found that the percussion system gave from 14 to
24 feet per second increased velocity over the flint type of
ignition.

[Lewis 1956:160]

Percussion caps were available from a number of makers.   The Union
Metallic Cartridge Company, the Winchester Repeating Arms Company, and
the U.S. Cartridge Company were among the American manufacturers who
produced good quality and relatively cheap caps.   The French "G.D."
caps were preferred by some.   The English Eley Brothers' cap was more
expensive but felt to be of the highest quality.   The Hudson's Bay
Company stocked only Eley caps.   They were felt to be sure fire in even
the most adverse conditions: extreme hot or cold or extreme dryness or
wetness (Roberts 1947:84).

The cost of a percussion rifle is suggested by the contract prices paid for the Model 1841 rifle. The prices ran from about $11.50 to $13.00 per rifle (Russell 1957:189-190).

LEAD ROUND BALLS

Description

The lead round balls used with muzzle-loading weapons can be described in terms of their method of manufacture, their diameter, and their weight. Two general methods of manufature are of interest. The first is known as the shot tower method. Molten lead is poured through a strainer that separates the lead into droplets, which are allowed to fall down the length of a high tower. The gravitational force shapes the droplets into a spherical form, which upon hitting a pool of water below, condenses to a solid ball. These balls are then shifted through meshes of varying size. The second method is known as the mold technique. It involves pouring molten lead into a manufactured or homemade mold, which forms the ball. After cooling, the mold is opened and the lead balls removed. Any excess lead or sprue is cut away.

The unfired balls (figure 97 a to d) range in diameter from 1.03 cm to 1.25 cm. Their weights vary from 6.4 gm to 11.3 gm. The fired balls (figure 97 i to m) range in weight from 7.4 gm to 20.4 gm.

One of the lead balls (figure 97 d) has a copper "jacket" or exterior coat. This ball is 0.5 cm in diameter and weights 0.9 gm.

Materials associated with the molding of lead balls include lead sprue (figure 97 e to h) and an iron cherry (figure 97 n). The sprue vary in weight from 0.5 gm to 6.0 gm. Cherries were used for carving out the bullet mold.

Distribution

The distributional aspects of the lead round balls and associated materials are listed in table 41. The spatial distribution is depicted in figure 88 for the West Dump and in Figure 89 for the Main Dump.

Comments

The existing intact lead balls suggest manufacture in molds. The existence of lead sprue also indicate local mold manufacture of lead balls. The presence of a cherry indicates that molds were also locally produced.

Copper jacketed lead bullets did not appear until the 1880s and 1890s along with the advent of smokeless powder (Barnes 1972:318). The single bullet in this collection is similar to the Winchester Standard Shot "BB" (Barnes 1972:295), which was used with a variety of shotgun gauges. These gauge sizes included 10, 12, 16, and 20. The recommended game sizes were geese, turkey, and fox (Barnes 1972:293).

346

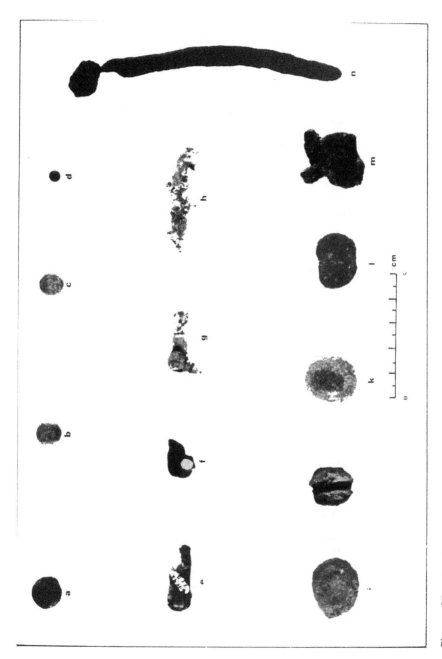

Figure 97. Lead Round Balls, Lead Sprue, and Cherry.

Table 41. Distribution of Lead Round Balls, Lead Sprue, and Cherry
by Dump, Unit Type, and Stratum

Item	Weight (gm)	Diameter (cm)	Frequency	Dump	Unit Type	Stratum
Ball	20.4	(fired)	1	West	Random	A
Ball	unknown	unknown	1	West	Random	B
Ball	7.3	1.06	1	West	Nonrandom	C
Ball	13.5	(fired)	1	West	Nonrandom	C
Ball	unknown	unknown	1	West	Random	C
Ball	7.4	(fired)	1	West	Nonrandom	D
Ball*	0.9	0.5	1	West	Random	D
Ball	11.3	1.25	1	Main	Nonrandom	B
Ball	unknown	unknown	2	Main	Random	B
Ball	6.4	1.03	1	Main	Nonrandom	C
Sprue	0.9	NA	1	West	Nonrandom	B
Sprue	6.0	NA	1	West	Nonrandom	C
Sprue	1.0	NA	1	West	Random	C
Sprue	3.2	NA	1	West	Random	D
Sprue	3.0	NA	1	Main	Nonrandom	D
Cherry	NA	NA	1	Main	Nonrandom	D

---

*The ball is copper jacketed.

METALLIC CARTRIDGES

Description and Comment

Six types of metallic cartridges (figure 98) are included within the dumps'
collections. These types are the .44 Henry Flat, the .56-50 Spencer, the
.56-56 Spencer, the .45 Colt, the .41 Short, and the .32 Teat Fire. The
.44 Henry Flat is represented by the most casings--five. All but one
exhibit the double pin strike marks of the Henry rifle. The exception
has a slightly longer casing. The Henry Flat was introduced between
1860 and 1861 (Barnes 1972:280) to accompany the lever action repeating
rifle invented by B. Tyler Henry. The Henry had a double firing pin to
ensure that the cartridge was ignited. This left a characteristic double
pin scar on the rim of Henry-fired cartridges. The casing of the original
Henry Flat was after a period of time lengthened. The length difference
and the absence of the double pin marks suggests that the one cartridge
was fired in a later rifle.

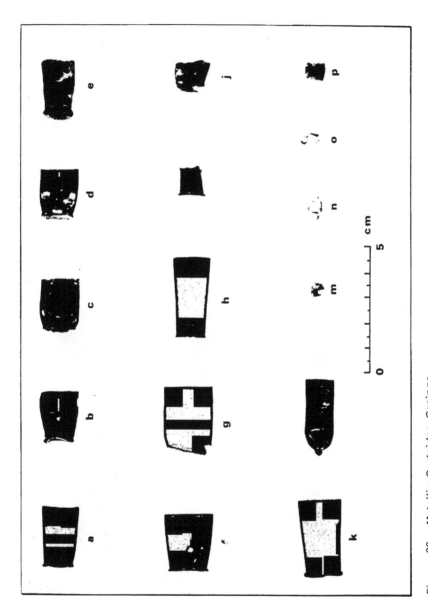

Figure 98. Metallic Cartridge Casings.

349

The .56-50 Spencer cartridge bears the headstamp, "F.V.V. & Co."
(figure 99 c). This cartridge was developed in late 1864 at the
Springfield Armory for use with the 1865 Model Spencer lever action
repeating rifle. It was issued to the troops fighting on the western
frontier (Barnes 1972:281). The headstamp belonged to the Fitch, Van
Vetchen & Co. of New York, which operated from 1862 to 1894
(Herskovitz 1978:48, 51). Spencer-fired cartridges retained a
characteristic mark:

A Spencer-fired cartridge was recognizable by the vague, oval
indentation it acquired on one side of the rim, just inside the
pin scar. A characteristic vertical scar, opposite the pin scar,
was made by the ejector and further identified Spencer-fired
cases.

[Moore 1973:96]

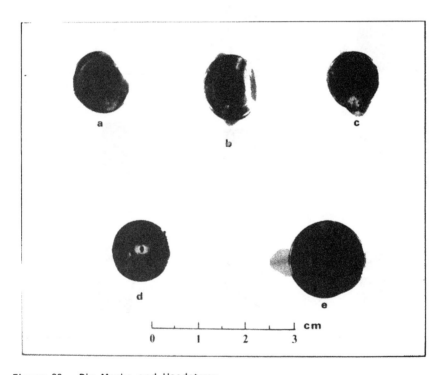

Figure 99. Pin Marks and Headstamp.

The .56-56 Spencer cartridges bear the characteristic marks noted by Moore. The .56-56 Spencer was designed as the original cartridge for the first spencer carbine, which was patented on March 6, 1860. The cartridge did not go into mass production until 1862 (Barnes 1972:281).

The .45 Colt had a Benet-type primer. It was developed for the "Peacemaker" single action revolver and introduced in 1873 (Barnes 1972:172). Adopted for military use in 1875, it remained in service until 1892.

The .41 Short was introduced along with the National Arms Company breech-loading derringer in 1863 or 1864. Thereafter, it was adopted for use with a variety of other derringer-type pocket pistols (Barnes 1972:279).

The .32 Teat Fire was patented on January 5, 1864, by D. Williamson. It was used with the front-loading National revolver (Logan 1948:54).

Distribution

The distributional aspects of the cartridge casing sample are listed in table 42. The spatial distribution of the casings is illustrated in figure 88 for the West Dump and in figure 89 for the Main Dump.

MISCELLANEOUS ITEMS

Description

Included within the miscellaneous weapons associated items are a lead powder cask plug, a lead gunflint pad, and powder flask tubes (figure 100). The plug weighs 9.9 gm. The pad is a roughly triangular piece of lead, which consists of a single sheet folded back onto itself. The base of the sheet is about 3.2 cm. The height is 3.2 cm. The pad is 1.8 mm thick. It weighs 6.5 gm. One of the copper tubes is 3.09 cm long and has an exterior diameter of about 0.95 cm. Its interior diameter is 0.65. The second tube consists of two fragments. The fragmentary length is 0.87 cm. The tube tapers in exterior diameter from 0.55 cm down to 0.44 cm. The interior diameter similarly tapers from 0.38 cm to 0.2 cm.

Distribution

The distributional aspects of the miscellaneous items are listed in table 43.

Table 42. Distribution of Metallic Cartridge Casings
by Dump, Unit Type, and Stratum

Item	Frequency	Dump	Unit Type	Stratum	Comment
.44 Henry Flat	1	West	Nonrandom	A	early rimfire
.44 Henry Flat	2	West	Random	A	early rimfire
.44 Henry Flat	1	West	Random	A	early rimfire
.44 Henry Flat	1	West	Nonrandom	B	late rimfire
.56-50 Spencer	1	West	Random	A	rimfire; headstamp, "F.V.V. & Co."
.56-56 Spencer	1	West	Random	A	rimfire
.56-56 Spencer	1	West	Random	C	rimfire
.45 Colt	1	West	Random	A	centerfire; Benet-type primer
.41 Short	1	West	Nonrandom	A	rimfire
.41 Short	1	West	Random	A	rimfire
.32 Teat Fire	1	West	Random	A	centerfire

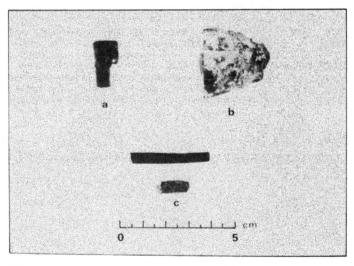

Figure 100. Miscellaneous Firearms Associated Items.

352

Table 43. Distribution of Miscellaneous Firearms Associated Items

Item	Frequency	Dump	Unit Type	Stratum
Lead cask plug	-	Main	Random	B
Lead gunflint pad		West	Random	D
Copper flask tube	1	Main	Random	B
Copper flask tube	1	Main	Random	C

THE TRANSPORTATION COMPONENT

INTRODUCTION

The transportation component of the artifact assemblage consists of all those items that were utilized on animals or as part of equipment involved in the movement of goods and personnel. Included within this section are harness buckles, horseshoes, horseshoe nails, and wagon wheel skeins.

HARNESS BUCKLES

Description

One iron harness buckle (figure 101a) was recovered from the West Dump. The approximate dimensions of this buckle are 4.5 cm by 3.5 cm. The tongue had been hinged to preclude lateral movement along the buckle.

HORSESHOES

Description

Three iron horseshoe fragments (figure 102) were excavated from the West Dump. The general terminology applicable to horseshoe attributes is illustrated in figure 103. The location of the fuller was discernible on only two of the fragments. On one, the crease occupied the quarter and part of the lower toe. On the other, it was placed between the lower toe and the upper heel sections. Forged heel calks were present on all the specimens. The thickness of all the shoes narrowed from the heel to the toe sections. One of the shoes was considerably smaller than the other two. Dimensional data are summarized in table 44.

In addition to the horseshoes themselves, three related iron fragments were noted (figure 101b & c). These had been produced by dubbing off shoes. Such objects have been described and defined by Robert Herskovitz:

> Dubbing or dubbing off is the process of cutting off the ends of the branches of a horse- or muleshoe so that the shoe does not extend beyond the rear of the hoof. These pieces are usually ½ in. thick and are 3/4 to 1-7/8 in. long. They are recognizable partly by their dimensions, but also because one end is relatively vertical while the other is at an angle, the result of having been cut with a blacksmith's hardy or a cold chisel.
>
> [Herskovitz 1978:83, 85]

Dimensional data are listed in table 45.

354

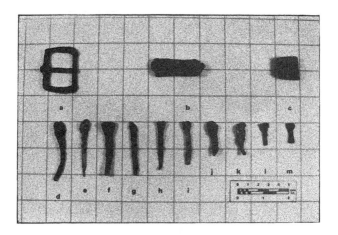

Figure 101.   Miscellaneous   Transportation   Component   Hardware   (a,
harness buckle; b & c, dubbing off fragments; d to m, horseshoe nails).

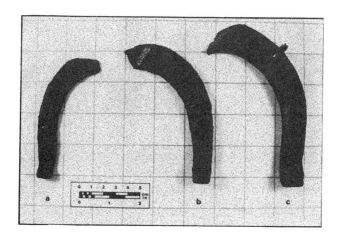

Figure 102.   Horseshoes.

355

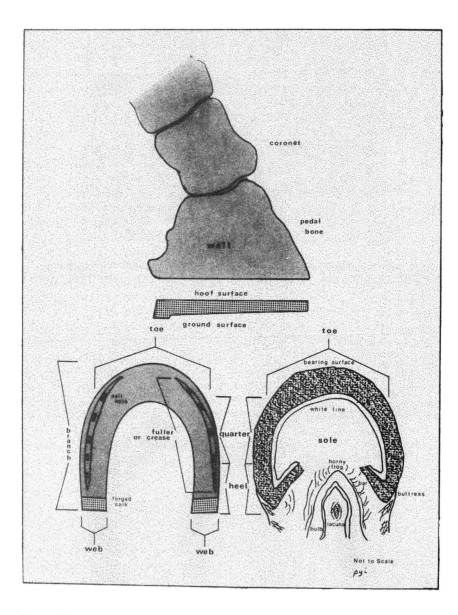

Figure 103.   Terminology of Features of or Related to the Horseshoe
(after Berge 1980:236, 237, 242, 243; Holmstrom 1971:76-78;
Watson 1977:72)

Table 44. Attributes of Horseshoe Fragments from the West Dump

Unit Category	Item	Length (cm)	Width (cm)	Calk location	Calk Height (cm)	Thickness at Calk (cm)	Fuller location
Nonrandom	C	10.7	NA	heel	1.6	1.0	toe
Random	A	9.8	NA	heel	1.2	0.5	undetermined
Random	B	12.3	NA	heel	1.9	1.2	vert toe to heel

Table 45. Attributes of Dubbing Off Fragments
from the West and Main Dumps

Area	Unit Category	Stratum	Width (cm)	Height (cm)	Fragment Length (cm)
West Dump			2.2	0.7	2.3
West Dump	Nonrandom	C	1.5	1.1	5.3
Main Dump	Random	E	1.7	1.3	2.3

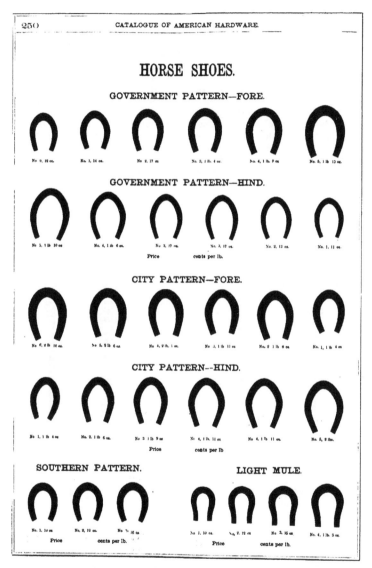

HORSE SHOES.

GOVERNMENT PATTERN—FORE.

GOVERNMENT PATTERN—HIND.

CITY PATTERN—FORE.

CITY PATTERN--HIND.

SOUTHERN PATTERN.

LIGHT MULE.

Figure 104.　　Horseshoes Sold in the Illustrated Catalogue of American Hardware of the Russell and Erwin Manufacturing Company, 1865.

HORSESHOE NAILS

Description

Eleven horseshoe nails (figure 101 d to m) were noted in the artifact assemblage. In addition to these, two more were observed still attached to one horseshoe fragment. Of the loose nails, all had been machine-cut. These nails can be divided into two general styles according to their physical shape. The first style (figure 105) consists of those nails whose head flares out to a thickness greater than the shank at the neck and then bevels down towards the top of the head. These have been referred to as rose-headed nails (Berge 1980:242-244). The second style (figure 105) consists of those nails whose head flares only slightly out from the thickness of the shank. These have been called countersunk nails (Berge 1980:243-244). Rose-headed nails are used with horseshoes that have not been fullered (Berge 1980:244). In addition to these styles, a category of unassignable fragments exists. These nails are those whose deterioration prevents a finer classification. The attributes of the nail sample have been summarized in table 46.

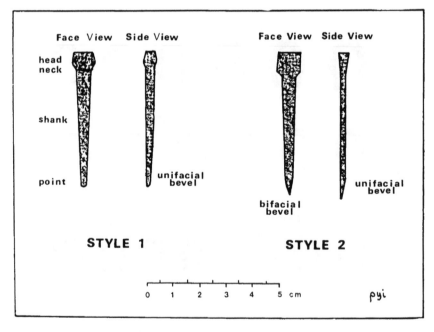

Figure 105. Horseshoe Nail Styles (Style 1, rose-head; Style 2, countersunk).

360

Table 46.   Attributes of Horseshoe Nails from the West and Main Dumps

Area	Unit Category	Stratum	Style	Total Length (cm)	Shank Length (cm)	Standard Size
West Dump	Random	A	2	5.2	4.4	8
Main Dump	Random	B	2	NA	NA	NA
West Dump	Random	C	1	4.9	4.1	8
Main Dump	Nonrandom	C	1	NA	NA	NA
Main Dump	Random	B	1	NA	NA	NA
West Dump	Nonrandom	A	?	5.5	NA	8
Main Dump	Random	B	?	5.3	NA	8
Main Dump	Random	B	?	NA	NA	NA
Main Dump	Random	B	?	NA	NA	NA
Main Dump	Random	C	?	NA	NA	NA
Main Dump	Nonrandom	B	?	5.9	NA	10

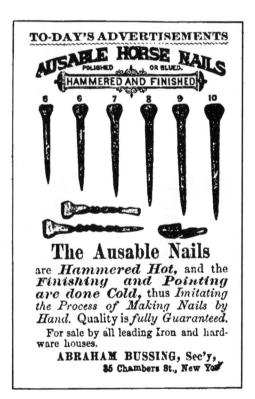

Figure 106.   Ausable Horse Nails Advertised in the Burlington Iowa Hawk-Eye, 1877.

361

WAGON WHEEL SKEINS

Description

Four fragments of iron skeins (figure 107) were observed. Two groups
can be defined. The first style (figure 108) consists of a single fragment
with a projecting spine. The second style (figure 108) consists of two
fragments and one probable fragment. This style possesses a ridge-like
spine that traverses the length of the fragment. With both styles, a
second spine opposite the remaining one probably existed. A measure of
the original dimensions of the skeins can be calculated utilizing
trigonometric relations. These dimensions along with other fragment
attributes are summarized in table 47.

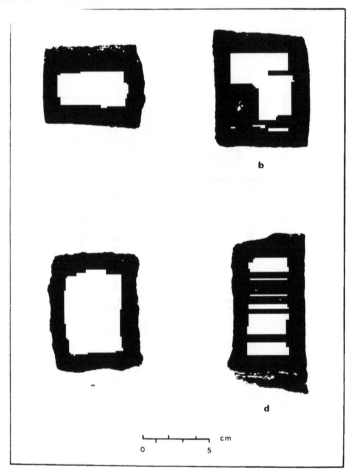

Figure 107. Wagon Wheel Skeins.

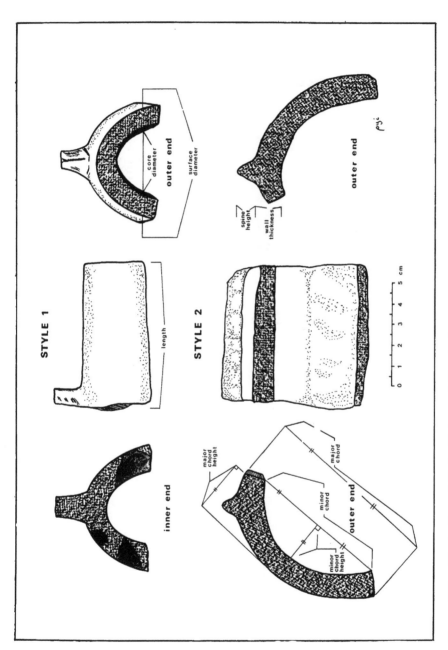

Figure 108. Illustration of Skein Styles and Terminology.

363

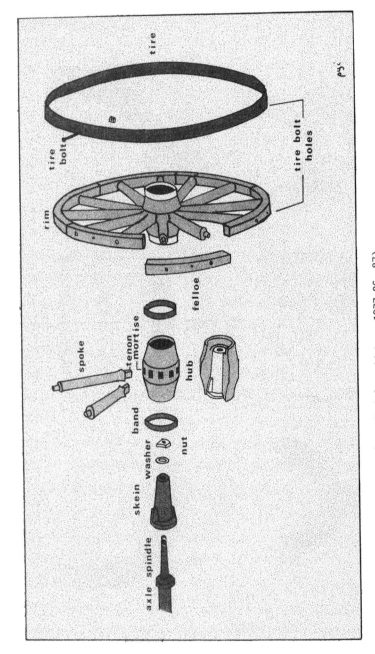

Figure 109. Wagon Wheel Parts (modified from Watson 1977:86, 87).

Comments

Skeins were utilized as shown in figure 109 as an intermediate connection between the wooden hub of the wheel and the iron spindle of the axle.

Table 47. Attributes of the Wagon Wheel Skein Fragments

Area	Unit Category	Stratum	Style	Length (cm)	Inner End				Outer End			
					Wall Thickness (cm)	Spine Height (cm)	Core Diameter (cm)	Surface Diameter (cm)	Wall Thickness (cm)	Spine Height (cm)	Core Diameter (cm)	Surface Diameter (cm)
West Dump	Nonrandom	C	2?	6.9	0.9	NA	14.0	15.6	1.6	NA	11.6	15.6
West Dump	Nonrandom	A	1	7.3	1.5	1.7	3.6	6.2	1.0	NA	3.8	5.6
Main Dump	Random	C	2	5.3	1.1	1.1	12.4	15.0	0.7	0.9	13.2	14.6
Main Dump	Random	D	2	6.5	1.0	1.0	7.6	9.2	1.5	1.0	6.4	8.8

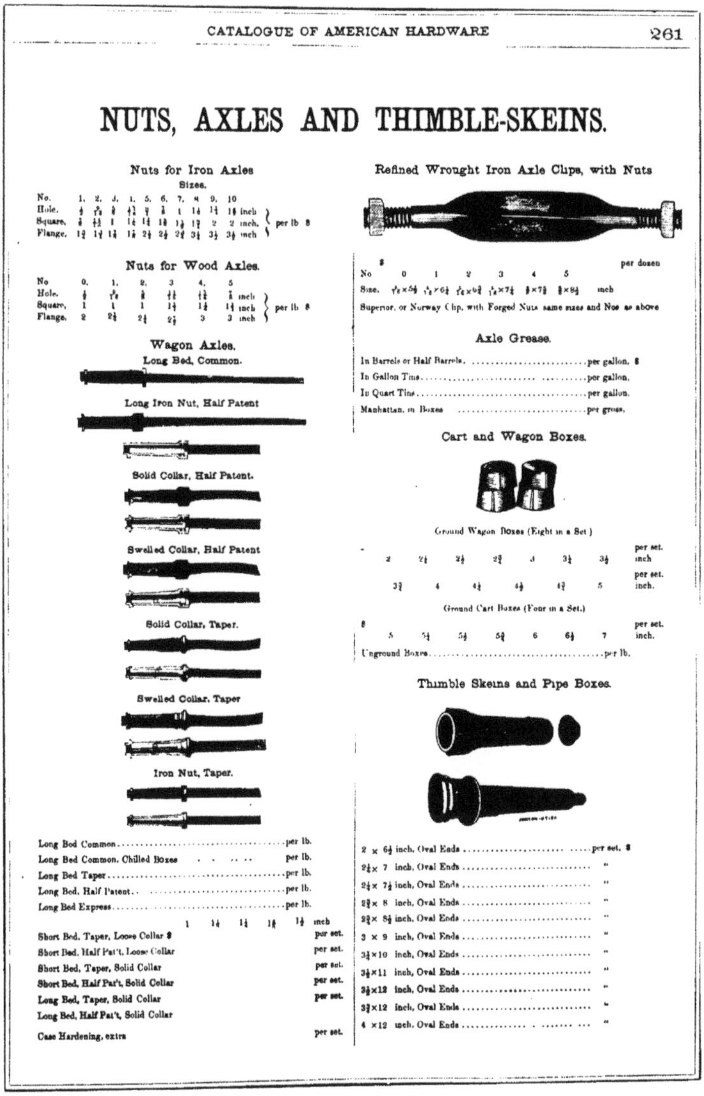

CATALOGUE OF AMERICAN HARDWARE 261

NUTS, AXLES AND THIMBLE-SKEINS.

Nuts for Iron Axles

Sizes.

No.	1.	2.	3.	4.	5.	6.	7.	8.	9.	10		
Hole.	1/2	9/16	5/8	11/16	3/4	7/8	1	1 1/8	1 1/4	1 3/8	inch	per lb $
Square.	7/8	15/16	1	1 1/8	1 1/4	1 3/8	1 1/2	1 3/4	2	2	inch.	
Flange.	1 1/2	1 5/8	1 3/4	1 7/8	2 1/4	2 1/2	2 3/4	3 1/4	3 1/2	3 1/2	inch	

Nuts for Wood Axles.

No	0.	1.	2.	3	4.	5		
Hole.	1/2	9/16	5/8	11/16	11/16	7/8	inch	per lb $
Square.	1	1	1	1 1/4	1 1/2	1 1/4	inch	
Flange.	2	2 1/4	2 1/4	2 1/2	3	3	inch	

Wagon Axles.

Long Bed, Common.

Long Iron Nut, Half Patent

Solid Collar, Half Patent.

Swelled Collar, Half Patent

Solid Collar, Taper.

Swelled Collar, Taper

Iron Nut, Taper.

Long Bed Common .... per lb.
Long Bed Common, Chilled Boxes .... per lb.
Long Bed Taper .... per lb.
Long Bed, Half Patent .... per lb.
Long Bed Express .... per lb.

	1	1 1/8	1 1/4	1 3/8	1 1/2 inch
Short Bed, Taper, Loose Collar $					per set.
Short Bed, Half Pat't, Loose Collar					per set.
Short Bed, Taper, Solid Collar					per set.
Short Bed, Half Pat't, Solid Collar					per set.
Long Bed, Taper, Solid Collar					per set.
Long Bed, Half Pat't, Solid Collar					
Case Hardening, extra					per set.

Refined Wrought Iron Axle Clips, with Nuts

$ per dozen

No	0	1	2	3	4	5	
Size.	5/16×5 1/2	5/16×6 1/4	7/16×6 3/4	7/16×7 1/4	1/2×7 3/4	1/2×8 1/2	inch

Superior, or Norway Clip, with Forged Nuts same sizes and Nos as above

Axle Grease.

In Barrels or Half Barrels .... per gallon, $
In Gallon Tins .... per gallon.
In Quart Tins .... per gallon.
Manhattan, in Boxes .... per gross.

Cart and Wagon Boxes.

Ground Wagon Boxes (Eight in a Set.)

$							per set.
	2	2 1/4	2 1/2	2 3/4	3	3 1/4	3 1/2 inch
							per set.
	3 3/4	4	4 1/4	4 1/2	4 3/4	5	inch.

Ground Cart Boxes (Four in a Set.)

$							per set.
	5	5 1/4	5 1/2	5 3/4	6	6 1/2	7 inch.

Unground Boxes .... per lb.

Thimble Skeins and Pipe Boxes.

2 × 6 1/2 inch, Oval Ends .... per set, $
2 1/4 × 7 inch, Oval Ends .... "
2 1/4 × 7 1/2 inch, Oval Ends .... "
2 3/8 × 8 inch, Oval Ends .... "
2 3/4 × 8 1/2 inch, Oval Ends .... "
3 × 9 inch, Oval Ends .... "
3 1/4 × 10 inch, Oval Ends .... "
3 1/2 × 11 inch, Oval Ends .... "
3 1/2 × 12 inch, Oval Ends .... "
3 3/4 × 12 inch, Oval Ends .... "
4 × 12 inch, Oval Ends .... "

Figure 110. Miscellaneous Wagon Hardware from the Illustrated Catalogue of American Hardware of the Russell and Erwin Manufacturing Company, 1865.

Distribution

The sportial distribution of the artifacts within the transportation component is depicted in figure 111 for the West Dump and in figure 112 for the main dump.

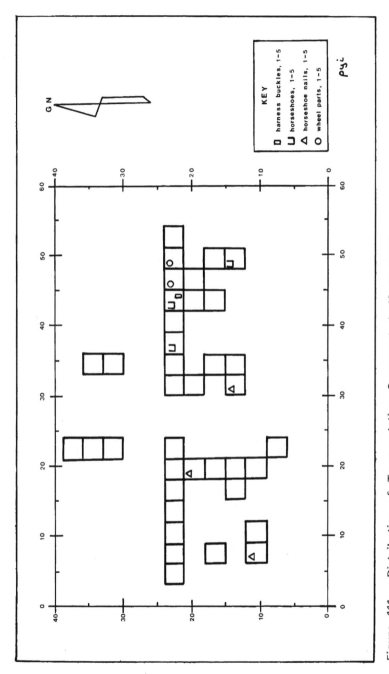

Figure 111. Distribution of Transportation Component Artifacts within the West Dump.

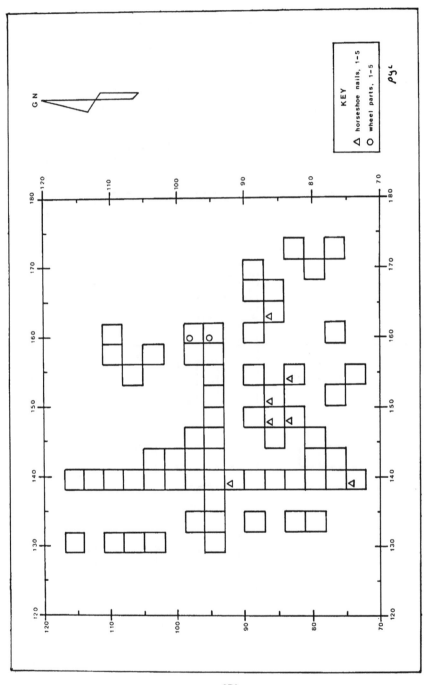

Figure 112. Distribution of Transportation Compenent Artifacts within the Main Dump.

INTRODUCTION

The structural component of the artifact assemblage consists of those items that were utilized in the construction and furnishing of structures. Included within this grouping are adobe bricks, hinges, hook and eye fasteners, latches, nails, and window glass.

ADOBE

Description

Numerous adobe fragments were encountered during the 1976 excavations. Unfortunately, the entire collection was not available for study during the current analysis. Three adobe fragments, however, from the larger collection were obtained for examination. These samples weighed 33.7 gm, 140.3 gm, and ca. 1 kg. The two lightest pieces had surface coatings of whitewash. At least two layers were evident. Each layer of whitewash was approximately 0.1 mm in thickness. The mode of application was not apparent. The adobe surfaces had not been prepared and were irregular in contour.

b

└─┴─┴─┴─┴─┘ c m
0   5

Figure 113.   Adobe Fragments from the West Dump.

371

The adobe matrix was comprised of a dried, semi-hard, and friable sandy clay loam. The color was reddish yellow and varied from 7.5YR6.5/6 to 7.5YR7/4 in hue, value, and chroma (Munsell Color 1975:np). Inclusions of grit-sized rock and of small pebbles were present. Traces of small rootlets were observed in the largest of the adobe fragments.

Distribution

While the earlier records did not systematically note either the number of the fragments or the weight of the recovered material, some notion of their spatial distribution could be reconstructed. Table 48 lists this data in tabular fashion while figure 114 for the West Dump and figure 115 for the Main Dump depict this distribution in a series of maps.

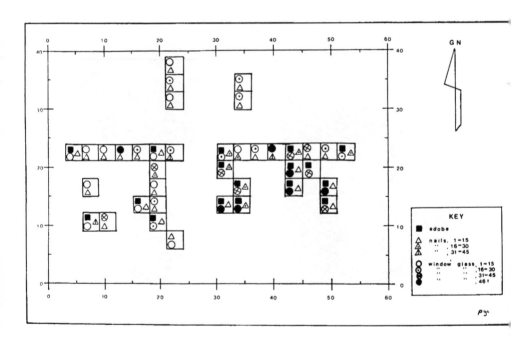

Figure 114. Distribution of Adobe, Nails, and Window Glass within the West Dump Excavations.

372

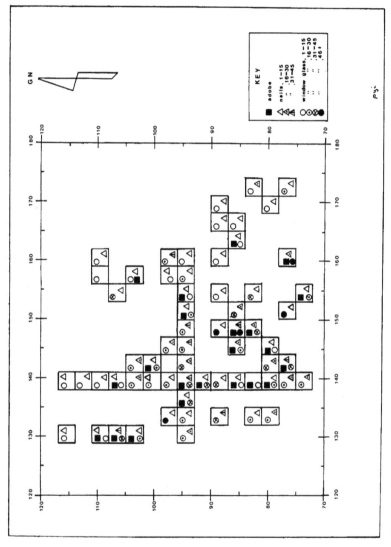

Figure 115. Distribution of Adobe, Nails, and Window Glass Within the Main Dump Excavations.

Table 48.   Distribution of Adobe Fragment Presence by Dump Area
and Excavation Category

Unit	West Dump			Main Dump		
Category	Present	Absent	Subtotal	Present	Absent	Subtotal
Random	12	8	20	13	29	42
Nonrandom	5	13	18	9	12	21
Total			38			63

Comments

Three tentative conclusions can be drawn from the examination of the
adobe samples.   First, the physical properties of the soil matrix suggest
that soils from the C2a, C3ca, and C4 strata of the Numa Series were
utilized (figure 116).   These strata occur, within a typical profile,
between 19 and 60 inches below the surface (U.S. Department of
Agriculture 1972:21).   The Numa Series is the dominant soil type within
the area of the fort.

Second, microscopic observation of the adobe matrix failed to detect
traces of either wool or grass temper.   Both of these materials had been
mentioned by various visitors and historians as having been included
within the adobe composition.   Dr. George Grinnell (1923:32), for
instance, had written, "He [Charles Bent] also sent up some wagon loads
of Mexican wool to mix with the clay of the brick, thus greatly
lengthening the life of the adobes."   On the other hand, Lieutenant J.W.
Apert (cited in Stinson 1965:52) had noted that the adobe consisted of
"clay and cut straw."

The absence, however, of any organic residue within the matrix suggests
that an adobe-making process that did not include such tempering may
have been employed.   Such a process has been described by Lewis
Garrard for the construction of Fort Mann in 1847:

> . . . making our own brick.   Some dug earth, others with the
> forewheels (tongue and hounds attached) of the cannon-wagon
> and a half-barrel, brought water from the river. . . .   We had
> two yoke of oxen to tramp the mud. . . .   The molds were
> sixteen inches long by eight in width and four in depth--the
> facsimile of brick molds on a larger scale.   These were filled
> with stiff mud and turned out on the smooth ground--the molds
> brought back, dipped in a barrel of water to free them of
> earthy particles, filled again, and so on ad infinitum. . . .
> Three hundred and twenty-six were the result of the day's
> labor.

[Garrard   1963:266-267]

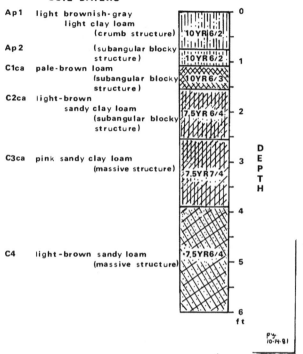

SOIL LAYERS

Ap1　light brownish-gray
　　　　light clay loam
　　　　(crumb structure)

Ap2　　　　　　(subangular blocky
　　　　　　　　structure)

C1ca　pale-brown loam
　　　　　　　　(subangular blocky
　　　　　　　　structure)

C2ca　light-brown
　　　　sandy clay loam
　　　　　　　(subangular blocky
　　　　　　　structure)

C3ca　pink sandy clay loam
　　　　　　　(massive structure)

C4　　light-brown sandy loam
　　　　　　　(massive structure)

Figure 116.　Typical Num Series Profile (USDA 1972:21).

Third, the presence of multiple coats of whitewash on two of the three adobe samples indicates that portions of the adobe walls had been, at some point, whitewashed and had, thereafter, been maintained through periodic reapplications. Although the coats were not tested, they probably consist of a mixture of lime, some type of size, and water. Historically, George Bent recalled (quoted in Stinson 1965:54) that the inside rooms had been whitewashed during his tenure at the fort (1843-1849). Moreover, Francis Parkman (1963:265), during his 1846 visit, noted, "the glazing sun was reflected down upon it [the plaza] from the high white walls around."

Most of the finished adobe that were recovered, however, by Jackson Moore, Jr. from the interior of the fort had been covered with white plaster rather than whitewashed. He, also, recovered evidence for red and yellow plaster. Traces of whitewash were rare. The distribution of this adobe is recapitulated by room in table 49.

No dimensional data for the adobe bricks was revealed by the samples examined. Moore, however, located floor bricks of 9x16x4 inches (1973:46). This appears to be approximately the common size for adobe bricks judging from the 8x16x4 inches used at Fort Mann and the 10x18x4 inches used at Johnny Ward's ranch (Fontana and Greenleaf 1962:30).

375

Table 49. Interior Fort Distribution of Excavated Adobe Finish
by Category and Room Designation
(Moore 1973:18, 22, 26, 31, 32, 35-38, 40, 44)

Finish Category	Room Designation															
	N2	N5	N6	E2	E3	E5	SE1	SE1A	S2	S4	S5	S6	S7	W2	W4	NW1
Plaster																
White	X	X	X		X	X			X	X	X	X		X	X	
Red				X		X			X	X						
Yellow				X					X							
Whitewash								X				X				X

In summary, the three adobe fragments, however limited, provide some evidence for the source, the composition, and the finish of at least part of the adobe, which at one time formed the walls of the fort. From the data excavated by Moore, the two whitewashed fragments would appear to represent a restricted rather than a common architectural occurrence.

HINGES

Description

Portions of three handwrought iron hinges were recovered. The first fragment (figure 117a) represents a segment from a relatively large strap hinge. Two holes remain and both appear to have been punched prior to the insertion of the fastening nail. The diameters and shapes of the holes suggest that two categories of nail were employed. The smaller, about 0.5 cm diameter, oval hole probaly was closed with an intermediate length nail. The larger, 1.1 cm diameter, circular hole probably accepted a relatively long spike.

The second fragment (figure 117b) is either a portion of the broad end of a triangular strap hinge or part of a side-arm of a butterfly hinge. The single remaining hole had been punched prior to closure. The small, oval aperature was about 0.6 cm in diameter.

The last hinge fragment (figure 117c) is a curved section, possibly from a serpentine-type strap hinge. One complete hole remains. This small, oval aperature was punched prior to use and was about 0.5 cm in diameter.

One circular-headed, iron hinge pin (figure 117f) was included in this sample. The shaft measured approximately 4 cm in length.

Distribution

The distribution of the hinge parts is summarized in table 50 along with the data from the hook and latch samples.

376

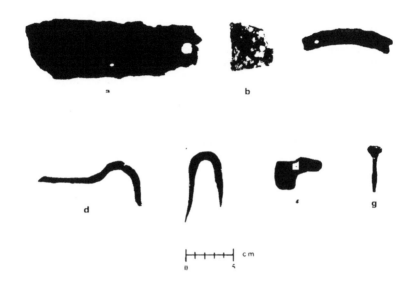

a   b

d   f   g

cm

0   5

Figure 117. Structural Hardware (a, b, and c, strap hinges; d and e, hook and staple "eye"; g, hinge pin; f, latch catch or keeper).

Comments

The relative size of the various hinge parts suggests certain types of usage. The large strap hinge arm probably was used on a relatively heavy door. Schiffer (1966:43) has observed that such hinges were the "strongest . . . developed for large and heavy doors. . . ." The smaller butterfly or strap hinge arm was most suitable for shutters, chests, or light doors. The serpentine strap hinge arm is too thin for other than use on relatively light weights. The hinge pin would have been suitable for weights such as a light door or shutter.

HOOK AND EYES

Description

A wrought iron hook and staple found in the Main Dump probably were used as a hook and eye closure (figure 117 d and e).

377

Distribution

The distribution of hook and eye parts is summarized in table 50.

Comments

The size of the hook suggests that this hook and eye combination were employed on a normal-sized shed or similar rough structure door·

LATCHES

Description

One wrought iron latch catch or keeper was recovered (figure 117f).

Distribution

The distribution of the latch part is recorded in table 50.

Comments

The latch catch fragment was probably welded to an escutcheon (e.g., Sonn 1979:220; Watson 1977:11) as part of a thumb latch mechanism (Schiffer 1966:7; Sonn 1979:215).

Table 50. Distribution of Hinge, Hook and Eye, and Latch Parts
by Excavation Area and Unit Category

	West Dump		Main Dump	
	Nonrandom	Random	Nonrandom	Random
Hinge				
Plain Strap				
Triangular Strap	1			
Curved Strap	1			
Hinge Pin				
Hook				1
Staple "Eye"				1
Latch Catch	—	—	—	1
Total	2	0		4

NAILS

Description

The nail sample consisted of 1,481 whole and fragment specimens. Of these, 557 (37.6 percent) were recovered from the West Dump and 924 (62.4 percent) from the Main Dump. The spatial distribution and density of these nails is illustrated in figures 114 and 115.

The nail collection can be grouped into four general categories according to the method of manufacture. These four categories were handwrought, machine-cut, wire, and unspecifiable fragments (Mercer 1976:1-10; Nelson 1968).

The first category, handwrought nails, was produced by pointing, cutting, and heading individual nails from long strips of iron called nail rods (Mercer 1976:4). The handwrought nails in this sample consist solely of round head and of round head and shaft sections. The overall size of the fragments suggests that the original nails were relatively large-sized spikes (figure 118a and b).

Machine-cut nails comprise the second category. They were made by inserting a strip of plate iron into a mechanical cutter, which "rising and falling rapidly, clipped off the end of the plate iron crosswise into narrow, tapering, rectangular slices or nails" (Mercer 1976:6). Such nails were, at first, hand-headed and, later, headed mechanically. The few nails for which the method of heading could be discerned appeared to be both manually and mechanically headed. The machine-cut nails can be sorted into four subcategories. These divisions are headless (figure 118c, d, and e), common (figure 118i to o), clinch (figure 118f, g, and h), and unspecifiable fragments.

Pennyweight or length was measureable on only 28 of the machine-cut nails. The headless nails were approximately 9d while the common nails clustered between 7d and 9d. Since none of the clinch nails were intact, no lengths could be ascertained. The overall distribution of nail lengths is shown in figure 119.

Wire nails were manufactured mechanically by advancing steel wire into a gripper die, which headed the nail; then, moving the wire forward and finally shearing off the appropriae nail length (Nelson 1968:7). The pennyweights of the measureable wire nails were 6d, 16d, 25d, and 30d.

The fourth category consisted of those nails that were identifiable as to function by their general shape only. No finer designation could be assigned to these due to their poor state of preservation.

Distribution

The distribution of nails by the method of manufacture is summarized in table 51. The largest percentage of the samples from both the West (76.5 percent) and the Main (74.8 percent) dumps was composed of fragments for which no specific classification could be assigned. The largest

379

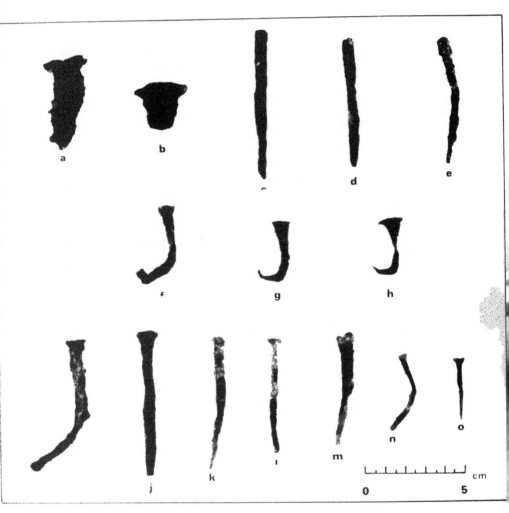

Figure 118. Nails and Spikes (a and b, handwrought spike fragments; c, d, and e, headless machine-cut nails; f, g, and h, machine-cut clinch nails; i to o, common machine-cut nails).

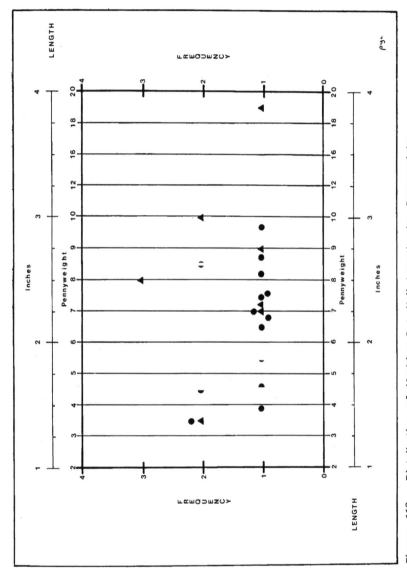

Figure 119. Distribution of Machine-Cut Nail Lengths by Pennyweight and Inch (West Dump;   Main Dump).

381

segment of the remaining nails consisted of machine-cut nails. This segment was 16.9 percent of the West Dump sample and 20.9 percent of the Main Dump sample.

Table 51. Distribution of Nail Categories
by Excavation Area and Unit Category

Nail Category	West Dump			Main Dump		
	Nonrandom	Random	Subtotal	Nonrandom	Random	Subtotal
Handwrought Spike	11	30	41	14	22	36
Machine-Cut						
Headless	0	0	0	2	1	3
Common	14	19	33	3	18	21
Clinch	1	0	1	2	0	2
Unspecified	45	15	60	56	111	167
Wire		0			3	4
Unspecified	254	167	421	196	495	691
Total	326	231	557	274	650	924

The frequency distribution of nails by strata is listed in table 52 for the West Dump and in table 53 for the Main Dump. An adjusted measure of frequency, nail density by strata, was calculated to compensate for the unequal number of times that any given stratum appears within the various excavation units. This figure is probably a somewhat better measure of the relative richness of each stratum in regards to nails than is the raw frequency. This measure is listed in tables 54 and 55.

Table 52. Stratigraphic Distribution of Spikes (S), Machine-Cut (M),
Wire (W), and Unspecified (U) Nails
in the West Dump by Unit Category

Stratum	Nonrandom					Random				
	S	M	W	U	Subtotal	S	M	W	U	Subtotal
OB*	0	0	0	24	24	1	3	0	7	11
A	5	31	1	82	119	5	19	0	65	89
B	0	2	0	39	41	7	6	0	29	42
C	5	21	0	96	122	11	5	0	41	57
D	1	6	0	13	20	6	1	0	25	32
Total	11	60	1	254	326	30	34	0	167	231

*Artifacts from Stratum OB represent only a partial retention of material.

382

Table 53. Stratigraphic Distribution of Spikes (S), Machine-Cut (M), Wire (W), and Unspecified (U) Nails in the Main Dump by Unit Category

Stratum	Nonrandom					Random				
	S	M	W	U	Subtotal	S	M	W	U	Subtotal
A*	0	2	0	0	2	2	3	0	11	16
B	1	20	0	36	57	9	34	0	119	162
C	5	28	1	85	119	3	53	0	157	213
D	4	4	0	46	54	7	25	2	152	186
E	4	3	0	27	34	1	10	0	48	59
F	NA	NA	NA	NA	NA	0	2	0	3	5
G	NA	NA	NA	NA	NA	0	2	1	0	3
H	0	6	0	2	8	0	1	0	5	6
Total	14	63	1	196	274	22	130	3	495	650

*Artifacts from Stratum A represent only a partial retention of excavated material.

Table 54. Relative Stratigraphic Density of Spikes (S), Machine-Cut (M), Wire (W), and Unspecified (U) Nails in the West Dump by Unit Category

Stratum	Nonrandom				Random			
	S	M	W	U	S	M	W	U
OB	NA	NA	NA	NA	NA	NA	NA	NA
A	0.3	1.7	0.1	4.6	0.7	1.0	0	3.4
B	0	0.3	0	6.5	0.5	0.9	0	4.1
C	0.6	2.6	0	12.0	0.8	0.4	0	3.2
D	0.1	0.8	0	1.6	0.7	0.1	0	2.8

Table 55. Relative Stratigraphic Density of Spikes (S), Machine-Cut (M), Wire (W), and Unspecified (U) Nails in the Main Dump by Unit Category

Stratum	Nonrandom				Random			
	S	M	W	U	S	M	W	U
A	NA	NA	NA	NA	NA	NA	NA	NA
B	0.1	1.0	0	1.8	0.3	1.0	0	3.6
C	0.3	1.5	0.1	4.5	0.1	1.6	0	4.6
D	0.2	0.2	0	2.6	0.2	0.7	0.1	4.5
E	0.3	0.2	0	1.9	0.1	0.5	0	2.4
F	NA	NA	NA	NA	0	1.0	0	1.5
G	NA	NA	NA	NA	0	2.0	1.0	0
H	0	3.0	0	1.0	0	1.0	0	5:0

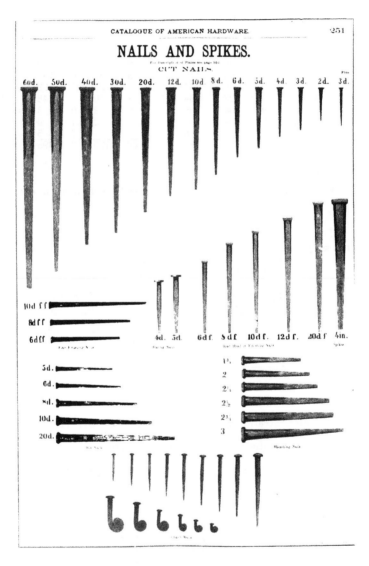

Figure 120. Illustrated Catalogue of American Hardware of the Russell and Erwin Manufacturing Company, 1865.

Comments

Two tentative conclusions can be derived from the study of the nail sample. First, the ordinal ranking of the nails by method of manufacture suggests, assuming that this order accurately represents the distribution of categories within the unspecifiable nail segment, that nails were items of importation from the more settled region to the east rather than objects of local production.

Second, the nail sample reflects, at least, part of the range of possible uses of nails at the fort. The size of the handwrought spike fragments indicates employment in comparatively heavy woodwork. Such spikes may have been similar to the "great nails," which were studded into the fort gates (Grinnell 1923:38, 40).

Headless nails were used primarily for various types of interior finish (Fontana and Greenleaf 1962:58). The pennyweight of the nails in this collection, approximately 9d, suggests that they may have been utilized in flooring (Fontana and Greenleaf 1962:57; J. Walker 1971:73).

Common nails were employed for a wide variety of purposes depending upon their length. They typically range in pennyweight from 2d to 60d. The measureable nails, however, clustered between 7d and 9d. These intermediate lengths were commonly applied to light framing in buildings and to boxes and crates (Fontana and Greenleaf 1962:57; J. Walker 1971:73).

Clinch nails were utilized in a number of special circumstances. They were often "used in the facings of window shutters; in the battens of doors; in the overlap of boards (old style) in lathed room partitions; or on door latches, etc. . . ." (Mercer 1976:4). The relatively large head remnants indicate that the nails in this collection were probably employed with some type of door latch.

Machine-cut nails, spikes, and handwrought nails were found by both Moore (1973:18, 19, 22, 24) and Leonard (1978:23, 40, 54, 57, 72) in their excavations of the fort interior. In addition to the nail categories represented in the trash dumps' collections, Leonard (1978:97) found an L-headed sprig. Both Moore (1973:22, 24) and Leonard (1978:54) discovered machine-cut nails in association with Stagecoach Period, 1861-1881, plank-and-joist floors.

WINDOW GLASS

Description

The window glass sample was not available for examination. From the existing records, however, the spatial distribution and the relative density of the fragments could be defined. This information is presented in figures 114 and 115. Some 1,065 fragments were recovered from the West Dump; 1,466 fragments were excavated from the Main Dump. The majority were recovered from the upper strata.

Distribution

The distribution of glass by strata is listed in tables 56 and 57. A measure of relative desnity has been included to compensate for the differences in the number of times that the various strata appear within the excavation units.

Comments

Based upon excavation evidence, Moore (1973:15) felt that window glass of some type had been used at the fort from the very beginning. His work (1973:15, 18, 19, 22, 35, 42) uncovered flat glass in a number of interior rooms (E5, N2, N4, S2, W3). Most of the window glass recovered by Leonard (1978:124) came from disturbed contexts. His glass sample had a mean thickness of approximately 1/6 inch.

Table 56. Stratigraphic Distribution and Relative Stratigraphic Density of Window Glass in the West Dump by Unit Category

Stratum	Nonrandom Frequency	Density	Random Frequency	Density
OB*	0	NA	63	NA
A	305	16.9	294	15.5
B	101	16.8	23	3.3
C	74	9.3	112	8.6
D	46	5.8	47	5.2
Total	526	NA	539	NA

---

*Not all of the material excavated from Stratum OB was retained.

Table 57. Stratigraphic Distribution and Relative Stratigraphic Density of Window Glass in the Main Dump by Unit Category

Stratum	Nonrandom Frequency	Density	Random Frequency	Density
A*	3	NA	40	NA
B	158	7.9	346	10.5
C	220	11.6	347	10.2
D	34	1.9	236	6.9
E	16	1.1	38	1.9
F	NA	NA	3	1.5
G	NA	NA	2	2.0
H	10	5.0	13	13.0
Total	441		1,025	

---

*Not all material recovered from Stratum A was retained.

Two types of glass were generally available during the first half of the 19th century (Wilson 1976:150-1164). These were cylinder glass (figure 121) and crown glass (figure 122). The former was made by blowing a large cylindrical bubble, which was later cut and heated to turn it into a flat sheet. The latter glass was formed by blowing a bubble and then spinning it into a disk. This later was cut into the appropriate sizes. Flat glass, due to breakage and due to high overland freight charges, probably was a relatively expensive item (Innes 1976:3) by the time it reached Bent's Fort.

Figure 121. Cylinder or Broad Glass Manufacture. (Wood engraving from "Scenes in a Glass Foundry," by Theo. R. Davis, Harpers Weekly, January, 1884. Reproduced in Wilson 1976:151.)

In 1971, John Walker suggested that window glass increased in thickness during the 19th century (1971:78). Since then, David and Jennifer Chance (1976:252) and Karl Roenke (1978:116) have offered tables of modal values of thickness corresponding to various periods. A study of the glass literature suggests that this tendency can be more specifically defined in terms of cylinder glass. This refinement and the limits of its applicability are discussed at length elsewhere (Inashima 1980:6-13). A regression equation was defined as a result of this refinement, $d = 1767 + 54.5 \, x$. That is, the date, $\underline{d}$, is equal to the sum of the constant 1767 plus the product of the constant 54.5 times the mean glass thickness measured to the tenth of a millimeter. When this formula was applied to the converted mean thickness reported by Leonard (1978:124), a date of 1857 was calculated. This corresponds relatively well to the disturbed materials, which probably represent glass from the 1833 to 1849 Bent Period and the 1861 to 1881 Stagecoach Period whose median date is 1854. The application of this method to the spatial and stratigraphic

Figure 122. Crown Glass Manufacture (a, rolling the "eye"; b, flattening the globe of glass; c, attaching a punty to the flattened end of the globe; d, spinning the globe into a flat disk of glass (Diderot 1959:plates 241, 242, 243, 245)).

distribution of glass fragments may have some use for verifying or establishing the chronology of various archeological contexts at the fort.

REDFORD GLASS COMPANY'S
PRICES CURRENT OF CROWN WINDOW GLASS,
MANUFACTURED AT REDFORD, CLINTON CO., N.Y.

REDFORD SIZE.	Whole sale Price per Light.	REDFORD SIZE.	Whole sale Price per Light.	REDFORD SIZE.	Whole sale Price per Light.	REDFORD SIZE.	Whole sale Price per Light.	REDFORD SIZE.	Whole sale Price per 100 ft.
22 by 17	1 25	19 by 15	0 74	16 by 14	0 54	13 by 13	0 36	10 by 8	16 00
22 .. 16	1 04	19 .. 14	0 69	16 .. 13	0 50	13 .. 12	0 33	9 .. 9	16 00
22 .. 15	0 95	19 .. 13	0 63	16 .. 12	0 45	13 .. 11	0 30	9 .. 8	16 00
22 .. 14	0 87	19 .. 12	0 57	16 .. 11	0 40	13 .. 10	0 26	9 .. 7	15 00
22 .. 13	0 80	19 .. 11	0 53	16 .. 10	0 36	13 .. 9	0 23	8 .. 8	14 00
22 .. 12	0 73	18 .. 15	0 69	16 .. 9	0 33	13 .. 8	0 19	8 .. 7	14 00
21 .. 16	0 96	18 .. 14	0 63	15 .. 13	0 44	12 .. 12	0 30	8 .. 6	13 00
21 .. 15	0 87	18 .. 13	0 59	15 .. 12	0 40	12 .. 11	0 26	7 .. 6	10 00
21 .. 14	0 80	18 .. 12	0 55	15 .. 11	0 36	12 .. 10	0 23	7 .. 5	10 00
21 .. 13	0 73	18 .. 11	0 50	15 .. 10	0 33	12 .. 9	0 18	7 .. 4	9 00
21 .. 12	0 67	18 .. 10	0 45	15 .. 9	0 30	12 .. 8	0 15	6 .. 4	9 00
20 .. 16	0 87	17 .. 15	0 63	15 .. 8	0 27	11 .. 11	0 23		
20 .. 15	0 80	17 .. 14	0 58	14 .. 14	0 40	11 .. 10	0 18		
20 .. 14	0 73	17 .. 13	0 54	14 .. 12	0 36	11 .. 9	0 15		
20 .. 13	0 67	17 .. 12	0 50	14 .. 11	0 33	11 .. 8	0 12		
20 .. 12	0 60	17 .. 11	0 45	14 .. 10	0 30	10 .. 10	0 14		
20 .. 11	0 57	17 .. 10	0 40	14 .. 9	0 20	10 .. 9	0 12		

SARANAC SIZE.	Whole sale Price per Light.	SARANAC SIZE.	Whole sale Price per Light.	SARANAC SIZE.	Whole sale Price per Light.	SARANAC SIZE.	Whole sale Price per Light.	SARANAC SIZE.	Whole sale Price per 100 ft.
22 by 17	94 cts.	19 by 15	55 cts	16 by 14	37 cts.	13 by 13	27 cts.	10 by 8	14 00
22 .. 16	78 ..	19 .. 14	50 ..	16 .. 13	34 ..	13 .. 12	24 ..	9 .. 9	14 00
22 .. 15	71 ..	19 .. 13	45 ..	16 .. 12	31 ..	13 .. 11	21 ..	9 .. 8	14 00
22 .. 14	65 ..	19 .. 12	41 ..	16 .. 11	29 ..	13 .. 10	20 ..	9 .. 7	13 00
22 .. 12	55 ..	19 .. 11	37 ..	16 .. 10	26 ..	13 .. 9	17 ..	8 .. 8	13 00
22 .. 13	55 ..	18 .. 15	50 ..	16 .. 9	24 ..	13 .. 8	14 ..	8 .. 7	13 00
21 .. 16	72 ..	18 .. 14	45 ..	15 .. 13	31 ..	12 .. 12	21 ..	8 .. 6	11 00
21 .. 15	63 ..	18 .. 13	41 ..	15 .. 12	28 ..	12 .. 11	20 ..	7 .. 6	9 00
21 .. 14	60 ..	18 .. 12	37 ..	15 .. 11	26 ..	12 .. 10	17 ..	7 .. 5	9 00
21 .. 13	55 ..	18 .. 11	31 ..	15 .. 10	24 ..	12 .. 9	14 ..	7 .. 4	8 00
21 .. 12	50 ..	18 .. 10	30 ..	15 .. 9	21 ..	12 .. 8	12 ..	6 .. 4	8 00
20 .. 16	65 ..	17 .. 15	45 ..	15 .. 8	18 ..	11 .. 11	17 ..		
20 .. 15	60 ..	17 .. 14	41 ..	14 .. 13	28 ..	11 .. 10	14 ..		
20 .. 14	55 ..	17 .. 13	37 ..	14 .. 12	26 ..	11 .. 9	11 ..		
20 .. 13	50 ..	17 .. 12	34 ..	14 .. 11	24 ..	11 .. 8	9 ..		
20 .. 12	45 ..	17 .. 11	31 ..	14 .. 10	21 ..	10 .. 10	11 ..		
20 .. 11	41 ..	17 .. 10	28 ..	14 .. 9	20 ..	10 .. 9	9 ..		

SIZES —10 by 8 and under, are packed in boxes of 50 feet each. 10 by 9, to 14 by 13, are packed in boxes of 30 lights each. 15 by 8, to 18 by 15, are packed in boxes of 30 lights each. 19 by 11 and upwards, are packed in boxes of 25 lights each. All sizes cut to order, not named in the Price Current, will be at the same rate as regular sizes. Fractional parts of inches will be charged as whole inches.

The Redford Crown Glass is made from WHITE FLINT SAND, obtained in the vicinity of the Works, and is the only Crown Glass made from that species of Sand in this country. It is capable of standing every change of climate—nor will it lose its lustre by age.

The REDFORD CROWN GLASS is distinguished from ordinary Crown Glass, by its uncommon evenness and beauty of surface—by its superior transparency and lightness of color—by its great thickness, and the general excellence of the materials which compose it. This Glass possesses a remarkable lustre, which causes it to reflect like the purest specimens of Plate Glass. Its surface not being polished after being blown, retains its enamel, brilliancy and hardness, and is not liable to the objection which applies to Plate Glass, of being easily and permanently bedimmed by dust; being all made of double thickness, will be found on comparison cheaper and stronger than Foreign or Cylinder Glass. The subscribers have spared no pains to make this one of the first establishments in the United States. Orders addressed to them or their Agents will be executed with care and prompt attention.

COOK, LANE, CORNING & CO.
Agent.   TROY, N Y, January 9, 1837.

Figure 123. Broadside for the Redford Glass Company, 1837. The cost of flat glass by the time it reached Bent's Fort was probably considerably higher (Wison 1976:162).

389

THE MISCELLANEOUS ARTIFACT COMPONENT

INTRODUCTION

The Miscellaneous Artifact Component consists of three categories of items. These categories are: those identifiable items that could not be assigned to any of the other components and that were not sufficiently numerous to devote a separate discussion to; those articles that were nonamorphous but were unidentifiable; and those artifacts that were unidentifiable and amorphous. Included within this component are abraders, adzs, and barbed wire.

IDENTIFIABLE ITEMS

Description

The identifiable items include a wide range of materials. Most relate to some specific activities that may have been carried out at the fort.

Abrader. There are three fragments (figure 124) of historic abraders. The first is rectangular block of purple sandstone. All of its surfaces are smoothed except along the line of fracture. The width is 4.48 cm and the thickness is 1.58 cm. The length is incomplete. The stone weighs 54.6 gm. The second is a rectangular block of purple sandstone. All of the faces are smoothed except along the line of fracture. The surface is

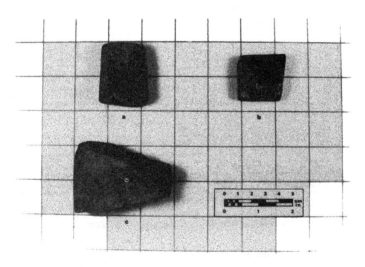

Figure 124. Miscellaneous Iron Artifacts.

somewhat grainy. The width is 3.38 cm and the thickness is 1.03 cm. The length is incomplete. The stone weighs 22.4 gm. The third is a rectangular block of purple sandstone. The upper and lower surfaces have been smoothed. The ends and sides have been chipped. The thickness is 2.59 cm. The width and the length are incomplete. The stone weighs 136.3 gm.

Adz. Two adz-like shafted blades were observed. Both had been made of wrought iron. The first (figure 125a) has a moderately wide edge with a unifacial bevel. The edge is 5.25 cm wide. The second (figure 125b) adz has a narrow edge, which measures about 2.27 cm in width. It has a unifacial edge. Adz blades of this size were commonly employed for coopering activities and might, also, have been utilized for other light woodworking.

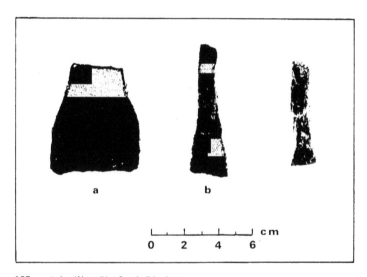

Figure 125. Adz-like Shafted Blades.

Barbed Wire.   Several fragments of barbed wire were noted.   These fragments represented at least two discernible styles.   The first style (figure 126a) was formed by twisting two double strands of wire together into a braided wire.   A wire barb was incorporated at intervals into the wire.   The single remnant of this style is similar to a number of double strand braided barbed wire types.   It is most closely akin to the "Two Twisted Two Lines Twisted Together Resembling Four Strand Braid" patented by J.B. Cleaveland on November 22, 1892 (Glover 1977:np). The other types to which it may be associated are (1) the "Brotherton Barb on Two Strand Twisted with Two Smooth Strand" patented by J. Brotherton on September 3, 1887; (2) the "Glidden Four line Wire" patented on November 24, 1874; and (3) the "Double Tack Wire" patented by H.M. Underwood on August 6, 1878.   The poor condition of this fragment precludes a more definitive identification.

The second style of barbed wire (figure 126b) is a single strand of wire with an attached wire barb.   This style is similar to at least four barbed wire types patented during the 19th century (Glover 1977:np).   These patented types are (1) the "Baker's Single Strand" patented by G.C. Baker on February 27, 1883; (2) the "Rogers Common Patent" patented by C.D. Rogers on January 10, 1888; (3) the "Glidden Reissue No. 6913"

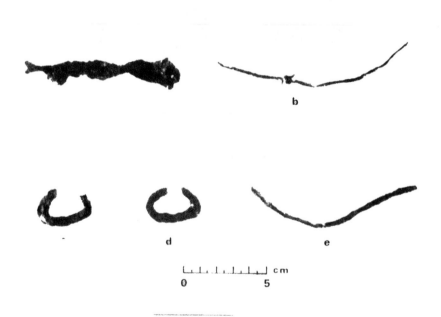

Figure 126.   Wire and Chain Links.

392

patented by J.F. Glidden on February 8, 1876; and (4) an unnamed wire patented by Charles D. Rogers on January 10, 1888.

Bell. This bell (figure 127a) consists of two sections of copper crimped together. The top section has a small loop brazed on for stringing. The bottom section has two holes placed in it. The overall form of the bell is egg-shaped. The bell is approximately 2.67 cm in length and 1.64 cm in width at its widest point.

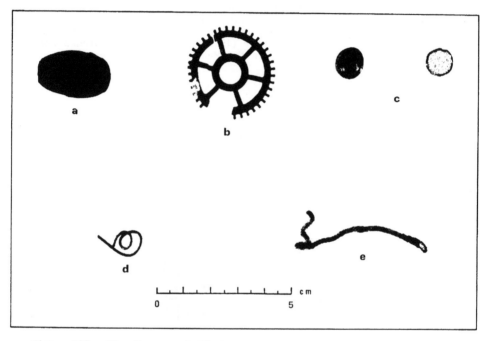

Figure 127. Miscellaneous Artifacts.

Brass Nails. Short dome-headed brass nails are represented primarily by head fragments. Of the 16 nails (figure 128a), only three had sections of the shaft attached. These shafts measured about three-quarters inch in length. The dome heads were about 1.0 cm in diameter. The shafts had squared cuts. Brass-headed nails of this size were "used for upholstering or for nailing on the patent wood chair seats" (Sears Roebuck 1897:np); they were also common items of trade to the Indians.

Chain. Two general styles of chain link were noted (figure 126c and d). The first style of chain link consisted of a strand of iron that had been formed into an oval shape and then had been partially twisted.

Links of this style varied in length from 2.2 cm to 4.5 cm. The second style of chain link was one that had been shaped into an oval form but had not been twisted. The single example measured about 3.5 cm in length.

Chisel. A single chisel-like implement was observed. The item had a unifacial beveled edge on an oval shaft (figure 125c). The edge was about 1.57 cm in width. The implement was handwrought. The size of the edge suggests a light woodworking application.

Clock. A clock-like gear was recovered (figure 127b). It is made of a copper alloy. The diameter from tooth edge to tooth edge is about 3.41 cm. Based upon the fragmentary gear, there were 42 teeth. The shaft hole is 0.75 cm. Moore had earlier (1973:110) recovered a bronze clock hand mounted on an iron pin from the Main Dump and a brass clock key from the interior fort.

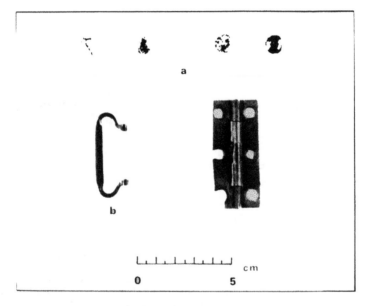

Figure 128. Furniture-Related Artifacts.

Cloth. Cloth was represented by fragments of a coarsely woven green fabric. Threads of a heavy green thread (figure 129) had been woven over a light brown thread. Neither were identifiable as to material.

394

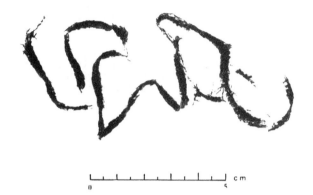

Figure 129.   Green Fabric Fragments.

Container.   A   single   iron   container   was   observed.   The   container
consisted of 28 fragments, which weight 106 gms.   The condition of the
item precluded a more specific identification.

Corn.   Charred fragments of corn cobs were recovered.   A detailed view
of these fragments is shown in figure 130.   Corn was provided by a
number of local Mexican farms as well as from more southerly Mexican
sources as a part of the trade process.

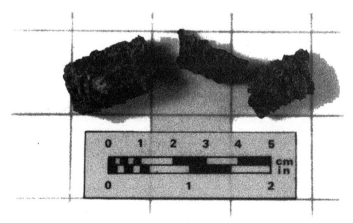

Figure 130.   Charred Corn Cob Fragments.

395

Handles. Two styles of handles were found. The first style (figure 132a) is a wrought iron handle fragment. The fragment is about 11.53 cm in length and 1.05 cm in thickness. The rectangular cross section of the shaft is about 2.79 cm wide; at the end, it is about 3.45 cm wide and has a pear-shaped hole. A number of utensil and tool applications are possible for such a handle.

The second style (figure 128b) is a copper alloy furniture handle. The length of the loop is 4.4 cm at its maximum. The distance between the two attachment arms is 3.3 cm. The width of the handle is 1.8 cm. The holes formed by the open curl of the attachment arms are about 0.17 cm in diameter. The back of the handle is marked "PATENT 1855" (figure 131a).

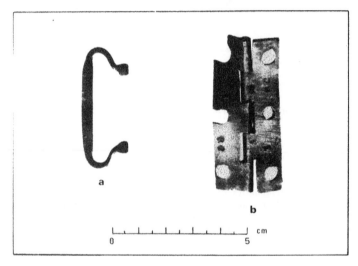

Figure 131. Detail of Drawer Handle Back.

Hinge. The single butt hinge recovered is made of brass. It measures 2.54 cm by 5.72 cm. The attachment holes (figure 128c) are of two sizes. Those on the ends are about 0.54 cm; those in the middle are 0.36 cm. The exterior surface of the aperatures are beveled suggesting that the holes had been created by punching. There are longitudinal striations on the face and oblique striations on the back. The edges of the sides and ends have oblique striations. The hinge pin is about 0.25 cm in diameter. The back of the hinge is impressed with a mark "23 RC" on both wings (figure 131b).

Insulator. A single, small porcelain insulator fragment was found. The shape is similar to eletrical insulators used to handle relatively low voltages. The interior is marked in relief "--SA," probably "USA."

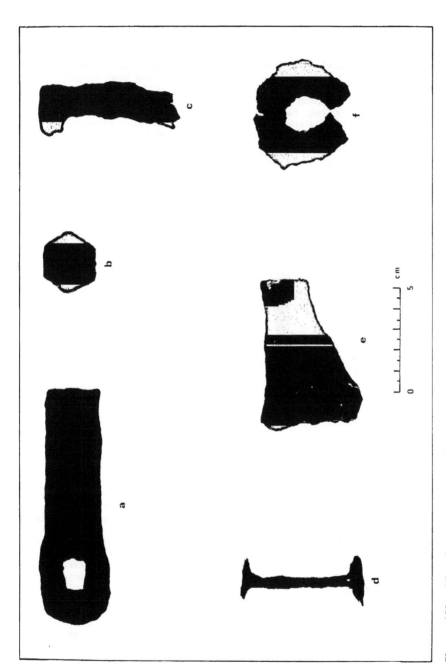

Figure 132.   Miscellaneous Iron Artifacts.

397

Nut.   The single nut is a hexagonal one with a width of 2.67 cm (figure
132b).   Part of a threaded bolt remains attached to the nut.

Pencils.   Fragments of pencils of two types of materia were noted.   The
first set (figure 133a and b) consisted of lead that had been shaped into
writing implements (cf. Hsu and Hanson 1975:147, 149).   Both were about
3.8 cm long.   The second pencil fragment (figure 133c) was made of
slate.   Pencils were not recorded by Moore; however, he recovered
fragments of drawing slates from excavations of the interior fort.
Included on the fragments were parts of a model alphabet, a sketch of a
fringed buckskin leg and moccasin shod foot, and the date 1846 or 1848
(Moore 1973:110, 111).

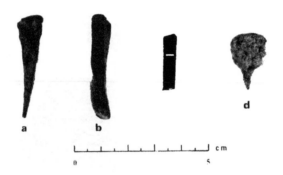

Figure 133.   Miscellaneous Lead Artifacts.

Rivets.   Two varieties of rivets were noted.   The first was made of iron
(figure 132d).   It was relatively large, having a length of about 6 cm.
Its size suggests that it was utilized for joining wood to wood or metal
plate to wood.   The second variety of rivets was made of a copper alloy.
The two rivet fragments of this variety (figure 127c) are primarily short
head sections.   Their partially distorted head diameters are 1.1 cm and
1.04 cm.   One rivet has a measureable shaft diameter of 0.57 cm and a
shaft length of 0.65 cm.   These rivets would have been employed for
light joining work.

Seal.   A small lead seal weighing 6.7 gm was observed (figure 133d).

Spike.   The single railroad spike-like head fragment that was recovered
probably was utilized on a wagon (figure 132c).

398

Stove Plate. A single fragment of cast iron was identified as a possible fragment of stove plate (figure 132e).

Washers. Fragments of iron washers were recovered (figure 132f). Only one fragment was sufficiently intact to measure. Its exterior diameter was about 5.27 cm. Its interior hole was about 1.78 cm in diameter. The relatively large size of the washers suggests possible application in wagon construction.

Wire. Both iron and copper were included within this collection. A single corroded iron fragment (figure 126c) was recovered. Two tarnished and three intact fragments of copper alloy wire (figure 127d and c) were found. Two of these had wire diameters of about 0.22 cm. Their lengths were about 6.5 cm and 17.0 cm. Both had ends that were twisted suggesting that they had been braided around a second wire at some earlier time. The third measureable copper alloy wire had a diameter of 0.14 cm. Copper wire was also included within the items that may have been traded to the Indians.

Distribution

The distributional aspects of the "Identifiable Items" are listed in table 58. The spatial distributiona of the artifacts have been combined with the other artifacts within this component and displayed for the combined strata in figure 134 for the West Dump and in figure 135 for the Main Dump.

Table 58. Distribution of Identifiable Items
by Dump, Unit Type, and Stratum

Item	Material	Frequency	Dump	Unit Type	Stratum
Abrader	sandstone	1	West	Nonrandom	B
Abrader	sandstone	1	West	Random	C
Abrader	sandstone		Main	Random	C
Adz	iron		West	Nonrandom	C
Adz	iron		Main	Random	C
Barb Wire (Style 1)	iron		Main	Nonrandom	B
Barb Wire (Style 2)	iron	1	Main	Nonrandom	A
Barb Wire (Style 2)	iron	1	Main	Random	C
Barb Wire (Style 2)	iron	1	Main	Random	G
Bell	copper		West	Random	A

Item	Material	Frequency	Dump	Unit Type	Stratum
Brass Nail	brass	3	West	Nonrandom	A
Brass Nail	brass	3	West	Random	A
Brass Nail	brass	2	West	Nonrandom	B
Brass Nail	brass	1	West	Random	B
Brass Nail	brass	1	West	Nonrandom	C
Brass Nail	brass	1	West	Random	C
Brass Nail	brass	1	West	Nonrandom	D
Brass Nail	brass	2	Main	Nonrandom	B
Brass Nail	brass	1	Main	Random	C
Brass Nail	brass	1	Main	Random	E
Chain Link (Style 1)	iron	2	West	Nonrandom	A
Chain Link (Style 1)	iron	1	Main	Nonrandom	
Chain Link (Style 1)	iron	1	Main	Random	B
Chain Link (Style 2)	iron		West	Nonrandom	C
Chisel	iron		West	Nonrandom	A
Clock Gear	copper alloy	2*	West	Nonrandom	C
Cloth	unidentified	1	West	Nonrandom	C
Container	iron	28*	Main	Nonrandom	H
Corn			West	Nonrandom	D
Corn		2	Main	Nonrandom	C
Corn		1	Main	Random	C
Handle	iron	1	West	Nonrandom	A
Handle	copper alloy	1	West	Nonrandom	A
Hinge	brass		Main	Random	D
Insulator	porcelain		Main	Random	B
Nut	iron		Main	Nonrandom	B
Pencil	lead	1	West	Nonrandom	A
Pencil	lead		Main	Random	C
Pencil	slate	1	West	Random	A
Rivet	iron	1	West	Random	C
Rivet	copper alloy	1	Main	Nonrandom	D
Rivet	copper alloy	1	Main	Random	D

400

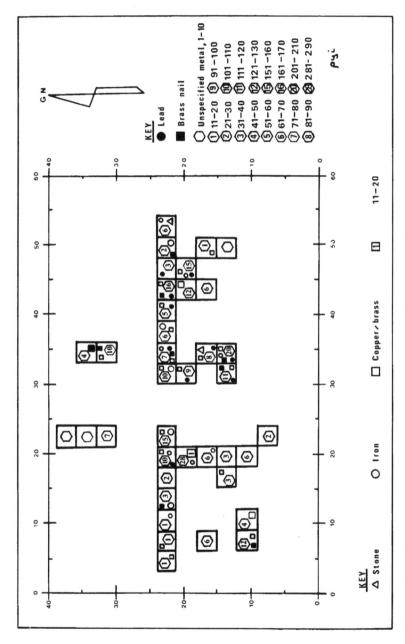

Figure 134. Distribution of Miscellaneous Artifacts within the West Dump.

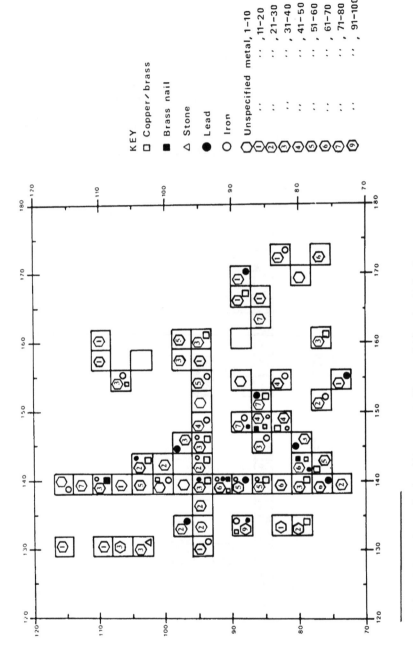

Figure 135. Distribution of Miscellaneous Artifacts within the Main Dump.

402

Item	Material	Frequency	Dump	Unit Type	Stratum
Seal	lead	1	West	Random	C
Spike	iron	1	Main	Random	C
Stove Plate	iron	1	West	Nonrandom	A
Washer	iron	1	West	Nonrandom	A
Washer	iron	1	West	Nonrandom	D
Washer	iron	1	Main	Nonrandom	D
Wire	iron	1	Main	Random	D
Wire	copper alloy	1	West	Random	A
Wire	copper alloy	1	West	Nonrandom	C
Wire	copper alloy	1	West	Random	C
Wire	copper alloy	1	Main	Nonrandom	D

UNIDENTIFIED NON-AMORPHOUS ARTIFACTS

Description

A number of artifacts possess distinct forms; however, they were not identified during the current study. These items are grouped below in terms of their material composition.

Brass or Copper Alloy.   Seven artifacts made of brass or of copper alloy have distinct shapes.   The first is a cylindrical rod (figure 136a) made of a copper alloy.   It has a fragment length of 6.5 cm and a rod diameter of 0.65 cm.   The second item is a cam-like fragment (figure 136b) made of a copper alloy.   The third artifact (figure 136c) is a fragment of plate about 2.5 cm by 1.3 cm by 0.1 cm.   The back has an impressed mark, "PATENT."   The fourth item (figure 136d) is an open oval-shaped artifact with a length of 2.0 cm and a width of 1.3 cm.   The fifth (figure 136e) is a plate-like fragment.   The sixth (figure 136f) is a brass disk-shaped artifact with a center pinhole.   Its diameter is 1.94 cm.   The border of the face is slightly roughened suggesting that a dial or some other type of object may have occupied the center portion of the disk.   The seventh item (figure 136g) is a copper alloy plate with a needle-shaped unidentified silvery metal attached.   The plate is 1.34 cm by 0.99 cm and has beveled side edges.   The needle is 2.74 cm long and bisects the plate perpendicular to the long axis.

403

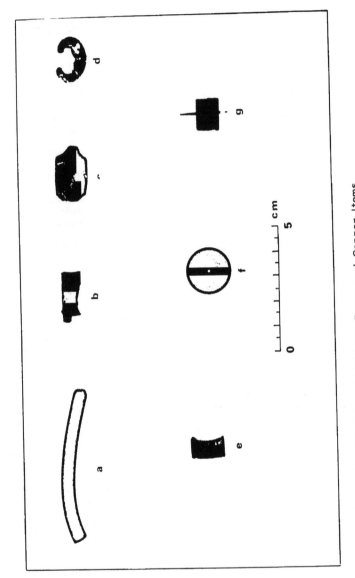

Figure 136.   Unidentified Non-Amorphous Brass and Copper Items.

404

Iron.   There are six categories of unidentified iron objects.   The first
consists of tabular bar fragments (figure 137a).   One fragment has
dimensions of 6.1 cm by 3.3 cm by 1.0 cm.   A second has dimensions of
1.43 cm by 3.17 cm by 5.43 cm.   The sides of this item are beveled.
These fragments suggest smithing activities.   The second group (figure
137b) is comprised of a circular rod.   The diameter of the rod is 1.52 cm
and its fragmentary length is 12.5 cm.   The third item (figure 137c) is a
flat, winged object.   The span along the wings is 15 cm.   The metal is
3.5 mm thick.   The central circular section has a rough diameter of 7.38
cm.   The hole in the middle of this section has a diameter of 2.72 cm.
The fourth group (figure 137d) consists of band-like fragments.   Two
fragments have measureable widths of 2.8 cm.   One of these has a
measureable thickness of 2.2 mm.   A third fragment has a width of 3.8
cm and a thickness of 6.8 mm.   These fragments suggest possible wagon
hardware.   The fifth group (figure 137e) consists of wedge or
shim-shaped small objects.   The sixth category (figure 137f, g, and h) is
spring-like fragments.   There are three artifacts within this category.
The first is a spring-like piece mounted on a backplate.   The second is
an "S"-shaped item.   The third is a fragment with curled edges.

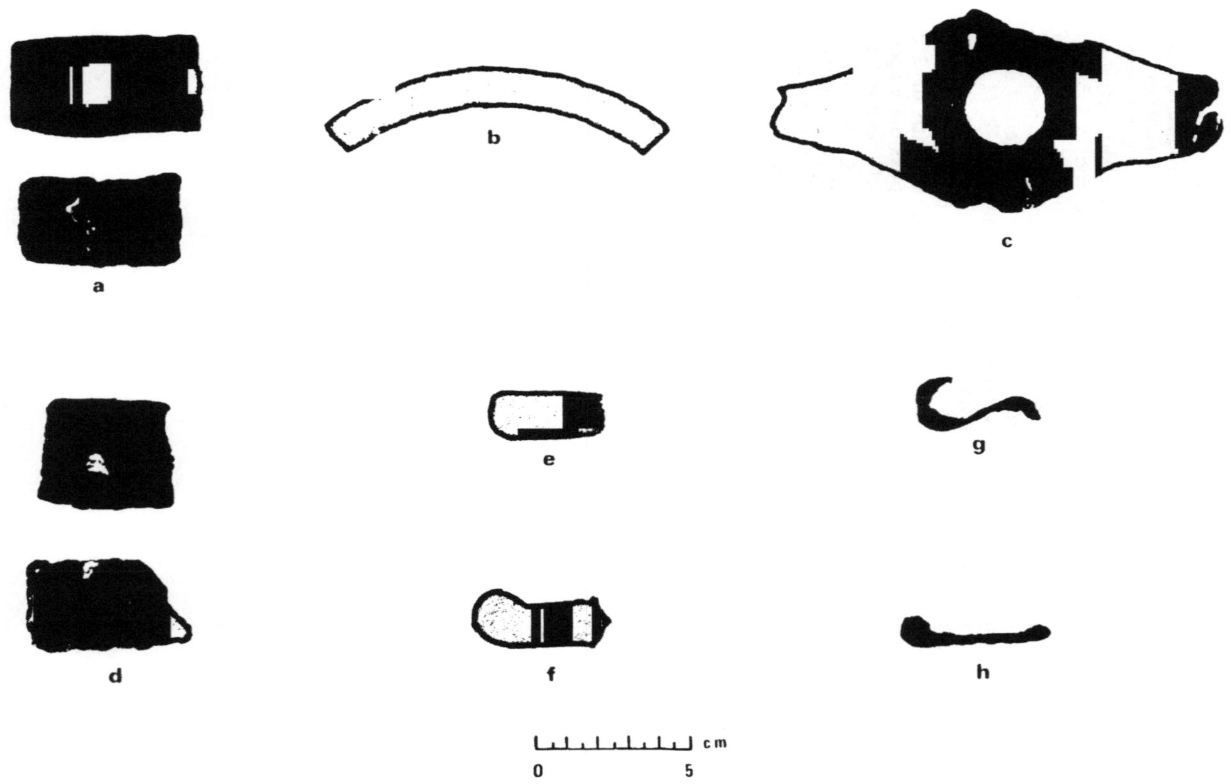

Figure 137. Unidentified Non-Amorphous Artifacts.

Lead. There are two unidentified lead items. The first is a sheet of lead measuring approximately 4.0 cm long (figure 138a). The sheet has a series of regularly placed pinholes. There is a slight ridge along part of the outer edge of the fragment, which suggests that the sheet may have been attached to a container. The second artifact (figure 138b) is a tabular chunk. It is about 2.68 cm by 2.34 cm by 0.65 cm. The ends are beveled in one direction; the sides in the opposite direction.

Other Materials. There are three categories of unidentified objects made of wood and stone. The first item (figure 138c) is a tabular fragment of petrified wood. The sides appear to have been rubbed or polished to create the tabular form. Its dimensions are 5.53 cm by 2.03 cm by 1.28 cm. The second artifact (figure 138d) is a fragmentary wooden ring. The exterior diameter of the ring is 4.25 cm. The diameter of the wood shaft is 0.6 cm. The third cateogry (figure 138e to h) is a series of apparently natural, black rock, which have been highly polished. These vary in weight from 0.5 gm to 2.3 gm. Their shapes vary from oval to tubular to spherical.

Distribution

The distributional aspects of the unidentified non-amorphous artifacts are listed in table 10-2. The spatial distribution of these items, combined with the other artifacts within this component, is depicted for the combined strata in figure 10-10 for the West Dump and in figure 10-11 for the Main Dump.

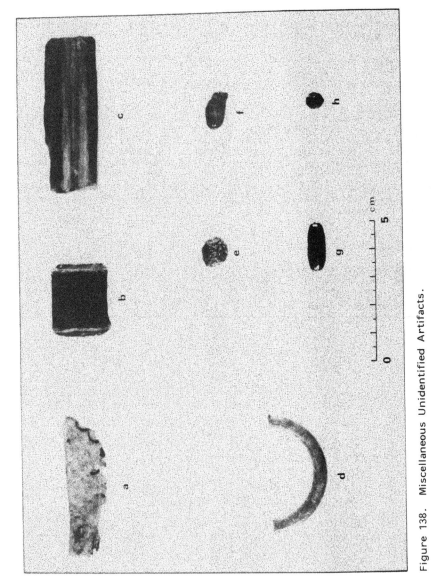

Figure 138. Miscellaneous Unidentified Artifacts.

Table 59. Distribution of Unidentified Non-Amorphous Artifacts
by Dump, Unit Type, and Stratum

Material	General Shape	Frequency	Dump	Unit Type	Stratum
Copper alloy	rod		Main	Nonrandom	E
Copper alloy	cam-like		West	Nonrandom	A
Copper alloy	plate		West	Random	C
Copper alloy	oval		West	Nonrandom	C
Copper alloy	plate		Main	Random	C
Brass	disk		West	Random	A
Copper alloy	plate/needle				
Iron	tabular bar		West	Nonrandom	B
Iron	tabular bar		Main	Random	B
Irn	rod		Main	Nonrandom	C
Iron	winged plate		Main	Random	C
Iron	band	4	West	Nonrandom	
Iron	band	1	West	Nonrandom	
Iron	band	1	West	Nonrandom	A
Iron	band	2	West	Random	B
Iron	band	1	Main	Random	B
Iron	band	1	Main	Random	D
Iron	shim		West	Nonrandom	C
Iron	shim		Main	Random	B
Iron	spring	1	West	Nonrandom	
Iron	spring	1	West	Random	B
Iron	spring		Main	Random	C
Lead	tabular chunk		Main	Nonrandom	B
Lead	strainer		Main	Random	D
Petrified Wood	tabular chunk		Main	Nonrandom	D
Wood	ring		West	Random	C

409

Material	General Shape	Frequency	Dump	Unit Type	Stratum
Stone	tubular object	2	West	Nonrandom	A
Stone	tubular object	3	West	Random	A
Stone	tubular object	1	West	Nonrandom	C
Stone	tubular object	1	West	Random	C
Stone	tubular object	1	Main	Nonrandom	C
Stone	tubular object	1	Main	Random	C
Stone	tubular object	1	Main	Random	D

AMORPHOUS ARTIFACTS

Description

A number of artifacts are either too fragmentary for identification or represent natural objects that retain no discernible physical indications of cultural use. The latter materials, however, may, through ethnohistorical analogy, have been culturally employed even though the objects themselves provide no direct indications of such use.

Calcite. Fragments of calcite varying between 0.4 gm and 213.4 gm were noted. Calcite is the most common of all carbonate minerals (Chesterman 1978:432). The Native American pottery contains a micaceous material in some of the styles that may be crushed calcite (figures 139 and 151a).

Charcoal. Fragments of charcoal were noted in the field notes for some of the excavated units. Samples (figure 14d) retained in this collection suggest the use of relatively thin wood stock. Given the relative scarcity of wood within the region, it is unlikely that this material represents wood used to burn trash. More likely, it derives from stove and hearth wastes. As in most frontier locations, loally prepared charcoal would have been used to fire the blacksmith's forge. There is no indication that any of the charcoal noted is a product of the charcoal preparation process.

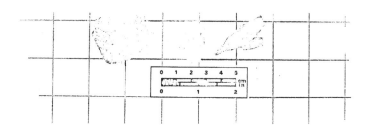

Figure 139. Calcite Fragments.

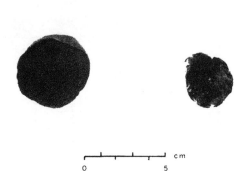

Figure 140. Charcoal.

411

Copper. Fragments of copper are present primarily in the form of sheet scrap. These fragments could represent trim scrap from the production of trade bells, etc. A listing of the copper fragments is provided in table 60.

Horn. Several horn tips were noted among the osteological material retained with the studied collection. Such tips were removed during the initial process in the preparation of horn slabs. In the context of recovery, however, these tips probably represent the local manufacture of powder horns.

Iron. Fragments of iron are present in a variety of forms from sheet scrap to cylindrical to corroded clumps. A listing of the iron fragments is provided in table 61.

Lead. Fragments of lead appear in a variety of non-ordered forms. Most of the fragments are probably the result of waste from the production of bullets and shot. The lead fragments are listed in table 62.

Leather. A single cluster of heavily burnt leather was noted.

Shell. A number of mollusk shell fragments (figure 141) varying in weight from 0.2 gm to 22.4 gm were noted. Such shells might have been used for such purposes as buttons, beds, and other ornaments.

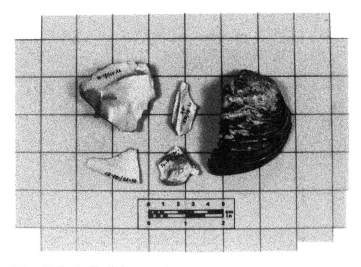

Figure 141. Mollusk Shell Fragments.

412

Slag and Clinker.   Slag and clinker (figure 142) were noted in many of
the excavated units.   Some of the material suggested forge wastes.

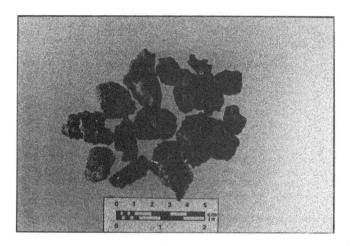

Figure 142.   Blacksmith's Forge Waste Slag.

Table 60.   Distribution of Copper Fragments
by Dump, Unit Type, and Stratum

Dump	Unit Type	Stratum	Frequency
West	Random	OB	1
West	Nonrandom	A	6
West	Random	A	11
West	Nonrandom	B	4
West	Random	B	5
West	Nonrandom	C	28
West	Random	C	6
West	Nonrandom	D	1
West	Random	D	2
Main	Random	A	1
Main	Nonrandom	B	1
Main	Random	B	1
Main	Nonrandom	C	4
Main	Random	C	3
Main	Nonrandom	D	1
Main	Random	D	6
Main	Random	E	4
Main	Random	H	1

West Dump Subtotal   64
Main Dump Subtotal   22

Total   86

413

Table 61. Distribution of Iron Fragments
by Dump, Unit Type, and Stratum

Dump	Unit Type	Stratum	Frequency
West	Random	OB	32
West	Nonrandom	A	586
West	Random	A	452
West	Nonrandom	B	74
West	Random	B	195
West	Nonrandom	C	502
West	Random	C	462
West	Nonrandom	D	245
West	Random	D	280
Main	Random	A	46
Man	Nonrandom	B	182
Main	Random	B	474
Main	Nonrandom	C	338
Main	Random	C	357
Main	Nonrandom	D	100
Main	Random	D	347
Main	Nonrandom	E	44
Main	Random	E	81
Main	Random	F	70
Main	Nonrandom	H	18
Main	Random	H	8

West Dump Subtotal 2,828
Main Dump Subtotal 2,065

Total   4,893

Table 62. Distribution of Lead Fragments
by Dump, Unit Type, and Stratum

Dump	Unit Type	Stratum	Frequency
West	Nonrandom	A	1
West	Random	A	4
West	Nonrandom	C	5
Main	Random	A	1
Main	Random	B	2
Main	Random	C	2
Main	Nonrandom	D	1
Main	Random	D	4

West Dump Subtotal 10
Main Dump Subtotal 10

Total   20

414

THE NATIVE AMERICAN COMPONENT

INTRODUCTION

The Native American Component of the artifact assemblage consists of those items that were manufactured by the indigenous population. Included within this component are a variety of lithic tools and fragments of pottery.

LITHICS

Description

The lithic collection can be divided into several categories. The first group consists of those items that have recognizable functional forms. The second group consists of those items that have no distinct functional attributes. In discussing the lithic artifacts various characteristics have been noted. Maximum length, maximum width, and maximum thickness of each item have been recorded in order to provide some measure of size. Likewise, where possible, a measure of each item's weight in grams was noted. In the case of tools, the length of the working edge, its location (distal or lateral edge), and edge angle were measured. Material and other comments, where applicable, were made.

Biface.   A single bifacially chipped artifact (figure 145) was noted. The biface was made of a gray quartzite and was fragmentary. The fragment weighed 12.0 gm and measured 2.1 cm by 3.4 cm by 1.25 cm. The curved working edge was about 3.4 cm long and had an edge angle of 75°.

Core.   A number of cores were noted (figure 144). These cores fall into two general groups. The first consists of cobbles or pebbles from which flakes have been struck. The second consists of decortication flakes from which additional flakes have been taken. Two cores of the first type were observed. The first is a nodule of variegated black flint. The stone weighs 58.6 gm. Its dimensions are 3.65 cm by 4.22 cm by 2.82 cm. The second is a pebble core of variegated gray and red chert. It weighs 12.7 gm and has maximal dimensions of 3.24 cm by 2.12 cm by 1.88 cm.

The remainder of the cores are based upon decortication flakes. There are three such cores. The first is made of a black sedimentary stone, possibly argillite. The stone weighs 77.2 gms and has dimensions of 6.5 cm by 5.16 cm by 2.61 cm. The second is made of a honey-colored jasper. It weighs 15.9 gm and has dimensions of 4.25 cm by 2.69 cm by 1.47 cm. It has a utilized edge of 2.08 cm length along one lateral edge. The edge angle is 75°. The third core is made of a honey-colored quartz. It weighs 11.3 gm and has dimensions of 3.35 cm by 2.15 cm by 1.57 cm.

Drill.   A single drill-type implement was observed (figure 146 a). It was made from gray chert. The total length of the implement was 3.3

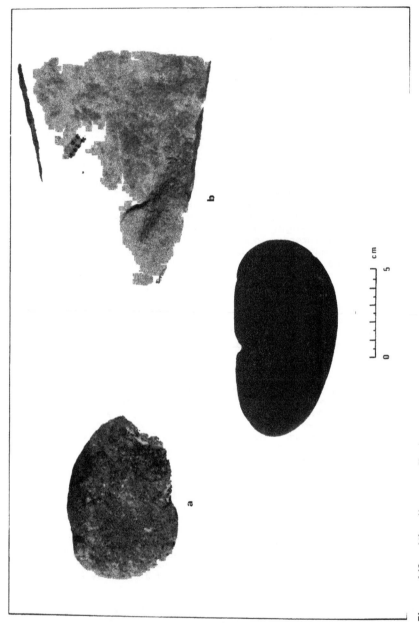

Figure 143. Miscellaneous Tools.

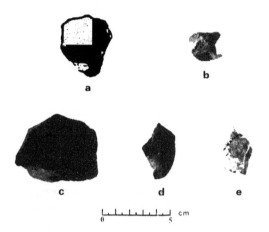

Figure 144. Miscellaneous Cores.

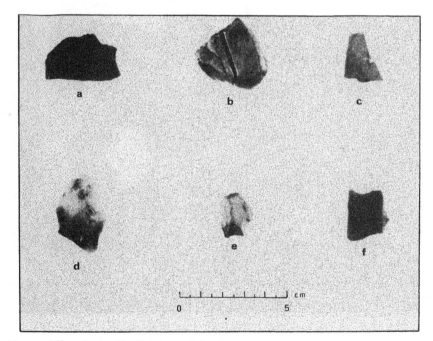

Figure 145. Projectile Points and Preforms.

417

cm. The shaft length was 2.0 cm. The base had a maximum width of 1.09 cm. The shaft width was about 0.42 cm. The piece was 0.43 cm thick at its greatest. It weighed 1.1 gm.

Hammerstone. A single quartzite hammerstone was noted (figure 143 a). The cobble was tabular ovoid in shape. About 8 cm of its edge had been heavily battered. Two spots retained traces of light pecking. The approximate dimensions were 9.5 cm by 7.0 cm by 3.0 cm. The piece weighed 293.2 gm.

Knife. A small, semi-circular milk quartz flake (figure 146 b) had been shaped into a knife-type form. The working edge was about 2.09 cm in length and had an angle of 30°. The overall dimensions were 1.79 cm by 1.88 cm by 0.51 cm. The item weighed 1.5 gm.

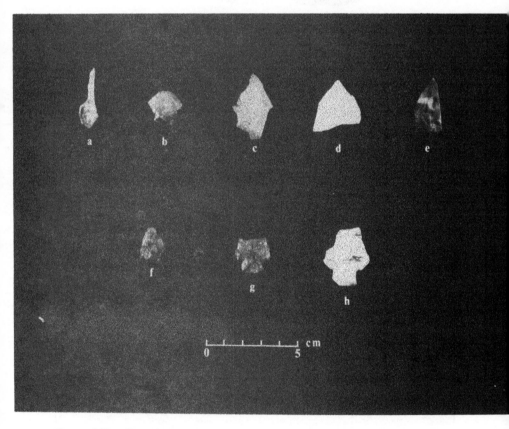

Figure 146. Scrapers.

Miscellaneous Crusher/Pounder.   A small patinated milk quartz pebble
(figure 145 b) retained pecked end surfaces suggesting a crushing or
pounding function.   The item weighed 21.0 gm and had dimensions of 2.85
cm by 2.73 cm by 0.62 cm.   In shape, it was triangular and tabular.

Ornament.   A fragment of a pendant-like object was noted (figure
145 c).   The stone was a light gray sandstone.   It had an obliquely
drilled hole.

Perforator.   Three artifacts with sharp-pointed appendages were noted
(figure 146 c, d, & e).   The first was made of a brown sedimentary
rock.   It was a cortex flake and weighed 4.1 gm.   Its overall dimensions
were 3.54 cm by 2.15 cm by 0.58 cm.   The second was an unidentified
white stone.   It weighed 5.3 gm and had dimensions of 2.61 cm by 2.98
cm by 0.84 cm.   The last was made of Chuska, an exotic material found
in   Arizona   and   New   Mexico   (Dennis   Stanford   1982:personal
communication).   It weighed 4.0 gm and had dimensions of 2.93 cm by 1.5
cm by 0.79 cm.

Preform.   Two preforms were noted.   The first (figure 145 d) was a
roughly point-shaped form made of a variegated rose and white quartz.
The preform weighed 6.1 gm and had dimensions of 3.53 cm by 2.53 cm
by 0.58 cm.   The edges had been bifacially flaked.   The second (figure
145 e) is a variegated gray and rose chert roughed out into a
sidescraper-like form.   The item weighs 2.8 gm and measures 1.96 cm by
1.51 cm by 0.73 cm.

Projectile Point.   Three projectile point fragments (figure 146 f, g, & h)
were noted.   The first was made of a variegated brown and purple
quartzite.   This is a local stone known as Dakota quartzite (Stanford
1982:personal communication).   This was corner notched.   The point had
a width of 1.91 cm at the lobes.   The width of the stem varied from 1.07
below the lobes 1.18 cm at the end.   The stem was expanding and
thinned.   The fragment weighed 2.2 gm and was 0.48 cm thick.   The
second is a stemmed point made of Texas alabase (Stanford 1982: personal
communication).   The stem is thinned and relatively straight.   The
fragment is 0.37 cm thick.   The point is 2.5 cm wide at the lobes.   The
stem varied from 1.24 cm to 1.33 cm in width.   The fragment is about 3.4
gm in weight.   The third is a variegated brown and red quartzite point
tip fragment, which weighed 1.3 gm.   Its dimensions were 1.75 cm by
1.41 cm by 0.41 cm.

Scrapers.   Both end and side scrapers were observed (figure 147 a to
f).   A small sidescraper is made of a white chert-like material.   It weighs
1.4 gm and has dimensions of 1.83 cm by 1.39 cm by 0.48 cm.   It has a
working edge of 1.4 cm and an edge angle of 75°.   A thumbnail
endscraper is made of light gray translucent flint.   It has dimensions of
1.12 cm by 1.24 cm by 0.35 cm and weighs 0.7 gm.   The working edge is
6.5 mm and has an angle of 75°.   A second endscraper is made of
variegated rose quartz.   It has dimensions of 3.55 cm by 2.72 cm by 0.92
cm.   It has a working edge of 2.15 cm and an angle of 80°-90°.   It
weighs 8.8 gm.   Another endscraper is made from a honey-colored jasper
cortex flake.   The dimensions are 2.73 cm by 1.09 cm by 0.74 cm.   It
weighs 2.5 gm.   The working edge is 8.4 mm and has an angle of 75°.   A

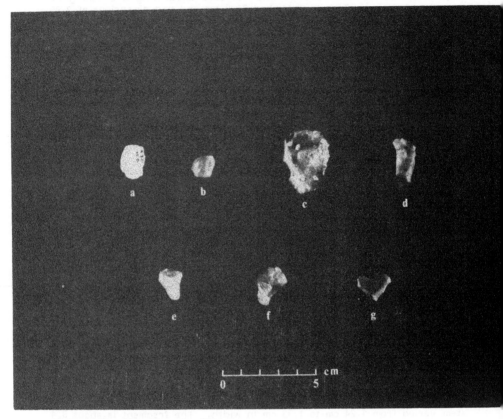

Figure 147. Miscellaneous Stone.

secondary lateral edge has a length of 1.36 cm and an angle of 40°. A fourth endscraper is made of gray chert. It has dimensions of 1.7 cm by 1.33 cm by 0.6 cm and weighs 1.3 gm. Its working edge is 8.8 mm and has an angle of 50°. The last endscraper is made of a translucent gray flint. It has dimensions of 2.22 cm by 1.52 cm by 0.54 cm and weighs 1.8 gm. The working edge is 8.8 mm and has an angle of 80°.

Spokeshave. Three spokeshaves were noted. The first is a tabular ovoid stone of a purple fine grained quartzite (figure 143 c). The edge has been unifacially chipped along the medial section to produce a beveled edge with a central semi-circular region. This region is about 5.8 mm in diameter. The edge angle is 75°. The overall dimensions are 11.0 cm by 6.0 cm by 1.0 cm. The stone weighs 111.4 gm.

The second spokeshave (figure 145 f) is made of a gray quartzite. The working edge is 1.0 cm and has an angle of 60°. The stone weighs 3.9 gm and has dimensions of 2.03 cm by 2.46 cm by 0.77 cm. The third (figure 147 g) is a gray chert with dimensions of 1.71 cm by 1.46 cm by 0.49 cm. It weighs 1.6 gm. The working edge is 8.4 mm and the angle is 75°.

Tabular Slab. This slab (figure 143 b) is triangular in shape and has chipped edges. The faces have both been smoothed. The dimensions are 16.5 cm by 11.0 cm by 2.3 cm. The material is a light to dark gray sandstone. Such slabs were used for cooking slabs and other purposes (Swannack 1969:141).

Utilized Flakes. A large number of the flakes (figure 148) from the collection had been utilized. The angles of the utilized edges varied from 30° to 90°. The flakes varied from between 0.4 gm to 6.2 gm in weight. Use of both distal and lateral edges was noted. The specific attributes of each flake are noted in table 64.

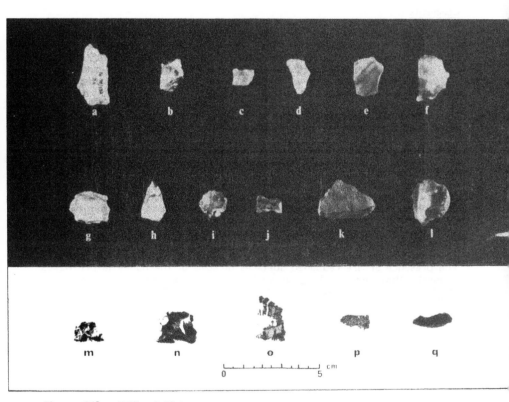

Figure 148. Utilized Flakes.

421

Miscellaneous Debitage. Included within this category are both unutilized flakes and chunk-shaped debitage. These vary in weight from 0.9 gm to 11.7 gm. The detailed attributes of each item are listed in table 65.

Indeterminate Objects. Some of the lithic remains are of unknown cultural value. Most have been split and some have been fire cracked. Only one shows indications of some rough chipping and may be a crude digging implement. This stone is a white sedimentary material. The attributes of these items are listed in table 66.

Distribution

The distributional aspects of the lithics collection are listed in tables 63 to 66. The spatial distribution for combined strata is depicted in figure 149 for the West Dump and in figure 150 for the Main Dump.

Comments

The Dakota quartzite point is a historic Apache point (Dennis Stanford 1982:personal communication). No chronological significance can be assigned to any of the other lithic items. The presence of artifacts made of Texas alabase and Arizona/New Mexico chuska suggests some movement of populations. Most of the lithics appear to have been made from small-sized cobbles or pebbles.

Moore (1973:111) recorded fragments of black flint and quartzite points. He also noted stemmed triangular points made of iron barred hoops.

Edwin Wilmsen (1972:202) has suggested some general functional categories for flake tools based upon edge angle. These groupings are 26°-35°, 46°-55°, and 66°-75°. The 26°-35° group is seen as being used primarily for cutting activities. The 46°-55° group is noted as being used for a variety of uses including skinning and hide scraping; heavy cutting of wood, bone, and horn; and tool-back blunting. The 66°-75° group is felt to have been employed for wood and bone working. While all of the edge angle groups are reprsented in this collecion, most fall within the second or general purpose group.

The presence of fire reddened surfaces of some of the honey jasper flakes suggests that fire cracking of cobbles may have been practiced. Fire cracking of stones has been employed for facilitating the knapping process.

Table 63. Distribution of Lithic Tool Ge Forms by Dump, Unit Type, and Stratum

Form	Material	Maximum Length (cm)	Maximum Width (cm)	Maximum Thickness (cm)	Weight (gm)	Edge Length (cm)	Edge Angle	Comments
Biface	gy quartzite	2.1	3.4	1.25	12.0	3.4	75°	fragment MRA
Ge	black flint	3.65	4.22	2.82	58.6			MRB
Ge	gray/red bt	3.24	2.12	1.88	12.7			MRD
Ge	gtite	5.16	6.50	2.61	77.2	2.08	75°	MRC
Ge	honey jasper	4.25	2.69	1.47	15.9			MRB
Ge	honey quartz	3.35	2.15	1.57	11.3			WRB
Drill	gy chert	3.3	1.09	0.42	1.1			MRC
Hammerstone	gray quartzite	9.5	7.0	3.0	293.2			MRC
Knife	milk qz	1.79	1.88	0.51	1.5	2.09	30°	WC
Crusher	milk quartz	2.85	2.73	0.62	21.0			MRB
Ornament	gray sandstone	2.5	1.6	0.7	3.4			WRB fragment
	bwn ndry	3.54	2.15	0.58	4.1			MRC
	unidentifid ha	2.61	2.98	0.84	5.3			MRC
	ha	2.93	1.50	0.79	4.0			MRB
Em	ee quartz	3.53	2.53	0.58	6.1			MRD
Em	gray/rose chert	1.96	1.51	0.73	2.8			MRE
Projectile Point	ha quartzite	NA	1.91	0.48	2.2			RC fragment
Projectile Point	Texas alabase	NA	2.5	0.37	3.4			WC fragment
Projectile Point	brown/red qtzite	NA	1.41	0.41	1.3			MNRH fragment
gar	white chert	1.83	1.39	0.48	1.4	1.4	5°	MRD
Endscraper	gy flint	1.12	1.24	0.35	0.7	0.65	75°	MRB
Endscraper	ee quartz	3.55	2.72	0.92	8.8	2.15	6- 8°	MNRD
Endscraper	honey jar	2.73	1.09	0.74	2.5	0.84	75°	WA
						1.36	8°	secondary lateral edge
Endscraper	gray chert	1.7	1.33	0.6	1.3	0.88	50°	MRC
Endscraper	gray flint	2.22	1.52	0.54	1.8	0.88	80°	MRB
Spokeshave	purple quartzite	11.0	6.0	1.0	111.4	0.58	75°	MRD
Spokeshave	gray quartzite	2.03	2.46	0.77	3.9	1.0	60°	MRB
Spokeshave	gray chert	1.71	1.46	0.49	1.6	0.84	5°	RB
Tabular Slab	gray sandstone	16.5	11.0	2.3	NA			WRA

423

Table 64. Distribution of Utilized Flakes by Dump, Unit Type, and Stratum

Dump	Unit Type	Stratum	Material	Maximum Length (cm)	Maximum Width (cm)	Maximum Thickness (cm)	Weight (gm)	Utilized Length (cm)	Edge Angle	Comments
West	Nonrandom	A	brown quartzite	2.47	1.74	0.38	2.3	3.24	50°-80°	distal edge
West	Nonrandom	A	gray flint	2.22	1.59	0.36	1.5	1.6	90°	distal edge
West	Nonrandom	B	honey jasper	1.35	0.93	0.43	0.8	1.09	30°	distal edge
West	Nonrandom	B	yellow flint	1.08	0.83	0.16	0.4	0.63 / 0.8 / 0.85 / 0.86	6° / 45° / 50° / 75°	
West	Ikm	D	tbl de	1.79	1.05	0.36	0.9	0.52	30°	
West	Ikm	D	tbl de	2.22	0.73	0.63	1.1	1.3	40°	cortex flake
Main	Ikm	B	tan chert	2.13	1.71	0.54	2.5	0.81 / 0.89	40° / 40°	fire reddened; cortex flake
Main	Bm	B	honey jasper	2.41	1.73	0.72	2.9	1.74 / 1.5	45° / 50°	fire reddened
Main	Bm	B	honey jasper	1.59	1.41	0.58	1.5	0.77 / 0.40	45° / 75°	
Main	Ikm	C	gy flint	1.88	1.02	0.18	0.7	1.1	45°	distal edge
Main	Ikm	C	honey jasper	3.06	2.02	0.68	4.2	1.33 / 2.26 / 2.73	50° / 50° / 6°	
Main	Nonrandom	C	honey jasper	2.05	2.4	0.90	4.4	1.82	60°	cortex flake
Main	Ikm	C	gray chert	1.3	6.5	0.2	0.3	0.6	30°	cortex flake; distal edge
Main	Ikm	C	brown quartz	2.44	1.45	1.29	5.0	0.68	75°	
Main	Bm	C	hornblende	1.7	1.24	0.39	1.1	1.68	45°	cortex fl ke
Main	Bm	D	honey jasper	2.25	1.31	0.5	1.4	1.81	80°	dital ge
Main	Ikm	D	jasper	2.25	1.84	0.74	4.5	1.65 / 0.86	6° / 30°	dital ge
Main	Ikm	E	honey jasper	1.85	1.28	0.66	1.6	.49 / 0.89	60° / 50°	tbl ge
Main	Bm	E	hornblende	2.22	1.99	0.48	2.9	0.90	40°	dital ge
Main	Bm	H	gray chert	3.25	1.66	0.87	6.2	1.98	75°	cortex flake

Note: All utilized edges are lateral unless otherwise noted.

424

Table 65. Distribution of Miscellaneous Debitage by Dump, Unit Type, and Stratum

Dump	Unit Type	Stratum	Material	Maximum Length (cm)	Maximum Width (cm)	Maximum Thickness (cm)	Weight (gm)	Comments
West	Random	A	gray flint	1.07	0.94	0.86	1.2	chunk
West	Nonrandom	A	hornblende	1.73	1.16	0.37	0.8	
West	Nonrandom	A	honey jasper	1.25	1.24	0.35	0.8	cortex flake
West	Nonrandom	A	chert	1.82	0.92	0.47	1.2	cortex flake, fire reddened
West	Nonrandom	B	hornblende	1.56	1.27	0.55	1.2	
West	Nonrandom	C	gray flint	2.35	1.15	0.7	2.3	
West	Random	C	gray chert	0.87	0.64	0.16	0.2	
Main	Nonrandom	B	honey jasper	2.35	2.45	0.71	4.7	
Main	Random	B	honey jasper	0.95	0.83	0.23	0.2	
Main	Random	C	white chert	1.29	0.90	0.24	0.4	
Main	Random	C	jasper	0.73	0.64	0.24	0.2	fire reddened
Main	Random	C	gray chert	1.61	1.23	0.48	1.2	
Main	Nonrandom	D	honey jasper	2.04	2.0	0.77	2.7	
Main	Random	D	gray flint	1.23	0.82	0.32	0.3	
Main	Random	D	brown jasper	2.53	2.55	1.14	7.5	cortex chunk
Main	Random	E	gray flint	1.6	1.24	0.46	0.9	
Main	Random	E	gray quartz	1.53	1.41	0.63	1.7	
Main	Random	E	gray quartz	3.1	2.34	1.48	11.7	chunk

425

Table 66. Distribution of Indeterminate Lithic Forms by Dump, Unit Type, and Stratum

Dump	Unit Type	Stratum	Material	Maximum Length (cm)	Maximum Width (cm)	Maximum Thickness (cm)	Weight (gm)	Comments
West	Nonrandom	A	quartz crystal	2.25	1.16	0.78	3.4	chunk
West	Nonrandom	D	buff sed. rock	5.85	4.25	3.04	110.0	split cobble
West	Random	D	white sed. rock	14.15	12.15	4.12	NA	chipped cobble
Main	Nonrandom	B	gray/brown chalcedony	1.58	1.32	1.12	2.8	chunk
Main	Random	B	unid. igneous	2.93	2.2	2.06	10.9	chunk
Main	Random	B	quartz	2.78	2.5	1.54	12.9	fire reddened chur
Main	Random	B	Wulfenite	1.75	0.64	0.6	1.3	chunk
Main	Rand o	B	honey jasper	7.13	5.03	2.57	102.9	split cobble
Main	Nonrandom	C	gray quartzite	4.75	6.93	3.45	122.4	split c bble
Main	Random	C	white quartz	1.63	0.89	0.46	1.1	chunk
Main	Random	C	gy chalcedony	1.94	1.38	0.68	3.4	split pbble
Main	Random	C	milk quartz	1.4	1.65	0.79	1.9	chunk
Main	Random	C	milk quartz	1.85	1.37	0.93	3.0	chunk

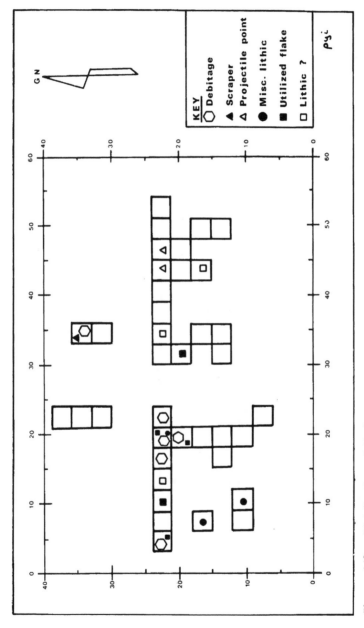

Figure 149. Distribution of Native American Artifacts in the West Dump.

427

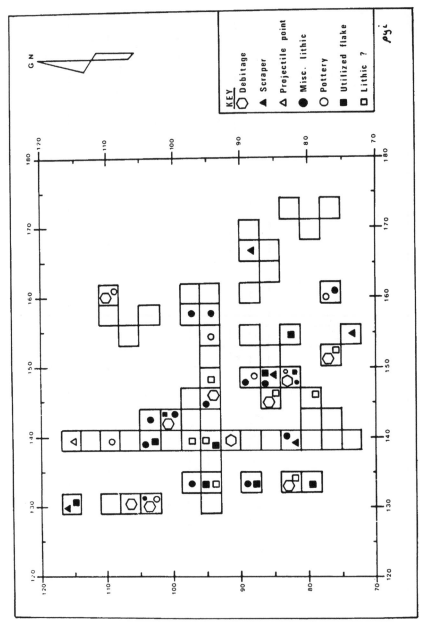

Figure 150. Distribution of Native American Artifacts in the Main Dump.

POTTERY

Description

Four styles of pottery were identified. Distinctions were based primarily upon surface appearance. Style One (figure 151 a) is a pottery with a micaceous surface. There were two sub-styles noted. Sub-style "a" had a wall thickness varying from 0.44 cm to 0.47 cm. Both the interior and exterior surfaces were undecorated. The temper was crushed calcite. The paste was a pale brown (10 YR 6.5/3) in color. The body had a hardness of approximately 4. The lip of the rim was flat. A shallow bowl type vessel was suggested by the shade of the shards.

Sub-style "b" had a wall thickness of 0.49 cm. The exterior surface resembled micaceous schist due to a heavy presence of crushed calcite in the paste and to a darkening of the paste with some form of blacking. The outer 0.37 cm of the body is gray (10 YR 4.5/1). The interior surface was also heavily micaceous and appeared brick red (2.5 YR 5.5/6). The red portion of the body was about 0.12 cm thick. The temper was a mixture of crushed calcite and quartz grit. The body had a hardness of about 4.

Figure 151. Native American Pottery.

429

Style Two (figure 151 b) consists of pottery that has polished surfaces at least one of which has been colored black. There are two sub-styles within this style. Sub-style "a" has a wall thickness that varies from 0.49 cm to 0.56 cm. Both the interior and exterior surfaces have been colored black and are highly polished. The temper is a mixture of sand, quartz grit, and an unidentified carbonized material. The paste is gray (5 YR 5.5/1) in color. The body has a hardness of approximately 4.

Sub-style "b" has a wall thickness of 0.54 cm. Although both surfaces have been polished, only the interior has been colored black. The temper is sand and quartz grit. The paste is a very pale brown (10 YR 7/3) in color. The body hardness is about 4.

Style Three (figure 151 c) is a decorated ware with a black on white exterior treatment on the exterior surface. The interior is undecorated. The wall thickness varies from 0.54 cm to 0.57 cm. The temper is sand and quartz grit. The paste is a light gray (5 YR 6.5/1) in color. The body hardness is about 4.

Style Four (figure 151 d) is an undecorated ware with polished interior and exterior surfaces. Flecks of a micaceous material are evident on the surfaces. The wall thickness is 0.6 cm. The temper is a mixture of sand and quartz grit. The paste is a bright red (2.5 YR 6/8) in color. The body hardness is about 4.

Distribution

The distributional aspects of the pottery sherds are listed in table 67. The spatial distribution of the shards for combined strata is depicted in figure 149 for the West Dump and in figure 150 for the Main Dump.

Comments

All of the limited number of sherds within the dumps' assemblages were examined by Dennis Stanford of the Smithsonian Institution Department of Anthropology. All of the sherds were assigned to the historic period. Styles One and Four pottery were attributed to being Apache in nature. No Native American pottery was reported by Moore (1973) for his excavations of the fort interior.

Table 67. Distribution of Native American Pottery by Dump, Unit Type, and Stratum

Style	Sub-Style	Surface Treatment Interior	Exterior	Paste	Temper	Wall Thickness (cm)	Hardness	Frequency	Dump	Unit Type	Stratum
1	a			pale brown 10YR6.5/3	crushed calcite	0.44-0.47	4	4	Main	Random	E
1	b			gray 10YR4.5/1	crushed calcite	0.49	4	1	Main	Random	D
2	a	polished carbon black	polished carbon black	gray 5YR5.5/1	sand, grit	0.49	4	1	Main	Random	B
2	a	polished carbon black	polished carbon black	gray 5YR5.5/1	sand, grit	0.56	4	1	Main	Nonrandom	C
2	b	polished carbon black	polished	pale brown 10YR7/3	sand, grit	0.54	4	1	Main	Random	D
3		polished carbon black	black on white	lt. gray 5YR6.5/1	sand, grit	0.54-0.57	4	1	Main	Nonrandom	B
4		polished	polished	lt. red 2.5YR6/8	sand, grit	0.6	4	1	Main	Random	D

REFERENCES

Albright, John, and Douglas D. Scott
1974   Historic Furnishing Study: Historical and Archeological Data,
        Fort Larned National Historic Site, Kansas.   United States
        Department of the Interior.   National Park Service.   Denver
        Service   Center.   Historic   Preservation   Team.   Denver,
        Colorado.

Anderson, Adrienne
1968   The   Archeology   of   Mass   Produced   Footwear.   Historical
        Archaeology 2:56-65.

Angus-Butterworth, L.M.
1958   Glass.   In A History of Technology.   Charles Singer et al.,
        Eds. Oxford: Clarendon Press.   Vol. IV.   Pp. 358-378.

Anonymous
1957   More About Bent's Old Fort.   Colorado Magazine 34:2:144-149.

Apschnikat, Ken
n.d.   Pamplin Red Clay Pipes.   Ms on File at the Appomattox Court
        House National Historical Park.   National Park Service.

Atterbury, Paul, Ed.
1978   English Pottery and Porcelain: An Historical Survey.   New
        York: Universe Books.

Babits, L.E.
1976   The Evolution and Adoption of Firearm Ignition Systems in
        Eastern North America: An Ethnohistorical Approach.   The
        Chesopiean 14:3-4:40-82.

Baldwin, Joseph K.
1973   Patent and Proprietary Medicine Bottles of the Nineteenth
        Century. New York: Thomas Nelson Inc.

Barber, Edwin A.
1904   Marks of American Potters.   Philadelphia: Patterson & White
        Company.

1909   The Pottery and Porcelain of the United States.   Reprinted
        1976. New York: Feingold & Lewis.

Barnes, Frank C.
1972   Cartridges of the World.   Northfield, Illinois: DBI Books,
        Inc.

Bealer, Alex W.
1976   The Tools that Built America.   New York: Bonanza Books.

Beck, Horace C.
1973   Classification and Nomenclature of Beads and Pendants.   York,
(1928) Pennsylvania: George Shumway Publishers.

Bell, Robert E., E.B. Jelks, and W.W. Newcomb
1967   A Pilot Study of Wichita Indian Archaeology and Ethnohistory.
Final Report to the National Science Foundation, Grant GS-964.

Berge, Dale L.
1980   Simpson Springs Station: Historical Archaeology in Western
Utah.   United States Bureau of Land Management.   Utah State
Office.   Salt Lake City, Utah.

Blakeslee, Donald J.
1975   The Plains Interband Trade System: An Ethnohistorical and
Archeological Investigation.   Unpublished Ph.D. Dissertation.
Department   of   Anthropology.   University   of
Wisconsin-Milwaukee.

Bowman, Orval
1967   Earthenware   Beverage   Bottles.   Western   Collector.   June
1967:35-41.

Brose, David J.
1967   The   Custer   Road   Dump   Site: An   Exercise   in   Victorian
Archaeology.   Michigan Archaeologist 13:2:37-83.

Brown, Stuart E., Jr.
1968   The Guns of Harpers Ferry.   Berryville, Virginia: Virginia
Book Company.

Buten, David
1976   Wedgwood: Guide   to   Marks   and   Dating.   Merion,
Pennsylvania: Buten Museum of Wedgwood.

Campbell, Ian M.
1972   The Red Wines of Bordeaux.   In How to Choose and Enjoy
Wine.   Augustus Muir, Ed.   New York: Bonanza Books.   Pp.
24-47.

Campbell, J. Duncan
1965   Military Buttons: Long-lost Heralds of Fort Mackinac's Past.
Mackinac History Leaflet No. 7.

Campbell, Robert, and N.H. Mager, Eds.
1973   How to Work with Tools and Wood.   New York: Pocket Books.
(1965)

Chance, David H., and Jennifer V. Chance
1976   Kanaka Village/Vancouver Barracks 1974.   Reports in Highway
Archaeology No. 3.   Office of Public Archaeology, Institute for
Environmental Studies, University of Washington.   Seattle.

Chapel, Charles E.
1961   Guns of the Old West. New York: Coward-McCann, Inc.

Chesterman, Charles W.
1978   The Audubon Society Field Guide to North American Rocks and Minerals. New York: Alfred A. Knopf.

Citizen Dolomieu
1960   Report on the Art of Making Gunflints (Fire Flint). Carlyle
(1796- S. Smith, Translator. Missouri Archaeologist 22:50-61.
1797)

Clement, Arthur W.
1944   American Ceramics, 1607-1943. Brooklyn Institute of Arts and Science. Brooklyn Museum. New York.

1947   Our Pioneer Potters. New York, Pennsylvania: Maple Press Company.

Collard, Elizabeth
1967   Nineteenth Century Pottery and Porcelain in Canada. Montreal: McGill University Press.

Condit, Carl W.
1968   American Building: Material and Techniques from the First Colonial Settlements to the Present. Chicago: University of Chicago Press.

Copeland, Robert
1980   Spoke's Willow Pattern and Other Designs after the Chinese. New York: Rizzoli International Publications, Inc.

Cosentino, Geraldine, and Regina Stewart
1976   Bottles. New York: Golden Press.

1977   Kitchenware. New York: Golden Press.

Coysh, A.W.
1972   Blue-Printed Earthenware, 18001850. London: David and Charles.

1974   Blue and White Transfer Ware: 1780-1840. London: David and Charles (Publishers) Limited.

Crawford, Prudence
1978   Buttons: Spin-Offs from the Decorative Arts. In The Encyclopedia of Collectibles: Buttons to Chess Sets. Andrea DiNoto, Ed. Alexandria, Virginia. Time-Life Books. Pp. 6-17.

Davey, Peter, Ed.
1979   The Archaeology of the Clay Tobacco Pipe II: The United States of America. BAR International Series 60. Oxford, England.

Dick, Herbert W.
1956   The Excavations of Bent's Fort, Otero County, Colorado.
        Colorado Magazine 33:181-196.

Dillon, John G.W.
1924   The Kentucky Rifle. Washington, D.C.: National Rifle
        Association.

Drumm, Stella M., Ed.
1962   Down the Santa Fe Trail and Into Mexico: The Diary of Susan
        Shelby Magoffin, 1846-1847. New Haven, Connectivut: Yale
        University Press.

Earle, Alice M.
1973   China Collecting in America. Rutland, Vermont: Charles E.
(1892) Tuttle Company, Inc.

Feinman, Jeffrey
1979   Sears, Roebuck and Company 1909 Catalog. New York:
        Ventura Books, Inc.

Fontana, Bernard L.
1965   The Tail of a Nail: On The Ethnological Interpretation of
        Historic Artifacts. Florida Anthropologist 18:3:2:85-101.

Fontana, Bernard L., and J. Cameron Greenleaf
1962   Johnny Ward's Ranch: A Study in Historic Archaeology. The
        Kiva 28:1-115.

Foshee, Rufus
1982   What Is Mochaware? Country Living 5:4:58-112.

Foster-Harris
1955   The Look of the Old West. New York: Viking Press.

Francis Bannerman Sons
1980   Bannerman Catalogue of Military Goods-1927. Northfield,
        Illinois. DBI Books, Inc.

Frison, George C., and Bruce A. Bradley
1980   Folsom Tools and Technology at the Hanson Site, Wyoming.
        Albuquerque: University of New Mexico Press.

Fuller, Claud E.
1958   The Rifled Musket. Harrisburg, Pennsylvania: The Stackpole
        Company.

Gardner, Paul V.
1977   American Glass. Washington, D.C.: Smithsonian Institution
        Press.

Garrard, Lewis
1968   Wah-To-Wah.   Palo Alto, California: American West Publishing
(1850) Company.

Glover, Jack
1977   The "Barbed Wire" Bible.   Sunset, Texas: Cow Puddle Press.

Godden, Geoffrey A.
1964   Encyclopedia of British Pottery and Porcelain Marks.   New
York: Bonanza Books.

1966a   Antique Glass and China.   New York: A.S. Barnes and
Company.

1966b   An Illustrated Encyclopedia of British Pottery and Porcelain.
New York: Crown Publishers, Inc.

1971   The Illustrated Guide to Mason's Patent Ironstone China and
Related Wares - Stone China, New Stone, Granite China and
Their Manufacturers.   New York: Praeger Publishers.

1975   British Pottery: An Illustrated Guide.   New York: Crown
Publishers, Inc.

Gordon, Elinor
1977   Collecting Chinese Export Porcelain.   New York: Universe
Books.

Greer, Georgeanna H.
1981   American Stonewares: The Art and Craft of Utilitarian
Potters.   Exton, Pennsylvania: Schiffer Publishing Ltd.

Gregg, Josiah
1967   The Commerce of the Prairies.   Lincoln: University of
(1926) Nebraska Press.

Gregory, Hiram A., and Clarence H. Webb
1965   European Trade Beads from Six Sites in Natchitoches Parish,
Louisiana.   Florida Anthropologist 18:3:2:15-44.

Guilland, Harold F.
1971   Early American Folk Pottery.   Philadelphia: Chilton Book
Company.

Hafen, LeRoy R.
1952   Fort St. Vrain.   Colorado Magazine 29:4:241-255.

1954   When Was Bent's Fort Built?   Colorado Magazine 31:1:105-119.

Haggar, Reginald G.
1950   English Country Pottery.   London: Phoenix House Limited.

Hamilton, Henry W., and Jean T. Hamilton
1972   Clay Pipes from Pamplin. Missouri Archaeologist 34:1-2:1-47.

Hamilton, T.M.
1960   Additional Comments on Gunflints. Missouri Archaeologist 22:73-80.

1976   Firearms on the Frontier: Guns at Fort Michilimackinac, 1715-1781. Mackinac Island State Park Commission. Reports on Mackinac History and Archaeology No. 5.

Hanson, Lee H., Jr.
1970   Gunflints from the Macon Plateau. Historical Archaeology 4:51-58.

1971   Pipes from Rome, New York. Historical Archaeology 5:92-99.

Hanson, Lee, and Dick Ping Hsu
1971   Nineteenth Century Transfer Printed Earthenwares. Historical Archaeology 5:74-91.

1975   Casemates and Cannonballs: Archeological Investigations at Fort Stanwix, Rome, New York. National Park Service Publications in Archeology 14. Washington, D.C.: Government Printing Office.

Hatch, Alden
1956   Remington Arms: The American Industry. New York: Rinehard and Company, Inc.

Hayden, Brian, Ed.
1979   Lithic Use-Wear Analysis. New York: Academic Press, Inc.

Hayes, Alden C., and James A. Lancaster
1975   Badger House Community. Mesa Verde National Park. Archeological Research Series Seven-E. Wetherill Mesa Studies. United States Department of the Interior. National Park Service. Washington, D.C.: Government Printing Office.

Heite, Edward F.
1971   Pipes from the Pamplin Factory in Appomattox County, Virginia. Quarterly Bulletin of the Archaeological Society of Virginia 25:3:195-196.

Herskovitz, Robert M.
1978   Fort Bowie Material Culture. Anthropological Papers of the University of Arizona No. 31. Tucson, Arizona.

Hicks, James E.
1962   U.S. Military Firearms, 1776-1956. La Canada, California: James E. Hicks & Son.

438

Holmstrom, J.G.
1904   Modern Blacksmithing. Chicago: Frederick J. Drake and
        Company.

Hsu, Dick Ping
1982   Personal Communication.

Hughes, G. Bernard
1977   Pocket Book of China. New York: Country Life.

Hughes, Bernard, and Therle Hughes
1968   The Collector's Encyclopedia of English Ceramics. London:
        Abbey Library.

Humphrey, Richard V.
1969   Clay Pipes from Old Sacramento. Historical Archaeology
        3:12-33.

Huntington Hopkins Company
  1890   Illustrated Catalogue and Price List of Hardware, Iron, Steel,
          Coal, Pipe, Pipe Fittings, Machinists' and Builders' Supplies.

Hyde, George E.
1968   Life of George Bent: Written from His Letters. Norman:
        University of Oklahoma Press.

Inashima, Paul Y.
1980   Analysis and Description of the Artifacts from Block 226,
        Washington, D.C. Washington, D.C.: Pennsylvania Avenue
        Development Corporation.

Innes, Lowell
1976   Pittsburgh Glass: 1797-1891. Boston: Houghton Mifflin
        Company.

Israel, Fred L., Ed.
1968   Sears, Roebuck Catalogue. New York: Chelsea House
(1897) Publishers.

Jarves, Deming
1865   Reminiscences of Glass-Making. Reprinted 1968. New York:
        Beatrice C. Weinstock.

Johnson, David F.
1948   Uniform Buttons. Vol. I & II. Watkins Glen, New York:
        Century House.

Jones, Olive
1971   Glass bottle Push-ups and Pontil Marks. Historical
        Archaeology 5:62-73.

Judge, W. James
1973   Paleo Indian Occupation of the Central Rio Grande Valley in
        New Mexico. Albuquerque: University of New Mexico Press.

439

Kauffman, Henry J.
1950   Early American Copper, Tin, and Brass. New York: Medill McBride Company.

1960   The Pennsylvania-Kentucky Rifle. New York: Bonanza Books.

1966   Early American Ironware: Cast and Wrought. New York: Weathervane Books.

1968   American Copper and Brass. Camden, N.J.: Thomas Nelson.

Ketchum, William C., Jr.
1975   A Treasury of American Bottles. Indianapolis, Indiana: Bobbs-Merrill Company, Inc.

Kidd, Kenneth E.
1979   Glass Bead-Making From the Middle Ages to the Early 19th Century. National Historic Parks and Sites Branch. Parks Canada. History and Archaeology No. 30. Ottawa, Canada.

Kidd, Kenneth E., and Martha A. Kidd
1970   A Classification System for Glass Beads for the Use of Field Archeologist. Canadian Historic Sites: Occasional Papers in Archaeology and History No. 1.

Kottman, Arthur
1979   Insulators. In The Encyclopedia of Collectibles. Inkwells to Lace. Alexandria, Virginia: Time-Life Books. Pp. 16-23.

Kovel, Ralph, and Terry Kovel
1973   Know Your Antiques. New York: Crown Publishers, Inc.

Larrabee, Edward M.
1961   Archeological Exploration of the Court House Building and Square, Appomattox Court House National Historical Park, Appomattox, Virginia, from July through September 1960. National Park Service.

Lavender, David
1954   Bent's Fort. Garden City, New York: Dolphin Books.

Lehner, Lois
1978   Ohio Pottery and Glass Marks and Manufacturers. Des Moines, Iowa. Wallace-Holmestead Book Co.

Leonard, Robert W., Jr.
1976   Archaeological Surveillance and Excavations: Bent's Old Fort National Historic Site, La Junta, Colorado. Contract Report CS-2000-6-0016. Prepared for the National Park Service. Denver Service Center. Denver, Colorado.

Lewis, Berkeley R.
1956   Small Arms and Ammunition in the U.S. Service. Washington,
        D.C.: The Smithsonian Institution.

Lief, Alfred
n.d.   A Close-up of Closures: History and Progress. New York:
        Glass Container Manufacturers Institute.

Little, W.L.
1969   Staffordshire Blue. New York: Crown Publishers, Inc.

Logan, Hershel C.
1959   Cartridges. New York: Bonanza Books.

Lord, Francis A.
1982   Civil War Collector's Encylcopedia: Arms, Uniforms, and
        Equipment of the Union and Confederacy. Secaucus, New
        Jersey: Castle.

Lorrain, Dessamae
1968   An Archaeologist's Guide to Nineteenth Century American
        Glass. Historical Archaeology 2:35-44.

Luscomb, Sally C.
1967   The Collector's Encyclopedia of Buttons. New York: Bonanza
        Books.

Macintosh, Duncan
1977   Chinese Blue and White Porcelain. Rutland, Vermont: Charles
        E. Tuttle Company, Publishers.

Martin, Patrick E.
1977   An Inquiry into the Locations and Characteristics of Jacob
        Bright's Trading House and William Montgomery's Tavern.
        Arkansas Archeological Survey Research Series No. 11.

McKearin, George P., and Helen
1948   American Glass. New York: Crown Publishers, Inc.

McKearin, Helen, and Kenneth M. Wilson
1978   American Bottles & Flasks and Their Ancestry. New York:
        Crown Publishers, Inc.

McKee, Harley J.
1973   Introduction to Early American Masonry: Stone, Brick, Mortar
        and Plaster. National Trust/Columbia University Series on the
        Technology of Early American Building No. 1. Washington,
        D.C.

Meltzer, David
1982   Personal Communication.

Mercer, Henry C.
1976   The Dating of Old Houses. Reprint of a Paper Read at a
(1923) Meeting of the Bucks County Historical Society. October 13,
        1923. New Hope, Pennsylvania.

Miller, George L.
1979   Classification and Economic Scaling of 19th Century Ceramics.
        Ms. on File, National Historic Parks and Sites Branch, Parks
        Canada. Ottawa, Canada.

Moore, Jackson W., Jr.
1963   The Archeology of Fort Smith I. United States Department of
        the Interior. National Park Service. Southeast Region.
        Richmond, Virignia.

1973   Bent's Old Fort: An Archeological Study. Boulder, Colorado:
        Pruett Publishing Company.

1982   Personal Communication.

Moore, N. Hudson
1974   The Old China Book. Rutland, Vermont: Charles E. Tuttle
(1903) Co., Inc.

Motz, Lee, and Peter D. Schulz
19__   European "Trade" Beads from Old Sacramento. In Papers on
        Old Sacramento Archeology. Peter D. Schulz and Betty J.
        Rivers, Eds. Department of Parks and Recreation. California
        Archeology Reports No. 19. Sacramento, California. Pp.
        49-68.

Munsey, Cecil
1970   The Illustrated Guide to Collecting Bottles. New York:
        Hawthorn Books, Inc. Publishers.

Murray, Robert A.
1964   Glass Trade Beads at Fort Laramie. Wyoming Archeologist
        7:13-19.

Myers, Susan H.
1977   A Survey of Traditional Pottery. Manufacture in the
        Mid-Atlantic and Northeastern United States. Northeast
        Historical Archaeology 6:1-2:1-13.

1978   The John Paul Remensnyder Collection of American Stoneware.
        Smithsonian Istitution. Washington, D.C.

Nadeau, Remi
1967   Fort Laramie and the Sioux Indians. Englewood Cliffs, New
        Jersey: Prentice-Hall, Inc.

442

National Park Service
1963   Historical Base Map: Bent's Old Fort National Historic Site,
        Colorado. United States Department of the Interior. National
        Park Service. Division of Landscape Architecture. Western
        Office, Division of Design and Construction.

Nelson, Lee H.
1968   Nail Chronology as an Aid to Dating Old Buildings. American
        Association for State and Local History Technical Leaflet 48.

Newman, T. Stell
1970   A Dating for Post-Eighteenth Century Bottles. Historical
        Archaeology 4:70-75.

Noel Hume, Audrey
1974   Archaeology and the Colonial Gardner. Williamsburg, Virginia:
        The Colonial Williamsburg Foundation.

Noel Hume, Audrey, Merry W. Abbitt, Robert H. McNulty, Isabel Davies,
and Edward Chappell
1973   Five Artifact Studies. Colonial Williamsburg Occasional Papers
        in Archaeology Volume I. Charlottesville: University of
        Virginia Press.

Noel Hume, Ivor
1969   A Guide to Artifacts of Colonail America. New York: Alfred
        A. Knopf.

1973   Creamware to Pearlware: A Williamsburg Perspective. In
        Ceramics in America. Ian M.G. Quimby, Ed. Winterthur
        Conference Report 1972. Charlottesville: University Press of
        Virginia.

Olsen, Stanley J.
1963   Dating Early Plain Buttons by Their Form. American Antiquity
        28:4:551-554.

Olsen, Stanley J., and J.D. Campbell
1962   Uniform Buttons as Interpretive Aids for Military Sites.
        Curator 5:4:346-352.

Omwake, H. Geiger
1965   Analysis of 19th Century White Kaolin Pipe Fragments from
        Mero Site, Dour County, Wisconsin. Wisconsin Archeologist
        46:2:125-139.

Osgood, Cornelius
1971   The Jug and Related Stoneware of Bennington. Rutland,
        Vermont: Charles E. Tuttle Company.

Oswald, Adrian
1960   The Archaeology and Economic History of English Clay Tobacco
        Pipes. Journal of the Archeological Association 23:40-102.

443

Oswald, Adrian
1961   The Evolution and Chronology of English Clay Tobacco Pipes.
        Archaeological Newsletter 7:3:55-62.

Palmer, Arlene M.
1976   A Winterthur Guide to Chinese Export Porcelain. New York:
        Crown Publishers, Inc.

Parkman, Frances
1963   The Oregon Trail. Garden City, New York: Garden City
(1892) Books.

Parsons, John e.
1952   Henry Deringer's Pocket Pistol. New York: William Morrow
        and Company.

1969   The First Winchester. New York: Winchester Press.

Peacock, Primrose
1978   Discovering Old Buttons. Bucks, England: Shire Publications
        Ltd.

Pepper, Adeline
1971   The Glass Gaffers of New Jersey. New York: Charles
        Scribner's Sons.

Petersen, Charles E., Ed.
1976   Building Early America: Contributions Toward the History of
        a Great Industry. Radnor, Pennsylvania: Chilton Book
        Company.

Petersen, Eugene T.
1963   Clay Pipes: A Footnote to Mackinac's History. Mackinac
        History Leaflet No. 1.

Petsche, Jerome E.
1974   The Steamboat Bertrand: History, Excavation, and
        Architecture. National Park Service Publications in Archeology
        11. Washington, D.C.: Government Printing Office.

Polak, Ada
1975   Glass: Its Tradition and Its Makers. New York: G.P.
        Putnam's Sons.

Price, Cynthia R.
1979   19th Century Ceramics . . . in the Eastern Ozark Border
        Region. Center for Archaeological Research Monograph Series
        No. 1. Southwest Missouri State University. Springfield,
        Missouri.

Robacker, Earl F., and Ada F. Robacker
1978   Spatterware and Sponge: Hardy Perennials of Ceramics.
        London: Thomas Yoseloff Ltd.

Roberts, Ned H.
1947   The   Muzzle-Loading   Cap   Lock   Rifle.   Harrisburg,
        Pennsylvania: The Stackpole Company.

Roenke, Karl G.
1978   Flat Glass: Its Use as a Dating Tool for Nineteenth Century
        Archaeological Sites in the Pacific Northwest and Elsewhere.
        Memoir No. 4.   Northwest Anthropological Research Notes.

Russell, Carl P.
1957   Guns on the Early Frontier: A History of Firearms from
        Colonial Times.   Berkeley: University of California Press.

Russell and Erwin Manufacturing Company
1980   Illustrated Catalogue of American Hardware of the Russell and
(1865) Erwin Manufacturing Company.   Facsimile Edition.   Association
        for Preservation Technology.

Sears, Roebuck Catalogue
1902   Reprinted 1969.   New York: Bounty Books.

Sears, W.H.
1954   Cowboy Life at Bent's New Fort and on the Arkansas.
        Colorado Magazine 31:1:193-201.

Schiffer, Herbert
1966   Early American Hardware.   Whitford, Pennsylvania: Whitford
        Press.

Schiffer, Herbert, et al.
1975   Chinese Export Porcelain: Standard Patterns and Forms, 1780
        to 1880.   Exton, Pennsylvania: Schiffer Publishing Limited.

Schulz, Peter .D., Betty J. Rivers, Mark M. Hales, Charles . Litzinger,
and Elizabeth A. McKee
1980   The   Bottles   of   Old   Sacramento: A   Study   of
        Nineteenth-Century Glass and Ceramic Retail Containers.   Part
        I.   California Department of Parks and Recreation Archeological
        Reports No. 20.   Sacramento, California.

Semenov, S.A.
1976   Prehistoric Technology: An Experimental Study of the Oldest
        Tools and Artifacts from Traces of Manufacture and Wear.
        Translated by M.W. Thompson.   New York: Barnes & Noble
        Books.

Smith, Carlyle S.
1960   Two 18th Century Reports on the Manufacture of Gunflints in
        France: Translator's Note.   Missouri Archaeologist 22:40-49.

Smith, Elmer, Compiler
1972   Pottery: A Utilitarian Folk Craft.   Lebanon, Pennsylvania:
        Applied Arts Publishers.

Smith, G. Hubert
1972   Like-a-Fishhook Village and Fort Berthold, Garrison Reservoir, North Dakota. United States Department of the Interior. National Park Service. Anthropological Papers 2. Washington, D.C.: Government Printing Office.

Smith, Joseph J.
1974   Regional Aspects of American Folk Pottery. York, Pennsylvania: Historical Society of York County.

Sonn, Albert H.
1979   Early American Wrought Iron. New York: Bonanza Books.
(1928)

South, Stanley
1964   Analysis of the Buttons from Brunswick Town and Fort Fisher. Florida Anthropologist 17:2:113-133.

1977   Method and Theory in Historical Archeology. New York: Academic Press, Inc.

Spargo, John
1974   Early American Pottery and China. Rutland, Vermont:
(1926) Charles E. Tutle Company.

Spector, Janet D.
1976   The Interpretive Potential of Glass Trade Beads in Historic Archaeology. Historical Archaeology 10:17-27.

Sprague, Marshall
1976   Colorado: A Bicentennial History. New York: W.W. Norton & Company, Inc.

Stanford, Dennis
1982   Personal Communication.

Stewart, Regina, and Geraldine Cosentino
1977   Stoneware. New York: Golden Press.

Stinson, Dwight E., Jr., Jackson W. Moore, Jr., and Charles S. Pope
1965   Historic Structures Report: Historic Reconstruction Bent's Old Fort, La Junta, Colorado. United States Department of the Interior. National Park Service.

Stone, Lyle M.
1974   Fort Michilimackinac, 1715-1781: An Archaeological Perspective on the Revolutionary Frontier. Publications of the Museum. Michigan State University. East Lansing, Michigan.

Stradling, Diana, and J. Garrison Stradling, Eds.
1977   The Art of the Potter: Redware and Stoneware. New York: Main Street/Universe Books.

Streeter, Donald
1971   Early American Wrought Iron Hardware: Norfolk Latches.
        APT 3:4:12-39.

1973   Early American Wrought Iron Hardware: H and HL Hinges,
        Together with Mention of Dovetails and Cast Iron Butt Hinges.
        APT Bulletin 5:1:22-49.

Sudbury, Byron
1977   History of the Pamplin Area Tobacco Pipe Industry. Quarterly
        Bulletin of the Archaeological Society of Virginia 32:2:1-35.

1979   Historic Clay Tobacco Pipemakers in the United States of
        America. In The Archaeology of the Clay Tobacco Pipe II:
        The United States of America. Peter Davey, Ed. BAR
        International Series 60. Oxford, England. Pp. 151-341.

1982   Personal Communication.

Sussman, Lynne
1979   Ceramics of Lower Fort Garry: Operations 1-31. National
        Historic Parks and Sites Branch. Parks Canada. History and
        Archaeology No. 24. Ottawa, Canada.

Swannack, Jervis D., Jr.
1969   Wetherill Mesa Excavations: Big Juniper House. Archeological
        Research Series No. Seven-C. United States Department of
        the Interior. National Park Service. Washington, D.C.:
        Government Printing Office.

Swenson, G.W.P.
1972   Pictorial History of the Rifle. New York: Bonanza Books.

Switzer, Ronald R.
1974   The Betrand Bottles: A Study of 19th-Century Glass and
        Ceramic Containers. United States Department of the Interior.
        National Park Service Publications in Archeology No. 12.
        Washington, D.C.: Government Printing Office.

Teague, George A., and Lynette O. Shenk
1977   Excavations at Harmony Borax Works. National Park Service.
        Western Archeological Center. Publications in Anthropology
        No. 6.

Toulouse, Julian H.
1969a   A Primer on Mold Seams. Western Collector 7:11:526-535.

1969b   A Primer on Mold Seams. Western Collector 7:12:578-587.

1971   Bottle Makers and Their Marks. New York: Thomas Nelson
        Inc.

Troy, Jack
1977   Salt-Glazed Ceramics. London: Pitman Publishing.

U.S. Soil Conservation Service
1972   Soil Survey of Otero County, Colorado.   United States
        Department of Agriculture.   Soil Conservation Service.
        Washington, D.C.: Government Printing Office.

Van der Sleen, W.G.N.
1967   A Handbook on Beads. York, Pennsylvania: George Shumway
        Publishers.

Van Rensselaer, Stephen
1947   American Firearms: An Histology of American Gunsmiths,
        Arms Manufacturers & Patenters with Detailed Description of
        Their Arms. Watkins Glen, New York: Century House.

1948   American Firearms: The Colt Supplement. Watkins Glen, New
        York: Century House.

Walker, Frank R.
1931   The Building Estimator's Reference Book.   Chicago: Frank
        R. Walker Company, Publishers.

Walker, Iain C.
1966   TD Pipes - A Preliminary Study.   Quarterly Bulletin of the
        Archaeological Society of Virginia 20:4:86-102.

1977   Clay Tobacco-Pipes, with Particular Reference to the Bristol
        Industry.   National Historical Parks and Sites Branch.   Parks
        Canada.   History and Archaeology No. 11. Ottawa, Canada.

Walker, John
1971   Excavations of the Arkansas Post Branch of the Bank of the
        State of Arkansas.   United States Department of the Interior.
        National Park Service. Washington, D.C.

Watkins, Lura Woodside
1950   Early New England Potters and Their Wares.   Cambridge,
        Massachusetts: Harvard University Press.

Watson, Aldren A.
1977   The Village Blacksmith. New York: Thomas Crowell.

Waugh, Alec
1969   Wines and Spirits. New York: Time-Life Books.

Weatherbee, Jean
1980   A Look at White Ironstone.   Des Moines, Iowa:
        Wallace-Homestead Book Company.

Webster, Donald B.
1971   Decorated Stoneware Pottery of North America.   Rutland,
        Vermont: Charles E. Tuttle Company.

Williams, Petra
1978   Staffordshire   Romantic   Transfer   Patterns.   Jeffersontown,
       Kentucky: Fountain House East.

Williamson, Harold F.
1952   Winchester: The Gun that Won the West.   Washington, D.C.:
       Combat Forces Press.

Wills, Geoffrey
1978   English Pottery and Porcelain.   Enfield, England.

Wilmsen, Edwin N.
1972   Lithic   Analysis   in   Paleoanthropology.   In   Contemporary
       Archaeology.   Mark P. Leone, Ed.   Carbondale: Southern
       Illinois University Press.   Pp. 195-205.

1974   Lindenmeir: A   Pleistocene   Hunting   Society.   New   York:
       Harper & Row, Publishers.

Wilson, Bill, and Betty Wilson
1968   Spirit   Bottles   of   the   Old   West.   Amador   City,   California:
       Antique and Hobby Publishing Company.

Wilson, Kenneth M.
1976   Window Glass in America.   In Building Early America.   Charles
       E.   Petersen,   Ed.   Radnor,   Pennsylvania: Chilton   Book
       Company.   Pp. 150-164.

Wilson, Rex L.
1971   Clay Tobacco Pipes from Fort Laramie National Historic Site
       and   Related   Locations.   Office   of   Archeology   and   Historic
       Preservation.   National Park Service.   Washington, D.C.

Witthoft, John.
1966   A   History   of   Gunflints.   Pennsylvania   Archaeologist
       36:1-2:12-49.

449

As the nation's principal conservation agency, the Department of the Interior has basic responsibilities to protect and conserve our land and water, energy and minerals, fish and wildlife, parks and recreation areas, and to ensure the wise use of all these resources. The department also has major responsibility for American Indian reservation communities and for people who live in island territories under U.S. administration.

Publication services were provided by the graphics staff of the Denver Service Center. NPS D-31 June 1985